CHOCTAW BY BLOOD

ENROLLMENT CARDS

1898-1914

VOLUME V

TRANSCRIBED BY

JEFF BOWEN

NATIVE STUDY
Gallipolis, Ohio
USA

Originally published:
Baltimore, Maryland
2015

Reprinted by:

Native Study LLC
Gallipolis, OH
www.nativestudy.com

Library of Congress Control Number: 2020911767

ISBN: 978-1-64968-008-2

Made in the United States of America.

This series is dedicated to
Mike Marchi,
who keeps my spirits up.

CREEK CENSUS.

SECOND NOTICE.

Members of the Dawes Commission will be present at the following times and places for the purpose of enrolling Creek citizens, as required by Act of Congress of June 10, 1896:

At Muskogee, Nov. 8 to 30, 1897, inclusive.
At Wagoner, Nov. 8 to 13, " inclusive.
At Eufaula, Nov. 8 to 13, " inclusive.
At Sapulpa, Nov. 15 to 20, " inclusive.
At Wetumpka, Nov. 15 to 20, " inclusive.
At Okmulgee, Nov. 22 to 30, " inclusive.

All persons who have not heretofore enrolled before the Dawes Commission should appear and enroll. Parents and guardians can enroll their families and wards.

TAMS BIXBY,
FRANK C. ARMSTRONG,
A. S. McKENNON,
THOS. B. NEEDLES,
Commissioners.

The above illustration is similar in nature to what was found throughout Indian Territory for different tribes as far as postings on bulletin boards, public centers, or wherever they could be read so people would be notified of where and when they needed to be for enrollment with the Dawes Commission.

This is a picture of the Dawes Commission at Camp Jones in Stonewall, Indian Territory on September 8, 1898.

The images below are of two of the original cards given on the microfilm. The cards given in this book have been formatted to fit on one page and still give all the information found on the original cards.

Introduction

This series of Choctaw Enrollment Cards for the Five Civilized Tribes 1898-1914 has been transcribed from National Archive Film M-1186 Rolls 39-46.

The series contains more than 6100 Choctaw enrollment cards. All of the cards list age, sex and degree of blood, the parties' Dawes Roll Numbers, and date of enrollment by the Secretary of Interior for each person. The contents also give the enrollee's parents' names as well as miscellaneous notes pertaining to the enrollee's circumstances, when needed. Most entries indicate whether or not a spouse is an Intermarried White, with the initials I.W.

Enrollment wasn't as simple a process as most would think just by going through these pages. The relationships between the Five Tribes and the Dawes Commission were weak at best. There were political battles going on between the tribes and the U.S. Government as it was, but the struggles didn't stop there. Each tribe had its own political factions pulling it from every direction. On top of everything else, people from every corner of the United States were trying to figure how to get in on the spoils (Money and Land Allotment) by means of political favor. Kent Carter, author of *The Dawes Commission*, describes the continuous effort required to enroll the different tribes and the pressure the Commission incurred from people all over the country who tried to insinuate themselves into the equation:

"In May 1896 the Dawes Commission Returned To Indian Territory for its third visit, establishing its headquarters at Vinita in the Cherokee Nation. It now had to process applications for citizenship in addition to negotiating allotment agreements; these circumstances make the narrative of events more confusing because the commission attempted the two tasks concurrently. The commissioners resumed making their usual speeches to tribal officials and public gatherings to promote negotiations, but now they inevitably had to respond to questions about how the application process for citizenship would work. They also began receiving letters from people all over the United States asking how they could 'get on the rolls' so they could 'get Indian land'."[1]

For the actual process of Choctaw enrollment, "A commission was appointed in each county of the Choctaw Nation under an act of September 18 to make separate rolls of citizens by blood, by intermarriage, and freedmen; it was to deliver them to recently elected Chief Green McCurtain by October 20, but he rejected them even before they were completed because of charges that people were being left off for political reasons. On October 30, the National Council authorized establishment of a five-member

---

[1] *The Dawes Commission* by Kent Carter, page 15, para. 1

commission to revise the rolls within ten days and then directed McCurtain to turn them over to the Dawes Commission on November 11, 1896. The Choctaws hired the law firm of Stuart, Gordon, and Hailey, of South McAlester to represent the tribe at all proceedings held by the Dawes Commission,"[2] another indication that throughout the Commission's efforts there was always controversy between the tribes and the negotiators.

When completed, this multi-volume series will contain thousands of names, all of them accounted for in the indexes carefully prepared by the author. Hopefully this work will help many researchers find their ancestors and satisfy the questions that so many have had about their Native American heritage.

Jeff Bowen
Gallipolis, Ohio
NativeStudy.com

---

[2] *The Dawes Commission* by Kent Carter, page 16, para. 5

Choctaw By Blood Enrollment Cards 1898-1914

RESIDENCE: Bok Tuklo   COUNTY.   **Choctaw Nation**   **Choctaw Roll**   CARD NO.
POST OFFICE: Luk-fa-tah, I.T.   *(Not Including Freedmen)*   FIELD NO. **1201**

Dawes' Roll No.	NAME	Relationship to Person	AGE	SEX	BLOOD	TRIBAL ENROLLMENT Year	County	No.
3257	1 Kanashambie, Stephen 38	First Named	35	M	Full	1896	Bok Tuklo	7554
3258	2 Wilson, Rhoda 17	Niece	14	F	"	1896	" "	13429
	3							
	4 ENROLLMENT OF NOS. 1 and 2 HEREON							
	5 APPROVED BY THE SECRETARY OF INTERIOR Dec 12, 1902							
	6							
	7							
	8							
	9							
	10							
	11							
	12							
	13							
	14							
	15							
	16							
	17							

TRIBAL ENROLLMENT OF PARENTS

Name of Father	Year	County	Name of Mother	Year	County
1 Kanashambie	Ded	Bok Tuklo	Elima	Ded	Bok Tuklo
2 Joel Wilson	"	" "	Betsy Wilson	"	" "
3					
4					
5					
6					
7					
8		No1 on 1896 roll as Stephen Kanashambe			
9					
10		For child of No2 see NB (Apr 26'06) Card No. 33			
11					
12					
13					
14					
15					
16				Date of Application for Enrollment	Apr. 29-99
17					

Choctaw By Blood Enrollment Cards 1898-1914

RESIDENCE: Red River COUNTY.
POST OFFICE: Janis, I.T.

Choctaw Nation

Choctaw Roll *(Not Including Freedmen)*

CARD NO.
FIELD NO. **1202**

Dawes' Roll No.	NAME	Relationship to Person First Named	AGE	SEX	BLOOD	TRIBAL ENROLLMENT Year	County	No.
3259	1 Jefferson, Julius 36	First Named	33	M	Full	1896	Red River	7046
3260	2 " , Winnie 28	Wife	25	F	"	1896	" "	7047
3261	3 " , Maggie 11	Dau	8	"	"	1896	" "	P.R. 351
3262	4 " , Catharine 9	"	6	"	"	1896	" "	7048
15659	5 " , Simpson 7	Son	4	M	"			
~~3263~~	6 ~~" , Solomon~~ *DIED PRIOR TO SEPTEMBER 25, 1902*	"	2	"	"			
3264	7 " , Anna 2	Dau	15mo	F	"			
	8							
	9							
	10							
	11							
	12							
	13							
	14							
	15							
	16							
	17							

ENROLLMENT OF NOS. 1 2 3 4 6 and 7 HEREON APPROVED BY THE SECRETARY OF INTERIOR Dec 12, 1902

ENROLLMENT OF NOS. ~~5~~ HEREON APPROVED BY THE SECRETARY OF INTERIOR Dec.-2-1904

TRIBAL ENROLLMENT OF PARENTS

	Name of Father	Year	County	Name of Mother	Year	County
1	Adam Jefferson	Dead	Red River	Ish-ta-la-ma	Dead	Red River
2	Felin Tushka	"	" "	Silway Tushka	1896	" "
3	No 1			No 2		
4	No 1			No 2		
5	No 1			No 2		
6	~~No 1~~			~~No 2~~		
7	No 1			No 2		
8						
9	No.6 died July 20, 1899: Enrollment cancelled by Department Sept. 16, 1904.					
10	No3 on 1893 Pay roll as Mykie Jefferson, Red River Co Page 41, No.351					
11	Also on 1896 roll, Page 320, No. 12326, " " " as Maggie Tushka					
12	No.7 Born Jan. 25, 1901: enrolled May 1, 1902					
13	No 4 on 1896 roll as Catherine Jefferson					
	No5 Proof of birth received and filed Dec. 2, 1901					
14	Proof of death filed Dec. 6, 1902				#1 to 6 inc	
15	No6 died July 20, 1899:				Date of Application for Enrollment.	
16					Apr. 29/99	
17	P.O. Norwood, I.T. 1/19/07					

Choctaw By Blood Enrollment Cards 1898-1914

RESIDENCE: Red River COUNTY.
POST OFFICE: Goodwater, I.T.

Choctaw Nation

Choctaw Roll
(Not Including Freedmen)

CARD NO.
FIELD NO. **1203**

	NAME		Relationship to Person	AGE	SEX	BLOOD	TRIBAL ENROLLMENT		
							Year	County	No.
1	Wilson, Willie	25	First Named	22	M	1/8	1896	Red River	13671
2	" , Ollie M	18	Wife	16	F	I.W.			
3	" , Willie	1	Son	1mo	M	1/16			
4									
5									
6									
7									
8		ENROLLMENT							
9		OF NOS. 1 and 3 HEREON APPROVED BY THE SECRETARY OF INTERIOR Dec 12, 1902							
10									
11		ENROLLMENT							
12		OF NOS. 2 HEREON APPROVED BY THE SECRETARY OF INTERIOR Sep. 12, 1903							
13									
14									
15									
16									
17									

TRIBAL ENROLLMENT OF PARENTS

	Name of Father	Year	County	Name of Mother	Year	County
1	Willie Wilson	Dead	Non Citz	Lou Wilson	Dead	Red River
2	Bob Phillips	"	" "	Sally Phillips	1896	Non Citz
3	No 1			No 2		
4						
5						
6		No.3 Enrolled June 3, 1901				
7		For children of Nos. 1&2 see NB (March 3, 1905) #1002				
8						
9						
10						
11						
12						
13						
14						
15						
16				Date of Application for Enrollment	Apr. 29/99	
17						

3

Choctaw By Blood Enrollment Cards 1898-1914

RESIDENCE: Red River COUNTY.
POST OFFICE: Goodwater, I.T.

Choctaw Nation

Choctaw Roll CARD NO.
(Not Including Precedent) FIELD NO. 1204

Dawes' Roll No.		NAME		Relationship to Person First Named	AGE	SEX	BLOOD	TRIBAL ENROLLMENT		
								Year	County	No.
226	1	Phillips, Tobe	25		22	M	I.W.			
3267	2	" Annie	21	Wife	18	F	1/8	1896	Red River	13672
3268	3	" Julia Margarett	2	Dau	4mo	F	1/16			
3269	4	" Jeffie J	1	Son	2mo	M	1/16			
3270	5	" Dora	3	Dau	2½	F	1/16			
	6									
	7	ENROLLMENT								
	8	OF NOS. 2 3 4 and 5 HEREON								
	9	APPROVED BY THE SECRETARY OF INTERIOR DEC 12 1902								
	10	ENROLLMENT								
	11	OF NOS. 1 HEREON APPROVED BY THE SECRETARY								
	12	OF INTERIOR SEP 12 1903								
	13									
	14									
	15									
	16									
	17									

TRIBAL ENROLLMENT OF PARENTS

	Name of Father	Year	County	Name of Mother	Year	County
1	Bob Phillips	Dead	Non Citz	Sallie Phillips	1896	Non Citz
2	Willie Wilson	"	" "	Lou Fulsom	Dead	Red River
3	No 1			No 2		
4	Nº1			Nº2		
5	Nº1			Nº2		
6						
7	No2 on 1896 roll as Anna Wilson					
8	For child of Nos 1&2 see NB (Apr 26-06) Card #461					
9	" " " " " " " (Mar 3-05) " #1007					
10	A daughter, Dora, born Nov 2/99, on card D544.					
11	No.3 Enrolled June 28, 1901					
12	Nº4 Born March 3, 1902: Enrolled May 20 1902					
13	Nº5 Born Nov. 2, 1899: enrolled on Choctaw card #D.544, Dec. 19, 1899, and transferred to this card May 21, 1902					
14						#1&2
15						Date of Application for Enrollment.
16						Apr. 29/99
17	[illegible] I.T. 4/13/0[ ]					

4

RESIDENCE: Eagle COUNTY.
POST OFFICE: Eagletown, I.T.

Choctaw Nation

Choctaw Roll
(Not Including Freedmen)

CARD NO.
FIELD NO. 1205

Dawes' Roll No.	NAME	Relationship to Person	AGE	SEX	BLOOD	TRIBAL ENROLLMENT		
						Year	County	No.
3271	1 Jones, Grayson 24	First Named	21	M	Full	1896	Eagle	6943
3272	2 " Wincy 25		22	F	"	1893	"	P.R. 141
	3							
	4	ENROLLMENT						
	5	OF NOS. 1 and 2 HEREON APPROVED BY THE SECRETARY						
	6	OF INTERIOR DEC 12 1902						
	7							
	8							
	9							
	10							
	11							
	12							
	13							
	14							
	15							
	16							
	17							

TRIBAL ENROLLMENT OF PARENTS

	Name of Father	Year	County	Name of Mother	Year	County
1	Isom Jones	1896	Eagle	Sillis Ghoing	1896	Eagle
2	Martin Cooper	1896	"	Mean Cooper	Dead	"
3						
4	No 2 died April 25, 1902: Enrollment cancelled by Department May 2-1906					
5	No2 on 1893 Pay roll as Wincy Cooper, Page 13, No 141, Eagle County					
6	No 1 " 1896 " " Crason Jones.					
7						
8	No 2 Died April 25, 1902: proof of death filed Dec. 12, 1902					
9						
10						
11						
12						
13						
14						
15						
16				Date of Application for Enrollment Apr 29/99		
17						

5

Choctaw By Blood Enrollment Cards 1898-1914

RESIDENCE: Red River COUNTY. **Choctaw Nation** Choctaw Roll CARD NO.
POST OFFICE: Goodwater, I.T. *(Not Including Freedmen)* FIELD NO. 1206

Dawes' Roll No.		NAME		Relationship to Person First Named	AGE	SEX	BLOOD	TRIBAL ENROLLMENT		
								Year	County	No.
3273	1	King, Arlington	22	First Named	19	M	Full	1896	Red River	7566
	2									
	3	ENROLLMENT								
	4	OF NOS. 1 HEREON APPROVED BY THE SECRETARY								
	5	OF INTERIOR DEC 12 1902								
	6									
	7									
	8									
	9									
	10									
	11									
	12									
	13									
	14									
	15									
	16									
	17									

TRIBAL ENROLLMENT OF PARENTS

	Name of Father	Year	County	Name of Mother	Year	County
1	Silas King	Dead	Red River	Melissie King	1896	Red River
2						
3						
4						
5	No 1 is now husband of Zona Byington on 7-1035 11/28/02					
6	For child of No.1 see NB (March 3 1905) #886					
7						
8						
9						
10						
11						
12						
13						
14						
15						
16				Date of Application for Enrollment	Apr. 29/99	
17						

6

RESIDENCE: Towson COUNTY.
POST OFFICE: Fowlerville, I.T.

Choctaw Nation

Choctaw Roll
(Not Including Freedmen)

CARD No.
FIELD No. 1207

Dawes' Roll No.	NAME	Relationship to Person	AGE	SEX	BLOOD	TRIBAL ENROLLMENT		
						Year	County	No.
3274	1 Jacobs, Rhoda ³²	First Named	29	F	Full	1896	Towson	185
3275	2 Austin, Benjamin ⁵	Son	2	M	"	1896	"	231
3276	3 Jacobs, Colman ¹	Son	3mo	M	"			
	4							
	5							
	6	ENROLLMENT						
	7	OF NOS. 1 2 and 3 HEREON APPROVED BY THE SECRETARY						
	8	OF INTERIOR DEC 12 1902						
	9							
	10							
	11							
	12							
	13							
	14							
	15							
	16							
	17							

TRIBAL ENROLLMENT OF PARENTS

	Name of Father	Year	County	Name of Mother	Year	County
1	Joseph Hokabe	1896	Towson	Susan Hokabe	Dead	Towson
2	Tobias Austin	Dead	"	No 1		
3	Houston B Jacobs	1896	"	Nº1		
4						
5						
6						
7	No. 1 is now the wife of Houston B Jacobs on Choctaw					
8	Card #1065. Evidence of marriage filed Aug 1, 1902.					
9	Nº3 Born May 5, 1902: enrolled Aug. 1, 1902.					
10						
11						
12						
13						
14					#1&2	
15					Date of Application for Enrollment.	
16					Apr. 29/99	
17	P.O. Rufe, I.T. 5/21/07					

Choctaw By Blood Enrollment Cards 1898-1914

Choctaw Nation

Choctaw Roll CARD NO.
(Not Including Freedmen) FIELD NO. 1208

Dawes' Roll No.	NAME	Relationship to Person First Named	AGE	SEX	BLOOD	TRIBAL ENROLLMENT Year	County	No.
3277	1 Austin Louie 27	First Named	24	M	Full	1896	Towson	187
3278	2 " Pauline 21	Wife	18	F	"	1896	"	4735
	3							
	4							
	5							
	6							
	7							
	8							
	9							
	10							
	11							
	12							
	13							
	14							
	15							
	16							
	17							

ENROLLMENT
OF NOS. 1 and 2 HEREON
APPROVED BY THE SECRETARY
OF INTERIOR DEC 12 1902

TRIBAL ENROLLMENT OF PARENTS

Name of Father	Year	County	Name of Mother	Year	County
1 Tobias Austin	Ded	Towson	Becky Austin	Ded	Towson
2 Nicholas Garland	"	San Bois		"	San Bois
3					
4					

No 2 On 1896 roll as Pauline Garland also on 1896 roll
Page 113, No 4654 as Pauline Garland, Sans Bois Co
No1 is a bull brother of Lena Austin on
Chickasaw Card No 1415. She has
been declared to be a Chickasaw by the
Chickasaw Commission and other witnesses
For child of Nos 1&2 see NB (March 3 1905) #1320

Date of Application
for Enrollment.

Apr. 29"99

8

Choctaw By Blood Enrollment Cards 1898-1914

RESIDENCE: Red River COUNTY. **Choctaw Nation** Choctaw Roll CARD No.
POST OFFICE: Goodwater I.T. (Not Including Freedmen) FIELD No. 1209

Dawes' Roll No.	NAME	Relationship to Person First Named	AGE	SEX	BLOOD	TRIBAL ENROLLMENT Year	County	No.
DEAD.	1 Thomas Jason DEAD.		46	M	Full	1896	Red River	12338
3279	2 Johnson Elsie ⁵³	Wife	50	F	"	1896	" "	12339
3280	3 Thomas Hudson ¹⁰	Son	7	M	"	1896	" "	12340
3281	4 Harner Wilmon DIED PRIOR TO SEPTEMBER 25, 1902	S.Son	10	"	"	1896	" "	5670
3282	5 Watkins, Gibson ¹⁹	S. "	16	"	"	1893	" "	P.R. 705
	6							
	7	ENROLLMENT OF NOS. 2 3 4 and 5 HEREON						
	8	APPROVED BY THE SECRETARY						
	9	OF INTERIOR DEC 12 1902						
	10							
	11	No 1 HEREON DISMISSED UNDER						
	12	ORDER OF THE COMMISSION TO THE FIVE						
	13	CIVILIZED TRIBES OF MARCH 31, 1905.						
	14							
	15							
	16							
	17							

TRIBAL ENROLLMENT OF PARENTS

	Name of Father	Year	County	Name of Mother	Year	County
1	John Thomas	Ded	Red River	Sissy	Ded	Red River
2	Pisa-lu-ka-bi	"	" "	Millie Nelson	"	" "
3	No 1			No 2		
4	Starling Waib	De'd	Eagle	No 2		
5	Rogers[sic] Fisher	"	Red River	No 2		
6						
7						
8			No 4 on 1896 roll as Wilburn Harner			
9			No 5 " 1893 Pay roll as Gibson Watkin			
10	No2 now the wife of No.2 on Choctaw Card #606, Anthony Johnson Evidence of marriage					
11	filed July 21ˢᵗ 1902.					
12	No 1 died in 1900; proof of death filed Dec 3, 1902					
13	No 4 " Aug 2, 1902: " " " " " " "					
14	No.4 died Aug 2, 1902: Enrollment cancelled by Department Dec 24 1904					
15						
16					Date of Application for Enrollment.	Apr 29/99
17						

9

Choctaw By Blood Enrollment Cards 1898-1914

Choctaw Nation

Choctaw Roll (Not Including Freedmen)

CARD No. FIELD No. 1210

Dawes' Roll No.	NAME	Relationship to Person First Named	AGE	SEX	BLOOD	TRIBAL ENROLLMENT Year	County	No.
DEAD.	1 Ho-k-abe Joseph DEAD.		65	M	Full	1896	Towson	5503
3283	2 " Sallie 25	Dau	22	F	"	1896	"	5504
3284	3 Missie DIED PRIOR TO SEPTEMBER 25, 1902	"	16	"	"	1896	"	5506
3285	4 Meshaya James 14	G.Son	11	M	"	1893	"	P.R. 273
Dead DEAD.	5 Aaron Thomas DEAD.	Ward	12	"	"	"	"	55
	6							
	7 ENROLLMENT							
	8 OF NOS. 2 3 and 4 HEREON APPROVED BY THE SECRETARY							
	9 OF INTERIOR DEC 12 1902							
	10							
	11 No. 1 and 5 HEREON DISMISSED UNDER							
	12 ORDER OF THE COMMISSION TO THE FIVE CIVILIZED TRIBES OF MARCH 31, 1905.							
	13							
	14							
	15							
	16							
	17							

TRIBAL ENROLLMENT OF PARENTS

	Name of Father	Year	County	Name of Mother	Year	County
1	Ya ho ka bi	Ded	Towson		Ded	Towson
2	No 1		Sine[sic]	Sine	"	"
3	No 1		"	"	"	"
4	Hicks Meshaya	Ded	Towson	Iney	"	"
5	Pitman Aaron	"	"	Hiney	"	"
6						
7			See pay rolls 55# and 273# for Towson Co for			
8			No^s 4 and 5			
9			No4 on 1893 Pay roll as Jim Heshaya.			
10	No3 died October 25, 1901: Enrollment cancelled by Department May 2, 1906					
11			No4 also on 1896 roll, Page 215,			
12			No 8606, as James Mishaya			
13	No 1 died Aug. 1899: proof of death filed Dec 3, 1902					
14	No 3 " Oct25, 1901: " " " " " " "					
15	No 5 " Sept – 1899: " " " " " " "				Date of Application for Enrollment.
16						Apr. 29 "99
17						

Choctaw By Blood Enrollment Cards 1898-1914

RESIDENCE: Eagle   COUNTY.   **Choctaw Nation**

POST OFFICE: Eagletown, I.T.

Choctaw Roll *(Not Including Freedmen)*

CARD NO.   FIELD NO. **1211**

Dawes' Roll No.	NAME	Relationship to Person First Named	AGE	SEX	BLOOD	TRIBAL ENROLLMENT Year	County	No.
3286	1 Jones, Isham ⁵³	First Named	50	M	Full	1896	Eagle	6934
3287	2 " , Sillis ⁵³	Wife	50	F	"	1896	"	6935
3288	3 " , Thomas ²¹	Son	18	M	"	1896	"	6933
3289	4 " , Amos ²⁰	"	17	"	"	1896	"	6937
3290	5 " , Sylvester ¹⁷	"	14	"	"	1896	"	6931
3291	6 " , Eastman ¹³	"	10	"	"	1896	"	6936
	7							
	8	ENROLLMENT						
	9	OF NOS. 12345and6 HEREON APPROVED BY THE SECRETARY						
	10	OF INTERIOR Dec 12, 1902						
	11							
	12							
	13							
	14							
	15							
	16							
	17							

TRIBAL ENROLLMENT OF PARENTS

Name of Father	Year	County	Name of Mother	Year	County
1 Louis Jones	Dead	Eagle	E-mollie	Dead	Eagle
2 John Going	"	"	Monte-ma	"	"
3 No 1			No 2		
4 No 1			No 2		
5 No 1			No 2		
6 No 1			No 2		
7					
8	No2 on 1896 roll as Silis Jones				
9	No2 died April 26, 1902: Proof of death filed Dec 12, 1902				
10	No4 " Jan'y 24, 1901: " " " " " " "				
	For child of No.3 see NB (March 3, 1905) #1019.				
11					
12					
13					
14					
15					
16				Date of Application for Enrollment	Apr. 29/99
17					

11

Choctaw By Blood Enrollment Cards 1898-1914

RESIDENCE: Red River COUNTY. **Choctaw Nation** **Choctaw Roll** CARD NO.
POST OFFICE: Goodwater I.T. *(Not Including Freedmen)* FIELD NO. 1212

Dawes' Roll No.	NAME	Relationship to Person First Named	AGE	SEX	BLOOD	TRIBAL ENROLLMENT		
						Year	County	No.
DEAD 1	~~Wade Nancy~~		70	F	Full	1896	~~Red River~~	~~13669~~
2								
3								
4	No. 1 HEREON DISMISSED UNDER							
5	ORDER OF THE COMMISSION TO THE FIVE							
6	CIVILIZED TRIBES OF MARCH 31, 1905.							
7								
8								
9								
10								
11								
12								
13								
14								
15								
16								
17								

TRIBAL ENROLLMENT OF PARENTS

	Name of Father	Year	County	Name of Mother	Year	County
1		Ded				
2						
3						
4						
5						
6						
7			No.1 Died July 30, 1900. Evidence of death filed April 25, 1901			
8						
9						
10						
11						
12						
13						
14						
15						
16					Date of Application for Enrollment	Apr. 29"99
17						

CANCELLED

Died prior to Sept 25 '02

12

Choctaw By Blood Enrollment Cards 1898-1914

RESIDENCE: Red River COUNTY. **Choctaw Nation** **Choctaw Roll** CARD No.
POST OFFICE: Goodwater I.T. (Not Including Freedmen) FIELD No. 1213

Dawes' Roll No.	NAME	Relationship to Person First Named	AGE	SEX	BLOOD	TRIBAL ENROLLMENT		
						Year	County	No.
3292	1 Loman Josiah DIED PRIOR TO SEPTEMBER 25, 1902		20	M	Full	1896	Red River	8070
	2							
	3	ENROLLMENT						
	4	OF NOS. 1 HEREON APPROVED BY THE SECRETARY						
	5	OF INTERIOR DEC 12 1902						
	6							
	7							
	8							
	9							
	10							
	11							
	12							
	13							
	14							
	15							
	16							
	17							

TRIBAL ENROLLMENT OF PARENTS

	Name of Father	Year	County	Name of Mother	Year	County
1	Joson Loman	1896	Red River	Suky Loman	Ded	Red River
2						
3						
4						
5	No.1 died Sept. 10, 1902. Proof of death filed Oct. 25, 1902					
6	No.1 died Sept. 10, 1902; Enrollment cancelled by Department Sept. 16, 1904					
7						
8						
9						
10						
11						
12						
13						
14						
15						
16					Date of Application for Enrollment.	Apr. 28"99
17						

13

RESIDENCE: Red River COUNTY.	Choctaw Nation	Choctaw Roll (Not Including Freedmen)	CARD NO.
POST OFFICE: Kully Tuk-lo I.T.			FIELD NO. 1214

Dawes Roll No	NAME		Relationship to Person First Named	AGE	SEX	BLOOD	TRIBAL ENROLLMENT		
							Year	County	No.
3293	1 Ward William S.	37	First Named	34	M	Full	1896	Red River	13619
3294	2 " Sillan	41	Wife	38	F	"	1896	" "	13629
DEAD.	3 " Harris		Son	18	M	"	1896	" "	13621
3295	4 " Moses	19	"	16	"	"	1896	" "	13629
3296	5 " Silena	15	Dau	12	F	"	1896	" "	13630
3297	6 " Sissy	8	"	5	"	"	1896	" "	13622
3298	7 " Reed	5	Son	2	M	"			
3299	8 " Simon	3	Son	1mo	M	"			
	9								
	10	ENROLLMENT OF NOS. 12 4567 and 8 HEREON APPROVED BY THE SECRETARY OF INTERIOR DEC 12 1902							
	11								
	12								
	13								
	14 For child of Nos 1&2 see NB (Mar 3-05) #879								
	15								
	16								
	17								

TRIBAL ENROLLMENT OF PARENTS

	Name of Father	Year	County	Name of Mother	Year	County
1	Sam Kaniyotabi	1896	Red River	"Sally"	1896	Red River
2	James Gravy	Ded	Bok Tuklo	Jane Gravy	1896	Bok Tuklo
3	No 1			No 2		
4	No 1			No 2		
5	No 1			No 2		
6	No 1			No 2		
7	No 1			No 2		
8	No 1			No 2		
9			No 2 on 1896 roll as Cillin Ward			
10			No 5 " " " " Celliny "			
11			No 1 " 1896 " " W. S. "			
12			No 8 born November 13, 1899; transferred to this card May 24, 1902			
13			Simon, son of Nos 1-2, born			
14			Nov 13/99 on Card No D-542			#1 to 7 inc
15			No 3 is duplicate of No 1 on 7-1215			Date of Application for Enrollment.
16						Apr. 28"99
17	P.O. Idabel IT 4/10/05					

Choctaw By Blood Enrollment Cards 1898-1914

RESIDENCE: Red River COUNTY. **Choctaw Nation** Choctaw Roll CARD NO.
POST OFFICE: Kully Tuk-lo I.T. (Not Including Freedmen) FIELD NO. **1215**

Dawes' Roll No.	NAME	Relationship to Person	AGE	SEX	BLOOD	Year	County	No.
3300	1 Ward, Harris 21	First Named	18	M	Full	1893	Red River	P.R. 710
3301	2 " , Mary 19	Wife	16	F	"	1896	" "	13191
3302	3 " , Lorancy 3	Dau	5mo	F	"			
3303	4 " , Robert 2	Son	6mo	M	"			
	5							
	6							
	7							
	8							
	9							
	10							
	11							
	12							
	13							
	14							
	15							
	16							
	17							

ENROLLMENT OF NOS. 1 2 3 and 4 HEREON APPROVED BY THE SECRETARY OF INTERIOR Dec 12, 1902

TRIBAL ENROLLMENT OF PARENTS

	Name of Father	Year	County	Name of Mother	Year	County
1	Willie Ward	1896	Red River	Sillan Ward	1896	Red River
2	Billy Williams	Ded	Eagle	Siney Williams	Ded	Eagle
3	No 1			No 2		
4	No 1			No 2		
5						
6		No 2 on 1896 roll as Mary B. Williams also on				
7		1896 roll page 356 No. 13599 as Mary William Red River Co.				
8						
9		No 1 is Duplicate of No 3 on Choc Card #1214.				
10						
11						
12		No.3 Enrolled May 24, 1900.				
13		No.4 Enrolled Aug 9, 1901.				
14					#1&2	
15					Date of Application for Enrollment.	
16					Apr. 29"99	
17						

15

RESIDENCE: **Red River** COUNTY.
POST OFFICE: **Goodwater I.T.**

Choctaw Nation

Choctaw Roll CARD NO.
(Not Including Freedmen) FIELD NO. **1216**

Dawes' Roll No.	NAME	Relationship to Person First Named	AGE	SEX	BLOOD	TRIBAL ENROLLMENT Year	County	No.
3304	1 Williams Michael 31	First Named	28	M	Full	1896	Red River	13597
3305	2 " Sillan 43	Wife	40	F	"	1896	" "	13598
~~3306~~	DIED PRIOR TO SEPTEMBER 25, 1903 3 ~~Simpson~~	~~Bro~~	~~12~~	~~M~~	~~"~~	~~1893~~	~~Eagle~~	P.R. 355
3307	4 Harley, Jane 12	Ward	9	F	"	1896	Red River	5667
	5							
	6 ENROLLMENT							
	7 OF NOS. 1 2 3 and 4 HEREON APPROVED BY THE SECRETARY							
	8 OF INTERIOR DEC 12 1902							
	9							
	10							
	11							
	12							
	13							
	14							
	15							
	16							
	17							

TRIBAL ENROLLMENT OF PARENTS

	Name of Father	Year	County	Name of Mother	Year	County
1	Billy Williams	De'd	Eagle	Siney Williams	Ded	Eagle
2	Thomas Harley	1896	Red River	Yousen Harley	"	Red River
3	~~Billy Williams~~	~~Ded~~	~~Eagle~~	~~Siney Williams~~	~~Ded~~	~~Eagle~~
4	Calvin Harley	"	Red River	Amy Harley	"	Red River
5						
6						
7			No 1 on 1896 roll as Michael William			
8			No 2 " " " " Cillen "			
9			No 3 " 1893 Pay roll as Simpson Homma			
10			No 3 died May 16-1900: proof of death filed Dec 3, 1902			
11			No.3 died May 16, 1900: Enrollment cancelled by Department Sept 16,1904			
12						
13						
14						
15					Date of Application for Enrollment.	
16						
17					Apr. 29 "99s	

16

RESIDENCE: Red River COUNTY.			**Choctaw Nation**			**Choctaw Roll** (Not Including Freedmen)	CARD No.	
POST OFFICE: Kullituklo, I.T.							FIELD No. 1217	

Dawes' Roll No.	NAME	Relationship to Person First Named	AGE	SEX	BLOOD	TRIBAL ENROLLMENT		
						Year	County	No.
3308	1 Amos, William 59	First Named	56	M	Full	1896	Red River	312
3309	2 DIED PRIOR TO SEPTEMBER 25, 1902 , Susan	Wife	45	F	"	1896	" "	313
3310	3 " , Amancy 28	Dau	25	"	"	1896	" "	315
3311	4 DIED PRIOR TO SEPTEMBER 25, 1902 , Esias	Son	17	M	"	1893	" "	P R 4
3312	5 Harley, Maggie 26	Ward	23	F	"	1896	" "	5656
3313	6 Robert, David 9	"	6	M	"	1896	" "	10809
14648	7 Amos, Kana 1	son of No 3	1	M	"			
14649	8 Dyer, Granson 1	son of No 5	5mo	M	"			
	9 ENROLLMENT OF NOS. HEREON APPROVED BY THE SECRETARY OF INTERIOR					ENROLLMENT OF NOS. 7 and 8 HEREON APPROVED BY THE SECRETARY OF INTERIOR May 20, 1903		
	10							
	11							
	12 For child of No5 see NB (Apr 26,06) Card #525							
	13 " " " " " " (Mar 3,05) " #878							
	14							
	15 No2 died July 14,1902: No4 died March							
	16 19,1902: Enrollment cancelled by							
	17 Department July 8, 1904.							

	TRIBAL ENROLLMENT OF PARENTS						
	Name of Father	Year	County	Name of Mother	Year	County	
1	Ishtahnube	Dead	Red River	Po-she-mar	Dead	Red River	
2	Wa-ka-ya	"	" "	Siney Wakaya	"	" "	
3	No 1			Susie Amos	"	" "	
4	No 1			No 2			
5	Calvin Harley	Dead	Red River	Liney Allen	Dead	Red River	
6	David Robert			Mary Kana-atube	"	" "	
7	Solomon Allen			No 3			
8	Louis Dyer			No 5			
9							
10	No3 on 1896 roll as Amanda Amos						
11	No4 " 1893 Pay roll as Esanis Amos Page 1 No 4 Red River Co						
12	No5 " 1896 roll as Mikey Harley						
13	No7 born July 2, 1901; enrolled Dec 2, 1902						
14	No2 died July 14, 1902; Proof of death filed Dec 4, 1902						
15	No4 " March 9, 1902; " " " " 4, 1902						
16	No.5 is now wife of Louis Dyer Choctaw Card #1169 evidence of marriage filed Dec. 8, 1902						1 to 6 inc
17	No8 Born July 30, 1902, Proof of birth filed Dec 24, 1902.					Date of Application for Enrollment.	Apr. 29/99
	No6 living with Celia Juzar (on 7-1195) at Kullituklo						
	For child of No3 see NB (Apr 26-06) Card #870.						

No5 P.O. Norwood I.T. 4/10/05

Choctaw By Blood Enrollment Cards 1898-1914

RESIDENCE: Red River   COUNTY.

POST OFFICE: Kullituklo, I.T.

Choctaw Nation

Choctaw Roll
(Not Including Freedmen)

CARD NO.

FIELD NO. **1218**

Dawes' Roll No.	NAME	Relationship to Person	AGE	SEX	BLOOD	TRIBAL ENROLLMENT		
						Year	County	No.
3314	1 Thomas, Philiston 25	First Named	22	M	Full	1896	Red River	12288
3315	2 " , Sallie 26	Wife	23	F	"	1893	Bok Tuklo	P R 256
3316	3 Willis, Jones 14	Nephew	11	M	"	1893	Eagle	583
	4							
	5 ENROLLMENT							
	6 OF NOS. 1 2 and 3 HEREON APPROVED BY THE SECRETARY							
	7 OF INTERIOR Dec 12, 1902							
	8							
	9							
	10							
	11							
	12							
	13							
	14							
	15							
	16							
	17							

TRIBAL ENROLLMENT OF PARENTS

	Name of Father	Year	County	Name of Mother	Year	County
1	Josiah Thomas	Dead	Bok Tuklo	Silway Thomas	1896	Red River
2	Silas Anderson	1896	" "	Amy Tikbombe	Ded	" "
3	Joe Willis	Dead	Red River	Tennessee Willis	"	" " "
4						
5						
6	No 1 on 1896 roll as Philliston Thomas					
7	No 2 on 1893 Pay roll as Sillie Anderson, Page 41, No.256, Bok Tuklo Co.					
8	No 3 " 1893 " " " John Thomas " 63 No.583, Eagle Co.					
9						
10						
11						
12						
13						
14					Date of Application for Enrollment.	
15						
16					Apr. 29/99	
17						

18

RESIDENCE: Red River   COUNTY.   **Choctaw Nation**   Choctaw Roll   CARD NO.

POST OFFICE: Kullituklo, I.T.   (Not Including Freedmen)   FIELD NO.   1219

Dawes' Roll No.	NAME	Relationship to Person	AGE	SEX	BLOOD	TRIBAL ENROLLMENT		
						Year	County	No.
3317	1 Kaniatobe, Sam ⁵⁹	First Named	56	M	Full	1896	Red River	7579
3318	2 " Sallie ⁵⁸	Wife	55	F	"	1896	" "	7580
DEAD.	3 ~~Picken, Isabel~~ DEAD.	~~Niece~~	~~26~~	~~"~~	~~"~~	~~1896~~	~~" "~~	~~10418~~
	4							
	5	ENROLLMENT ~~OF NOS. 1 and 2~~ HEREON APPROVED BY THE SECRETARY OF INTERIOR DEC 12 1902						
	6							
	7							
	8							
	9	No. 3 HEREON DISMISSED UNDER ORDER OF THE COMMISSION TO THE FIVE ~~CIVILIZED TRIBES OF MARCH 31, 1905.~~						
	10							
	11							
	12							
	13							
	14							
	15							
	16							
	17							

TRIBAL ENROLLMENT OF PARENTS

	Name of Father	Year	County	Name of Mother	Year	County
1	Kaniatobe	Dead	Red River	E-mi-l-to-na	Dead	Red River
2	Pisa-bun-aby	"	" "	Pe-sa-hu-na	"	" "
3	~~Ellis Picken~~	~~"~~	~~" "~~	~~Elsie Picken~~	~~"~~	~~" "~~
4						
5						
6	Is not Isabel Picken dead?					
7	See letter of Sam Kaniatobe of Dec. 7th, 1900.					
8	No.3 Died June 30, 1900. Evidence of death filed Feby. 14, 1901.					
9						
10						
11						
12						
13						
14					Date of Application for Enrollment.	
15						
16					Apr. 29/99	
17						

Choctaw By Blood Enrollment Cards 1898-1914

RESIDENCE: Red River   **Choctaw Nation**   **Choctaw Roll**   CARD NO.
POST OFFICE: Kullituklo, I.T.   *(Not Including Freedmen)*   FIELD NO. 1220

Dawes' Roll No.	NAME	Relationship to Person First Named	AGE	SEX	BLOOD	TRIBAL ENROLLMENT Year	County	No.
3319	1 Hopakonobi, Elizabeth	Named	55	F	Full	1896	Red River	5683
3320	2 Billy, Frances 11	Ward	8	"	"	1896	" "	1376
	3							
	4							
	5							
	6							
	7							
	8							
	9							
	10							
	11							
	12							
	13							
	14							
	15							
	16							
	17							

ENROLLMENT
OF NOS. 1 and 2 HEREON
APPROVED BY THE SECRETARY
OF INTERIOR DEC 12 1902

TRIBAL ENROLLMENT OF PARENTS

	Name of Father	Year	County	Name of Mother	Year	County
1	Pisa-bun-aby	Dead	Red River	Pesa-hu-na	Dead	Red River
2	Tom Billy	"	" "	Jency Billy	"	" "
3						
4						
5						
6						
7						
8						
9						
10						
11						
12						
13						
14						
15				Date of Application for Enrollment.		
16				Apr. 29/99		
17						

Choctaw By Blood Enrollment Cards 1898-1914

RESIDENCE: Red River   COUNTY.   **Choctaw Nation**   **Choctaw Roll** CARD NO.
POST OFFICE: Goodwater, I.T.   (Not Including Freedmen)   FIELD NO. 1221

Dawes' Roll No.	NAME	Relationship to Person	AGE	SEX	BLOOD	TRIBAL ENROLLMENT		
						Year	County	No.
3321	1 Byington, Moody 21	First Named	18	M	Full	1896	Red River	1353
3322	2 " Annie 24	Wife	21	F	"	1896	" "	13685
3323	3 " Sibbie 4	Dau	8mo	"	"			
14650	4 " Francis 1	"	18mo	"	"			
	5							
	6	ENROLLMENT OF NOS. 1 2 and 3 HEREON APPROVED BY THE SECRETARY OF INTERIOR DEC 12 1902						
	7							
	8							
	9							
	10	ENROLLMENT OF NOS. 4 HEREON APPROVED BY THE SECRETARY OF INTERIOR MAY 20 1903						
	11							
	12							
	13							
	14							
	15							
	16							
	17							

TRIBAL ENROLLMENT OF PARENTS

	Name of Father	Year	County	Name of Mother	Year	County
1	Thos. Byington	Dead	Red River	Sallie Byington	1896	Red River
2	Ah-no-hun-taby	"	Eagle	Chiffie	1896	" "
3	No 1			No 2		
4	No 1			No 2		
5						
6						
7		No2 on 1896 as Anna Wade				
8		No4 Born April 17, 1901		Enrolled Oct. 25, 1902		
9		For child of Nos 1&2 see NB (March 3, 1905) #1087				
10						
11						
12						
13						
14				Date of Application for Enrollment.		
15						
16				Apr. 29/99		
17						

Choctaw By Blood Enrollment Cards 1898-1914

RESIDENCE: Red River COUNTY.
CE: Goodwater, I.T. **Choctaw Nation**
Choctaw Roll *(Not Including Freedmen)*
CARD NO.
FIELD NO. 1222

	NAME	Relationship to Person First Named	AGE	SEX	BLOOD	TRIBAL ENROLLMENT		
						Year	County	No.
1	Webster, Michael ⁴⁹		46	M	Full	1896	Red River	13420
2								
3								
4								
5		ENROLLMENT						
6		OF NOS. 1 HEREON APPROVED BY THE SECRETARY						
7		OF INTERIOR DEC 12 1902						
8								
9								
10								
11								
12								
13								
14								
15								
16								
17								

TRIBAL ENROLLMENT OF PARENTS

	Name of Father	Year	County	Name of Mother	Year	County
1	Wilson Webster	Dead	Blue	Sarah Christie	Dead	Bok Tuklo
2						
3						
4						
5	Husband of No 1 on Choc card No 1191					
6						
7						
8						
9						
10						
11						
12						
13						
14						
15						
16				Date of Application for Enrollment	Apr. 29/99	
17	P.O. Glover, Okla 2/21/10					

Choctaw By Blood Enrollment Cards 1898-1914

RESIDENCE: Red River 7/20/14 COUNTY. **Choctaw Nation** **Choctaw Roll** *(Not Including Freedmen)* CARD NO. FIELD NO. 1223
POST OFFICE: Janis, I.T.

Dawes' Roll No.	NAME	Relationship to Person First Named	AGE	SEX	BLOOD	TRIBAL ENROLLMENT		
						Year	County	No.
3325	1 Brown, Seldon 24	First Named	21	M	Full	1896	Red River	1407
	2							
	3							
	4	ENROLLMENT						
	5	OF NOS. 1 HEREON APPROVED BY THE SECRETARY						
	6	OF INTERIOR DEC 12 1902						
	7							
	8							
	9							
	10							
	11							
	12							
	13							
	14							
	15							
	16							
	17							

TRIBAL ENROLLMENT OF PARENTS

	Name of Father	Year	County	Name of Mother	Year	County
1	John Brown	Dead	Red River	Susan Brown	Dead	Red River
2						
3						
4						
5						
6						
7						
8						
9	For child of No 1 see NB (Apr 26-06) Card #345					
10						
11						
12						
13						
14						
15						
16					Date of Application for Enrollment	Apr. 29/99
17						

23

Choctaw By Blood Enrollment Cards 1898-1914

Dawes' Roll No.	NAME	Relationship to Person	AGE	SEX	BLOOD	TRIBAL ENROLLMENT		
						Year	County	No.
3326	1 Haiakanubbi, Hamplin ³⁹	First Named	36	M	Full	1896	Red River	5660
3327	2 " Lucy Ann ³⁹	Wife	36	F	"	1896	" "	5661
3328	3 " Wellington ¹⁹	Son	16	M	"	1896	" "	5662
	4							
	5							
	6							
	7							
	8							
	9							
	10							
	11							
	12							
	13							
	14							
	15							
	16							
	17							

> ENROLLMENT
> OF NOS. 1 2 and 3 HEREON
> APPROVED BY THE SECRETARY
> OF INTERIOR DEC 12 1902

TRIBAL ENROLLMENT OF PARENTS

	Name of Father	Year	County	Name of Mother	Year	County
1	Haiakanubbi	Dead	Red River		Dead	Eagle
2	Ellis	"	Bok Tuklo	Pe-sa-ka-che-hoke	"	Bok Tuklo
3	No 1			No 2		
4						
5						
6	No1 on 1896 roll as Amblin Haiakanubbi					
7	No2 " 1896 " " Louisiana "					
8	Nº3 is now the husband of Mary Williston on Choctaw card #521 Aug. 28, 1902. For child of No.3 see NB (March 3 1905) #955.					
9						
10						
11						
12						
13						
14					Date of Application for Enrollment.	
15						
16					Apr 29/99	
17						

Choctaw By Blood Enrollment Cards 1898-1914

RESIDENCE: Red River COUNTY.
POST OFFICE: Goodwater, I.T.

Choctaw Nation

Choctaw Roll
(Not Including Freedmen)

CARD NO.
FIELD NO. 1225

Dawes' Roll No.	NAME	Relationship to Person	AGE	SEX	BLOOD	TRIBAL ENROLLMENT Year	County	No.
3329	1 Williams, Dennis 21	First Named	18	M	Full	1896	Red River	13600
	2							
	3							
	4							
	5							
	6							
	7							
	8							
	9							
	10							
	11							
	12							
	13							
	14							
	15							
	16							
	17							

ENROLLMENT
OF NOS. 1 HEREON
APPROVED BY THE SECRETARY
OF INTERIOR DEC 12 1902

TRIBAL ENROLLMENT OF PARENTS

	Name of Father	Year	County	Name of Mother	Year	County
1	Benj. Williams	Dead	Eagle	Siney Williams	Dead	Eagle
2						
3						
4			No 1 on 1896 Roll as Dennis William			
5						
6						
7						
8						
9						
10						
11						
12						
13						
14						
15					Date of Application for Enrollment.	
16					Apr. 29/99	
17						

25

Choctaw By Blood Enrollment Cards 1898-1914

RESIDENCE: Cedar   COUNTY. **Choctaw Nation**   **Choctaw Roll**   CARD NO.

POST OFFICE: Doaksville, I.T.   *(Not Including Freedmen)*   FIELD NO. 1226

Dawes' Roll No.	NAME	Relationship to Person First Named	AGE	SEX	BLOOD	TRIBAL ENROLLMENT		
						Year	County	No.
3330	1 Wesley, Edward 21	First Named	18	M	Full	1896	Cedar	13144
	2							
	3 ENROLLMENT							
	4 OF NOS. 1 HEREON APPROVED BY THE SECRETARY							
	5 OF INTERIOR DEC 12 1902							
	6							
	7							
	8							
	9							
	10							
	11							
	12							
	13							
	14							
	15							
	16							
	17							

TRIBAL ENROLLMENT OF PARENTS

	Name of Father	Year	County	Name of Mother	Year	County
1	Jonis Wesley	Dead	Cedar	Winnie Wesley	1896	Cedar
2						
3						
4						
5	N°1 is now husband of Lizzie Jackson on Choctaw card #915 Oct. 15, 1902					
6						
7						
8						
9						
10						
11						
12						
13						
14						
15						
16				Date of Application for Enrollment.		Apr. 29.99
17						

Choctaw By Blood Enrollment Cards 1898-1914

RESIDENCE:	Bok Tuklo	COUNTY.	**Choctaw Nation**		**Choctaw Roll**	CARD NO.	
POST OFFICE:	Lukfata, I.T.				*(Not Including Freedmen)*	FIELD NO.	1227

Dawes' Roll No.	NAME	Relationship to Person First Named	AGE	SEX	BLOOD	TRIBAL ENROLLMENT		
						Year	County	No.
3331	1 Pislin, Alexander DIED PRIOR TO SEPTEMBER 25, 1902		18	M	Full	1896	Bok Tuklo	10398
	2							
	3							
	4	ENROLLMENT OF NOS. 1 HEREON APPROVED BY THE SECRETARY OF INTERIOR DEC 12 1902						
	5							
	6							
	7							
	8							
	9							
	10							
	11							
	12							
	13							
	14							
	15							
	16							
	17							

TRIBAL ENROLLMENT OF PARENTS

	Name of Father	Year	County		Name of Mother	Year	County
1	Pislin	Dead	Bok Tuklo		Sincy Pislin	Dead	Bok tuklo
2							
3							
4							
5							
6		In penitentiary.					
7							
8		On 1896 roll as Aleck Pislin					
9							
10		No 1 Died in 1899; proof of death filed Dec 5, 1902					
11		No.1 died – – 1899: Enrollment cancelled by Department July 8, 1904.					
12							
13							
14							
15							
16					Date of Application for Enrollment	Apr. 29/99	
17							

RESIDENCE: **Eagle** COUNTY. **Choctaw Nation** **Choctaw Roll** CARD NO.
POST OFFICE: **Eagle Town I.T.** *(Not Including Freedmen)* FIELD NO. **1228**

Dawes' Roll No.	NAME	Relationship to Person	AGE	SEX	BLOOD	TRIBAL ENROLLMENT		
						Year	County	No.
3332	1 McKinney John ³¹	First Named	28	M	Full	1896	Eagle	9303
3333	2 " Ishlea ³⁸	Wife	35	F	"	1896	"	9304
3334	3 " Simmie ⁹	Dau	6	"	"	1896	"	9301
3335	4 Anderson Selina	S. Dau	21	"	"	1893	"	P.R. 733
	5							
	6							
	7	ENROLLMENT						
	8	OF NOS. 1 2 3 and 4 HEREON APPROVED BY THE SECRETARY						
	9	OF INTERIOR DEC 12 1902						
	10							
	11							
	12							
	13							
	14							
	15							
	16							
	17							

TRIBAL ENROLLMENT OF PARENTS

	Name of Father	Year	County	Name of Mother	Year	County
1	Sam Pisahekabi	Ded	Eagle	Eyatona	1896	Eagle
2	Ya-ho-kebabi	"	"	Oklaeshi	Ded	"
3	No 1			No 2		
4	Camel Anderson	"	"	No 2		
5						
6			No 2 Enrolled on 1896 roll as Sisten McKinney			
7			No 3 " " " " " Seama "			
8			No 4 on 1893 Pay roll as "Silina", Page 77, No 733, Eagle County			
9			Nº 4 also on 1896 Choctaw census roll page 9, #345 as Selina Apotantubbe			
10			No4 died May 4, 1899; proof of death filed Dec. 9, 1902			
11			No.4 died May 4, 1899; Enrollment cancelled by Department July 8, 1904			
12			For child of No.1 see NB (March 3, 1905) #875			
13						
14						
15						
16				Date of Application for Enrollment Apr. 29" 99		
17						

Choctaw By Blood Enrollment Cards 1898-1914

RESIDENCE: Bok Tuk-lo   COUNTY. **Choctaw Nation**   **Choctaw Roll**   CARD NO.
POST OFFICE: Luk-fa-tah I.T.   *(Not Including Freedmen)*   FIELD NO.   1229

Dawes' Roll No.	NAME	Relationship to Person	AGE	SEX	BLOOD	TRIBAL ENROLLMENT		
						Year	County	No.
3336	1 Pislin Guelis 22	First Named	19	M	Full	1896	Bok Tuklo	10397
	2							
	3	ENROLLMENT						
	4	OF NOS. 1 HEREON APPROVED BY THE SECRETARY						
	5	OF INTERIOR DEC 12 1902						
	6							
	7							
	8							
	9							
	10							
	11							
	12							
	13							
	14							
	15							
	16							
	17							

TRIBAL ENROLLMENT OF PARENTS

	Name of Father	Year	County	Name of Mother	Year	County
1	"Pislin"	Ded	Bok Tuklo	Siney	Ded	Bok Tuklo
2						
3						
4						
5						
6			On 1896 roll as Shillis Pislin			
7						
8						
9						
10						
11						
12						
13						
14						Date of Application for Enrollment.
15						
16						Apr. 29 99
17						

Choctaw By Blood Enrollment Cards 1898-1914

RESIDENCE: Cedar   COUNTY.   **Choctaw Nation**   **Choctaw Roll**   CARD NO.
POST OFFICE: Doaksville, I.T.   *(Not Including Freedmen)*   FIELD NO.   1230

Dawes' Roll No.	NAME	Relationship to Person First Named	AGE	SEX	BLOOD	TRIBAL ENROLLMENT		
						Year	County	No.
3337	1 Peter, Gooden ²²		19	M	Full	1893	Nashoba	P.R. 274
	2							
	3							
	4	ENROLLMENT						
	5	OF NOS. 1 HEREON APPROVED BY THE SECRETARY						
	6	OF INTERIOR DEC 12 1902						
	7							
	8							
	9							
	10							
	11							
	12							
	13							
	14							
	15							
	16							
	17							

TRIBAL ENROLLMENT OF PARENTS

	Name of Father	Year	County	Name of Mother	Year	County
1	Davison Peter	1896	Nashoba	Elsey Houston	1896	Cedar
2						
3						
4						
5						
6						
7		On 1893 Pay roll a Cotton Haais, Page 23, No 274, Nashoba Co.				
8		No1 also on 1896 Census Roll No 10363 as Gooden Pisaletubbi				
9						
10						
11						
12						
13						
14						Date of Application for Enrollment.
15						
16						Apr. 29" 99
17						

Choctaw By Blood Enrollment Cards 1898-1914

RESIDENCE: Bok Tuklo   COUNTY.   **Choctaw Nation**   **Choctaw Roll**   CARD NO.
POST OFFICE: Lukfata, I.T.   (Not Including Freedmen)   FIELD NO.   1231

Dawes' Roll No.	NAME	Relationship to Person	AGE	SEX	BLOOD	TRIBAL ENROLLMENT		
						Year	County	No.
3338	1 Colbert, William J ²¹	First Named	18	M	Full	1896	Nashoba	2492
3339	2 " Sinie ²³	Wife	20	F	"	1896	Bok Tuklo	13437
	3							
	4							
	5	ENROLLMENT						
	6	OF NOS. 1 and 2 HEREON APPROVED BY THE SECRETARY						
	7	OF INTERIOR DEC 12 1902						
	8							
	9							
	10							
	11							
	12							
	13							
	14							
	15							
	16							
	17							

TRIBAL ENROLLMENT OF PARENTS

Name of Father	Year	County	Name of Mother	Year	County
1 Jonas Colbert	Dead	Nashoba	Sallie Colbert	Dead	Nashoba
2 Ismon Willis	1896	Bok Tuklo	May J. Willis	"	Bok Tuklo
3					
4					
5					
6	No1 on 1896 roll as Wᵐ J Colbert				
7	No2 " 1896 " " Sinie Willis				
8					
9					
10					
11					
12					
13					
14				Date of Application for Enrollment.	
15					
16				Apr. 29/99	
17					

31

Choctaw By Blood Enrollment Cards 1898-1914

RESIDENCE: Towson COUNTY.
POST OFFICE: Fowlerville, I.T.

Choctaw Nation

Choctaw Roll
(Not Including Freedmen)

CARD NO.
FIELD NO. 1232

Dawes' Roll No.	NAME	Relationship to Person First Named	AGE	SEX	BLOOD	TRIBAL ENROLLMENT		
						Year	County	No.
3340	1 Murphy, Joe 39	First Named	36	M	Full	1896	Towson	8600
3341	2 " Molsey 40	Wife	37	F	"	1896	"	8601
	3							
	4	ENROLLMENT						
	5	OF NOS. 1 and 2 HEREON APPROVED BY THE SECRETARY						
	6	OF INTERIOR DEC 12 1902						
	7							
	8							
	9							
	10							
	11							
	12							
	13							
	14							
	15							
	16							
	17							

TRIBAL ENROLLMENT OF PARENTS

Name of Father	Year	County	Name of Mother	Year	County
1 Stephen Murphy	Dead	Towson	Serena Murphy	Dead	Towson
2 Bar-ti-tubbee	"	Kiamitia	Ta-ho-na	"	Kiamitia
3					
4					
5					
6					
7					
8					
9					
10					
11					
12					
13					
14			Date of Application for Enrollment.		
15					
16			May 1/99		
17					

RESIDENCE: Red River COUNTY. **Choctaw Nation** **Choctaw Roll** CARD No.
POST OFFICE: Shawnee Town I.T. _(Not Including Freedmen)_ FIELD No. 1233

Dawes' Roll No.	NAME	Relationship to Person	AGE	SEX	BLOOD	TRIBAL ENROLLMENT		
						Year	County	No.
3342	1 Fisher, Hicks ⁴¹	First Named	38	M	Full	1896	Red River	4212
3343	2 " Elizabeth ³¹	Wife	28	F	"	1896	" "	4213
DEAD	3 " Harris	S. Son	15	M	"	1896	" "	4218
3344	4 " Robert ³	Son	1	M	"			
	5							
	6	ENROLLMENT						
	7	OF NOS. 1 2 and 4 HEREON						
	8	APPROVED BY THE SECRETARY OF INTERIOR DEC 12 1902						
	9							
	10	No. 3 HEREON DISMISSED UNDER						
	11	ORDER OF THE COMMISSION TO THE FIVE						
	12	CIVILIZED TRIBES OF MARCH 31, 1905.						
	13							
	14							
	15							
	16							
	17							

TRIBAL ENROLLMENT OF PARENTS

	Name of Father	Year	County	Name of Mother	Year	County
1	Mon-la-tub-bi	Ded	Bok Tuk-lo	Ya-kab-im-nia	Ded	Red River
2	Simon Wallin	"	" " "	Lucy Wallin	"	Bok Tuk-lo
3	No 1			Sose Fisher	"	Red River
4	No 1			No 2		
5						
6						
7			No 4 Enrolled February 4, 1901.			
8			No 3 Died September 15, 1900. Evidence of death filed April 16, 1901.			
9						
10						
11						
12						
13						
14						#1 to 3
15						Date of Application for Enrollment.
16						May 1-99
17						

Choctaw By Blood Enrollment Cards 1898-1914

RESIDENCE: **Red River**   COUNTY.   **Choctaw Nation**   **Choctaw Roll**   CARD NO.

POST OFFICE: **Shawnee Town I.T.**   *(Not Including Freedmen)*   FIELD NO.   **1234**

Dawes' Roll No.	NAME	Relationship to Person First Named	AGE	SEX	BLOOD	TRIBAL ENROLLMENT		
						Year	County	No.
3345	1 Clay Betsy 53	First Named	50	F	Full	1896	Red River	2651
	2							
	3							
	4							
	5							
	6							
	7							
	8							
	9							
	10							
	11							
	12							
	13							
	14							
	15							
	16							
	17							

ENROLLMENT
OF NOS.   1   HEREON
APPROVED BY THE SECRETARY
OF INTERIOR DEC 12 1902

TRIBAL ENROLLMENT OF PARENTS

	Name of Father	Year	County	Name of Mother	Year	County
1	Craven	Ded	Mississippi	Yakohtina	Ded	Bok Tuklo
2						
3						
4						
5						
6						
7						
8						
9						
10						
11						
12						
13						
14						
15					Date of Application for Enrollment.	
16					May 1-99	
17						

34

Choctaw By Blood Enrollment Cards 1898-1914

RESIDENCE: Red River   COUNTY.
POST OFFICE: Shawnee Town I.T.

Choctaw Nation

Choctaw Roll CARD NO.
(Not Including Freedmen) FIELD NO. **1235**

Dawes' Roll No.	NAME	Relationship to Person First Named	AGE	SEX	BLOOD	TRIBAL ENROLLMENT Year	County	No.
3346	1 Clay Calvin ³⁸	First Named	35	M	Full	1896	Red River	2648
3347	2 " Bycey ²⁷	Wife	24	F	"	1896	" "	2649
Dead	3 " Arthur DEAD.	Son	4	M	"	1896	" "	2650
3348	4 " Isabella ¹	Dau	3wks	F	"			
	5							
	6 ENROLLMENT							
	7 OF NOS. 1 2 and 4 HEREON							
	APPROVED BY THE SECRETARY							
	8 OF INTERIOR DEC 12 1902							
	9							
	10 No. 3 HEREON DISMISSED UNDER							
	ORDER OF THE COMMISSION TO THE FIVE							
	11 CIVILIZED TRIBES OF MARCH 31, 1905.							
	12							
	13							
	14							
	15							
	16							
	17							

TRIBAL ENROLLMENT OF PARENTS

	Name of Father	Year	County	Name of Mother	Year	County
1	Simon Clay	Ded	Red River	Betsy Clay	1896	Red River
2	Payson Williston	"	" "	Sarah Williston	Ded	" "
3	No 1			No 2		
4	№1			№2		
5						
6	No.2 on Choctaw roll as Bycy Clay.					
7						
8						
9						
10	No.3 died June 28, 1899. Proof of death filed March 28, 1904					
11	№4 Born Aug. 22, 1902; enrolled Sept. 15, 1902					
12						
13						
14					#1 to 3 inc	
15					Date of Application for Enrollment.	
16					May 1-99	
17						

Choctaw By Blood Enrollment Cards 1898-1914

RESIDENCE: Towson COUNTY.   **Choctaw Nation**   **Choctaw Roll** CARD NO.
POST OFFICE: Garvin, I.T.   *(Not Including Freedmen)*   FIELD NO. 1236

Dawes' Roll No.	NAME		Relationship to Person	AGE	SEX	BLOOD	TRIBAL ENROLLMENT		
							Year	County	No.
I.W 1093	1 Birlen, Stephen	48	First Named	45	M	I W	1896	Red River	14314
I.W 1094	2 " Rebecca	25	Wife	22	F	I W	1896	Bok Tuklo	14694
3349	3 " Albert	9	Son	6	M	3/8	1896	Red River	1378
3350	4 " Filena	5	Dau	2	F	3/8			
	5								
	6	ENROLLMENT							
	7	OF NOS. 3 and 4 HEREON							
	8	APPROVED BY THE SECRETARY OF INTERIOR DEC 12 1902							
	9								
	10	ENROLLMENT							
	11	OF NOS. ~ 1 and 2 ~HEREON							
	12	APPROVED BY THE SECRETARY OF INTERIOR NOV 16 1904							
	13								
	14	Child of Nos 1 and 2 on Choctaw							
	15	card D#833							
	16	For child of Nos 1&2 see NB(Apr 26'06) #1085							
	17								

TRIBAL ENROLLMENT OF PARENTS

	Name of Father	Year	County	Name of Mother	Year	County
1	Joe Birlen	Dead	Non Citz	Catherine Birlen	Dead	Non Citz
2	Jackson Holder	"	" "	Mandy Holder		" "
3	No 1			Betsy Birlen	Dead	Bok Tuklo
4	No 1			" "	"	" "
5						
6	No1 – License not recorded. Married to					
7	Betsy James, now deceased, in 1895 In=			Betsy Birlin	1896	Red River
8	termarried with Rebeca James, his present					
9	wife, who claims to be an intermarried citizen, June 21, 1898.					
10	No1 on 1896 roll as Stephen Birlow					
11	No2 Intermarried with Alfred					
12	James, a Choctaw Citz, now deceased, on April 8, 1895. Alfred James, 1896 Boktuklo[sic]					
13	No2 on 1896 roll as Rebecca James					
14	No3 " 1896 " " Albert Birlow					
15						
16				Date of Application for Enrollment May 1/99		
17						

36

Choctaw By Blood Enrollment Cards 1898-1914

RESIDENCE: Bok Tuk-Lo COUNTY.

POST OFFICE: Luk-fa-tah I.T.

Choctaw Nation

Choctaw Roll
(Not Including Freedmen)

CARD NO.

FIELD NO. **1237**

Dawes' Roll No.	NAME	Relationship to Person First Named	AGE	SEX	BLOOD	TRIBAL ENROLLMENT		
						Year	County	No.
3351	1 McGee, Austin 63	First Named	60	M	Full	1896	Bok Tuk-lo	9289
3352	2 DIED PRIOR TO SEPTEMBER 25, 1902 , Louisa	Wife	30	F	1/2	1896	" " "	9290
3353	3 " , Lizzie 14	Dau	11	"	3/4	1896	" " "	9291
3354	4 DIED PRIOR TO SEPTEMBER 25, 1902 , Ed	Son	9	M	3/4	1896	" " "	9292
	5							
	6 ENROLLMENT							
	7 OF NOS. 1 2 3 and 4 HEREON APPROVED BY THE SECRETARY							
	8 OF INTERIOR Dec. 12, 1902							
	9							
	10							
	11							
	12 No.2 died March 20, 1900; No.4 died in 1900; Enrollment cancelled by Department							
	13 July 8, 1904.							
	14							
	15							
	16							
	17							

TRIBAL ENROLLMENT OF PARENTS

	Name of Father	Year	County	Name of Mother	Year	County
1	McGee	Ded	Bok Tuk-lo	A-lah-ta-ho-na	Ded	Eagle
2	Davis Na-tak-cho-pa	"	" " "	Wolscy Clay	1896	Bok Tuk-lo
3	No 1			No 2		
4	No 1			No 2		
5						
6						
7						
8			No.1 on 1896 roll as Austin McKee			
9			No.2 " " " " Louisa "			
10			No.3 " " " " Lizzie "			
			No.4 " " " " Ed "			
11			No.2 died March 20, 1900; Proof of death filed Dec. 6, 1902.			
12						
13						
14						
15						
16				Date of Application for Enrollment May 1-99		
17						

Choctaw By Blood Enrollment Cards 1898-1914

RESIDENCE: Cedar   COUNTY.   **Choctaw Nation**   **Choctaw Roll** CARD NO.
POST OFFICE: Doaksville I.T.   (Not Including Freedmen)   FIELD NO. 1238

Dawes' Roll No.	NAME	Relationship to Person First Named	AGE	SEX	BLOOD	TRIBAL ENROLLMENT		
						Year	County	No.
3355	1 Tims, Columbus ⁴³	First Named	40	M	3/4	1896	Cedar	12072
	2							
	3	ENROLLMENT						
	4	OF NOS. 1 HEREON APPROVED BY THE SECRETARY						
	5	OF INTERIOR DEC 2 1902						
	6							
	7							
	8							
	9							
	10							
	11							
	12							
	13							
	14							
	15							
	16							
	17							

TRIBAL ENROLLMENT OF PARENTS

	Name of Father	Year	County	Name of Mother	Year	County
1	E.W. Tims	1896	Towson	Polly Tims	Ded	Towson
2						
3						
4						
5						
6						
7						
8						
9						
10						
11						
12						
13						
14						
15					Date of Application for Enrollment.	
16					May 1-99	
17						

RESIDENCE: Eagle COUNTY:
POST OFFICE: Eagle Town I.T. **Choctaw Nation** Choctaw Roll *(Not Including Freedmen)*

CARD NO.
FIELD NO. 1239

Dawes' Roll No.	NAME	Relationship to Person	AGE	SEX	BLOOD	TRIBAL ENROLLMENT Year	County	No.
3356	1 Ontaiyabi Stephen 63	First Named	60	M	Full	1896	Eagle	9928
3357	2 " Netsie 48	Wife	45	F	"	1896	"	9929
	3							
	4	ENROLLMENT						
	5	OF NOS. 1 and 2 HEREON APPROVED BY THE SECRETARY						
	6	OF INTERIOR DEC 12 1902						
	7							
	8							
	9							
	10							
	11							
	12							
	13							
	14							
	15							
	16							
	17							

TRIBAL ENROLLMENT OF PARENTS

Name of Father	Year	County	Name of Mother	Year	County
1 Ontaiyabi	Ded	Bok Tuk lo	"Katy"	Ded	Bok Tuk lo
2 Geo. Tihbambi	"	" " "	Anolimana	"	" " "
3					
4					
5					
6					
7					
8					
9					
10		No 1 on 1896 roll as Stephen Ontohyobe			
11		No 2 " " " " Netsie			
12					
13					
14				Date of Application for Enrollment,	
15					
16				May 1 99	
17					

39

RESIDENCE: Eagle COUNTY.
POST OFFICE: Eagle Town I.T.

Choctaw Nation

Choctaw Roll
(Not Including Freedmen)

CARD NO.
FIELD NO. 1240

Dawes' Roll No.	NAME	Relationship to Person First Named	AGE	SEX	BLOOD	TRIBAL ENROLLMENT Year	County	No.
3358	1 Hleotambi ⁶⁵	First Named	62	M	Full	1896	Eagle	5608
3359	2 Betsy ~~DIED PRIOR TO SEPTEMBER 25, 1902~~	Wife	61	F	"	1896	"	5606
3360	3 Nancy ~~DIED PRIOR TO SEPTEMBER 25, 1902~~	Niece	11	"	"	1896	"	5609
	4							
	5							
	6							
	7							
	8							
	9							
	10							
	11							
	12							
	13							
	14							
	15							
	16							
	17							

ENROLLMENT
OF NOS. 1 2 and 3 HEREON
APPROVED BY THE SECRETARY
OF INTERIOR DEC 17 1902

TRIBAL ENROLLMENT OF PARENTS

	Name of Father	Year	County	Name of Mother	Year	County
1	Elehomahi	Ded	Eagle	He-na-ke	Ded	Eagle
2	~~Ta-nap-no-wa~~	"	~~Mississippi~~	~~Mon-to-na~~	"	~~Mississippi~~
3	~~James Yo-chi-mon~~	"	~~Eagle~~	~~Louisa Yo-chi-mon~~	"	~~Eagle~~
4						
5						
6						
7		Surnames of Nos 1 2 and 3 on 1896 roll as Hleohtambi				
8		~~No. 2 died – – 1901 No 3 died – – 1900; Enrollment cancelled by Department July 8, 1904~~				
9						
10						
11						
12						
13						
14					Date of Application for Enrollment.	
15						
16					May 1" 99	
17						

RESIDENCE:	Eagle	COUNTY.	**Choctaw Nation**	Choctaw Roll	CARD NO.	
POST OFFICE:	Eagle Town, I.T.			*(Not Including Freedmen)*	FIELD NO. 1241	

Dawes' Roll No.	NAME	Relationship to Person	AGE	SEX	BLOOD	TRIBAL ENROLLMENT		
						Year	County	No.
3361	1 Hleohtambi Esias ³⁷	First Named	34	M	Full	1896	Eagle	5617
3362	2 " Olacie ³³	Wife	30	F	"	1896	"	5643
	3							
	4 ENROLLMENT							
	5 OF NOS. 1 and 2 HEREON APPROVED BY THE SECRETARY							
	6 OF INTERIOR DEC 12 1902							
	7							
	8							
	9							
	10							
	11							
	12							
	13							
	14							
	15							
	16							
	17							

TRIBAL ENROLLMENT OF PARENTS

	Name of Father	Year	County	Name of Mother	Year	County
1	Hleotambi	1896	Eagle	Betsy Hleotambi	1896	Eagle
2	Josiah Crossbill	1896	Bok Tuk lo	Silyn Crossbill	Ded	Bok Tuklo
3						
4						
5						
6						
7						
8						
9						
10			No 2 on 1896 roll as Oleasy hleohtambi[sic]			
11						
12						
13						
14					Date of Application for Enrollment.	
15						
16					May 1-99	
17						

41

RESIDENCE: Eagle   COUNTY.
POST OFFICE: Luk-fa-tah, I.T. Lukfata, I.T.

Choctaw Nation

Choctaw Roll
(Not Including Freedmen)

CARD NO.
FIELD NO. **1242**

Dawes' Roll No.	NAME	Relationship to Person First Named	AGE	SEX	BLOOD	TRIBAL ENROLLMENT		
						Year	County	No.
3363	1 Alemohtubbi, Israel 40	First Named	37	M	Full	1896	Eagle	281
3364	2 " Leon 34	Wife	31	F	"	1896	"	289
3365	3 " Elus 12	Son	9	M	"	1896	"	271
3366	4 " Litty 10	Dau	7	F	"	1896	"	290
3367	5 ~~" Silis~~ DIED PRIOR TO SEPTEMBER 25, 1902	"	3	"	"	1896	"	299
3368	6 " Ilas	"	3mo	"	"			
15975	7 " Sidney 1	Son	1	M	"			
	8							
	9	ENROLLMENT OF NOS. 12345and6 HEREON APPROVED BY THE SECRETARY OF INTERIOR Dec. 12, 1902						
	10							
	11							
	12	ENROLLMENT OF NOS. ~~7~~ HEREON APPROVED BY THE SECRETARY OF INTERIOR Jun 16, 1906						
	13							
	14							
	15							
	16							
	17							

TRIBAL ENROLLMENT OF PARENTS

	Name of Father	Year	County	Name of Mother	Year	County
1	Alemohtubbi	Ded		"Ona"	Ded	Eagle
2				"Bissie"	"	Bok Tuk-lo
3	No 1			No 2		
4	No 1			No 2		
5	No 1			No 2		
6	No 1			No 2		
7	No 1			No 2		
8			No 2 on 1896 roll as Leannie Alemohtubbi			
9			No.3 " " " " Eleus "			
10			No.5 " " " " Silis "			
11	No.5 died July 8, 1901; Enrollment cancelled by Department July 8, 1904					
12	No.7 was born Nov. 11th,1901: application received and name placed on					
13	this card March 25, 1905, under provision of Act of Congress, Approved March 3, 1905.					
14						Date of Application for Enrollment.
15				No 7		
16				**GRANTED**		May 1-99
17				Apr. 25,1906.		

Choctaw By Blood Enrollment Cards 1898-1914

RESIDENCE: Cedar COUNTY.		Choctaw Nation				Choctaw Roll	CARD NO.	
POST OFFICE: Doaksville I.T.						(Not Including Freedmen)	FIELD NO. 1243	

Dawes' Roll No.		NAME	Relationship to Person First Named	AGE	SEX	BLOOD	TRIBAL ENROLLMENT		
							Year	County	No.
369	1	Billy, Naaman ~~DIED PRIOR TO SEPTEMBER 25, 1902~~ 33	First Named	30	M	Full	1896	Cedar	1082
370	2	" Ellen 31	Wife	28	F	"	1896	"	1083
3371	3	" Nora 3	Dau	5mo	F	"			
	4								
	5	ENROLLMENT							
	6	OF NOS. 1 2 and 3 HEREON APPROVED BY THE SECRETARY							
	7	OF INTERIOR DEC 12 1902							
	8								
	9								
	10								
	11								
	12								
	13								
	14								
	15								
	16								
	17								

TRIBAL ENROLLMENT OF PARENTS

	Name of Father	Year	County	Name of Mother	Year	County
1	~~Johnnis Billy~~	~~Ded~~	~~Cedar~~	~~Netsy Jacob~~	~~Ded~~	~~Cedar~~
2	Chelonie	"	Towson	Ela-yo-to-na	"	"
3	No.1			No.2		
4						
5						
6				No.3 Enrolled Aug. 30th, 1900		
7				For child of No 2 see NB (Apt 26-06) Card #847		
8						
9				No2 is now wife of Noel Nehka Choc #900 10/2/02		
10				No1 died Aril 8, 1900; proof of death filed Dec 5, 1902		
11				No.2 died April 8, 1900: Enrollment cancelled by Department July 8, 1904		
12						
13						
14						
15						
16				Date of Application for Enrollment	182 May 1"99	
17						

Choctaw By Blood Enrollment Cards 1898-1914

RESIDENCE: Eagle   COUNTY.   **Choctaw Nation**   **Choctaw Roll** _(Not Including Freedmen)_   CARD NO. FIELD NO. **1244**

POST OFFICE: Eagletown, I.T.

Dawes' Roll No.	NAME	Relationship to Person First Named	AGE	SEX	BLOOD	TRIBAL ENROLLMENT		
						Year	County	No.
3372	1 Fobb, Watkin ⁹	First Named	26	M	Full	1896	Eagle	4187
3373	2 " Alice ~~DIED PRIOR TO SEPTEMBER 25, 1902~~	Wife	20	F	"	1896	"	4195
3374	3 " Lucy ⁶	Dau	3	"	"	1896	"	4176
	4							
	5	ENROLLMENT						
	6	OF NOS. 1 2 and 3 HEREON APPROVED BY THE SECRETARY						
	7	OF INTERIOR DEC 12 1907						
	8							
	9							
	10							
	11							
	12							
	13							
	14							
	15							
	16							
	17							

TRIBAL ENROLLMENT OF PARENTS

	Name of Father	Year	County	Name of Mother	Year	County
1	Louis Fobb	Dead	Eagle	Lizzie Fobb	Dead	Eagle
2	Simeon Jefferson	1896	"	Mary Jefferson	"	"
3	No 1			No 2		
4						
5						
6						
7	No 2 died May 9, 1902; proof of death filed Dec 3, 1902					
8	No 2 died May 9, 1902; Enrollment cancelled by Department July 8, 1904					
9						
10						
11						
12						
13						
14						
15					Date of Application for Enrollment.	
16					May 1/99	
17						

Choctaw By Blood Enrollment Cards 1898-1914

Choctaw Nation

Choctaw Roll (Not Including Freedmen)

CARD NO.
FIELD NO. 1245

Dawes' Roll No.	NAME	Relationship to Person First Named	AGE	SEX	BLOOD	TRIBAL ENROLLMENT		
						Year	County	No.
3375	₁ John, Hagan	First Named	38	M	Full	1896	Towson	6798
3376	₂ " Lena	Wife	30	F	"	1896	Bok Tuklo	6283
3377	₃ Died prior to September 25, 1902 Simon	Son	6	M	"	1896	Towson	6755
3378	₄ Ishtiahonobbe Hettie	S.Dau.	9	F	"	1896	"	6284
3379	₅ Died prior to September 25, 1902 John Mary	Dau	1mo	F	"			
	6							
	7							
	8	ENROLLMENT						
	9	OF NOS. 1,2,3 4 and 5 HEREON APPROVED BY THE SECRETARY						
	10	OF INTERIOR DEC 12 1902						
	11							
	12							
	13							
	14							
	15							
	16							
	17							

TRIBAL ENROLLMENT OF PARENTS

	Name of Father	Year	County	Name of Mother	Year	County
1	John Hopyishubbee	Dead	Towson		Dead	Towson
2	Lorin Untemabe	"	Bok Tuklo	Rosie Untemabe	"	Bok Tuklo
3	Nº 1			Liley John	"	Towson
4	Tom Ishtiahonobbe	Dead	Bok Tuklo	Nº 2		
5	Nº 1			Nº 2		
6						
7			Nº 2 on 1896 roll as Leniy Ishtiahonobbe			
8			Nº 5 Enrolled Aug. 31ˢᵗ 1900			
9						
10			Nº 3 died July 20, 1900; proof of death filed Dec. 3, 1902			
11			Nº 5 died Sept. 22, 1902; proof of death filed Dec. 3, 1902			
12						
13			Nº 3 died July 20, 1900: Nº 5 died Sept 22, 1902: Enrollment cancelled by Department			
14				July 3, 1904		
15			For children of Nº 1 see N.B. (Mar 3, 1905) Card Nº 51			
16				DATE OF APPLICATION FOR ENROLLMENT. May 1/99		
17						

45

Choctaw By Blood Enrollment Cards 1898-1914

RESIDENCE: Towson COUNTY.
POST OFFICE: Fowlerville I.T.

Choctaw Nation

Choctaw Roll (Not Including Freedmen)

CARD NO.
FIELD NO. **1246**

Dawes' Roll No.	NAME		Relationship to Person First Named	AGE	SEX	BLOOD	TRIBAL ENROLLMENT		
							Year	County	No.
3380	1 Loman, Thomas	73	First Named	70	M	Full	1896	Towson	7917
I W 227	2 Loman, Susan	26	Wife	24	F	I.W.	1896	"	14764
3381	3 Loman, Oscar	5	Son	1½	M	1/2			
14925	4 Loman, Annie	2	Dau	29mo	F	1/2			
	5								
	6	ENROLLMENT OF NOS. 1 and 3 HEREON APPROVED BY THE SECRETARY OF INTERIOR Dec 12, 1902							
	7								
	8			For child of No2 see NB (Mar 3rd 1905) Card No.51.					
	9								
	10	ENROLLMENT OF NOS. 2 HEREON APPROVED BY THE SECRETARY OF INTERIOR Sep 12, 1903		No 2 on 1896 roll as Susan Loman					
	11								
	12								
	13	ENROLLMENT OF NOS. 4 HEREON APPROVED BY THE SECRETARY OF INTERIOR Oct. 15, 1903							
	14								
	15								
	16								
	17								

TRIBAL ENROLLMENT OF PARENTS

	Name of Father	Year	County	Name of Mother	Year	County
1	E-lo-ma	Dead	Red River	Marsie Eloma	Dead	Red River
2	Tom Furgeson	"	Non Citz	Frances Furgeson	"	Non Citz
3	No 1			No 2		
4	No 1			No 2		
5						
6						
7						
8			Nos.1 and 2 were married July 1, 1895 by John			
9			Edwards, Minister of the Gospel. No.1 is a			
10			full blood Choctaw, his wife is a United States Citz. His house was burned and			
11			certificate of Marriage with it. These facts			
12			are shown by sworn testimony of himself and Amos Yale. See testimony.			
13			No.4 Proof of birth 11/26/02.			
14		No4 Born Nov. 28, 1900. Application made Nov. 26, 1902 Proof of				
15		birth filed April 2, 1903.				
16					Date of Application for Enrollment May 1/99	
17	Garvin I.T. 12/2/02					

46

Choctaw By Blood Enrollment Cards 1898-1914

RESIDENCE: Bok Tuklo   COUNTY.   **Choctaw Nation**   Choctaw Roll   CARD NO.

POST OFFICE: Lukfata, I.T.   *(Not Including Freedmen)*   FIELD NO. **1247**

Dawes' Roll No.	NAME	Relationship to Person	AGE	SEX	BLOOD	TRIBAL ENROLLMENT		
						Year	County	No.
3382	₁ James, Calvin ⁵³	First Named	50	M	1/2	1896	Bok Tuklo	6916
3383	₂ " Janey ⁵³	Wife	50	F	Full	1896	" "	6917
3384	₃ Herndon, Isabelle ¹⁹	Dau	16	"	3/4	1896	" "	6918
3385	₄ James, Shub ¹⁵	Son	12	M	3/4	1896	" "	6919
I.W. 1289	₅ Herndon, John C. ³³	Husband of No.3	33	M	I.W.			
	6							
	7 ENROLLMENT OF NOS. 1 2 3 and 4 HEREON APPROVED BY THE SECRETARY OF INTERIOR Dec 12 1902							
	10							
	11 ENROLLMENT OF NOS. 5 HEREON APPROVED BY THE SECRETARY OF INTERIOR Mar 14 1905							
	14							
	15							
	16							
	17 On July 23, 1902 No.5 was married to No.3							

TRIBAL ENROLLMENT OF PARENTS

	Name of Father	Year	County	Name of Mother	Year	County
₁	Bob James		Towson		Dead	Towson
₂	O-sha-she-huma	Dead	Kiamitia	Feh-na-hohke	"	Kiamitia
₃	No 1			No 2		
₄	No 1			No 2		
₅	Harrison Herndon		non citizen	Alice Herndon		non citizen
₆						
₇						
₈						
₉	For child of Nos 3&4 see NB (Apr 26-06) Card #736					
₁₀	No1 on 1896 roll as Garvin James					
₁₁	No4 " 1896 " " Sheb "					
₁₂	No.3 married to John C. Herndon on Choctaw Card #D-779, on July 23, 1902					
₁₃	Evidence of marriage with Choctaw #D 779, Filed Aug 29, 1902.					
₁₄	No.5 originally listed for enrollment on Choctaw Card D-779 Aug 29,1902; transferred to this card Jan. 28, 1905. See decision of Jan. 12, 1905					
₁₅	Record as to enrollment of No.5 forwarded Department Mar. 14, 1906.					
₁₆	Record returned. See opinion of Assistant Attorney General of March 15, 1906 in case of Omer R. Nicholson				May 1/99	
₁₇	No.5 P.O. Glover I.T. 2/4/04					

For child of Nos 3&5 see N.B. (Mar 3-05) Card #106

47

Choctaw By Blood Enrollment Cards 1898-1914

RESIDENCE: Red River COUNTY.
POST OFFICE: Shawneetown, I.T.

Choctaw Nation

Choctaw Roll
(Not Including Freedmen)

CARD NO.
FIELD NO. **1248**

Dawes' Roll No.	NAME		Relationship to Person	AGE	SEX	BLOOD	TRIBAL ENROLLMENT		
							Year	County	No.
3386	1 Hotinlobi, Joe	27	First Named	24	M	Full	1896	Red River	5726
3387	2 " Lasin	36	Wife	33	F	"	1893	Nashoba	P.R. 925
3388	3 Oklahambi, Mary	14	Niece	11	"	"	1896	Eagle	9934
3389	4 " Joseph	8	Nephew	5	M	"	1896	"	9935
	5								
	6	ENROLLMENT							
	7	OF NOS. 1 2 3 and 4 HEREON							
	8	APPROVED BY THE SECRETARY OF INTERIOR Dec 12 1902							
	9								
	10								
	11								
	12								
	13								
	14								
	15								
	16								
	17								

TRIBAL ENROLLMENT OF PARENTS

	Name of Father	Year	County	Name of Mother	Year	County
1	Ho-tin-lobi	Dead	Bok Tuklo	Louisiana Hotinlobi	Dead	Red River
2	Wm Meashetubbi	1896	Wade	Sally Meashetubbi	"	Wade
3	Ramsey Oklahambi	Dead	Red River	Miney Oklahambi	"	Red River
4	" "	"	" "	" "	"	" "
5						
6						
7			No2 on 1893 Pay roll as Lucin Stephens, Page 80			
8			No 925, Nashoba County. She is also known as Sissy			
9			For child of No.3 see NB (Mar. 3 1905 #877			
10						
11						
12						
13						
14				Date of Application for Enrollment.		
15				May 1/99		
16						
17	No.3 P.O. Goodwater I.T. 4/10/05					

48

Choctaw By Blood Enrollment Cards 1898-1914

RESIDENCE: Eagle COUNTY.   **Choctaw Nation**   **Choctaw Roll** CARD NO.
POST OFFICE: Eagletown, I.T.   (Not Including Freedmen)   FIELD NO. **1249**

Dawes' Roll No.	NAME		Relationship to Person	AGE	SEX	BLOOD	TRIBAL ENROLLMENT		
							Year	County	No.
3390	1 Wesley, Elias	38	First Named	35	M	Full	1896	Eagle	13442
3391	2 " Betty	26	Wife	23	F	"	1896	"	13450
3392	3 " Malissy	22	Niece	19	"	"	1896	"	13451
3393	4 " Lucy	21	"	18	"	"	1896	"	13448
3394	5 " John	2	Son	11mo	M	"			
	6								
	7	ENROLLMENT OF NOS. 1 2 3 4 and 5 HEREON APPROVED BY THE SECRETARY OF INTERIOR Dec 12 1902							
	8								
	9								
	10								
	11								
	12								
	13								
	14								
	15								
	16								
	17								

TRIBAL ENROLLMENT OF PARENTS

	Name of Father	Year	County	Name of Mother	Year	County
1	Ah-ne-tubby	Dead	Eagle	Ta-ma-huna	Dead	Eagle
2	Austin McGee	1896	Bok Tuklo	Jennie McGee	"	"
3	Le-a-mus	Dead	Eagle	Emily Leamus	"	"
4	"	"	"	"	"	"
5	No.1			No.2		
6						
7						
8						
9			No 4 also on 1896 roll, Page 353			
10			No 13447, Eagle Co.			
11			No.5 Enrolled July 29, 1901.			
12			No4 is the wife of Otson Tonihka on Choctaw Card #897, and mother of Richmond Tonihka on same card. See letter from Jeff Gardner filed Oct. 11, 1902			
13			For child of No.1 see NB (March 3, 1905) #971			
14						
15					Date of Application for Enrollment.	
16				For Nos 1 to 4 inc	May 1/99	
17						

49

RESIDENCE: Eagle COUNTY.	**Choctaw Nation**	Choctaw Roll *(Not Including Freedmen)*	CARD No.
POST OFFICE: Eagletown, I.T.			FIELD No. **1250**

Dawes' Roll No.	NAME	Relationship to Person First Named	AGE	SEX	BLOOD	TRIBAL ENROLLMENT		
						Year	County	No.
DEAD	1 Wade, Nicholas E **DEAD**		41	M	Full	1896	Eagle	13462
14651	2 Stephen, Linas 27	Wife	24	F	"	1896	"	13474
3395	3 Wade, Barnet 25	Son	22	M	"	1896	"	13464
3396	4 " Formy[sic] 23	"	20	"	"	1896	"	113471
3397	5 " Bitny[sic] 10	Dau	7	F	"	1896	"	13467
3398	6 " Williston	Son	5	M	"	1896	"	13473
3399	7 " Frances 7	Dau	4	F	"	1896	"	13468
14652	8 Stephen, Crety 2	Son	6mo	M	"			
	9 ENROLLMENT							
	10 OF NOS. 3 4 5 6 and 7 HEREON APPROVED BY THE SECRETARY							
	11 OF INTERIOR Dec 12 1902							
	12 ENROLLMENT							
	13 OF NOS. 2 and 8 HEREON APPROVED BY THE SECRETARY							
	14 OF INTERIOR May 20 1903						No	
	15 No. 1 hereon dismissed under order of							
	16 the Commission to the Five Civilized							
	17 Tribes of March 31, 1905.							

DIED PRIOR TO SEPTEMBER 25, 1908

TRIBAL ENROLLMENT OF PARENTS

	Name of Father	Year	County	Name of Mother	Year	County
1	E-ya-hoke-tubby	Dead	Eagle	Okla-hay-she	Dead	Eagle
2	Isom Jones	1896	"	Sillis Jones	1896	"
3	No 1			Elsie Wade	Dead	"
4	No 1			" "	"	"
5	No 1			No 2		
6	No 1			No 2		
7	No 1			No 2		
8	Lemus Stephen	1896	Eagle	No 2		
9	No.6 died - -, 1900. Enrollment cancelled by Department July 8, 1904					
10	No2 on 1896 roll as Lemus Wade					
11	No5 " 1896 " " Bickny "					
12	No1 died July 10, 1900. proof of death filed Dec 3, 1902 No6 died in 1900 " " " " " "					
13	No.2 is now the wife of Lemus Stephen on Choctaw Card #833. Evidence of					
14	marriage filed Aug 10, 1901. (For child of No.2 see NB Apr26-06) Card #584					
15	No 8 Enrolled Aug 10, 1901.					
16	No 3 is the husband of Emiline Harrison #1 to 7 inc. on Choctaw Card #694, August 30, 1901 Date of Application for Enrollment May 1/99					
17						

Choctaw By Blood Enrollment Cards 1898-1914

RESIDENCE: Eagle   COUNTY.   **Choctaw Nation**   Choctaw Roll _(Not Including Freedmen)_   CARD No.

POST OFFICE: Eagletown, I.T.   FIELD No. 1251

Dawes' Roll No.	NAME	Relationship to Person	AGE	SEX	BLOOD	TRIBAL ENROLLMENT		
						Year	County	No.
3400	1 Wesley, Lenas 27	First Named	24	M	Full	1896	Eagle	13446
	2							
	3 ENROLLMENT OF NOS. 1 HEREON							
	4 APPROVED BY THE SECRETARY OF INTERIOR DEC 12 1902							
	5							
	6							
	7							
	8							
	9							
	10							
	11							
	12							
	13							
	14							
	15							
	16							
	17							

TRIBAL ENROLLMENT OF PARENTS

	Name of Father	Year	County	Name of Mother	Year	County
1	Ah-nit-tubbee	Dead	Eagle	Ta-ma-huna	Dead	Eagle
2						
3						
4						
5		On 1896 roll as Lemus Wesley				
6		No.1 is now husband of Salean Tonihka 7-897				
7		For child of No.1 see NB (March 3 1905) #1148				
8						
9						
10						
11						
12						
13						
14						Date of Application for Enrollment.
15						
16						May 1/99
17						

Choctaw By Blood Enrollment Cards 1898-1914

RESIDENCE: Eagle COUNTY.
POST OFFICE: Eagletown, I.T.

Choctaw Nation

Choctaw Roll
(Not Including Freedmen)

CARD NO.
FIELD NO. 1252

Dawes' Roll No.	NAME	Relationship to Person	AGE	SEX	BLOOD	TRIBAL ENROLLMENT		
						Year	County	No.
3401	1 Wesley, Elsey 33	First Named	30	F	Full	1896	Eagle	13443
	2							
	3	ENROLLMENT						
	4	OF NOS. 1 HEREON APPROVED BY THE SECRETARY						
	5	OF INTERIOR DEC 12 1902						
	6							
	7							
	8							
	9							
	10							
	11							
	12							
	13							
	14							
	15							
	16							
	17							

TRIBAL ENROLLMENT OF PARENTS

	Name of Father	Year	County	Name of Mother	Year	County
1	Ah-nit-tubbee	Dead	Eagle	Ta-ma-huna	Dead	Eagle
2						
3						
4						
5						
6						
7						
8						
9						
10						
11						
12						
13						
14						
15				Date of Application for Enrollment		
16				May 1/99		
17						

Choctaw By Blood Enrollment Cards 1898-1914

RESIDENCE: Red River   COUNTY.   **Choctaw Nation**   **Choctaw Roll**   CARD NO.

POST OFFICE: Kullituklo, I.T.   *(Not Including Freedmen)*   FIELD NO.   1253

Dawes' Roll No.	NAME	Relationship to Person First Named	AGE	SEX	BLOOD	TRIBAL ENROLLMENT		
						Year	County	No.
3402	1 Wilson, Ward 25	First Named	22	M	Full	1896	Red River	13613
3403	2 " Sarphin 33	Wife	30	F	"	1896	" "	13616
3404	3 Willis, Wallace 8	S.Son	6	M	"	1896	" "	13618
3405	4 ~~DIED PRIOR TO SEPTEMBER 25, 1902~~ Inis	S.Dau	1	F	"			
	5							
	6							
	7	ENROLLMENT OF NOS. 1 2 3 and 4 HEREON						
	8	APPROVED BY THE SECRETARY						
	9	OF INTERIOR DEC 12 1902						
	10							
	11							
	12							
	13							
	14							
	15							
	16							
	17							

TRIBAL ENROLLMENT OF PARENTS

	Name of Father	Year	County	Name of Mother	Year	County
1	Wright Mintichuby	Dead	Eagle	Winey Mintichuby	1896	Eagle
2	Bar-na-by	"	Red River	Ma-sey	Dead	Red River
3	Davis Willis	"	" "	No 2		
4	~~Julius Jefferson~~	~~1896~~	" "	No 2		
5						
6						
7	No2 on 1896 roll as Sarphim Willis					
8	No.2 is dead; see N.B. (Apr. 26,'06) card #270					
9	No4 Affidavit of birth to be supplied. Rec'd May 9/99					
10						
11						
12	No4 died in 1899, proof of death filed Dec 2, 1902					
13	~~No.4 died — —. 1899: Enrollment cancelled by Department July 8, 1904~~					
14					Date of Application for Enrollment.	
15	For child of No's 1&2, see N.B. (Apr. 26, 1906) Card #270				May 1/99	
16						
17	Lukfata I.T. 11/25/02					

Choctaw By Blood Enrollment Cards 1898-1914

RESIDENCE: Eagle COUNTY.
POST OFFICE: Lukfata, I.T.

Choctaw Nation

Choctaw Roll
(Not Including Freedmen)

CARD NO.
FIELD NO. 1254

Dawes' Roll No.		NAME	Relationship to Person First Named	AGE	SEX	BLOOD	TRIBAL ENROLLMENT		
							Year	County	No.
3406	1	Hleohtambi, Charley 41	First Named	38	M	Full	1896	Eagle	5607
3407	2	" Eliona 45	Wife	42	F	"	1896	"	5618
3408	3	" Selile 23	Dau	20	"	"	1896	"	5644
	4								
	5	ENROLLMENT							
	6	OF NOS. 1 2 and 3 HEREON APPROVED BY THE SECRETARY							
	7	OF INTERIOR DEC 12 1902							
	8								
	9								
	10								
	11								
	12								
	13								
	14								
	15								
	16								
	17								

TRIBAL ENROLLMENT OF PARENTS

	Name of Father	Year	County	Name of Mother	Year	County
1	Hleohtambi	1896	Eagle	Betsey Hleohtambi	1896	Eagle
2	Ah-took-che-nuby	Dead	"	Betsey Wilson	1896	"
3	No 1			Margaret Hleohtambi	Dead	"
4						
5						
6	No2 on 1896 roll as Eleciana Hleohtambi					
7	No3 " 1896 " " Silili "					
8						
9						
10						
11						
12						
13						
14				Date of Application for Enrollment.		
15						
16				May 1/99		
17						

Choctaw By Blood Enrollment Cards 1898-1914

RESIDENCE: Eagle   COUNTY.   **Choctaw Nation**   **Choctaw Roll**   CARD NO.

POST OFFICE: Lukfata, I.T.   (Not Including Freedmen)   FIELD NO. 1255

Dawes' Roll No.	NAME	Relationship to Person First Named	AGE	SEX	BLOOD	Year	County	No.
3409	1 Wilson, Betsy DIED PRIOR TO SEPTEMBER 25, 1902		75	F	Full	1896	Eagle	13494
3410	⊕ 2 " Wiley 41	Son Dau	38	M F	"	1896	"	13522
3411	3 " Mamie 37	Dau	34	F	"	1896	"	13536
	4							
	5	ENROLLMENT						
	6	OF NOS. 1 2 and 3 HEREON APPROVED BY THE SECRETARY						
	7	OF INTERIOR DEC 12 1902						
	8							
	9							
	10							
	11							
	12							
	13							
	14	⊕ Correction of Sex of No 2						
	15	made in accordance with						
	16	Dept letter I.O. No 3611-1919.						
	17							

TRIBAL ENROLLMENT OF PARENTS

	Name of Father	Year	County	Name of Mother	Year	County
1	Me-ash-in-tubby	Dead	Eagle	Ua-ka-tema	Died in Mississippi	
2	A-took-chi-nubbee	"	"	No 1		
3	"	"	"	No 1		
4						
5						
6						
7						
8	No3 on 1896 roll as Mannie Wilson					
9	No1 died Dec 3, 1901: proof of death filed Dec 15, 1902.					
10						
11						
12						
13						
14						
15						
16						
17						

Choctaw By Blood Enrollment Cards 1898-1914

RESIDENCE: Eagle COUNTY. **Choctaw Nation** **Choctaw Roll** CARD NO.
POST OFFICE: Eagletown, I.T. *(Not Including Freedmen)* FIELD NO. 1256

Dawes' Roll No.	NAME	Relationship to Person First Named	AGE	SEX	BLOOD	TRIBAL ENROLLMENT		
						Year	County	No.
3412	1 Tushka, Levi 23	First Named	20	M	Full	1896	Eagle	12236
3413	2 " Kissie 21	Sister	18	F	1/2	1896	"	12238
	3							
	4							
	5	ENROLLMENT						
	6	OF NOS. 1 and 2 HEREON APPROVED BY THE SECRETARY						
	7	OF INTERIOR DEC 12 1902						
	8							
	9							
	10							
	11							
	12							
	13							
	14							
	15							
	16							
	17							

TRIBAL ENROLLMENT OF PARENTS

	Name of Father	Year	County	Name of Mother	Year	County
1	Tushka	Dead	Red River	Netsey Tushka	Dead	Eagle
2	Henry Garvin	"	Non Citz	" "	"	"
3						
4						
5						
6						
7		No1 on 1896 roll as Levi Tashka				
8		No2 " 1896 " " Kissie "				
9						
10						
11						
12						
13						
14						
15					Date of Application for Enrollment.	
16					May 1/99	
17						

RESIDENCE: Eagle COUNTY.
POST OFFICE: Lukfata, I.T.

Choctaw Nation

Choctaw Roll (Not Including Freedmen)

CARD No.
FIELD No. 1257

Dawes' Roll No.	NAME	Relationship to Person	AGE	SEX	BLOOD	TRIBAL ENROLLMENT		
						Year	County	No.
3414	1 Alemohtubbi, David 41	First Named	38	M	Full	1896	Eagle	306
3415	2 " Inez 25	Wife	22	F	"	1893	"	P.R. 6
3416	3 " Steson 14	Son	11	M	"	1893	"	8
3417	4 " Emma 8	Dau	5	F	"	1896	"	273
3418	5 " Ina 5	"	1	"	"			
	6							
	7	ENROLLMENT OF NOS. 1 2 3 4 and 5 HEREON APPROVED BY THE SECRETARY OF INTERIOR Dec. 12, 1902.						
	8							
	9							
	10							
	11							
	12							
	13							
	14							
	15							
	16							
	17							

TRIBAL ENROLLMENT OF PARENTS

	Name of Father	Year	County	Name of Mother	Year	County
1	David Alemohtubbi	Dead	Eagle	Unat-a-mah	Dead	Eagle
2	James Wilson	"	"	Sally Wilson	"	"
3	No 1			Litey Alemohtubbi	1896	Nashoba
4	No 1			No 2		
5	No 1			No 2		
6						
7						
8	No2 on 1893 Pay roll as Agnes Alematube Page 1 No 6 Eagle County					
9	No3 " 1893 " " " Steson " " 1 No 8 " "					
10	No3 also on 1896 " " Kesin Alemohtubbi " 8 " 307 " "					
11						
12						
13						
14					Date of Application for Enrollment.	
15						
16					May 1/99	
17						

Choctaw By Blood Enrollment Cards 1898-1914

RESIDENCE: Eagle   COUNTY.   **Choctaw Nation**   Choctaw Roll   CARD NO.

POST OFFICE: Lukfata, I.T.   *(Not Including Freedmen)*   FIELD NO.   1258

Dawes' Roll No.	NAME	Relationship to Person First Named	AGE	SEX	BLOOD	TRIBAL ENROLLMENT Year	County	No.
3419	1 Thompson, Craymon [23]	First Named	20	M	Full	1896	Eagle	12254
	2							
	3							
	4	ENROLLMENT						
	5	OF NOS. 1 HEREON APPROVED BY THE SECRETARY						
	6	OF INTERIOR DEC 12 1902						
	7							
	8							
	9							
	10							
	11							
	12							
	13							
	14							
	15							
	16							
	17							

TRIBAL ENROLLMENT OF PARENTS

	Name of Father	Year	County	Name of Mother	Year	County
1	Thompson	Dead	Eagle	Louisa Thompson	Dead	Eagle
2						
3						
4						
5						
6						
7						
8						
9						
10						
11						
12						
13						
14						
15						
16				Date of Application for Enrollment.	May 1/99	
17						

Choctaw By Blood Enrollment Cards 1898-1914

RESIDENCE: Towson COUNTY.
POST OFFICE: Doaksville, I.T.

Choctaw Nation

Choctaw Roll (Not Including Freedmen)

CARD NO. FIELD NO. **1259**

Dawes' Roll No.	NAME	Relationship to Person	AGE	SEX	BLOOD	TRIBAL ENROLLMENT		
						Year	County	No.
3420	1 Aaron, Jim 21	First Named	18	M	Full	1893	Towson	P.R. 21
	2							
	3							
	4	ENROLLMENT						
	5	OF NOS. 1 HEREON APPROVED BY THE SECRETARY OF INTERIOR DEC 12 1902						
	6							
	7							
	8							
	9							
	10							
	11							
	12							
	13							
	14							
	15							
	16							
	17							

TRIBAL ENROLLMENT OF PARENTS

	Name of Father	Year	County	Name of Mother	Year	County
1	Stephen Aaron	Dead	Towson	Liley Aaron	Dead	Towson
2						
3						
4						
5	On 1893 Pay roll as Janie Aaron Page 2 No 21, Towson Co.					
6						
7						
8						
9						
10						
11						
12						
13						
14						
15					Date of Application for Enrollment.	
16					May 1/99	
17						

59

Choctaw By Blood Enrollment Cards 1898-1914

RESIDENCE: Nashoba COUNTY.
POST OFFICE: Alikchi I.T.

Choctaw Nation

Choctaw Roll (Not Including Freedmen)

CARD NO.
FIELD NO. 1260

Dawes' Roll No.	NAME	Relationship to Person First Named	AGE	SEX	BLOOD	TRIBAL ENROLLMENT		
						Year	County	No.
DEAD	1 Johnson Watson		55	M	Full	1896	Nashoba	6851
DEAD	2 " Tennissa	Wife	44	F	"	1896	"	6852
	3							
	4							
	5	DISMISSED						
	6	JAN 30 1907						
	7							
	8							
	9							
	10							
	11							
	12							
	13							
	14							
	15							
	16							
	17							

TRIBAL ENROLLMENT OF PARENTS

Name of Father	Year	County	Name of Mother	Year	County
1 Ish-tiata-bi	Ded	Nashoba		De'd	Nashoba
2 Fi-lam-i-tabi	"	"	"Hoki"	"	"
3					
4					
5	1/20/03 No proof of death in jacket				
6	No2 on 1896 roll as Tennessee Johnson				
7					
8					
9					
10					
11					
12					
13					
14					
15					Date of Application for Enrollment.
16					May 1-99
17					

Choctaw By Blood Enrollment Cards 1898-1914

RESIDENCE: Red River COUNTY. **Choctaw Nation** **Choctaw Roll** CARD NO.
POST OFFICE: Kully-Tuk-lo I.T. (Not Including Freedmen) FIELD NO. 1261

Dawes' Roll No.	NAME		Relationship to Person	AGE	SEX	BLOOD	TRIBAL ENROLLMENT		
							Year	County	No.
3421	1 Talvatona	53	First Named	50	F	Full	1896	Red River	12311
3422	2 Boling Billy	27	Son	24	M	"	1896	" "	1367
	3								
	4	ENROLLMENT							
	5	OF NOS. 1 and 2 HEREON APPROVED BY THE SECRETARY							
	6	OF INTERIOR DEC 12 1902							
	7								
	8								
	9								
	10								
	11								
	12								
	13								
	14								
	15								
	16								
	17								

TRIBAL ENROLLMENT OF PARENTS

	Name of Father	Year	County	Name of Mother	Year	County
1	"Ale-moh-tabi"	Ded	Eagle	Mintihema	De'd	Eagle
2	"Steka"	"	"	No 1		
3						
4						
5						
6	For child of No.1 see NB (March 3, 1905) #1446					
7						
8						
9						
10						
11						
12						
13						
14						
15						
16				Date of Application for Enrollment	May 1-99	
17						

61

Choctaw By Blood Enrollment Cards 1898-1914

RESIDENCE: Eagle COUNTY.
POST OFFICE: Luk-fa-tah I.T.

Choctaw Nation

Choctaw Roll
(Not Including Freedmen)

CARD NO.
FIELD NO. 1262

Dawes' Roll No.	NAME	Relationship to Person First Named	AGE	SEX	BLOOD	TRIBAL ENROLLMENT		
						Year	County	No.
3423	1 Wilson Tobias 27	First Named	24	M	Full	1896	Eagle	13549
3424	2 " Tom 15	Bro	12	"	"	1896	"	13547
	3							
	4							
	5	ENROLLMENT OF NOS. 1 and 2 HEREON APPROVED BY THE SECRETARY OF INTERIOR DEC 12 1902						
	6							
	7							
	8							
	9							
	10							
	11							
	12							
	13							
	14							
	15							
	16							
	17							

TRIBAL ENROLLMENT OF PARENTS

	Name of Father	Year	County	Name of Mother	Year	County
1	Commise Wilson	Ded	Eagle	Winny Wilson	De'd	Eagle
2	" "	"	"	" "	"	"
3						
4						
5						
6						
7						
8						
9						
10						
11						
12						
13						
14						
15					Date of Application for Enrollment.	
16					May 1-99	
17						

RESIDENCE: Bok Tuklo   **COUNTY.**   **Choctaw Nation**   **Choctaw Roll**   **CARD NO.**
POST OFFICE: Luk-fa-tah I.T.   *(Not Including Freedmen)*   **FIELD NO.** 1263

Dawes Roll No.	NAME	Relationship to Person	AGE	SEX	BLOOD	TRIBAL ENROLLMENT		
						Year	County	No.
2578 1	Johnson Isabel ²¹	First Named	18	F	Full	1896	Kiamatia[sic]	6771
2								
3	ENROLLMENT OF NOS. 1 HEREON APPROVED BY THE SECRETARY OF INTERIOR DEC 12 1902							
4								
5								
6								
7								
8								
9								
10								
11								
12								
13								
14								
15								
16								
17								

TRIBAL ENROLLMENT OF PARENTS

	Name of Father	Year	County	Name of Mother	Year	County
1	Tom Johnson	Ded	Kiamatia[sic]	Sibbie Johnson	Ded	Kiamatia[sic]
2						
3						
4						
5	No.1 on Choctaw roll as Isabelle Johnson					
6	No1 is now wife of Byington Williams 7-534					
7						
8						
9						
10						
11						
12						
13						
14						
15						
16				Date of Application for Enrollment May 1"99		
17						

63

Choctaw By Blood Enrollment Cards 1898-1914

RESIDENCE: Eagle   COUNTY.   **Choctaw Nation**   **Choctaw Roll**   CARD NO.
POST OFFICE: Luk fa tah I.T.   *(Not Including Freedmen)*   FIELD NO. 1264

Dawes' Roll No.	NAME		Relationship to Person	AGE	SEX	BLOOD	TRIBAL ENROLLMENT		
							Year	County	No.
3425	1 Wilson William P.	46	First Named	43	M	Full	1896	Eagle	13559
3426	2 " Jacob	19	Son	16	"	"	1896	"	13501
3427	3 " Isabelle	17	Dau	14	F	"	1896	"	13532
3428	4 " Mary	15	"	12	"	"	1896	"	13503
3429	5 " Frank	13	Son	10	M	"	1896	"	13538
3430	6 " Easter	11	Dau	8	F	"	1896	"	13512
3431	7 " Walter	9	Son	6	M	"	1896	"	13527
	8								
	9	ENROLLMENT OF NOS. 123456and7 HEREON APPROVED BY THE SECRETARY OF INTERIOR DEC 12 1902							
	10								
	11								
	12								
	13								
	14								
	15								
	16								
	17								

TRIBAL ENROLLMENT OF PARENTS

	Name of Father	Year	County	Name of Mother	Year	County
1	Wilson Matihena	De'd	Eagle	Betsy	De'd	Eagle
2	No 1			Lila Wilson	"	"
3	No 1			" "	"	"
4	No 1			" "	"	"
5	No 1			" "	"	"
6	No 1			" "	"	"
7	No 1			" "	"	"
8						
9						
10			No1 On 1896 toll as Wm P. Wilson			
11			No.1 is now the husband of Littie Goings on Choctaw Card #871. July 20,1901			
12						
13			For child of No3 see NB (Apr 26-06) Card # 691			
14			" " " No1 " " (Mar 3-05) " #1143			
15						Date of Application for Enrollment.
16						May 1"99
17						

Choctaw By Blood Enrollment Cards 1898-1914

RESIDENCE: Red River   COUNTY.   **Choctaw Nation**   **Choctaw Roll** (Not Including Freedmen)   CARD NO.

POST OFFICE: Garvin I T   FIELD NO. 1265

Dawes' Roll No.	NAME	Relationship to Person First Named	AGE	SEX	BLOOD	TRIBAL ENROLLMENT		
						Year	County	No.
IW228 ₁	Holman Charles R. ²⁸	First Named	25	M	I.W.		Non Citz	
3432 ₂	" Sarah ²³	Wife	20	F	3/4	1896	Towson	13161
3433 ₃	~~Rosa~~ DIED PRIOR TO SEPTEMBER 25, 1902	Dau	8mo	"	3/8			
3434 ₄	~~Ben Denison~~ DIED PRIOR TO SEPTEMBER 25, 1902	Son	2mo	M	3/8			
	5							
	6	ENROLLMENT OF NOS. 2 3 and 4 HEREON APPROVED BY THE SECRETARY OF INTERIOR DEC 12 1902						
	7							
	8							
	9	ENROLLMENT OF NOS. 1 HEREON APPROVED BY THE SECRETARY OF INTERIOR SEP 12 1903						
	10							
	11							
	12							
	13							
	14							
	15							
	16							
	17							

TRIBAL ENROLLMENT OF PARENTS

	Name of Father	Year	County	Name of Mother	Year	County
1	James Holman	1896	Non Citz	Sarah Holman	De'd	Non Citz
2	Daniel Webster	1896	" "	Lavisa Webster	"	Towson
3	No 1			No 2		
4	No 1			No 2		
5						
6						
7						
8						
9						
10						
11	No 2 on 1896 roll as Sarah Webster					
12	No.4 Enrolled Aug 24, 1901.					
13	For child of Nos 1&2, see N.B. (Apr. 26, 1906) Card No.58					
14	No3 died March 5, 1900; proof of death filed Dec 2, 1902 No4 " March 8, 1902; " " " " " "					
15	No3 died March 5,1900;No4 died March 8,1902; Enrollment cancelled by Department July 8,1904					
16	For child of Nos 1&2 see NB (Mar 3,1905) #517 Date of Application for Enrollment May 1-99					
17						

65

Choctaw By Blood Enrollment Cards 1898-1914

RESIDENCE: Eagle COUNTY.
POST OFFICE: Eagle Town I T

Choctaw Nation

Choctaw Roll (Not Including Freedmen)

CARD NO.
FIELD NO. 1266

Dawes Roll No.	NAME		Relationship to Person	AGE	SEX	BLOOD	TRIBAL ENROLLMENT		
							Year	County	No.
3435	1 Byington Alfred	58	First Named	55	M	Full	1896	Eagle	1259
3436	2 " Phillis	43	Wife	40	F	"	1896	"	1309
3437	3 Wilson Joe	15	S Son	12	M	"	1896	"	13502
	4								
	5								
	6								
	7								
	8								
	9								
	10								
	11	ENROLLMENT OF NOS. 1 2 and 3 HEREON							
	12	APPROVED BY THE SECRETARY							
	13	OF INTERIOR DEC 12 1902							
	14								
	15								
	16								
	17								

TRIBAL ENROLLMENT OF PARENTS

	Name of Father	Year	County	Name of Mother	Year	County
1	Albert Byington	Ded	Blue	Basie Byington	Ded	Eagle
2	Elikanclaitabi	"	Eagle	Cha-fa-ho-na	"	"
3	Jacob Lewis	"	"	No 2		
4						
5						
6						
7		No 2 on 1896 roll as Philis Byington				
8						
9						
10						
11						
12						
13						
14					Date of Application for Enrollment.	
15						
16					May 1-99	
17						

RESIDENCE: Nashoba   COUNTY.   **Choctaw Nation**   **Choctaw Roll**   CARD No.

POST OFFICE: Alikchi I.T.   *(Not Including Freedmen)*   FIELD No. 1267

Dawes' Roll No.		NAME	Relationship to Person First Named	AGE	SEX	BLOOD	TRIBAL ENROLLMENT		
							Year	County	No.
3438	1	Battiest Sibbie		70	F	Full	1896	Nashoba	1174
3439	2	" Frances ¹⁷	G. Dau	14	"	"	1896	"	1175
3440	3	" Aaron ¹⁶	" Son	13	M	"	1896	"	1176
	4								
	5	ENROLLMENT							
	6	OF NOS. 1 2 and 3 HEREON APPROVED BY THE SECRETARY							
	7	OF INTERIOR DEC 2 1902							
	8								
	9								
	10								
	11								
	12								
	13								
	14								
	15								
	16								
	17								

TRIBAL ENROLLMENT OF PARENTS

	Name of Father	Year	County	Name of Mother	Year	County
1		Ded	Mississippi	Minto hoyo	Ded	Nashoba
2	William Battiest	"	Nashoba	Amy Battiest	"	"
3	" "	"	"	" "	"	"
4						
5						
6						
7	No 1 died March 1900: proof of death filed Dec 16, 1902					
8	No 2 is now wife of Hinson King on Choc #1061					
9	No.1 died March 4, 1900: Enrollment cancelled by Department July 8, 1904					
10	For child of No 2 see NB Apr 26'06 #1271					
11						
12						
13						
14						
15						Date of Application for Enrollment.
16						May 1"99
17						

Choctaw By Blood Enrollment Cards 1898-1914

RESIDENCE: Towson COUNTY. **Choctaw Nation** **Choctaw Roll** *(Not Including Freedmen)* CARD NO.
POST OFFICE: Doaksville, I.T. FIELD NO. **1268**

Dawes' Roll No.	NAME	Relationship to Person First Named	AGE	SEX	BLOOD	TRIBAL ENROLLMENT Year	TRIBAL ENROLLMENT County	No.
3441	1 Tims, Willie 26	First Named	23	M	3/4	1896	Towson	12118
3442	2 " Mary 24	Wife	21	F	Full	1896	"	7942
3443	3 " Roberson 2	Son	3mo	M	7/8			
	4							
	5							
	6	ENROLLMENT						
	7	OF NOS. 1 2 and 3 HEREON APPROVED BY THE SECRETARY						
	8	OF INTERIOR Dec 12 1902						
	9							
	10							
	11							
	12							
	13							
	14							
	15							
	16							
	17							

TRIBAL ENROLLMENT OF PARENTS

	Name of Father	Year	County	Name of Mother	Year	County
1	Vincent Tims	Dead	Towson	Emiline Tims	1896	Towson
2	King Lewis	"	"	Nancy Lewis	1896	
3	No.1			No.2		
4						
5						
6						
7		No2 on 1896 roll as Mawey Lewis				
8		No.3 Enrolled May 17, 1901.				
9		For child of Nos. 1&2 see N.B. (Apr 26'06) Card #274				
10		" " " " " " " (March 3'05) " #1424				
11						
12						
13						
14						
15					#1&2	
16				Date of Application for Enrollment	May 1/99	
17						

RESIDENCE: Eagle   COUNTY.   **Choctaw Nation**   **Choctaw Roll**   CARD NO.

POST OFFICE: Eagletown I.T.   *(Not Including Freedmen)*   FIELD NO.   1269

Dawes' Roll No.	NAME	Relationship to Person	AGE	SEX	BLOOD	TRIBAL ENROLLMENT		
						Year	County	No.
3444	1 Wade, Ben 39	First Named	36	M	Full	1896	Eagle	13469
3445	2 " Louina 43	Wife	40	F	"	1896	"	13463
3446	3 " Leasin 14	Dau	11	"	"	1896	"	13466
3447	4 " Sissy 12	"	9	"	"	1896	"	13472
	5							
	6	ENROLLMENT						
	7	OF NOS. 1 2 3 and 4 HEREON APPROVED BY THE SECRETARY						
	8	OF INTERIOR DEC 12 1902						
	9							
	10							
	11							
	12							
	13							
	14							
	15							
	16							
	17							

TRIBAL ENROLLMENT OF PARENTS

	Name of Father	Year	County	Name of Mother	Year	County
1	Ya-ho-ka-tubbee	Dead	Eagle	Kana-hama	1896	Eagle
2	Ah-le-muh-tubbee	"	"	Hoh-na	Dead	"
3	No 1			No 2		
4	No 1			No 2		
5						
6						
7			No2 on 1896 roll as Melvina Wade			
8			For child of No.1 see NB (March 3, 1905) #1530			
9						
10						
11						
12						
13						
14						
15						
16				Date of Application for Enrollment May 1/99		
17						

Choctaw By Blood Enrollment Cards 1898-1914

RESIDENCE: Eagle   COUNTY.   **Choctaw Nation**   **Choctaw Roll**   CARD NO.

POST OFFICE: Eagletown, I.T.   *(Not Including Freedmen)*   FIELD NO.   1270

Dawes' Roll No.	NAME	Relationship to Person	AGE	SEX	BLOOD	TRIBAL ENROLLMENT		
						Year	County	No.
3448	1 Kanahima ⁷¹	First Named	68	F	Full	1896	Eagle	7558
3449	2 Ward, Amy ¹⁰	Ward	7	"	"	1896	"	13480
	3							
	4	ENROLLMENT						
	5	OF NOS. 1 and 2 HEREON APPROVED BY THE SECRETARY						
	6	OF INTERIOR DEC 12 1902						
	7							
	8							
	9							
	10							
	11							
	12							
	13							
	14							
	15							
	16							
	17							

TRIBAL ENROLLMENT OF PARENTS

	Name of Father	Year	County	Name of Mother	Year	County
1	Aba-whee-ly	Dead	Nashoba	Ba-ta-le-huna	Dead	Nashoba
2	Lyman Ward	"	Eagle	Liswee Ward	"	Eagle
3						
4						
5						
6			No2 on 1896 roll as Emma Ward			
7						
8						
9						
10						
11						
12						
13						
14						
15						
16					Date of Application for Enrollment	May 1/99
17						

Choctaw By Blood Enrollment Cards 1898-1914

RESIDENCE: Bok Tuklo   **COUNTY.**   **Choctaw Nation**   **Choctaw Roll** *(Not Including Freedmen)*   **CARD NO.**

POST OFFICE: Lukfata, I.T.   **FIELD NO.** 1271

Dawes' Roll No.	NAME	Relationship to Person First Named	AGE	SEX	BLOOD	TRIBAL ENROLLMENT		
						Year	County	No.
3450	1 Banabbe 55	First Named	52	M	Full	1896	Bok Tuklo	1253
	2							
	3							
	4	ENROLLMENT OF NOS. 1 HEREON APPROVED BY THE SECRETARY OF INTERIOR DEC 12 1902						
	5							
	6							
	7							
	8							
	9							
	10							
	11							
	12							
	13							
	14							
	15							
	16							
	17							

TRIBAL ENROLLMENT OF PARENTS

	Name of Father	Year	County	Name of Mother	Year	County
1	Pa-la-taby	Dead	Bok Tuklo		Dead	Bok Tuklo
2						
3						
4						
5						
6						
7						
8						
9						
10						
11						
12						
13						
14						
15						
16					Date of Application for Enrollment	May 1/99
17						

Choctaw By Blood Enrollment Cards 1898-1914

RESIDENCE: Towson   COUNTY.
POST OFFICE: Doaksville, I.T.

Choctaw Nation

Choctaw Roll   CARD NO.
(Not Including Freedmen)   FIELD NO.   1272

Dawes' Roll No.	NAME		Relationship to Person	AGE	SEX	BLOOD	TRIBAL ENROLLMENT		
							Year	County	No.
3451	1	Aaron, Johnson 30	First Named	27	M	Full	1896	Towson	209
3452	2	" Sarah 28	Wife	25	F	"	1896	"	210
3453	3	" Moses 9	Son	6	M	"	1896	"	211
3454	4	" Annie 4	Dau	5mo	F	"			
14653	5	" Frances 1	Dau	11mo	F	"			
	6								
	7	ENROLLMENT							
	8	OF NOS. 1 2 3 and 4 HEREON APPROVED BY THE SECRETARY							
	9	OF INTERIOR DEC 12 1902							
	10								
	11								
	12	ENROLLMENT							
	13	OF NOS. 5 HEREON APPROVED BY THE SECRETARY							
	14	OF INTERIOR MAY 20 1903							
	15								
	16								
	17								

TRIBAL ENROLLMENT OF PARENTS

	Name of Father	Year	County	Name of Mother	Year	County
1	Stephen Aaron	Dead	Towson	Itey Aaron	Dead	Towson
2	Anderson McKinney	"	Jackson	Silway McKinney	"	Jackson
3	No 1			No 2		
4	No 1			No 2		
5	Nº1			Nº2		
6						
7		Nº5 Born Dec. 15 1901. Enrolled Nov. 17, 1902.				
8						
9		For child of No 1&2 see N.B. (Apr.26,1906) Card No. 203.				
		" " " " " " (Mar 3-1905) " " 100				
10						
11						
12						
13						
14						
15						#1 to 4
16						May 1/99
17	P.O. Fort Towson 3/22/05					

RESIDENCE: Bok Tuk-lo   COUNTY.   **Choctaw Nation**   **Choctaw Roll**   CARD No.
POST OFFICE: Luk fa-tah I.T.   *(Not Including Freedmen)*   FIELD No.   1273

Dawes' Roll No.	NAME	Relationship to Person	AGE	SEX	BLOOD	TRIBAL ENROLLMENT		
						Year	County	No.
3455	1 Lawitaya Hodges 44	First Named	41	M	Full	1896	Bok Tuklo	8006
3456	2 " Sophie 31	Wife	28	F	"	1896	" "	8007
3457	3 " John 5	Son	2	M	"			
3458	4 " Isabell 2	Dau	7mo	F	"			
	5							
	6	ENROLLMENT						
	7	OF NOS. 1 2 3 and 4 HEREON APPROVED BY THE SECRETARY						
	8	OF INTERIOR DEC 12 1902						
	9							
	10							
	11							
	12							
	13							
	14							
	15							
	16							
	17							

TRIBAL ENROLLMENT OF PARENTS

	Name of Father	Year	County	Name of Mother	Year	County
1	Lowitaya[sic]	Ded	Bok Tuklo	Lila	Ded	Bok Tuklo
2	Sho-nabi	"	" "	Winnie	"	" "
3	No 1			No 2		
4	No.1			No.2		
5						
6						
7			No.4 Enrolled December 15, 1900			
8						
9			No.2 died June 16, 1902; proof of death filed Dec 6, 1902			
10			No.2 died June 16, 1902: Enrollment cancelled by Department [remainder illegible]			
11						
12						
13						
14						
15						#1 to 3
16					Date of Application for Enrollment	May 1"99
17						

73

Choctaw By Blood Enrollment Cards 1898-1914

RESIDENCE: Red River COUNTY. **Choctaw Nation** Choctaw Roll (Not Including Freedmen) CARD NO. FIELD NO. 1274
POST OFFICE: Goodwater, I.T.

Dawes' Roll No.	NAME			Relationship to Person	AGE	SEX	BLOOD	TRIBAL ENROLLMENT		
								Year	County	No.
3459	1 McClure	Reuben	34	First Named	31	M	3/4	1896	Red River	9362
3460	2 " "	Ellen	29	Wife	26	F	Full	1896	" "	9363
3461	3 " "	Fannie	10	Dau	7	"	7/8	1896	" "	9364
3462	4 " "	Jennie	8	"	5	"	"	1896	" "	9365
3463	5 " "	Newton	6	Son	3	M	"	1896	" "	9366
3464	6 " "	Oscar	5	"	1	"	"			
3465	7 " "	Mollis	1	Son	6m	M	"			
	8									
	9									
	10									
	11	ENROLLMENT OF NOS. 1 2 3 4 5 6 and 7 HEREON APPROVED BY THE SECRETARY OF INTERIOR DEC 12 1902								
	12									
	13									
	14									
	15									
	16									
	17									

TRIBAL ENROLLMENT OF PARENTS

	Name of Father	Year	County	Name of Mother	Year	County
1	Wallace McClure	Ded	Red River	Isabel McClure	1896	Red River
2	Lewis Fobb	"	Eagle	Sophie Fobb	Ded	Eagle
3	No 1			No 2		
4	No 1			No 2		
5	No 1			No 2		
6	No 1			No 2		
7	No 1			No 2		
8						
9						
10						
11	No 3 enrolled on 1896 roll as Viney McClure					
12	No 4 " " " " " Jinnie " "					
13	No 5 " " " " " Babis " "					
14	No.7 Born Decr 28th 1901; Enrolled June 19th 1902					
15	For child of Nos. 1&2 see NB (March 3, 1905) #935				Date of Application for Enrollment. #1 to 6	
16				For Nos 1 to 6 incl.	May 1"99	
17						

74

Choctaw By Blood Enrollment Cards 1898-1914

RESIDENCE: Red River COUNTY.
POST OFFICE: Goodwater I.T.

Choctaw Roll
(Not Including Freedmen)

CARD NO.
FIELD NO. 1275

Dawes' Roll No.		NAME		Relationship to Person	AGE	SEX	BLOOD	TRIBAL ENROLLMENT		
								Year	County	No.
3466	1	McClure Isabel	76	First Named	73	F	Full	1896	Red River	9313
	2									
	3	ENROLLMENT								
	4	OF NOS. 1 HEREON APPROVED BY THE SECRETARY								
	5	OF INTERIOR DEC 12 1902								
	6									
	7									
	8									
	9									
	10									
	11									
	12									
	13									
	14									
	15									
	16									
	17									

TRIBAL ENROLLMENT OF PARENTS

	Name of Father	Year	County	Name of Mother	Year	County
1	"Ashley"	De'd	Eagle	"Peky"	Ded	Eagle
2						
3						
4						
5						
6						
7			No.1 on Choctaw roll as Isabelle McClure			
8						
9						
10						
11						
12						
13						
14						
15						
16				Date of Application for Enrollment	May 1"99	
17						

75

Choctaw By Blood Enrollment Cards 1898-1914

RESIDENCE: Eagle COUNTY.	POST OFFICE: Eagle Town I.T.	Choctaw Nation	Choctaw Roll (Not Including Freedmen)	CARD NO. FIELD NO. 1276

Dawes' Roll No.	NAME	Relationship to Person First Named	AGE	SEX	BLOOD	TRIBAL ENROLLMENT Year	County	No.
3467	1 To-tubbi Battiest 43	First Named	40	M	Full	1896	Eagle	12241
3468	2 " Kissie 33	Wife	10	F	"	1896	"	12242
3469	3 Jones Jimmie 20	Neph	17	M	"	1896	"	6941
	4							
	5							
	6	ENROLLMENT						
	7	OF NOS. 1 2 and 3 HEREON APPROVED BY THE SECRETARY						
	8	OF INTERIOR DEC 12 1902						
	9							
	10							
	11							
	12							
	13							
	14							
	15							
	16							
	17							

TRIBAL ENROLLMENT OF PARENTS

	Name of Father	Year	County	Name of Mother	Year	County
1	Jack Thompson	Ded	Eagle	Ma-ho-na	Ded	Eagle
2	Toantabi	Ded	"	Harriet	"	"
3	Jefferson Jones	"	"	Frances	"	"
4						
5						
6						
7						
8						
9						
10			No 2 on 1896 Roll as Kissi Tolubbi			
11						
12						
13						
14					Date of Application	
15						
16						May 1"99
17						

RESIDENCE: Eagle COUNTY.
POST OFFICE: Luk-fa-tah I.T.

Choctaw Nation

Choctaw Roll
(Not Including Freedmen)

CARD NO.
FIELD NO. 1277

Dawes' Roll No.	NAME		Relationship to Person First Named	AGE	SEX	BLOOD	TRIBAL ENROLLMENT		
							Year	County	No.
3470	1 Pisachubbi Case	25	First Named	22	M	Full	1893	Eagle	P.R. 564
3471	2 " Sarah	23	Wife	20	F	"	1893	Red River	72
3472	3 " Sebit	4	Dau	3mo	F	"			
3473	4 Taylor Latis	9	S "	6	"	"	1896	Red River	7029
	5								
	6								
	7	ENROLLMENT							
	8	OF NOS. 1 2 3 and 4 HEREON APPROVED BY THE SECRETARY							
	9	OF INTERIOR DEC 12 1902							
	10	No.2 on 1896 Choctaw census roll, Red River County, No. 7028							
	11	as Sarah Jones.							
	12								
	13								
	14								
	15								
	16								
	17								

TRIBAL ENROLLMENT OF PARENTS

	Name of Father	Year	County	Name of Mother	Year	County
1	Pisachubbi	Ded	Eagle	Neise	1896	Eagle
2	Bobb Tekabi	1896	Bok Tuklo	Pisatimma	Ded	Bok Tuklo
3	No 1			No 2		
4	Watson Taylor	1896	Red River	No 2		
5						
6						
7						
8	No 1 on p. 59 #564, 1893 Pay Roll Eagle County as King Pissachabbe					
9	No 2 on p 9 #72 1893 Pay Roll Red River County as Sarah Bob					
10	No 4 on p 73 #631 as Lodus Taylor					
11						
12	No 4 on 1896 roll as Latis Jones					
13						
14	No 1 on 1896 roll as Kase Wilson, Page 355				Date of Application for Enrollment.	
15	No 13561, Eagle Co.					
16	No 2 also on 1896 Choctaw Census roll as Sillin Wilson page 357 #13614				May 1" 99	
17						

Choctaw By Blood Enrollment Cards 1898-1914

RESIDENCE: Eagle COUNTY.
POST OFFICE: Luk-fa-tah I.T.

Choctaw Nation

Choctaw Roll
(Not Including Freedmen)

CARD NO.
FIELD NO. 1278

Dawes' Roll No.	NAME		Relationship to Person First Named	AGE	SEX	BLOOD	TRIBAL ENROLLMENT		
							Year	County	No.
3474	1 Pisachubbi Nancy	72	First Named	69	F	Full	1896	Eagle	10410
	2								
	3	ENROLLMENT							
	4	OF NOS. 1 HEREON APPROVED BY THE SECRETARY							
	5	OF INTERIOR DEC 12 1902							
	6								
	7								
	8								
	9								
	10								
	11								
	12								
	13								
	14								
	15								
	16								
	17								

TRIBAL ENROLLMENT OF PARENTS

	Name of Father	Year	County	Name of Mother	Year	County
1	Te-hol-ba-ta-bi	Ded	Eagle	Malindy	Ded	Mississippi
2						
3						
4						
5						
6						
7						
8						
9						
10						
11						
12						
13						
14						
15						
16				Date of Application for Enrollment.		May 1" 99
17						

Choctaw By Blood Enrollment Cards 1898-1914

RESIDENCE: Bok Tuklo   COUNTY. **Choctaw Nation**   **Choctaw Roll**   CARD NO.
POST OFFICE: Fowlerville, I.T.   *(Not Including Freedmen)*   FIELD NO. 1279

Dawes' Roll No.	NAME	Relationship to Person First Named	AGE	SEX	BLOOD	TRIBAL ENROLLMENT		
						Year	County	No.
3475	1 Kanashambe, Israel 48	First Named	45	M	Full	1896	Bok Tuklo	7548
3476	2 " Chostin 52	Wife	49	F	"	1896	Eagle	12243
3477	3 " Malissa 15	Dau	12	"	"	1896	Bok Tuklo	7556
	4							
	5	ENROLLMENT						
	6	OF NOS. 1 2 and 3 HEREON APPROVED BY THE SECRETARY						
	7	OF INTERIOR DEC 12 1902						
	8							
	9							
	10							
	11							
	12							
	13							
	14							
	15							
	16							
	17							

TRIBAL ENROLLMENT OF PARENTS

	Name of Father	Year	County	Name of Mother	Year	County
1	Kanashambe	Dead	Bok Tuklo	Linna	Dead	Bok Tuklo
2	A-po-an-tubbe	"	" "	Lucy	"	" "
3	No 1			Sinie Kanashambe	"	" "
4						
5						
6			No2 on 1896 roll as Chostin Thomas			
7			No3 " 1896 " " Milissa Kanashambe			
8						
9						
10						
11						
12						
13						
14						
15				Date of Application for Enrollment		
16				May 1 99		
17						

Choctaw By Blood Enrollment Cards 1898-1914

RESIDENCE: Bok Tuklo   COUNTY.   **Choctaw Nation**   Choctaw Roll   CARD NO.
POST OFFICE: Lukfata, I.T.   *(Not Including Freedmen)*   FIELD NO. **1280**

Dawes' Roll No.	NAME		Relationship to Person First Named	AGE	SEX	BLOOD	TRIBAL ENROLLMENT		
							Year	County	No.
3478	1 Watson, Thomas	50	First Named	47	M	Full	1896	Bok Tuklo	13431
3479	2 " Nicie	49	Wife	46	F	"	1896	" "	13432
3480	3 Anderson Winey	20	S.Dau	17	"	"	1896	" "	10394
3481	4 Mitchell, Elcie	12	"	9	"	"	1896	" "	8642
3482	5 Anderson, Isaac	1	Son of No.3	2mo	F	"			
	6								
	7	ENROLLMENT							
	8	OF NOS. 1 2 3 4 and 5 HEREON APPROVED BY THE SECRETARY							
	9	OF INTERIOR Dec 12 1902							
	10								
	11								
	12								
	13								
	14								
	15								
	16								
	17								

TRIBAL ENROLLMENT OF PARENTS

	Name of Father	Year	County	Name of Mother	Year	County
1	A-ba-la-teby	Dead	Bok Tuklo		Dead	Bok Tuklo
2	Henry Push	"	" "		"	" "
3	Pisahinlabi	"	" "	No 2		
4	Albert Mitchell	"	Red River	No 2		
5	Daniel Anderson	on Choctaw Card #1052		No 3		
6						
7						
8	No 3 on 1896 roll as Winney Pisahinlabi					
9	No 3 now the wife of Daniel Anderson on Choctaw Card #1052: Evidence of marriage filed June 28th 1902:					
10	No 5 Born April 7th 1902 Enrolled June 28th 1902					
11						
12						
13						
14						
15					For Nos	
16				Date of Application for Enrollment	1 to 4 Incl.	
17					May 1/99	

Choctaw By Blood Enrollment Cards 1898-1914

RESIDENCE: Cedar   COUNTY.   **Choctaw Nation**   Choct...
POST OFFICE: Doaksville, I.T.   *(Not Including Freedmen)*   FIELD NO. 1281

Dawes' Roll No.	NAME	Relationship to Person	AGE	SEX	BLOOD	TRIBAL ENROLLMENT		
						Year	County	No.
3483	1 Wilson, James ²⁷	First Named	24	M	Full	1896	Cedar	13159
3484	2 " Rosanna ²¹	Wife	18	F	3/4	1896	Towson	12119
3485	3 " Isbam ²	Son	2mo	M	7/8			
	4							
	5	ENROLLMENT						
	6	OF NOS. 1 2 and 3 HEREON APPROVED BY THE SECRETARY						
	7	OF INTERIOR DEC 12 1902						
	8							
	9							
	10							
	11							
	12							
	13							
	14							
	15							
	16							
	17							

TRIBAL ENROLLMENT OF PARENTS

	Name of Father	Year	County	Name of Mother	Year	County
1	Simon Wilson	Dead	Cedar	Melissie Wilson	Dead	Cedar
2	Benson Tims	"	Towson	Emiline Tims		Towson
3	No.1			No.2		
4						
5						
6						
7						
8						
9						
10	No.2 enrolled April 24, 1899 on Choctaw card #778 as Rosanna					
11	Tims and transferred to this card with her husband, Oct. 26, 1900.					
	No.3 Enrolled Oct. 26, 1900					
12	Evidence of marriage Nos. 1 and 2 to be supplied. Filed Aug 19, 1901.					
13	For child of Nos. 1&2 see N.B. (Apr. 26, 1906) Card No. 150.					
14	" " " " " " " " (Mar 3, 1905) " " 1171					
15				#1		
16				Date of Application for Enrollment May 1/99		
17						

81

Choctaw By Blood Enrollment Cards 1898-1914

RESIDENCE: Cedar	COUNTY.	**Choctaw Nation**	Choctaw Roll	CARD No.
POST OFFICE: Doaksville, I.T.			(Not Including Freedmen) FIELD No. 1282	

Dawes' Roll No.	NAME	Relationship to Person First Named	AGE	SEX	BLOOD	TRIBAL ENROLLMENT Year	County	No.
3486	1 Thompson, Henry W 28	First Named	25	M	Full	1896	Cedar	1207
	2							
	3	ENROLLMENT						
	4	OF NOS. 1 HEREON APPROVED BY THE SECRETARY						
	5	OF INTERIOR DEC 12 1902						
	6							
	7							
	8							
	9							
	10							
	11							
	12							
	13							
	14							
	15							
	16							
	17							

TRIBAL ENROLLMENT OF PARENTS

	Name of Father	Year	County	Name of Mother	Year	County
1	Simon Thompson	Dead	Cedar	Lucy Thompson	Dead	Cedar
2						
3						
4						
5						
6	On 1896 roll as Henry Thompson					
7	No1 Now the Husband of Illie Thompson on Choctaw Card #1288. Evidence of marriage filed July 16" 1902					
8						
9						
10						
11						
12						
13						
14						
15						
16				Date of Application for Enrollment.	May 1/99	
17						

Choctaw By Blood Enrollment Cards 1898-1914

RESIDENCE: Cedar   COUNTY.   **Choctaw Nation**   **Choctaw Roll**   CARD No.
POST OFFICE: Doaksville, I.T.   *(Not Including Freedmen)*   FIELD No. **1283**

Dawes' Roll No.	NAME	Relationship to Person First Named	AGE	SEX	BLOOD	TRIBAL ENROLLMENT Year	County	No.
3487	1 Thompson, Joseph P. ⁴⁰	First Named	37	M	Full	1896	Cedar	12073
3488	2 " Betsy ³¹	Wife	28	F	1/2	1896	"	12074
3489	3 " Alexander B ¹²	Son	9	M	3/4	1896	"	12075
3490	4 " Joel J ¹⁰	"	7	"	3/4	1896	"	12076
~~Dead~~	5 " ~~Ella N~~	~~Dau~~	~~5~~	~~F~~	~~3/4~~	~~1896~~	~~"~~	~~12077~~
3491	6 " Peter P ⁵	Son	2	M	3/4	1896	"	12080
3492	7 " Simon ³	"	7½ mo	M	3/4			
	8							
	9	ENROLLMENT	No. 5 hereon dismissed under order of					
	10	OF NOS. 1 2 3 4 6 and 7 HEREON APPROVED BY THE SECRETARY	the Commission to the Five Civilized					
	11	OF INTERIOR Dec 12 1902	Tribes of March 31, 1905					
	12							
	13	No 7 enrolled Dec 19/99						
	14	Affidavit irregular and						
	15	returned for correction. Returned corrected And						
	16	filed, Feby 20, 1900.						
	17							

TRIBAL ENROLLMENT OF PARENTS

	Name of Father	Year	County	Name of Mother	Year	County
1	John Thompson	Dead	Cedar	Betsy Thompson	Dead	Cedar
2	Vincent Tims	"	Towson	Emiline Tims	1896	Towson
3	No.1			No.2		
4	No.1			No.2		
5	~~No.1~~			~~No.2~~		
6	No.1			No.2		
7	No.1			No.2		
8						
9	No.1 on 1896 roll as Joseph Thompson					
10	No.3 " 1896 " " Alexander "					
11	No.4 " 1896 " " Joel "					
12	~~No.5 " 1896 " " Ella "~~ No.6 " 1896 " " Peter B. "					
13	No.5 Died May 22, 1899. Evidence of death filed April 18, 1901.					
14	For child of nos 1&2 see NB (March 3, 1905) #1410					
15					Date of Application for Enrollment.	
16					May 1/99	
17	P.O. Ft. Towson I.T. 4/29/05					

83

Choctaw By Blood Enrollment Cards 1898-1914

RESIDENCE: Red River COUNTY. **Choctaw Nation** Choctaw Roll (Not Including Freedmen) CARD NO.
POST OFFICE: Goodwater, I.T. FIELD NO. **1284**

Dawes' Roll No.		NAME		Relationship to Person First Named	AGE	SEX	BLOOD	TRIBAL ENROLLMENT		
								Year	County	No.
IW1497	1	Willis, Frances M	52	First Named	49	M	I.W.	1896	Eagle	15177
	2						I.W.			
	3									
	4									
	5	ENROLLMENT								
	6	OF NOS. ~~~ 1 ~~~ HEREON APPROVED BY THE SECRETARY								
	7	OF INTERIOR Nov 27 1905								
	8									
	9									
	10									
	11	No 1 Formerly husband of Rosa Ella Robinson Choctaw Roll 15873								
	12									
	13									
	14									
	15									
	16									
	17									

TRIBAL ENROLLMENT OF PARENTS

	Name of Father	Year	County	Name of Mother	Year	County
1	Andrew Willis	Dead	Non Citz	Bunneta Willis	Dead	Non Citz
2						
3						
4	Adopted by Act of Council, approved October 24, 1888, as husband of Rose					
5	Ella, daughter of Z.T. and Fannie Davis. Act was shown to					
6	Commissioner McKennon (Certified copy filed Jan 18 1904					
7	Supplemental testimony taken Jan 28th 1904 Former wife and two children on Choctaw Card #5695					
8						
9	Notify G.A. Spaulding Garvin I.T of action 8/26/05					
10						
11						
12						
13						
14						
15	P.O. Hocha Town 1/28/04			Date of Application for Enrollment.		
16				April 24/99		
17	P.O. Ultuna Thule, Ark 1/13/03.					

Choctaw By Blood Enrollment Cards 1898-1914

| RESIDENCE: Cedar | COUNTY. | Choctaw Nation | Choctaw Roll | CARD NO. |
| POST OFFICE: Doaksville, I.T. | | | (Not Including Freedmen) | FIELD NO. 1285 |

Dawes' Roll No.	NAME	Relationship to Person First Named	AGE	SEX	BLOOD	TRIBAL ENROLLMENT		
						Year	County	No.
DEAD Dead	1 Carby, Nicholas DEAD	Named	39	M	Full	1896	Cedar	2444
3493	2 " Eli 19	Son	16	"	"	1893	Kiamitia	454
3494	3 Josiah DIED PRIOR TO SEPTEMBER 25, 1902	"	13	"	"	1893	"	754
	4							
	5							
	6							
	7							
	8							
	9							
	10							
	11							
	12							
	13							
	14							
	15							
	16							
	17							

ENROLLMENT
OF NOS. 2 and 3 HEREON
APPROVED BY THE SECRETARY
OF INTERIOR Dec 12 1902

No. 1 hereon dismissed under order of
the Commission to the Five Civilized
Tribes of March 31, 1905.

No 1 On 1896 roll as Nicholas Curby

TRIBAL ENROLLMENT OF PARENTS

	Name of Father	Year	County	Name of Mother	Year	County
1	Louis Carby	Dead	Kiamitia	Si-yoh-ke	Dead	Blue
2	No 1			Betsy Carby	"	Kiamitia
3	No 1			" "	"	"
4						
5			No2 on 1893 Pay roll, Page 56, No 454, Kiamitia Co			
6			No3 " 1893 " " " 92 " 754 " " as Josiah Thompson			
7			No.2 on 1896 Choctaw roll as Elie Mihyachubbe page 218: #8728.			
			No.3 " " " " " Josiah " " " " #8729.			
8			No1 died in 1900: proof of death filed Dec. 8, 1902			
9			No3 " Aug 16, 1899. " " " " " " "			
10			No.3 died Aug. 16, 1899: Enrollment cancelled by Department July 8, 1904			
11						
12						
13						
14						
15				Date of Application for Enrollment.		
16				May 1/99		
17				Nos 2 – 3 May 10/99		

85

Choctaw By Blood Enrollment Cards 1898-1914

RESIDENCE: Towson COUNTY.
POST OFFICE: Fowlerville, I.T.

Choctaw Nation

Choctaw Roll
(Not Including Freedmen)

CARD No.

FIELD NO. 1280

Dawes' Roll No.	NAME		Relationship to Person First Named	AGE	SEX	BLOOD	TRIBAL ENROLLMENT		
							Year	County	No.
I.W. 562	1 Obannon, Jack	35		32	M	I.W.	1896	Towson	14313
3495	2 " Isabel	53	Wife	50	F	1/2	1896	"	1086
	3								
	4	ENROLLMENT OF NOS. 2 HEREON APPROVED BY THE SECRETARY OF INTERIOR DEC 12 1902							
	5								
	6								
	7								
	8	ENROLLMENT OF NOS. 1 HEREON APPROVED BY THE SECRETARY OF INTERIOR FEB -8 1904							
	9								
	10								
	11								
	12								
	13								
	14								
	15								
	16								
	17								

TRIBAL ENROLLMENT OF PARENTS

	Name of Father	Year	County	Name of Mother	Year	County
1	Bill Obannon	Dead	Non Citz	Elizabeth Obannon	Dead	Non Citz
2	John James	"	Bok Tuklo	Sally James	"	Bok Tuklo
3						
4						
5						
6			No1 on 1896 roll as Jack O. Banon			
7			No2 " 1896 " " Isabell O. Banon.			
8						
9						
10						
11						
12						
13						
14						
15						
16				Date of Application for Enrollment May 1/99		
17	PO Valliant I T. 12/1/02					

Choctaw By Blood Enrollment Cards 1898-1914

RESIDENCE: Towson   COUNTY.

POST OFFICE: Garvin, I.T

Choctaw Nation

Choctaw Roll (Not Including Freedmen)

CARD NO.

FIELD NO.   1287

Dawes' Roll No.	NAME		Relationship to Person	AGE	SEX	BLOOD	TRIBAL ENROLLMENT		
							Year	County	No.
496	1 Wilson, Emma	26	First Named	23	F	1/2	1896	Towson	13184
497	2 " Edward	8	Son	5	M	1/4	1896	"	13186
498	3 " James	6	"	3	"	1/4	1896	"	13185
499	4 " Alma	5	Dau	1	F	1/4			
500	5 " J. Dace	3	Son	3mo	M	1/4			
501	6 " Willie H	1	Son	5wks	M	1/4			
	7								
	8								
	9								
	10								
	11								
	12								
	13								
	14								
	15								
	16								
	17								

ENROLLMENT
OF NOS. 12345and6 HEREON
APPROVED BY THE SECRETARY
OF INTERIOR   DEC 12 1902

TRIBAL ENROLLMENT OF PARENTS

	Name of Father	Year	County	Name of Mother	Year	County
1	Joe Everidge	1896	Kiamitia	Susie Everidge	Dead	Kiamitia
2	Edward H. Wilson	1896	Chick. Roll	No 1		
3	" " "	1896	" "	No 1		
4	" " "	1896	" "	No 1		
5	" " "	1896	" "	No 1		
6	" " "	1896	" "	No 1		
7						
8	Husband of No1 and father of her children on					
9	Chickasaw Card No 1413 transferred to Choctaw card 536					
10						
11	No4 Affidvit of birth to be supplied. Recd May 8/99					
12	No.6 Born Sept. 27, 1901: Enrolled Nov. 5 1901.					
13						
14	For child of No1 see NB (Apr 26-06) Card #459					
15	" " " " " (Mar 3 05) " #439				#1 to 4	
16					Date of Application for Enrollment May 1/99	
17	P.O. Fort Towson I.T. 3/30/05				No 5 enrolled Dec 14/99	

Choctaw By Blood Enrollment Cards 1898-1914

RESIDENCE: Towson COUNTY. **Choctaw Nation** Choctaw Roll CARD NO.
POST OFFICE: Doaksville, I.T. *(Not Including Freedmen)* FIELD NO. **1288**

Dawes' Roll No.	NAME	Relationship to Person First Named	AGE	SEX	BLOOD	TRIBAL ENROLLMENT		
						Year	County	No.
3502	1 Aaron, Selina 53	First Named	50	F	Full	1896	Towson	220
3503	2 " Martha	Dau	12	"	"	1896	"	221
3504	3 Thompson, Illie 18	G.Dau	15	"	"	1896	"	10353
3505	4 Pisahambe David 16	G.Son	13	M	"	1896	"	10354
3506	5 Gibson, Jane 14	G.Dau	11	F	"	1896	"	4744
3607	6 " Peter 6	G.Son	3	M	"	1896	"	4745
3508	7 Thompson, Hampton 1	Son of 3	8mo	M	"			
	8							
	9							
	10							
	11							
	12							
	13							
	14							
	15							
	16							
	17							

DIED PRIOR TO SEPTEMBER 25, 1902 (on line 2)

ENROLLMENT OF NOS. 123456and7 HEREON APPROVED BY THE SECRETARY OF INTERIOR

TRIBAL ENROLLMENT OF PARENTS

	Name of Father	Year	County	Name of Mother	Year	County
1	Jacob Taylor	Dead	Towson	Sukey Taylor	Dead	Towson
2	Felin Aaron	"	"	No.1		
3	Willie Pisahambe	"	"	Betsy Pisahambe	Dead	Towson
4	" "	"	"	" "	"	"
5	Gibson	"	"	Selina Gibson	"	"
6	"	"	"	" "	"	"
7	Henry W. Thompson	on Choctaw Card #1282		No.3		
8						
9						
10	No3 now the wife of Henry W. Thompson on Choctaw Card #1282: Evidence of marriage filed July 16th 1902					
11	No.7 Born Nov 12th 1901: Enrolled July 16th 1902.					
12	No2 died February, 1899: proof of death filed Dec. 2, 1902.					
13	No.2 died Feb. —, 1899: Enrollment cancelled by Department July 8, 1904					
14					#1 to 6 inc.	
15				Date of Application for Enrollment.		
16				May 1/99		
17						

RESIDENCE: Red River COUNTY.   **Choctaw Nation**   **Choctaw Roll** CARD NO.
POST OFFICE: Garvin, I.T.   (Not Including Freedmen)   FIELD NO. 1289

Dawes' Roll No.	NAME	Relationship to Person	AGE	SEX	BLOOD	TRIBAL ENROLLMENT		
						Year	County	No.
3509	₁ Dickson, Minerva ²⁴	First Named	21	F	1/2	1896	Towson	5474
3510	₂ Wilson, Frank ⁸	Son	5	M	1/4	1896	"	13375
3511	₃ " Eva ⁶	Dau	3	F	1/4	1896	"	13176
3512	₄ Pebsworth, Vivian ⁵	Dau	1	"	1/4			
	₅							
	₆	ENROLLMENT						
	₇	OF NOS. 1 2 3 and 4 HEREON APPROVED BY THE SECRETARY						
	₈	OF INTERIOR DEC 12 1902						
	₉							
	10							
	11							
	12							
	13							
	14							
	15							
	16							
	17							

TRIBAL ENROLLMENT OF PARENTS

	Name of Father	Year	County	Name of Mother	Year	County
₁	Dave Harkins	Dead	Non Citz	Rebecca Cotton	Dead	Towson
₂	Raphael Wilson	1896	Chick Roll	No 1		
₃	" "	1896	" "	No 1		
₄	Sam Pebsworth	1896	Non Citz	No 1		
₅						
₆						
₇	No1 on 1896 roll as Minerva Harkins.					
₈						
₉						
10						
11						
12						
13						
14						
15					Date of application for Enrollment.	
16					May 1/99	
17						

Choctaw By Blood Enrollment Cards 1898-1914

Choctaw Nation

Choctaw Roll
(Not Including Freedmen)

CARD NO.
FIELD NO. 1290

Dawes' Roll No.	NAME		Relationship to Person	AGE	SEX	BLOOD	TRIBAL ENROLLMENT		
							Year	County	No.
3513	1 Lewis, Nancy	73	First Named	70	F	Full	1896	Towson	7941
3514	2 Bobb Johnson	8	G.Son	5	M	"	1896	"	1109
3515	3 Washington Isham	15	Nep.	12	"	"	1893	"	P.R. 414
	4								
	5								
	6	ENROLLMENT OF NOS. 1 2 and 3 HEREON							
	7	APPROVED BY THE SECRETARY							
	8	OF INTERIOR DEC 12 1902							
	9								
	10								
	11								
	12								
	13								
	14								
	15								
	16								
	17								

TRIBAL ENROLLMENT OF PARENTS

	Name of Father	Year	County	Name of Mother	Year	County
1	Jacob	Ded	Towson		Ded	Mississippi
2	Frelin Bobb	"	"	Emily Bobb	"	Towson
3	Patterson Washington	"	"	Eny Washington	"	"
4						
5						
6						
7						
8						
9						
10						
11			No 2 on 1896 Roll as Johnson Bob			
12			No 3 on 1893 Pay Roll Towson Co			
13			as Isom Washington			
			No.3 also on 1896 Choctaw census roll, page 167, #6794 as Isham James.			
14						
15					Date of Application for Enrollment	
16					May 1" 99	
17						

Choctaw By Blood Enrollment Cards 1898-1914

RESIDENCE: Red River   COUNTY.   **Choctaw Nation**   **Choctaw Roll**   CARD NO.

POST OFFICE: Goodwater I.T.   (Not Including Freedmen)   FIELD NO. 1291

Dawes' Roll No.	NAME	Relationship to Person	AGE	SEX	BLOOD	TRIBAL ENROLLMENT Year	County	No.
3516	1 Watkins Mollie 50	First Named	47	F	Full	1896	Red River	13601
	2							
	3							
	4							
	5							
	6							
	7							
	8							
	9							
	10							
	11							
	12							
	13							
	14							
	15							
	16							
	17							

ENROLLMENT
OF NOS. 1 HEREON
APPROVED BY THE SECRETARY
OF INTERIOR DEC 12 1902

TRIBAL ENROLLMENT OF PARENTS

	Name of Father	Year	County	Name of Mother	Year	County
1		Ded		I-lip-hon-na	Ded	Jack Fork
2						
3						
4						
5						
6						
7						
8						
9						
10						
11						
12						
13						
14						
15						
16				Date of Application for Enrollment.	May 1" 99	
17						

Choctaw By Blood Enrollment Cards 1898-1914

RESIDENCE: Cedar COUNTY. **Choctaw Nation** Choctaw Roll CARD NO.
POST OFFICE: Alikchi I.T. (Not Including Freedmen) FIELD NO. 1292

Dawes' Roll No.	NAME	Relationship to Person First Named	AGE	SEX	BLOOD	TRIBAL ENROLLMENT		
						Year	County	No.
3517	1 Tom, Sally ⁵³	First Named	50	F	Full	1896	Cedar	12084
3518	2 " Jimmie ~~DIED PRIOR TO SEPTEMBER 25, 1902~~	Son	25	M	"	1896	"	12087
3519	3 " Jesse ²⁰	"	17	"	"	1896	"	12085
3520	4 " Sarah ¹⁸	Dau	15	F	"	1896	"	12086
	5							
	6	ENROLLMENT						
	7	OF NOS. 1 2 3 and 4 HEREON APPROVED BY THE SECRETARY						
	8	OF INTERIOR DEC 12 1902						
	9							
	10							
	11							
	12							
	13							
	14							
	15							
	16							
	17							

TRIBAL ENROLLMENT OF PARENTS

	Name of Father	Year	County	Name of Mother	Year	County
1	Ahekatabi	Ded	Cedar	Ishtemona	Ded	Cedar
2	~~Harrison Toms~~	"	"	~~No 1~~		
3	" "	"	"	No 1		
4	" "	"	"	No 1		
5						
6						
7						
8						
9			No2 died in 1900: proof of death filed Dec 5, 1902			
10			.No.2 died – –. 1900: Enrollment cancelled by Department [remainder illegible]			
11						
12						
13						
14						
15				Date of Application for Enrollment May 1 99		
16						
17	Spencerville I.T. 12/2/02					

Choctaw By Blood Enrollment Cards 1898-1914

RESIDENCE: **Nashoba** COUNTY. **Choctaw Nation** **Choctaw Roll** CARD NO.
POST OFFICE: **Alikchi, I.T.** *(Not Including Freedmen)* FIELD NO. **1293**

Dawes' Roll No.	NAME	Relationship to Person	AGE	SEX	BLOOD	TRIBAL ENROLLMENT		
						Year	County	No.
3521	1 Bathest Pitchlynn 28	First Named	25	M	Full	1896	Jacks fork[sic]	1982
	2							
	3							
	4	ENROLLMENT OF NOS. 1 HEREON APPROVED BY THE SECRETARY OF INTERIOR Dec 12 1902						
	5							
	6							
	7							
	8							
	9							
	10							
	11							
	12							
	13							
	14							
	15							
	16							
	17							

TRIBAL ENROLLMENT OF PARENTS

	Name of Father	Year	County	Name of Mother	Year	County
1	Me-he-tubbi	Ded	Nashoba	Sibbie	1896	Nashoba
2						
3						
4						
5	Nº1 is husband of Delilah Billy Choctaw card #801 Jany. 28, 1903					
6	Surname of Nº1 is Battiest					
7						
8						
9						
10						
11						
12						
13						
14					Date of Application for Enrollment.	
15						
16					May 1 – 99	
17						

Choctaw By Blood Enrollment Cards 1898-1914

RESIDENCE: Towson COUNTY. **Choctaw Nation** Choctaw Roll CARD NO.
POST OFFICE: Doaksville I.T. (Not Including Freedmen) FIELD NO. 1294

Dawes' Roll No.	NAME		Relationship to Person	AGE	SEX	BLOOD	TRIBAL ENROLLMENT		
							Year	County	No.
3522 522	1 Aaron Nebus	21	First Named	18	M	Full	1896	Towson	205
	2								
	3								
	4	ENROLLMENT							
	5	OF NOS. 1 HEREON APPROVED BY THE SECRETARY							
	6	OF INTERIOR DEC 12 1902							
	7								
	8								
	9								
	10								
	11								
	12								
	13								
	14								
	15								
	16								
	17								

TRIBAL ENROLLMENT OF PARENTS

	Name of Father	Year	County	Name of Mother	Year	County
1	Stephen Aaron	Ded	Towson	Susan Aaron	Ded	Towson
2						
3						
4						
5						
6						
7						
8						
9						
10						
11						
12						
13						
14						
15						
16						May 1 – 99
17						

94

Choctaw By Blood Enrollment Cards 1898-1914

Choctaw Nation

Choctaw Roll C
(Not Including Freedmen) FIEL.

Dawes' Roll No.	NAME	Relationship to Person	AGE	SEX	BLOOD	TRIBAL ENROLLMENT		
						Year	County	No.
3523	1 Nanomantube, Mary 60	First Named	57	F	Full	1896	Towson	9658
	2							
	3							
	4							
	5							
	6							
	7							
	8							
	9							
	10							
	11							
	12							
	13							
	14							
	15							
	16							
	17							

ENROLLMENT
OF NOS. 1 HEREON
APPROVED BY THE SECRETARY
OF INTERIOR DEC 12 1902

TRIBAL ENROLLMENT OF PARENTS

Name of Father	Year	County	Name of Mother	Year	County
1 Tar-ka-har-jo	Dead	in Mississippi		Dead	in Mississippi
2					
3					
4					
5					
6	On 1896 roll as Mary Nanamantube				
7					
8					
9					
10					
11					
12					
13					
14					
15					
16			Date of Application for Enrollment. May 1/99		
17					

Choctaw By Blood Enrollment Cards 1898-1914

RESIDENCE: Eagle   COUNTY.   **Choctaw Nation**   **Choctaw Roll**   CARD NO.
POST OFFICE: Eagletown, I.T.   *(Not Including Freedmen)*   FIELD NO. **1296**

Dawes' Roll No.	NAME	Relationship to Person	AGE	SEX	BLOOD	TRIBAL ENROLLMENT		
						Year	County	No.
3524	1 Wesley, Bicey ³³	First Named	30	F	Full	1893	Nashoba	P.R. 107
	2							
	3	ENROLLMENT						
	4	OF NOS. 1 HEREON APPROVED BY THE SECRETARY						
	5	OF INTERIOR Dec 12 1902						
	6							
	7							
	8							
	9							
	10							
	11							
	12							
	13							
	14							
	15							
	16							
	17							

TRIBAL ENROLLMENT OF PARENTS

	Name of Father	Year	County	Name of Mother	Year	County
1	Mishontutta Wesley	Dead	Cedar	Elizabeth Wesley	Dead	Cedar
2						
3						
4						
5						
6		On 1893 Pay roll as Phycia Bettast, Page 9, No 107, Nashoba Co also on				
7		1896 roll as Dicy Wisby, Page 352, No 13433, Bok Tuklo Co.				
8						
9						
10						
11						
12						
13						
14						
15						
16				Date of Application for Enrollment	May 1/99	
17						

Choctaw By Blood Enrollment Cards 1898-1914

RESIDENCE: Eagle   COUNTY.

POST OFFICE: Eagletown, I.T.

Choctaw Nation

Choctaw Roll *(Not Including Freedmen)*

CARD NO. FIELD NO. 1297

Dawes' Roll No.	NAME	Relationship to Person	AGE	SEX	BLOOD	TRIBAL ENROLLMENT		
						Year	County	No.
3525	1 Going, Semiya 43	First Named	40	F	Full	1893	Eagle	P.R. 279
	2							
	3 ENROLLMENT							
	4 OF NOS. 1 HEREON APPROVED BY THE SECRETARY							
	5 OF INTERIOR DEC 12 1902							
	6							
	7							
	8							
	9							
	10							
	11							
	12							
	13							
	14							
	15							
	16							
	17							

TRIBAL ENROLLMENT OF PARENTS

	Name of Father	Year	County	Name of Mother	Year	County
1	Isom Going	1896	Eagle		Dead	Eagle
2						
3						
4						
5		On 1893 Pay roll as Semaye Going, Page 29, No 279, Eagle Co.				
6		No 1 also on 1896 Choc census roll page 171 #6776 as Siney James.				
7						
8						
9						
10						
11						
12						
13						
14						
15						
16				Date of Application for Enrollment	May 1/99	
17						

97

Choctaw By Blood Enrollment Cards 1898-1914

RESIDENCE: Towson COUNTY. **Choctaw Nation** Choctaw Roll CARD No.
POST OFFICE: Doaksville, I.T. *(Not Including Freedmen)* FIELD No. 1298

Dawes' Roll No.	NAME		Relationship to Person First Named	AGE	SEX	BLOOD	TRIBAL ENROLLMENT		
							Year	County	No.
3526	1 Snead, Louis	40	First Named	37	M	Full	1896	Towson	11389
3527	2 " Emiline	40	Wife	37	F	"	1896	"	11390
3528	3 " Josephine	6	Dau	2	"	"			
3529	4 David, Wister	11	S.Son	8	M	"	1896	Towson	3379
3530	5 Snead, Dewey	3	Son	3mo	"	"			
	6								
	7	ENROLLMENT							
	8	OF NOS. 1 2 3 4 and 5 HEREON APPROVED BY THE SECRETARY							
	9	OF INTERIOR DEC 12 1902							
	10								
	11								
	12								
	13								
	14								
	15								
	16								
	17								

TRIBAL ENROLLMENT OF PARENTS

	Name of Father	Year	County	Name of Mother	Year	County
1	Pisa-tok-cubbee	Dead	Cedar	Lucy Ward	Dead	Cedar
2	Nano-man-tubbee[sic]	"	Towson	Mary Nanomantubbe	1896	Towson
3	No 1			No 2		
4	Loin David	Dead	Towson	No 2		
5	No 1			No 2		
6						
7						
8			No5 enrolled Dec 19/99 Affidavit			
9			irregular and returned for correction.			
10			Returned corrected and filed Feby 20, 1900.			
11						
12						
13						
14					Date of Application for Enrollment.	
15						
16					May 1/99	
17						

| RESIDENCE: Cedar | COUNTY. | **Choctaw Nation** | Choctaw Roll | CARD NO. |
| POST OFFICE: Doaksville, I.T. | | | *(Not Including Freedmen)* | FIELD NO. **1299** |

Dawes' Roll No.	NAME		Relationship to Person	AGE	SEX	BLOOD	TRIBAL ENROLLMENT		
							Year	County	No.
3531	1 Harland, Raybin	30	First Named	27	M	Full	1896	Cedar	5422
3532	2 " Jennie	37	Wife	34	F	"	1896	"	4090
3533	3 " Agnes	6	Dau	2	"	"			
3534	4 Frazier, Martha	21	S.Dau	18	"	"	1896	"	4091
3535	5 " Betsie	14	"	11	"	"	1896	"	4092
3536	6 " Rebecca	9	"	6	"	"	1896	"	4093
7									
8									
9									
10									
11									
12									
13									
14									
15									
16									
17									

ENROLLMENT
OF NOS. 1 2 3 4 5 and 6 HEREON
APPROVED BY THE SECRETARY
OF INTERIOR Dec. 12, 1902

TRIBAL ENROLLMENT OF PARENTS

	Name of Father	Year	County	Name of Mother	Year	County
1	Bill Harland	Dead	Cedar	Ishtona Harlan[sic]	Dead	Cedar
2	Johnson Young	"	"	Annie Young	"	"
3	No 1			No 2		
4	Aaron Frazier	Dead	Cedar	No 2		
5	" "	"	"	No 2		
6	Henry LeFlore	1896	"	No 2		
7						
8						
9	No 1 on 1896 roll as Raybin Harlin					
10	No 2 " 1896 " " Jennie Frazier					
11	No 6 " 1896 " " Bakie "					
12	No 4 is now the wife of Louis Campbell on Choctaw Card 1069; Evidence of marriage filed					
13						Nov 15 1902
14						
15						
16						Date of Application
17						for Enrollment. May 1/99

Choctaw By Blood Enrollment Cards 1898-1914

RESIDENCE: Towson COUNTY.
POST OFFICE: Doaksville I T.

Choctaw Nation

Choctaw Roll
(Not Including Freedmen)

CARD NO.
FIELD NO. **1300**

Dawes' Roll No.	NAME	Relationship to Person First Named	AGE	SEX	BLOOD	TRIBAL ENROLLMENT Year	County	No.
3537	1 Aaron Austin 28	First Named	25	M	Full	1896	Towson	206
3538	2 " Elsie 35	Wife	32	F	"	1896	"	207
~~3539~~	~~3 Sibbie~~ DIED PRIOR TO SEPTEMBER 25, 1902	~~Dau~~	~~6~~	"	"	~~1896~~	"	~~208~~
3540	4 Ahayotubbe Leson 16	S Son	13	M	"	1896	"	234
	5							
	6							
	7							
	8							
	9							
	10							
	11							
	12							
	13							
	14							
	15							
	16							
	17							

ENROLLMENT OF NOS. 1 2 3 and 4 HEREON APPROVED BY THE SECRETARY OF INTERIOR Dec 12, 1902

TRIBAL ENROLLMENT OF PARENTS

	Name of Father	Year	County	Name of Mother	Year	County
1	Phelan Aaron	Ded	Towson	Sallie Aaron	Ded	Towson
2	Kalaha	"	Cedar		"	Cedar
3	~~No 1~~			~~No 2~~		
4	Solomon Ahayotubbe	Ded	Towson	No 2		
5						
6						
7						
8	No3 died in Feb. 1899: proof of death filed Dec. 2, 1902.					
9	No.3 died Feb. – 1899: Enrollment cancelled by Department July 8, 1904					
10						
11						
12						
13						
14						
15				Date of Application for Enrollment.		
16				May 2" 99		
17						

Choctaw By Blood Enrollment Cards 1898-1914

RESIDENCE: Towson COUNTY.
POST OFFICE: Doaksville I.T.

Choctaw Nation

Choctaw Roll
(Not Including Freedmen)

CARD NO.
FIELD NO. 1301

Dawes' Roll No.	NAME	Relationship to Person First Named	AGE	SEX	BLOOD	TRIBAL ENROLLMENT		
						Year	County	No.
3541	₁ Ahayotubbe Betsy ⁶³	First Named	60	F	Full	1896	Towson	230
3542	₂ Taylor Johnson ¹⁵	G.Son	12	M	"	1896	"	12129
	₃							
	₄ ENROLLMENT							
	₅ OF NOS. 1 and 2 HEREON APPROVED BY THE SECRETARY							
	₆ OF INTERIOR DEC 12 1902							
	₇							
	₈							
	₉							
	10							
	11							
	12							
	13							
	14							
	15							
	16							
	17							

TRIBAL ENROLLMENT OF PARENTS

	Name of Father	Year	County	Name of Mother	Year	County
1		Ded	Mississippi		Ded	Mississippi
2	Taylor Ahayotubbe	"	Towson	Selina	"	Towson
3						
4						
5						
6		No 1 on 1896 roll as Ahayotubbe				
7						
8						
9						
10						
11						
12						
13						
14					Date of Application for Enrollment.	
15						
16					May 2" 99	
17						

101

Choctaw By Blood Enrollment Cards 1898-1914

RESIDENCE: Eagle   COUNTY.

POST OFFICE: Eagle Town I.T.

Choctaw Nation

Choctaw Roll
(Not Including Freedmen)

CARD NO.

FIELD NO. **1302**

Dawes' Roll No.	NAME		Relationship to Person First Named	AGE	SEX	BLOOD	TRIBAL ENROLLMENT		
							Year	County	No.
3543	1 James Charles	30	First Named	27	M	Full	1896	Eagle	6978
3544	2 " Marcy	19	Wife	16	F	"	1896	"	1307
	3								
	4								
	5								
	6								
	7								
	8								
	9								
	10								
	11								
	12								
	13								
	14								
	15								
	16								
	17								

ENROLLMENT
OF NOS. 1 and 2 HEREON
APPROVED BY THE SECRETARY
OF INTERIOR Dec. 12, 1902

TRIBAL ENROLLMENT OF PARENTS

	Name of Father	Year	County	Name of Mother	Year	County
1	Wilson James	De'd	Eagle	Margaret James	1896	Eagle
2	Joseph Bobb	1896	"	Betty Bobb	Ded	"
3						
4						
5						
6		No 2 on roll of 1896 as Nancy Bobb				
7		No 1 was formerly husband of Nannie James Choctaw D 36				
8		No 1 also on 1896 roll Page 171, No 6974 Eagle Co.				
		No 1 and 2 are divorced				
9		No 1 is husband of Selina McAfee on 7-1084 11/27/02				
10						
11						
12						
13						
14					Date of Application *(for Enrollment.)*	
15						
16					May 2" 99	
17	P.O. Garvin I.T. 7/5/05					

102

Choctaw By Blood Enrollment Cards 1898-1914

RESIDENCE:	Eagle	COUNTY.	**Choctaw Nation**		**Choctaw Roll**	CARD NO.	
POST OFFICE:	Eagle Town I.T.				(Not Including Freedmen)	FIELD NO.	**1303**

Dawes' Roll No.	NAME		Relationship to Person	AGE	SEX	BLOOD	TRIBAL ENROLLMENT		
							Year	County	No.
3545	1 Fobb, Frances	22	First Named	19	F	Full	1896	Eagle	4190
3546	2 " Rhoda	5	Dau	mon 15	"	"			
	3								
	4	ENROLLMENT							
	5	OF NOS. 1 and 2 HEREON APPROVED BY THE SECRETARY OF INTERIOR							
	6								
	7								
	8								
	9								
	10								
	11								
	12								
	13								
	14								
	15								
	16								
	17								

TRIBAL ENROLLMENT OF PARENTS

	Name of Father	Year	County	Name of Mother	Year	County
1	John Fobb	Ded	Eagle	Sallie Fobb	Ded	Eagle
2	George James	1896	"	No 1		
3						
4						
5						
6		No 1 on 1896 roll as Francis Fobb.				
7						
8		For child of No1 see N.B. (Apr. 26-06) Card #848				
9						
10						
11						
12						
13						
14					Date of Application for Enrollment.	
15						
16					May 2-99	
17						

103

Choctaw By Blood Enrollment Cards 1898-1914

RESIDENCE: Eagle   COUNTY.
POST OFFICE: Eagle Town I.T.

Choctaw Nation

Choctaw Roll
(Not Including Freedmen)

CARD NO.
FIELD NO. **1304**

Dawes' Roll No.	NAME	Relationship to Person First Named	AGE	SEX	BLOOD	TRIBAL ENROLLMENT		
						Year	County	No.
3547	1 James, Margaret ⁵³	First Named	50	F	Full	1896	Eagle	6977
3548	2 " Jones ²⁵	Son	22	M	"	1893	"	P.R. 452
	3							
	4	ENROLLMENT						
	5	OF NOS. 1 and 2 HEREON APPROVED BY THE SECRETARY						
	6	OF INTERIOR Dec. 12, 1902						
	7							
	8							
	9							
	10							
	11							
	12							
	13							
	14							
	15							
	16							
	17							

TRIBAL ENROLLMENT OF PARENTS

	Name of Father	Year	County	Name of Mother	Year	County
1	Battes Fobb	Ded	Eagle	Toshoahona	Ded	Eagle
2	Wilson James	"	"	No 1		
3						
4						
5						
6	No 2 on 1893 Pay Roll as Joseph James					
7	No.2 in U.S. Penitentary[sic], Atlanta Ga. Aug. 8 1902					
8						
9	No 2 Discharged 9-21-08					
10						
11						
12						
13						
14						
15				Date of Application for Enrollment.	May 2" 99	
16						
17						

RESIDENCE: Towson COUNTY.	**Choctaw Nation**	Choctaw Roll	CARD NO.
POST OFFICE: Clear Creak I.T.		*(Not Including Freedmen)*	FIELD NO. **1305**

Dawes' Roll No.	NAME		Relationship to Person	AGE	SEX	BLOOD	TRIBAL ENROLLMENT		
							Year	County	No.
3549	₁ Gardner Edmond	25	First Named	22	M	1/2	1896	Towson	4733
IW511	₂ " Laura B.	21	Wife	18	F	I.W.	1896	"	14570
3550	₃ " Lela	4	Dau	4 mon	"	1/4			
3551	₄ DIED PRIOR TO SEPTEMBER 25, 1902 William J.		Son	1mo	M	1/4			
14654	₅ " Lydia	1	Dau	9mo	F	1/4			
	₆								
	₇	ENROLLMENT OF NOS. 1 3 and 4 HEREON APPROVED BY THE SECRETARY OF INTERIOR Dec. 12, 1902							
	₈								
	₉								
	₁₀	ENROLLMENT OF NOS. 5 HEREON APPROVED BY THE SECRETARY OF INTERIOR May 20 1903							
	₁₁								
	₁₂								
	₁₃	ENROLLMENT OF NOS. ~2~ HEREON APPROVED BY THE SECRETARY OF INTERIOR Dec. 24, 1903							
	₁₄								
	₁₅								
	₁₆								
	₁₇								

TRIBAL ENROLLMENT OF PARENTS

	Name of Father	Year	County	Name of Mother	Year	County
₁	Jerry Gardner	Ded	Towson	Jinnie Gardner	Ded	Towson
₂	Charley James	1896	Non Citz	Mary L James	"	Non Citz
₃	No 1			No 2		
₄	No 1			No 2		
₅	No 1			No 2		
₆						
₇						
₈						
₉						
₁₀			Affidavit to be supplied. Recd May 10/99			
₁₁						
₁₂			No.4 Enrolled July 13th 1900 No 5 Born Jany 28, 1902 enrolled Oct. 14, 1902			
₁₃			No 4 died December 2, 1901; proof of death filed Dec 2, 1902			
₁₄			No.4 died Dec. 2, 1901: Enrollment cancelled by Department July 8, 1904			
₁₅				Date of Application for Enrollment.		May 2 "99
₁₆						
₁₇	Valliant I.T. 11/28/02					

Choctaw By Blood Enrollment Cards 1898-1914

RESIDENCE: Nashoba COUNTY.
POST OFFICE: Alikchi I.T.

Choctaw Nation

Choctaw Roll
(Not Including Freedmen)

CARD NO.
FIELD NO. **1306**

Dawes' Roll No.		NAME		Relationship to Person	AGE	SEX	BLOOD	TRIBAL ENROLLMENT		
								Year	County	No.
3552	1	Bathest Allington	36	First Named	33	M	Full	1896	Eagle	1211
3553	2	" Samblin	11	son	8	"	"	1896	"	1212
	3									
	4									
	5	ENROLLMENT								
	6	OF NOS. 1 and 2 HEREON								
	7	APPROVED BY THE SECRETARY OF INTERIOR Dec. 12, 1902								
	8									
	9									
	10									
	11									
	12									
	13									
	14									
	15									
	16									
	17									

TRIBAL ENROLLMENT OF PARENTS

	Name of Father	Year	County	Name of Mother	Year	County
1	Ama-he-ta-bi	Ded	Nashoba	Sibbie	Ded	Nashoba
2	No 1			Lizzie Bathest	"	"
3						
4						
5						
6						
7						
8			No 2 on 1896 roll as Simpson Battiest			
9			No 1 " 1896 " " Allington "			
10			No 1 husband of Melwessie Columbus 7-718			
			For child of No.1 see N.B. (March 3, 1905) #948			
11			" " " " " " (April 26, 1906) #607			
12						
13						
14					Date of Application for Enrollment.	
15						
16					May 2" 99	
17						

Choctaw By Blood Enrollment Cards 1898-1914

RESIDENCE: Towson COUNTY.	Choctaw Nation	Choctaw Roll (Not Including Freedmen)	CARD NO.
POST OFFICE: Garvin I.T.			FIELD NO. 1307

Dawes' Roll No.	NAME	Relationship to Person First Named	AGE	SEX	BLOOD	TRIBAL ENROLLMENT		
						Year	County	No.
3554	1 Robert Silas 41	First Named	38	M	Full	1893	Jack's Fork	P.R. 634
3555	2 " Sarah 10	Dau	7	F	"	1893	" "	636
	3							
	4	ENROLLMENT						
	5	OF NOS. 1 and 2 HEREON APPROVED BY THE SECRETARY						
	6	OF INTERIOR DEC 12 1902						
	7							
	8							
	9							
	10							
	11							
	12							
	13							
	14							
	15							
	16							
	17							

TRIBAL ENROLLMENT OF PARENTS

	Name of Father	Year	County	Name of Mother	Year	County
1	John Robert	Ded	Towson	Achuk-ma-ho-yo	De'd	Red River
2	No 1			Mollie Robert	"	Kiamitia
3						
4						
5						
6	No 1 on 1896 Choctaw roll No 10860 Kiamitia Co.					
7	No 2 " 1896 " " " 10861 " "					
8				10/21 – 99		
9						
10						
11						
12						
13						
14						
15						
16				Date of Application for Enrollment May 2" 99		
17						

Choctaw By Blood Enrollment Cards 1898-1914

RESIDENCE: Cedar COUNTY. **Choctaw Nation** **Choctaw Roll** CARD NO.
POST OFFICE: Doaksville I.T. *(Not Including Freedmen)* FIELD NO. 1308

Dawes' Roll No.	NAME	Relationship to Person First Named	AGE	SEX	BLOOD	TRIBAL ENROLLMENT Year	TRIBAL ENROLLMENT County	TRIBAL ENROLLMENT No.
3556 ₁	Hayes Abel [DIED PRIOR TO SEPTEMBER 25, 1902]	First Named	42	M	Full	1896	Cedar	5419
3557 ₂	" Eliza ⁴³	Wife	40	F	"	1896	"	5420
3558 ₃	" Viney ⁸	Dau	5	"	"	1896	"	5421
₄								
₅								
₆	ENROLLMENT							
₇	OF NOS. 1 2 and 3 HEREON APPROVED BY THE SECRETARY							
₈	OF INTERIOR DEC 12 1902							
₉								
10								
11								
12								
13								
14								
15								
16								
17								

TRIBAL ENROLLMENT OF PARENTS

	Name of Father	Year	County	Name of Mother	Year	County
₁	Ma hli tabi	Ded	Kiamatia[sic]		De'd	Cedar
₂	"Lewis"	"		Betsy Lewis	"	"
₃	No 1			No 2		
₄						
₅						
₆						
₇			No 3 on 1896 roll as Fannie Hayes			
₈	No 1 died Feb 11, 1901; proof of death filed Dec 9, 1902					
₉	No.1 died Feb. 11, 1901: Enrollment cancelled by Department July 8, 1904.					
10						
11						
12						
13						
14						
15						
16				Date of Application for Enrollment,	May 2" 99	
17						

Choctaw By Blood Enrollment Cards 1898-1914

RESIDENCE: Red River COUNTY. **Choctaw Nation** Choctaw Roll CARD No.
POST OFFICE: Shawnee Town I.T. (Not Including Freedmen) FIELD No. 1309

Dawes' Roll No.	NAME		Relationship to Person	AGE	SEX	BLOOD	TRIBAL ENROLLMENT		
							Year	County	No.
3559	1 Shaw Collin	46	First Named	43	M	Full	1896	Red River	11467
3560	2 " Bessie	62	Wife	59	F	"	1896	" "	11440
3561	3 " Keith	20	Son	17	M	"	1896	" "	11441
3562	4 " Samuel	13	Son	10	M	"	1896	" "	11442
3563	5 " David	10	Son	7	M	"	1896	" "	11443
	6								
	7	ENROLLMENT							
	8	OF NOS. 1 2 3 4 and 5 HEREON APPROVED BY THE SECRETARY							
	9	OF INTERIOR DEC 12 1902							
	10								
	11								
	12								
	13								
	14								
	15								
	16								
	17								

TRIBAL ENROLLMENT OF PARENTS

	Name of Father	Year	County	Name of Mother	Year	County
1	Bob Shaw	Ded	Red River	Eleah	De'd	Red River
2	Amos John	"	Nashoba	Ishtahona	"	Bok Tuklo
3	No 1			No 2		
4	No 1			No 2		
5	No 1			No 2		
6						
7			Sis Ishtonake			
8	No3 husband of ∧ No2 on #7-1168					
9	For child of No.3 see NB (March 3 1905) #1370					
10						
11						
12						
13						
14						
15					Date of Application for Enrollment.	
16					May 2" 99	
17						

Choctaw By Blood Enrollment Cards 1898-1914

RESIDENCE: Red River COUNTY.　**Choctaw Nation**　Choctaw Roll CARD No.
POST OFFICE: Kully Tuklo I.T.　(Not Including Freedmen)　FIELD NO. 1310

Dawes' Roll No.	NAME	Relationship to Person First Named	AGE	SEX	BLOOD	TRIBAL ENROLLMENT		
						Year	County	No.
3564	1 Hampton Bennie 24	First Named	21	M	3/4	1896	Kiamatia[sic]	5746
	2							
	3							
	4							
	5							
	6							
	7							
	8							
	9							
	10							
	11							
	12							
	13							
	14							
	15							
	16							
	17							

ENROLLMENT
OF NOS. 1 HEREON
APPROVED BY THE SECRETARY
OF INTERIOR DEC 12 1902

TRIBAL ENROLLMENT OF PARENTS

Name of Father	Year	County	Name of Mother	Year	County
1 Benson Hampton	Ded	Red River	Mary Hampton	Ded	Kiamatia[sic]
2					
3					
4					
5 On 1896 Roll as Ben Hampton.					
6					
7					
8					
9					
10					
11					
12					
13					
14					Date of Application for Enrollment.
15					
16					May 2" 99
17					

Choctaw By Blood Enrollment Cards 1898-1914

RESIDENCE: Towson COUNTY.
POST OFFICE: Garvin I.T.

Choctaw Nation

Choctaw Roll
(Not Including Freedmen)

CARD NO.
FIELD NO. **1311**

Dawes' Roll No.	NAME	Relationship to Person	AGE	SEX	BLOOD	TRIBAL ENROLLMENT		
						Year	County	No.
3565	1 Yale Amos ⁵¹	First Named	48	M	Full	1896	Towson	14228
	2							
	3	ENROLLMENT						
	4	OF NOS. 1 HEREON APPROVED BY THE SECRETARY						
	5	OF INTERIOR DEC 12 1902						
	6							
	7							
	8							
	9							
	10							
	11							
	12							
	13							
	14							
	15							
	16							
	17							

TRIBAL ENROLLMENT OF PARENTS

Name of Father	Year	County	Name of Mother	Year	County
1 Elisha Yale	De'd	Kiamatia[sic]		De'd	Kiamatia
2					
3					
4					
5					
6					
7					
8					
9					
10					
11					
12					
13					
14					
15				Date of Application for Enrollment.		
16				May 2" 99		
17						

Choctaw By Blood Enrollment Cards 1898-1914

RESIDENCE: Towson   COUNTY.   **Choctaw Nation**   **Choctaw Roll**   CARD NO.

POST OFFICE: Garvin I.T.   *(Not Including Freedmen)*   FIELD NO. 1312

Dawes' Roll No.	NAME	Relationship to Person First Named	AGE	SEX	BLOOD	TRIBAL ENROLLMENT		
						Year	County	No.
3566	1 Homa Elijah 62		59	M	Full	1896	Towson	5470
	2							
	3							
	4							
	5							
	6							
	7							
	8							
	9							
	10							
	11							
	12							
	13							
	14							
	15							
	16							
	17							

ENROLLMENT
OF NOS. 1 HEREON
APPROVED BY THE SECRETARY
OF INTERIOR DEC 12 1902

TRIBAL ENROLLMENT OF PARENTS

Name of Father	Year	County	Name of Mother	Year	County
1 Solomon Homa	De'd	Kiamatia[sic]		De'd	Kiamatia[sic]
2					
3					
4					
5					
6					
7					
8					
9					
10					
11					
12					
13					
14					
15					
16			Date of Application for Enrollment. May 2" 99		
17					

112

Choctaw By Blood Enrollment Cards 1898-1914

RESIDENCE: Towson COUNTY.
POST OFFICE: Fowlerville, I.T.

Choctaw Nation

Choctaw Roll
(Not Including Freedmen)

CARD NO.

FIELD NO. 1313

Dawes' Roll No.	NAME	Relationship to Person	AGE	SEX	BLOOD	TRIBAL ENROLLMENT		
						Year	County	No.
3567	1 Jefferson, Mahaley ⁵⁰	First Named	47	F	Full	1896	Towson	6793
	2							
	3	ENROLLMENT						
	4	OF NOS. 1 HEREON APPROVED BY THE SECRETARY						
	5	OF INTERIOR DEC 12 1902						
	6							
	7							
	8							
	9							
	10							
	11							
	12							
	13							
	14							
	15							
	16							
	17							

TRIBAL ENROLLMENT OF PARENTS

	Name of Father	Year	County	Name of Mother	Year	County
1	Willis Washington	Dead	Towson	Lucy Washington	Dead	Towson
2						
3						
4						
5						
6						
7						
8						
9						
10						
11						
12						
13						
14						
15						
16				Date of Application for Enrollment	May 2/99	
17						

113

Choctaw By Blood Enrollment Cards 1898-1914

RESIDENCE: Bok Tuklo   COUNTY.   **Choctaw Nation**   **Choctaw Roll** CARD No.
POST OFFICE: Lukfata, I.T.   *(Not Including Freedmen)*   FIELD No. **1314**

Dawes' Roll No.	NAME	Relationship to Person First Named	AGE	SEX	BLOOD	TRIBAL ENROLLMENT Year	County	No.
3568	1 James, Joe 26	First Named	23	M	Full	1896	Bok Tuklo	6913
3569	2 DIED PRIOR TO SEPTEMBER 25, 1902 Nancy	Wife	31	F	"	1896	" "	6914
3570	3 " Marswis 6	Dau	3	"	"	1896	" "	6915
3571	4 " Simeon 4	Son	10mo	M	"			
	5							
	6	ENROLLMENT						
	7	OF NOS. 1 2 3 and 4 HEREON APPROVED BY THE SECRETARY						
	8	OF INTERIOR DEC 12 1902						
	9							
	10							
	11							
	12							
	13							
	14							
	15							
	16							
	17							

TRIBAL ENROLLMENT OF PARENTS

	Name of Father	Year	County	Name of Mother	Year	County
1	Alfred James	Dead	Bok Tuklo	Soyou Willis	1896	Bok Tuklo
2	Wilson Thomas	"	" "	Mary Cornelius	1896	" "
3	No 1			No 2		
4	No 1			No 2		
5						
6			No 2 on 1896 roll as Netsie James			
7			No 3 " 1896 " " Masaris "			
8	No. 2 died April 25, 1900: Enrollment cancelled by Department [remainder illegible]					
9			No 2 died April 25,1900: proof of death filed Dec 2, 1902			
10			No 1 is husband of Selina Durant Choc #1063			
11						
12			For child of No1 see NB (Mar 3-1905) Card No 19			
13						
14						
15					Date of Application for Enrollment.	
16					May 2/99	
17						

Choctaw By Blood Enrollment Cards 1898-1914

RESIDENCE: Towson COUNTY.	Choctaw Nation			Choctaw Roll	CARD NO.	
POST OFFICE: Fowlerville, I.T.				(Not Including Freedmen)	FIELD NO. 1315	

Dawes' Roll No.	NAME		Relationship to Person First Named	AGE	SEX	BLOOD	TRIBAL ENROLLMENT		
							Year	County	No.
2	1 Gardner, Alfred	26	First Named	23	M	1/2	1896	Towson	4734
8	2 " Mattie	22	Wife	19	F	I.W.			
3	3 DIED PRIOR TO SEPTEMBER 25, 1902 " Emma L.		Dau.	2mo	F	1/4			
3574	4 " Rena M	1	Dau	7mo	F	1/4			
	5								
	6	ENROLLMENT OF NOS. 1 3 and 4 HEREON APPROVED BY THE SECRETARY OF INTERIOR DEC 12 1902							
	7								
	8								
	9								
	10	ENROLLMENT OF NOS. ~2~ HEREON APPROVED BY THE SECRETARY OF INTERIOR JUN 13 1903							
	11								
	12								
	13								
	14								
	15								
	16								
	17								

TRIBAL ENROLLMENT OF PARENTS

	Name of Father	Year	County	Name of Mother	Year	County
1	Jerry Gardner	Dead	Towson	Jennie Gardner	Dead	Towson
2	Virgil Bartee	"	Non Citz	Deide Bartee	"	Non Citz
3	No 1			No 2		
4	Nº1			Nº2		
5						
6			No 3 Enrolled Sept 6th, 1900			
7			Nº4 Born Oct. 24,1901: enrolled May 31, 1902			
8						
9			No3 died August 16, 1902; proof of death filed Dec 2 1902			
10	No.3 died Aug 16, 1902: Enrollment cancelled by Department July 8, 1904.					
11			For child of Nºˢ 1&2 see N.B.(Apr.26,06) Card No. 2 6.			
12		"	" " " " " "	" (March3 1905) "	"	1092
13						
14					#1&2 Date of Application for Enrollment.	
15						
16					May 2/99	
17	Valliant I.T. 11/28/02					

115

Choctaw By Blood Enrollment Cards 1898-1914

RESIDENCE: Red River COUNTY. **Choctaw Nation** Choctaw Roll CARD NO.
POST OFFICE: Kullituklo, I.T. *(Not Including Freedmen)* FIELD NO. **1316**

Dawes' Roll No.	NAME	Relationship to Person First Named	AGE	SEX	BLOOD	TRIBAL ENROLLMENT Year	County	No.
3575	1 Coxwell, Johnson ²³	First Named	20	M	Full	1896	Red River	2677
	2							
	3							
	4							
	5							
	6							
	7							
	8							
	9							
	10							
	11							
	12							
	13							
	14							
	15							
	16							
	17							

ENROLLMENT
OF NOS. 1 HEREON
APPROVED BY THE SECRETARY
OF INTERIOR Dec 12 1902

TRIBAL ENROLLMENT OF PARENTS

Name of Father	Year	County	Name of Mother	Year	County
1 Daniel Coxwell	Dead	Red River	Sallie Coxwell	Dead	Red River
2					
3					
4					
5					
6					
7					
8					
9					
10					
11					
12					
13					
14					
15					
16					
17					

No.1 is now the husband of Ida Fobb – (formerly McIntosh) on
Choctaw card #1062 July 25, 1902
For child of No 1 see NB (March 3, 1905) #1465

Date of Application for Enrollment.
May 2/99

116

Choctaw By Blood Enrollment Cards 1898-1914

RESIDENCE: Eagle   COUNTY.
POST OFFICE: Eagletown, I.T.

Choctaw Nation
Choctaw Roll (Not Including Freedmen)

CARD NO.
FIELD NO. **1317**

Dawes' Roll No.	NAME	Relationship to Person First Named	AGE	SEX	BLOOD	TRIBAL ENROLLMENT		
						Year	County	No.
DEAD	₁ Carney, Albert		38	M	Full	1896	Eagle	2592
14655	₂ Homma, Jincy ³¹	Wife	28	F	"	1896	"	2615
3576	₃ Carney, Julius DIED PRIOR TO SEPTEMBER 25, 1902	Son	4	M	"	1896	"	2616
14656	₄ Ephraim DIED PRIOR TO SEPTEMBER 25, 1902	"	1mo	"	"			
3577	₅ Byington, Israel ⁹	S.Son	6	"	"	1896	Eagle	1282
14657	₆ Homma, Flora ¹	Dau of No2	6mo	F	"			
	₇							
	₈ ENROLLMENT OF NOS. 3 and 5 HEREON APPROVED BY THE SECRETARY OF INTERIOR Dec. 12, 1902							
	₁₀							
	₁₁ ENROLLMENT OF NOS. 2, 4 and 6 HEREON APPROVED BY THE SECRETARY OF INTERIOR May 20, 1903							
	₁₃							
	₁₄							
	No.₁₅ Hereon Dismissed under order of the ₁₆ Commission to the Five Civilized Tribes of March 31, 1905.							
	₁₇							

TRIBAL ENROLLMENT OF PARENTS

	Name of Father	Year	County	Name of Mother	Year	County
₁	Pe la by	Dead	Bok Tuklo	He o ho no	Dead	Eagle
₂	Sam Amos	"	Eagle	Meley Amos	"	"
₃	No 1			No 2		
₄	No 1			No 2		
₅	Maxwell Byington	Dead	Red River	No 2		
₆	Simeon Homma			No 2		
₇	No 3 died May 24 1902 ⎫ Enrollment cancelled by Department May 2 1906.					
₈	No 4 died May 18 1902 ⎭					
₉						
₁₀	No2 on 1896 roll as Jinsey Carney					
₁₁	No1 Died May 19, 1902, proof of death filed Nov. 11,1902					
₁₂	No2 is now wife of Simeon Homma on Choctaw card #625. Evidence of marriage filed Dec. 11,1901. These persons are also known by the surname of "Fobb"					
₁₃	No6 born July 9, 1902; enrolled Dec. 11, 1902					
₁₄	No 4 Evidence of birth on file 3/31/03					
₁₅	For child of No2 see N.B. (Apr. 26-06) Card #820			#1 to 5 inc		
₁₆				Date of Application for Enrollment May 2/99		
₁₇						

Choctaw By Blood Enrollment Cards 1898-1914

Choctaw Nation

Choctaw Roll (Not Including Freedmen)

CARD NO. FIELD NO. **1318**

Dawes' Roll No.	NAME	Relationship to Person First Named	AGE	SEX	BLOOD	TRIBAL ENROLLMENT		
						Year	County	No.
3579	₁ Bobb, Ellen *DIED PRIOR TO SEPTEMBER 25, 1902*	First Named	40	F	Full	1896	Towson	1093
3580	₂ James, Aaron ¹⁴	Son	11	M	"	1896	"	6765
3581	₃ Bobb, Mitchell ⁷	"	4	"	"	1896	"	1094
	₄							
	₅							
	₆	ENROLLMENT OF NOS. 1 2 and 3 HEREON APPROVED BY THE SECRETARY OF INTERIOR **Dec 12 1902**						
	₇							
	₈							
	₉							
	₁₀							
	₁₁							
	₁₂							
	₁₃							
	₁₄							
	₁₅							
	₁₆							
	₁₇							

TRIBAL ENROLLMENT OF PARENTS

	Name of Father	Year	County	Name of Mother	Year	County
₁	Jackson	Dead	Red River	I-yo-ka-la	Dead	Towson
₂	Patterson James	"	Towson	No 1		
₃	Ellis Bobb	1896	"	No 1		
₄						
₅			No 1 on 1896 roll as Aalin Bobb.			
₆						
₇						
₈			No 1 died Sept. 17, 1902; proof of death filed Dec. 2, 1902			
₉			Nos 1 and 3 are now wards of H.L. Fowler on Choctaw card D.#127.			
₁₀			Letters of guardianship filed December 3, 1902.			
₁₁		No.1 died Sept. 17, 1902. Enrollment cancelled by Department July 8 1904.				
₁₂						
₁₃						
₁₄				Date of Application for Enrollment.		
₁₅						
₁₆				May 2/99		
₁₇						

Choctaw By Blood Enrollment Cards 1898-1914

RESIDENCE: Eagle COUNTY.
POST OFFICE: Eagletown, I.T.

Choctaw Nation

Choctaw Roll (Not Including Freedmen)

CARD NO. FIELD NO. 1319

Dawes' Roll No.	NAME		Relationship to Person First Named	AGE	SEX	BLOOD	TRIBAL ENROLLMENT		
							Year	County	No.
3582	1 Fobb, Lee	41	First Named	38	M	Full	1896	Eagle	4175
3583	2 " Phillis	31	Wife	28	F	"	1896	"	4170
Dead	3 " Chaslin		Son	10	M	"	1896	"	4165
3584	4 " Jenkin	7	"	4	"	"	1896	"	4192
3585	5 " Robert	1	"	5mo	M	"			
	6								
	7	ENROLLMENT							
	8	OF NOS. 1 2 4 and 5 HEREON APPROVED BY THE SECRETARY							
	9	OF INTERIOR DEC 12 1902							
	10								
	11								
	12	No. 3 HEREON DISMISSED UNDER							
	13	ORDER OF THE COMMISSION TO THE FIVE							
	14	CIVILIZED TRIBES OF MARCH 31, 1905.							
	15								
	16								
	17								

TRIBAL ENROLLMENT OF PARENTS

	Name of Father	Year	County	Name of Mother	Year	County
1	Joe Fobb	Dead	Eagle	Hattie Jones	Dead	Eagle
2	Alfred Byington	1896	"	Fa-la-sen	"	"
3	No 1			No 2		
4	No 1			No 2		
5	Nº2			Nº2		
6						
7	No4 on 1896 roll as Jinkin Fobb					
8	No2 " 1896 " " Philis "					
9	Nº5 Born March 4, 1902: enrolled Aug. 22, 1902.					
10	No 3 died June 15,1899: proof of death filed Dec. 5, 1902					
	For child of Nos 1&2 see NB (March 3 1905) #1358					
11						
12						
13						
14					Date of Application for Enrollment.	
15						
16					May 2/99	
17						

Choctaw By Blood Enrollment Cards 1898-1914

Choctaw Nation

Choctaw Roll
(Not Including Freedmen)

CARD NO.
FIELD NO. 1320

	NAME	Relationship to Person First Named	AGE	SEX	BLOOD	TRIBAL ENROLLMENT		
						Year	County	No.
1	Jefferson, Cornelius ²³		20	M	Full	1896	Towson	6792
2								
3	ENROLLMENT							
4	OF NOS. 1 HEREON APPROVED BY THE SECRETARY							
5	OF INTERIOR DEC 12 1902							
6								
7								
8								
9								
10								
11								
12								
13								
14								
15								
16								
17								

TRIBAL ENROLLMENT OF PARENTS

	Name of Father	Year	County	Name of Mother	Year	County
1	Jamison Jefferson	Dead	Towson	Mahaley Jefferson	1896	Towson
2						
3						
4						
5	For child of No.1 see N.B. (Apr. 26,1906) Card No. 200.					
6						
7						
8						
9						
10						
11						
12						
13						
14					Date of Application for Enrollment.	
15						
16					May 2/99	
17						

Choctaw By Blood Enrollment Cards 1898-1914

RESIDENCE: Bok Tuklo	COUNTY.	Choctaw Nation	Choctaw Roll	CARD NO.	
POST OFFICE: Lukfata, I.T.			(Not Including Freedmen)	FIELD NO. **1321**	

Dawes' Roll No.	NAME	Relationship to Person	AGE	SEX	BLOOD	TRIBAL ENROLLMENT		
						Year	County	No.
3587	1 Louis, Johnson 26	First Named	23	M	Full	1896	Bok Tuklo	8010
	2							
	3							
	4	ENROLLMENT OF NOS. 1 HEREON APPROVED BY THE SECRETARY OF INTERIOR Dec. 12, 1902						
	5							
	6							
	7							
	8							
	9							
	10							
	11							
	12							
	13							
	14							
	15							
	16							
	17							

TRIBAL ENROLLMENT OF PARENTS

	Name of Father	Year	County	Name of Mother	Year	County
1	Silman Louis	1896	Bok Tuklo	Sukey Louis	Dead	Bok Tuklo
2						
3						
4						
5			No 1 is now husband of Susan Crosby on Choctaw			
6			Card #889 Nov 28/02.			
7						
8						
9						
10						
11						
12						
13						
14						
15				Date of Application for Enrollment.		
16					May 2/99	
17						

121

Choctaw By Blood Enrollment Cards 1898-1914

RESIDENCE: Red River COUNTY.   **Choctaw Nation** *(Not Including Freedmen)*   Choctaw Roll   CARD NO.

POST OFFICE: Janis, I.T.   FIELD NO. 1322

Dawes' Roll No.	NAME	Relationship to Person First Named	AGE	SEX	BLOOD	TRIBAL ENROLLMENT Year	County	No.
3588	1 Brown, Eastman ⁵⁰	First Named	47	M	Full	1896	Red River	1382
3589	2 Louisa [DIED PRIOR TO SEPTEMBER 25, 1902]	Wife	37	F	"	1896	" "	1383
3590	3 " Arnes ¹⁸	Son	15	M	"	1896	" "	1384
3591	4 " Kitsie ¹⁶	Dau	13	F	"	1896	" "	1385
3592	5 " Elias ¹²	Son	9	M	"	1896	" "	1386
3593	6 " Frank ¹¹	"	8	"	"	1896	" "	1387
3594	7 " Minnie ⁹	Dau	6	F	"	1896	" "	1388
3595	8 " Nicholas ⁷	Son	4	M	"	1896	" "	1389
3596	9 Eight [DIED PRIOR TO SEPTEMBER 25, 1902]	"	1	"	"			
3597	10 Emma [DIED PRIOR TO SEPTEMBER 25, 1902]	Ward	21	F	"	1896	" "	1372
	11 ENROLLMENT OF NOS. 1,2,3,4,5,6,7,8,9 and 10 HEREON APPROVED BY THE SECRETARY OF INTERIOR DEC 12 1902							
	12							
	13							
	14 No.2 died Feb. 29, 1900: No.9 died							
	15 May 1, 1900: No.10 died Sept. 8, 1900:							
	Enrollment cancelled by Department							
	16 July 8, 1904							
	17							

TRIBAL ENROLLMENT OF PARENTS

Name of Father	Year	County	Name of Mother	Year	County
1 Ish-noah	Dead	Red River	Bicey Brown	1896	Red River
2 Bah-na-by	"	Bok Tuklo	Amy Fisher	1896	" "
3 No 1			No 2		
4 No 1			No 2		
5 No 1			No 2		
6 No 1			No 2		
7 No 1			No 2		
8 No 1			No 2		
9 No 1			No 2		
10 Byington Brown	Dead	Red River	Elizabeth Brown	Dead	Red River
11	For child of No.4 see NB (March 3, 1905) #922				
12	No 3 on 1896 roll as Annie Brown				
13	No 4 " 1896 " " Ketsie "				
14	No2 died Feb 29,1900: proof of death filed Dec 2, 1902				
15	No9 " May 1, 1900: " " " " " " " "			Date of Application for Enrollment.	
16	No10 " Sept 8, 1900: " " " " " " " "			May 2/99	
17					

Choctaw By Blood Enrollment Cards 1898-1914

RESIDENCE: Red River   COUNTY.   **Choctaw Nation**   **Choctaw Roll**   CARD No.

POST OFFICE: Janis, I.T.   *(Not Including Freedmen)*   FIELD No.   1323

Dawes' Roll No.	NAME	Relationship to Person	AGE	SEX	BLOOD	TRIBAL ENROLLMENT		
						Year	County	No.
3598	1 Brown, Bicey ⁷⁸	First Named	75	F	Full	1896	Red River	1390
3599	2 " Josephine ²⁹	Dau	26	"	"	1896	" "	1391
	3							
	4	ENROLLMENT						
	5	OF NOS. 1 and 2 HEREON APPROVED BY THE SECRETARY OF INTERIOR DEC 12 1902						
	6							
	7							
	8							
	9							
	10							
	11							
	12							
	13							
	14							
	15							
	16							
	17							

TRIBAL ENROLLMENT OF PARENTS

	Name of Father	Year	County	Name of Mother	Year	County
1	Cornelius Kemp	Dead	Red River		Dead	Red River
2	Ish-noah	Dead	" "	No 1		
3						
4						
5						
6						
7						
8						
9						
10						
11						
12						
13						
14				Date of Application for Enrollment.		
15						
16				May 2/99		
17						

RESIDENCE: **Red River**   COUNTY.   **Choctaw Nation**   Choctaw Roll   CARD NO.

POST OFFICE: **Janis, I.T.**   *(Not Including Freedmen)*   FIELD NO.   **1324**

Dawes' Roll No.	NAME		Relationship to Person First Named	AGE	SEX	BLOOD	TRIBAL ENROLLMENT		
							Year	County	No.
3600	1 Moore, John	50	First Named	47	M	Full	1896	Red River	8685
DEAD	2 " Martha		Wife	40	F	"	1896	" "	8686
DEAD	3 " Philliston		Son	19	M	"	1896	" "	8687
3601	4 " Sealy	17	Dau	14	F	"	1896	" "	8690
3602	5 " Linnie	15	"	12	"	"	1896	" "	8691
3603	6 " Ainsworth	12	Son	9	M	"	1896	" "	8688
3604	7 " Rayson		"	7	"	"	1896	" "	8689
3605	8 " Sarlin	7	"	4	"	"	1896	" "	8692
	9								
	10								
	11								
	12								
	13								
	14								
	15								
	16								
	17								

DIED PRIOR TO SEPTEMBER 25, 1902

ENROLLMENT OF NOS. 1 4 5 6 7 and 8 HEREON APPROVED BY THE SECRETARY OF INTERIOR Dec 12 1902

No 2 and 3 hereon dismissed under order of the Commission to the Five Civilized Tribes of March 31, 1905.

TRIBAL ENROLLMENT OF PARENTS

	Name of Father	Year	County	Name of Mother	Year	County
1	A-che-no-ta	Dead	Red River	Una-ha-tema	1896	Red River
2	Thompson Wilson	1896	" "	Sillie Wilson	Dead	" "
3	No.1			No.2		
4	No.1			No.2		
5	No.1			No.2		
6	No.1			No.2		
7	No.1			No.2		
8	No.1			No.2		
9	No.2 Died April 28,1900. Evidence of death filed April 25, 1901					
10	No.3 Died April 21,1900. Evidence of death filed April 25, 1901					
11	No.1 is now the husband of Frances Coxwell on Choctaw card #1358 March 15,1902					
12	No.7 died July 3,1901; proof of death filed Dec. 2, 1902. No.7 died July 3, 1901: Enrollment cancelled by Department July 8, 1904					
13	For child of No.1 see NB (March 3, 1905) #930					
14	" " " " " " (April 26, 1906) #505					
15					Date of Application for Enrollment.	
16					May 2/99	
17						

Choctaw By Blood Enrollment Cards 1898-1914

RESIDENCE: Cedar   COUNTY.   **Choctaw Nation**   **Choctaw Roll**   CARD NO.
POST OFFICE: Doaksville, I.T.   *(Not Including Freedmen)*   FIELD NO.   1325

Dawes' Roll No.	NAME	Relationship to Person	AGE	SEX	BLOOD	TRIBAL ENROLLMENT		
						Year	County	No.
3606	1 Houston, Davison 53	First Named	50	M	Full	1896	Cedar	5466
3607	2 " Sophia 53	Wife	50	F	"	1896	"	5469
	3							
	4	ENROLLMENT						
	5	OF NOS. 1 and 2 HEREON APPROVED BY THE SECRETARY						
	6	OF INTERIOR DEC 12 1902						
	7							
	8							
	9							
	10							
	11							
	12							
	13							
	14							
	15							
	16							
	17							

TRIBAL ENROLLMENT OF PARENTS

	Name of Father	Year	County	Name of Mother	Year	County
1	E-mo-nah-aby	Dead	Cedar	Sally	Dead	Cedar
2	Thompson	"	"		Dead	Cedar
3						
4						
5	No 1 on 1896 roll as Lewieson Houston					
6	No 2 ' 1896 " " Sopha "					
7						
8						
9						
10						
11						
12						
13						
14						
15						
16				Date of Application for Enrollment May 2/99		
17						

125

Choctaw By Blood Enrollment Cards 1898-1914

RESIDENCE: **Red River** COUNTY.
POST OFFICE: **Janis, I.T.**

Choctaw Nation
(Not Including Freedmen)

Choctaw Roll No...
FIELD NO. **1326**

Dawes' Roll No.	NAME	Relationship to Person First Named	AGE	SEX	BLOOD	TRIBAL ENROLLMENT		
						Year	County	No.
3608	₁ Wilson, Ambrose ²³	DIED PRIOR TO SEPTEMBER 25, 1902	22	M	Full	1896	Red River	13658
3609	₂ Fisher, Viney ²³	Wife	20	F	"	1896	" "	1348
3610	₃ Fisher, Susan ¹	Dau of No 2	2mo	F	"			
	₄							
	₅	ENROLLMENT						
	₆	OF NOS. 1 2 and 3 HEREON APPROVED BY THE SECRETARY						
	₇	OF INTERIOR DEC 12 1902						
	₈							
	₉							
	10							
	11							
	12							
	13							
	14							
	15							
	16							
	17							

TRIBAL ENROLLMENT OF PARENTS

	Name of Father	Year	County	Name of Mother	Year	County
₁	Daniel Wilson	Dead	Red River	Malis Wilson	Dead	Red River
₂	Ellis Barney	"	" "	Isabelle Barney	1896	" "
₃	Wilson Fisher	1896	" "	No 2		
₄						
₅						
₆						
₇						
₈						
₉	No 2 wife of Alfred Tushka on 7-1117					
10	No2 on 1896 roll as Viney Barney.					
11	No 1 and 2 have been divorced and No2 is now the wife of Wilson Fisher on Choctaw Card #500. See letter of Wilson Fisher filed with papers herein Aug. 21, 1901.					
12	No.3 Enrolled Aug 21, 1901					
13	Evidence of divorce of No1 and 2 filed Sept. 6, 1901					
14	Marriage certificate of No.2 and Wilson Fisher on Choctaw Card No. 500 filed Sept. 6, 1901.					#1&2 Date of Application for Enrollment
15	No1 died in Jail at S. McAlester get proof of Jailor					
16	Nº1 Died Nov. 21, 1900. Proof of death filed Feby. 11, 1903.					May 2/99
17	No.1 died Nov. 21, 1900: Enrollment cancelled by Department July 8, 1904					

126

Choctaw By Blood Enrollment Cards 1898-1914

RESIDENCE: Eagle   COUNTY.   **Choctaw Nation**   CARD NO.

POST OFFICE: Eagletown, I.T.   **Choctaw Roll** *(Not Including Freedmen)*   FIELD NO. 1327

Dawes' Roll No.	NAME		Relationship to Person	AGE	SEX	BLOOD	TRIBAL ENROLLMENT		
							Year	County	No.
3611	1 Wilson, John	44	First Named	41	M	Full	1896	Eagle	13498
3612	2 DIED PRIOR TO SEPTEMBER 25, 1902 Ennis		Wife	33	F	"	1896	"	13536
3613	3 " Foston	21	Son	18	M	"	1896	"	13508
3614	4 " James	8	"	5	"	"	1896	"	13535
3615	5 " Frances	6	Dau	2	F	"	1896		
3616	6 " Roah	4	Son	1	M	"			
3617	7 " Senie	15	S.Dau	13	F	"	1896	"	13524
	8								
	9	ENROLLMENT							
	10	OF NOS. 1 2 3 4 5 6 and 7 HEREON APPROVED BY THE SECRETARY							
	11	OF INTERIOR DEC 12 1902							
	12								
	13								
	14								
	15								
	16								
	17								

TRIBAL ENROLLMENT OF PARENTS

Name of Father	Year	County	Name of Mother	Year	County
1 Emi-lya	Dead	Eagle	Ah-tegl	Dead	Eagle
2 Bill Sam	"	"	Winnie Sam	"	"
3 No 1			Nellie Wilson	"	"
4 No 1			No 2		
5 No 1			No 2		
6 No 1			No 2		
7 Jim Billy		Eagle	No 2		
8					
9					
10					
11					
12					
13	No.2 died – – 1901: Enrollment cancelled by Department Sept. 16. 1904.				
14					
15				Date of Application for Enrollment May 2/99	
16					
17					

127

Choctaw By Blood Enrollment Cards 1898-1914

RESIDENCE: Red River   COUNTY.   **Choctaw Nation**   Choctaw Roll   CARD NO.
POST OFFICE: Goodwater, I.T.   *(Not Including Freedmen)*   FIELD NO. **1328**

Dawes' Roll No.	NAME	Relationship to Person First Named	AGE	SEX	BLOOD	TRIBAL ENROLLMENT Year	County	No.
3618	1 King, Solomon ~~DIED PRIOR TO SEPTEMBER 25, 19~~ 35	First Named	36	M	Full	1896	Red River	7595
3619	2 ", Anna 34	Wife	31	F	"	1896	" "	7596
3620	3 ", Elsie 15	Dau	12	"	"	1896	" "	7598
3621	4 ", Wicklis 13	Son	10	M	"	1896	" "	7599
3622	5 ", Bessie 8	Dau	5	F	"	1896	" "	7600
3623	6 ", Emily 5	"	2	"	"			
3624	7 ", Charlisson Isaac 3	Son	14m	M	"			
	8							
	9							
	10							
	11							
	12							
	13							
	14							
	15							
	16							
	17							

ENROLLMENT
OF NOS. 1 2 3 4 5 6 and 7 HEREON
APPROVED BY THE SECRETARY
OF INTERIOR Dec. 12, 1902

No 1 died Aug.20,1902 Enrollment
cancelled by Department July 8, 1904.

No.3, 4 & 5 are living with
William S. Wardon 7-12-14.

TRIBAL ENROLLMENT OF PARENTS

	Name of Father	Year	County	Name of Mother	Year	County
1	~~Yak a no la~~	~~Dead~~	~~Red River~~	~~Ish ta ba we la~~	~~Dead~~	~~Red River~~
2	Ho-pa-kon-ubby	"	" "	Liswe Hopakonubby	1896	" "
3	No 1			No 2		
4	No 1			No 2		
5	No 1			No 2		
6	No 1			No 2		
7	No 1			No 2		
8						
9	No 4 on 1896 roll as Wilkin King					
10	No.5 " 1896 " " Beslin "					
11	No.7 Enrolled January 15, 1901.					
12	No 1 died August 10, 1902. Proof of death filed Dec. 2, 1902.					
13						
14						#1 to 6
15						Date of Application for Enrollment.
16						May 2/99
17						

E: Red River COUNTY. **Choctaw Nation** Choctaw Roll CARD NO.
ICE: Janis I.T. (Not Including Freedmen) FIELD NO. 1329

NAME	Relationship to Person	AGE	SEX	BLOOD	TRIBAL ENROLLMENT		
					Year	County	No.
1 William Johnson 45	First Named	42	M	Full	1896	Red River	13668
2							
3	ENROLLMENT						
4	OF NOS. 1 HEREON APPROVED BY THE SECRETARY						
5	OF INTERIOR DEC 12 1902						
6							
7							
8							
9							
10							
11							
12							
13							
14							
15							
16							
17							

This person said to have any heirs(sic) 1913 See letter 29491 from M.I. Mueller(sic)

TRIBAL ENROLLMENT OF PARENTS

	Name of Father	Year	County	Name of Mother	Year	County
1						
2						
3						
4						
5						
6						
7			Does not know either parent or where			
8			they lived or died –			
9						
10						
11						
12						
13						
14					Date of Application for Enrollment.	
15						
16					May 2" 99	
17						

Choctaw By Blood Enrollment Cards 1898-1914

Dawes' Roll No.	NAME		Relationship to Person First Named	AGE	SEX	BLOOD	TRIBAL ENROLLMENT		
							Year	County	No.
3626	1 Hicks, William	33	First Named	30	M	Full	1896	Cedar	5423
3627	2 " Anna	43	Wife	40	F	"	1896	"	7911
3628	3 Loman Frank	12	S.Son	9	M	"	1896	"	7912
	4								
	5	ENROLLMENT							
	6	OF NOS. 1 2 and 3 HEREON APPROVED BY THE SECRETARY							
	7	OF INTERIOR DEC 12 1902							
	8								
	9								
	10								
	11								
	12								
	13								
	14								
	15								
	16								
	17								

TRIBAL ENROLLMENT OF PARENTS

	Name of Father	Year	County	Name of Mother	Year	County
1	Hicks Mishaid	Ded	Cedar		De'd	Towson
2	Wilson Loman	"	"	Mollie Loman	"	Cedar
3	James Mullen	"	"	No 2		
4						
5						
6						
7			~~No 2 on 1896 Roll as Anna Loman~~			
8	No 1 and 2 are seperated[sic].					
9						
10						
11						
12						
13						
14						
15				Date of Application for Enrollment.		
16				May 2" 99		
17						

130

		Relationship to Person	AGE	SEX	BLOOD	TRIBAL ENROLLMENT		
	NAME					Year	County	No.
1	Billy Austin 23	First Named	20	M	Full	1896	Cedar	1084
2	" Eliza 31	Wife	28	F	"	1896	"	13131
3	Gabel Ansie DEAD.	S Dau	3	"	"			
4	Billy, Wesley 2	Son	3	M	"			
5	ENROLLMENT							
6	OF NOS. 1 and 2 HEREON APPROVED BY THE SECRETARY							
7	OF INTERIOR DEC 12 1902							
8								
9								
10	ENROLLMENT OF NOS. ___ 4 ___ HEREON							
11	APPROVED BY THE SECRETARY							
12	OF INTERIOR FEB 16 1904							
13								
14	No. 3 HEREON DISMISSED UNDER ORDER OF THE COMMISSION TO THE FIVE							
15	CIVILIZED TRIBES OF MARCH 31, 1905							
16								
17								

Choctaw Nation

E: Cedar COUNTY.
CE: Doaksville I.T.

Choctaw Roll CARD No.
(Not Including Freedmen) FIELD NO. 1331

TRIBAL ENROLLMENT OF PARENTS

	Name of Father	Year	County	Name of Mother	Year	County
1	John Hickman	Ded	Cedar	Eliza Hickman	1896	Cedar
2	Anthony Washington	"	Red River	Siney Nihka	1896	"
3	Willman Gabel	"	Cedar	No 2		
4	Nº1			Nº2		
5						
6						
7						
8			No 2 on 1896 Roll as Eliza Washington			
9	For child of Nos 1&2 see N.B. (Apr. 26, 1906) Card No. 52.					
10	No 3 died May 15, 1899; proof of death filed Dec 4, 1902.					
11	Nº4 Born Sept. 19, 1900. Application received at Garvin I.T. Nov. 28, 1902, only the affidavit of father being supplied. Affidavits of the mother received and					
12	Nº4 enrolled Aug. 11, 1903.					
13						
14					Date of A for Enr	
15						
16				Date of Application for Enrollment.	May 2, 1899	
17						

Choctaw By Blood Enrollment Cards 1898-1914

RESIDENCE: **Red River** COUNTY.
POST OFFICE: **Goodwater I.T.**

Choctaw Nation

Choctaw Roll
(Not Including Freedmen)

CARD NO.
FIELD NO. **1332**

Dawes' Roll No.	NAME	Relationship to Person First Named	AGE	SEX	BLOOD	TRIBAL ENROLLMENT Year	TRIBAL ENROLLMENT County	TRIBAL ENROLLMENT No.
3631	1 McClure Stephen 28	First Named	25	M	Full	1896	Red River	9359
14658	2 " Acy 25	Wife	22	F	"	1896	" "	1368
3632	3 " Lena 9	Dau	6	"	"	1896	" "	9360
3633	4 " Alex 7	Son	4	M	"	1896	" "	9361
14659	5 " Wesley 1	Son	1	M	"			
	6							
	7	ENROLLMENT						
	8	OF NOS. 1 3 and 4 HEREON APPROVED BY THE SECRETARY						
	9	OF INTERIOR DEC 12 1902						
	10							
	11							
	12	ENROLLMENT						
	13	OF NOS. 2 and 5 HEREON APPROVED BY THE SECRETARY						
	14	OF INTERIOR MAY 20 1903						
	15							
	16							
	17							

TRIBAL ENROLLMENT OF PARENTS

	Name of Father	Year	County	Name of Mother	Year	County
1	Elson McClure	1896	Red River	Elsie McClure	Ded	Red River
2	Silas Anson	1896	Bok Tuklo	Amy	"	Bok Tuk-lo
3	No 1			Frances McCann	"	" " " "
4	No 1			" " "	"	" " " "
5	No 1			No 2		
6						
7	No 2 on 1896 roll as Asay Boling					
8	No.1 father of Freeman McClure on Choctaw card #1334					
9	No 5 born June 15, 1901: enrolled Dec 2, 1902					
10						
11						
12						
13						
14					#1 to 4	
15					Date of Application for Enrollment.	
16					May 2-99	
17						

Choctaw By Blood Enrollment Cards 1898-1914

RESIDENCE: Eagle COUNTY.
POST OFFICE: Eagle Town, I.T.

Choctaw Nation

Choctaw Roll
(Not Including Freedmen)

CARD NO.
FIELD NO. **1333**

Dawes' Roll No.	NAME		Relationship to Person	AGE	SEX	BLOOD	TRIBAL ENROLLMENT		
							Year	County	No.
3634	1 Takalitubbi	48	First Named	45	M	Full	1896	Eagle	12232
	2								
	3	ENROLLMENT							
	4	OF NOS. 1 HEREON APPROVED BY THE SECRETARY							
	5	OF INTERIOR Dec. 12, 1902							
	6								
	7								
	8								
	9								
	10								
	11								
	12								
	13								
	14								
	15								
	16								
	17								

TRIBAL ENROLLMENT OF PARENTS

	Name of Father	Year	County	Name of Mother	Year	County
1	Ichukenatabi	Ded	Eagle	Holo	Ded	Eagle
2						
3						
4						
5						
6						
7						
8						
9						
10						
11						
12						
13						
14						
15						
16				Date of Application for Enrollment.		May 2" 99
17						

133

Choctaw By Blood Enrollment Cards 1898-1914

RESIDENCE: Red River   COUNTY.   **Choctaw Nation**   Choctaw Roll   CARD NO.
POST OFFICE: Goodwater, I.T.   *(Not Including Freedmen)*   FIELD NO. **1334**

Dawes' Roll No.	NAME	Relationship to Person First Named	AGE	SEX	BLOOD	TRIBAL ENROLLMENT Year	County	No.
DEAD	1 McClure, Mason DEAD		35	M	Full	1896	Red River	9315
3635	2 " " , Josephine 27	Wife	24	F	"	1896	" "	9316
3636	3 " " , Freeman 1	son of No.2	6wks	M	"			
	4							
	5 ENROLLMENT							
	6 OF NOS. 2 and 3 HEREON APPROVED BY THE SECRETARY							
	7 OF INTERIOR Dec. 12, 1902							
	8							
	9 No. 1 hereon dismissed under order of							
	10 the Commission to the Five Civilized							
	11 Tribes of March 31, 1905.							
	12							
	13							
	14							
	15							
	16							
	17							

TRIBAL ENROLLMENT OF PARENTS

	Name of Father	Year	County	Name of Mother	Year	County
1	Wallis McClure	Ded	Red River	Isabel McClure	1896	Red River
2	Abel Butter	1896	" "	"Swilla"	1896	Red River
3	Stephen McClure	1896	" "	No 2		
4						
5						
6	No3 Born Jany. 4, 1902: enrolled Feby 24, 1902.					
7	Father of No3 is Stephen McClure on Choctaw Card #1332					
8	No.1 Died Nov. 18, 1900: Proof of death filed April 3, 1902.					
9						
10						
11						
12						
13						
14					#1&2 Date of Application for Enrollment.	
15						
16					May 2" 99	
17						

RESIDENCE: Red River COUNTY. **Choctaw Nation** Choctaw Roll CARD NO.
POST OFFICE: Goodwater I.T. (Not Including Freedmen) FIELD NO. 1335

Dawes' Roll No.	NAME		Relationship to Person	AGE	SEX	BLOOD	TRIBAL ENROLLMENT		
							Year	County	No.
3637	₁ McClure Gleason	50	First Named	47	M	Full	1896	Red River	9353
14660	₂ " Lottie	45	Wife	42	F	"	1896	" "	9354
	3								
	4								
	5								
	6								
	7								
	8								
	9								
	10								
	11								
	12								
	13								
	14								
	15								
	16								
	17								

ENROLLMENT
OF NOS. 1 HEREON
APPROVED BY THE SECRETARY
OF INTERIOR DEC 12 1902

ENROLLMENT
OF NOS. 2 HEREON
APPROVED BY THE SECRETARY
OF INTERIOR MAY 20 1903

TRIBAL ENROLLMENT OF PARENTS

	Name of Father	Year	County	Name of Mother	Year	County
1	Wallis McClure	Ded	Red River	Isabel McClure	1896	Red River
2	John Wilson	"	" "	Achukmahona	Ded	" "
3						
4						
5						
6						
7						
8						
9						
10						
11						
12						
13						
14						
15				Date of Application for Enrollment.		
16				May 2" 99		
17						

135

Choctaw By Blood Enrollment Cards 1898-1914

RESIDENCE: Red River   COUNTY. **Choctaw Nation**   **Choctaw Roll** *(Not Including Freedmen)*   CARD NO.

POST OFFICE: Harris I.T.   FIELD NO. 1336

Dawes' Roll No.	NAME		Relationship to Person First Named	AGE	SEX	BLOOD	TRIBAL ENROLLMENT		
							Year	County	No.
I.W. **69**	1 McFarland J.B.	50	First Named	47	M	I.W.	1896	Red River	14870
3638	2 " Abbie	31	Wife	28	F	1/16	1896	" "	9331
3639	3 " John E.	8	Son	5	M	1/32	1896	" "	9332
3640	4 " Anna L.	5	Dau	2	F	1/32			
3641	5 " Ina Juanita	4	"	6wk	"	1/32			
3642	6 Kirby Murtie	13	S "	10	"	1/32	1896	" "	7587
3643	7 " Alice	12	S "	9	"	1/32	1896	" "	7588
3644	8 McFarland, Daniel Zac	1	Son	25da	M	1/32			
	9								
	10	ENROLLMENT							
	11	OF NOS. 234567and8 HEREON							
	12	APPROVED BY THE SECRETARY							
	13	OF INTERIOR DEC 12 1902							
	14	ENROLLMENT							
	15	OF NOS. ~~~ 1 ~~~ HEREON APPROVED BY THE SECRETARY							
	16	OF INTERIOR JUN 13 1903							
	17								

TRIBAL ENROLLMENT OF PARENTS

	Name of Father	Year	County	Name of Mother	Year	County
1	James A. McFarland	Ded	Non Citz	Mary Ann McFarland	Ded	Non Citz
2	Morris	"	" "	Carrie Hampton	1896	Red River
3	No 1			No 2		
4	No 1			No 2		
5	No 1			No 2		
6	Asa Kirby	Ded	Non Citz	No 2		
7	" "	"	" "	No 2		
8	No 1			No 2		
9						
10	For child of Nos 1&2 see NB (Apr 26-06) Card #682					
11	No 2 on 1896 roll as Abby McFarland					
12	No 3 " 1896 " " Jno E.					
	For child of Nos 1&2 see NB (March 3 1905) #1112					
13	No 1 admitted as an intermarried citizen by					
14	Dawes Commission, Choctaw Case #1261: No appeal					
15	No.8 Born October 11, 1901: Enrolled November 1, 1901.			Date of Application for Enrollment.		
16				May 2" 99		
17						

RESIDENCE: Eagle   COUNTY. **Choctaw Nation**   **Choctaw Roll**   CARD NO.
POST OFFICE: Eagle Town I.T.   (Not Including Freedmen)   FIELD NO. **1337**

Dawes' Roll No.	NAME	Relationship to Person	AGE	SEX	BLOOD	TRIBAL ENROLLMENT		
						Year	County	No.
3645	1 Billy Simon 47	First Named	44	M	Full	1896	Eagle	1315
3646	2 " Pikey 41	Wife	38	F	"	1896	"	6963
3647	3 " James 27	Son	24	M	"	1896	"	1286
3648	4 " George 16	"	13	"	"	1896	"	1276
3649	5 " Eleus 10	"	7	"	"	1896	"	1272
3650	6 Wilson Philip 15	S Son	12	"	"	1896	"	6964
~~3651~~	~~7 " Lenus~~ DIED PRIOR TO SEPTEMBER 25, 1902	~~" "~~	~~8~~	~~"~~	~~"~~	~~1896~~	~~"~~	~~6959~~
3652	8 " Caesar 10	" "	7	"	"	1896	"	6966
3653	9 Billy, Lena 2	Dau	2	F	"			
	10							
	11	ENROLLMENT						
	12	OF NOS. 1 2 3 4 5 6 7 8 and 9 HEREON APPROVED BY THE SECRETARY						
	13	OF INTERIOR DEC 12 1902						
	14							
	15							
	16							
	17							

TRIBAL ENROLLMENT OF PARENTS

	Name of Father	Year	County	Name of Mother	Year	County
1	Billy	Ded	Eagle	Finney	Ded	Eagle
2	Stephen Harrison	"	"	Chimulihoke	"	"
3	No 1			Susan Billy	"	"
4	No 1			" "	"	"
5	No 1			" "	"	"
6	Wilson			No 2		
7	"			No 2		
8	"			No 2		
9	N̊1			N̊2		
10						
11						
12		No 2 on 1896 roll as Pikey Jefferson				
13		No 5 " " " Ellen Billy				
14		No 6 " " " Philip Jefferson			#1 to 8		
15		No 7 " " " Lewis "			Date of Application for Enrollment.		
16		No 8 " " " Caesar "					
		N̊9 Born July 20, 1900: enrolled Sept. 5, 1902.			May 2" 99		
		N̊7 Died Jany 10, 1901, proof of death filed Dec 24, 1902					
17		No 7 died Jan 10, 1901: Enrollment cancelled by Department July 8, 1904					

Choctaw By Blood Enrollment Cards 1898-1914

RESIDENCE: Red River COUNTY. **Choctaw Nation** Choctaw Roll CARD NO.
POST OFFICE: Goodwater, I.T. (Not Including Freedmen) FIELD NO. **1338**

Dawes' Roll No.	NAME	Relationship to Person First Named	AGE	SEX	BLOOD	TRIBAL ENROLLMENT Year	County	No.
3654	1 Jefferson, Daniel 37		34	M	Full	1896	Red River	7049
3655	2 DIED PRIOR TO SEPTEMBER 25, 1902 , Jennie	Wife	32	F	"	1896	" "	7050
3656	3 " , Josephus 12	Son	9	M	"	1896	" "	7051
Dead	4 " , Susan	Dau	6	F	"	1896	" "	7052
	5							
	6 ENROLLMENT OF NOS. 1 2 and 3 HEREON							
	7 APPROVED BY THE SECRETARY OF INTERIOR Dec. 12, 1902.							
	8							
	9 No. 4 hereon dismissed under order of							
	10 the Commission to the Five Civilized							
	11 Tribes of March 31, 1905.							
	12							
	13							
	14							
	15							
	16							
	17							

TRIBAL ENROLLMENT OF PARENTS

	Name of Father	Year	County	Name of Mother	Year	County
1	Thomas Jefferson	Ded	Red River		Ded	Red River
2	Thompson Wilson	1896	" "	Kanahotima	"	" "
3	No 1			No 2		
4	No 1			No 2		
5						
6						
7						
8						
9						
10						
11			No.2 on 1896 roll as Jincy Jefferson			
12			No.4 " " " " Stephen "			
13			No.4 died August 11, 1899: Evidence of death filed May 17, 1901			
			No.2 died January 26, 1902 Proof of death filed Dec. 2, 1902.			
14			No.2 died Jan 25, 1902: Enrollment cancelled by Department July 8, 1904.			
15						
16				Date of Application for Enrollment.	May 2" 99	
17						

Choctaw By Blood Enrollment Cards 1898-1914

RESIDENCE: **Red River**　COUNTY. **Choctaw Nation**　**Choctaw Roll** *(Not Including Freedmen)*　CARD NO.
POST OFFICE: **Goodwater I.T.**　　FIELD NO. **1339**

Dawes' Roll No.	NAME	Relationship to Person First Named	AGE	SEX	BLOOD	TRIBAL ENROLLMENT Year	County	No.
3657	₁ Juzan Sattie ²⁸	First Named	25	F	Full	1896	Red River	9356
3658	₂ McClure Absolom ⁷	Son	4	M	"	1896	"　　"	9358
3659	₃ ~~Taylor~~ DIED PRIOR TO SEPTEMBER 25, 1902	Bro	16	M	"	1896	"　　"	9357
3660	₄ Juzan Isaac ¹	Son	7mo	M	"			
	5							
	6							
	7							
	8							
	9							
	10							
	11							
	12							
	13							
	14							
	15							
	16							
	17							

ENROLLMENT
OF NOS. 1 2 3 and 4 HEREON
APPROVED BY THE SECRETARY
OF INTERIOR DEC 12 1902

TRIBAL ENROLLMENT OF PARENTS

	Name of Father	Year	County	Name of Mother	Year	County
1	Isom McClure	Ded	Red River	Bicky McClure	Ded	Red River
2	Gleason McClure	1896	"　　"	No 1		
3	Isom McClure	Ded	"　　"	Bicky McClure	Ded	Red River
4	Philliston Juzan	1896	"　　"	N⁰1		
5						
6						
7						
8						
9						
10						
11	No 2 on 1896 roll as Absalom McClure.					
12	N⁰1 is now the wife of Philliston Juzan on Choctaw Card #965. Evidence of marriage filed Sept. 18, 1902.					
13	N⁰4 Born Feby. 14, 1902: enrolled Sept. 18, 1902.					
14	For child of No 1 see NB (March 3 1905) #905					
	No 3 died Dec., 1900; proof of death filed Dec 2, 1902.				Date of Application for Enrollment.	
15	No.3 died Dec –, 1900: Enrollment cancelled by Department July 8, 1904					
16					May 2" 99	
17	Kullituklo I.T. 11/28/02					

Shults, Okla. 1/20/14

Choctaw By Blood Enrollment Cards 1898-1914

	RESIDENCE: Eagle COUNTY.								
	POST OFFICE: Eagletown, I.T.		**Choctaw Nation**			Choctaw Roll *(Not Including Freedmen)*		CARD NO. FIELD NO. 1340	

Dawes' Roll No.	NAME	Relationship to Person First Named	AGE	SEX	BLOOD	TRIBAL ENROLLMENT		
						Year	County	No.
3661	1 Fobb, Impson 27	First Named	24	M	Full	1896	Eagle	4173
3662	2 Ellen ~~DIED PRIOR TO SEPTEMBER 25, 1902~~	Wife	16	F	"	1896	"	6965
3663	3 Adeline ~~DIED PRIOR TO SEPTEMBER 25, 1902~~	Dau	9mo	"	"			
	4							
	5	ENROLLMENT						
	6	OF NOS. 1 2 and 3 HEREON APPROVED BY THE SECRETARY						
	7	OF INTERIOR DEC 12 1902						
	8							
	9							
	10							
	11							
	12							
	13							
	14							
	15							
	16							
	17							

TRIBAL ENROLLMENT OF PARENTS

	Name of Father	Year	County	Name of Mother	Year	County
1	Louis Fobb	Dead	Eagle	Lizzie Fobb	Dead	Eagle
2	Simeon Jefferson	1896	"	Mary Jefferson	"	"
3	No 1			No 2		
4						
5						
6		No.2 on 1896 roll as Alin Jefferson				
7	No.2 died Aug.28,1901; No.3 died Aug.27,1902; Enrollment cancelled by Department July 8 1904					
8						
9						
10						
11						
12						
13						
14						
15						
16					Date of Application for Enrollment	May 2/99
17						

Choctaw By Blood Enrollment Cards 1898-1914

RESIDENCE: Red River   COUNTY.   **Choctaw Nation**   **Choctaw Roll**   CARD NO.
POST OFFICE: Goodwater, I.T.   *(Not Including Freedmen)*   FIELD NO.   1341

Dawes' Roll No.	NAME	Relationship to Person	AGE	SEX	BLOOD	TRIBAL ENROLLMENT		
						Year	County	No.
3664	1 Fobb, Eastman 24	First Named	21	M	Full	1896	Red River	4220
	2							
	3	ENROLLMENT						
	4	OF NOS. 1 HEREON APPROVED BY THE SECRETARY						
	5	OF INTERIOR DEC 12 1902						
	6							
	7							
	8							
	9							
	10							
	11							
	12							
	13							
	14							
	15							
	16							
	17							

TRIBAL ENROLLMENT OF PARENTS

	Name of Father	Year	County	Name of Mother	Year	County
1	Louis Fobb	Dead	Eagle	Sophia Fobb	Dead	Eagle
2						
3						
4						
5	No 1 is husband of Sallie Dyer on Choc #1196					
6	For child of No.1 see NB (March 3 1905) #266					
7						
8						
9						
10						
11						
12						
13						
14						Date of Application for Enrollment.
15						
16						May 2/99
17						

141

Choctaw By Blood Enrollment Cards 1898-1914

RESIDENCE: Red River COUNTY.   **Choctaw Nation**   Choctaw Roll   CARD NO.
POST OFFICE: Goodwater, I.T.   *(Not Including Freedmen)*   FIELD NO. 1342

Dawes' Roll No.	NAME		Relationship to Person First Named	AGE	SEX	BLOOD	TRIBAL ENROLLMENT		
							Year	County	No.
DEAD.	1 Thompson, Stephen	DEAD.	Named	26	M	Full	1896	Red River	12301
3665	2 " Wincey	31	Wife	28	F	"	1896	" "	12302
3666	3 " Lena	6	Dau	3	"	"	1896	" "	12303
3667	4 " Emma	4	"	3mo	"	"			
3668	5 " Robert	1	Son	15mo	M	"			
	6								
	7	ENROLLMENT OF NOS. 2 3 4 and 5 HEREON APPROVED BY THE SECRETARY OF INTERIOR DEC 12 1902							
	8								
	9								
	10	No. 1 HEREON DISMISSED UNDER ORDER OF THE COMMISSION TO THE FIVE CIVILIZED TRIBES OF MARCH 31, 1905							
	11								
	12								
	13								
	14								
	15								
	16								
	17								

TRIBAL ENROLLMENT OF PARENTS

	Name of Father	Year	County	Name of Mother	Year	County
1	Thompson Wilson	Dead	Red River	Ka-na-ho-tema	Dead	Red River
2	Adam Jefferson	"	" " "	Rhoda Jefferson	"	" " "
3	No 1			No 2		
4	No 1			No 2		
5	No 1			No 2		
6						
7	No 2 on 1896 roll as Winsy Thompson					
8	No.5 born March 31, 1901: Enrolled July 8, 1902.					
9	No.1 died Aug. 13, 1900: Proof of death filed July 8, 1904. For child of No.2 see NB (March 3 1905) #960					
10						
11						
12						
13						
14						
15					#1 to 4	
16					Date of Application for Enrollment May 2/99	
17						

Choctaw By Blood Enrollment Cards 1898-1914

RESIDENCE: Red River COUNTY.
POST OFFICE: Goodwater, I.T.

Choctaw Nation

Choctaw Roll CARD NO.
(Not Including Freedmen) FIELD NO. 1343

Dawes' Roll No.	NAME		Relationship to Person First Named	AGE	SEX	BLOOD	TRIBAL ENROLLMENT			
							Year	County		No.
3669	1 Wilson, Thomas	60	First Named	57	M	Full	1893	Red River		P.R. 819
3670	2 " Ilantima	53	Wife	50	F	"	1893	" "		820
3671	3 " Bessie Ann	39	Dau	36	"	"	1893	" "		821
	4									
	5	ENROLLMENT								
	6	OF NOS. 1 2 and 3 HEREON APPROVED BY THE SECRETARY								
	7	OF INTERIOR DEC 12 1902								
	8									
	9									
	10									
	11									
	12									
	13									
	14									
	15									
	16									
	17									

TRIBAL ENROLLMENT OF PARENTS

	Name of Father	Year	County	Name of Mother	Year	County
1	Ish-tan-tubbee	Dead	Red River		Dead	Red River
2		"			"	
3	No 1			No 2		
4						
5						
6			All on Page 92, 1893 Pay roll, Red River County			
7						
8			No3 on 1893 Pay roll as Bissiam Wilson			
9						
10			No2 claims she never knew her parents or where			
11			they died			
12						
13			No1 on 1896 roll as Thomas Ishtontobe, Page 154			
14			No 6298, Red River Co.			
15					Date of Application for Enrollment.	
16					May 2/99	
17						

143

Choctaw By Blood Enrollment Cards 1898-1914

RESIDENCE: Red River COUNTY. **Choctaw Nation** Choctaw Roll CARD NO.
POST OFFICE: Goodwater, I.T. (Not Including Freedmen) FIELD NO. 1344

Dawes' Roll No.	NAME		Relationship to Person First Named	AGE	SEX	BLOOD	TRIBAL ENROLLMENT		
							Year	County	No.
3672	1 Wilson, Nelson	36	First Named	33	M	Full	1896	Red River	13596
I.W. 702	2 " , Maggie	(24)	Wife	24	F	I.W.			
15397	3 " , Sillena	2	Dau	2	F	1/2			
	4								
	5								
	6								
	7	ENROLLMENT OF NOS. 1 HEREON APPROVED BY THE SECRETARY OF INTERIOR DEC 12 1902							
	8								
	9								
	10								
	11								
	12	ENROLLMENT OF NOS. 2 HEREON APPROVED BY THE SECRETARY OF INTERIOR MAY 7 1904							
	13								
	14			ENROLLMENT OF NOS. 3 HEREON APPROVED BY THE SECRETARY OF INTERIOR MAY 9 1904					
	15								
	16								
	17								

TRIBAL ENROLLMENT OF PARENTS

	Name of Father	Year	County	Name of Mother	Year	County
1	Thomas Wilson	1896	Red River	Ilomtima Wilsom	1896	Red River
2	A.J. McIntosh	Dead	non-citizen	Melissa McIntosh	Dead	non-citizen
3	No 1			No 2		
4						
5						
6						
7	No.1 is now husband of Maggie Wilson on Choctaw Card #D674 Nov 7 1901					
8	Nº1 is said to be father of Sillena Wilson on Choctaw Card #D675 Nov 7 1901					
9	Nº2 transferred from Choctaw card #D.674. See decision of Feby 27, 1904					
10	No3 transferred from Choctaw card D675. See decision of March 15, 1904.					
	For child of Nos 1&2 see NB (March 3 1905) #996					
11						
12						
13						
14					#1	
15					Date of Application for Enrollment.	
16					May 2/99	
17						

Choctaw By Blood Enrollment Cards 1898-1914

RESIDENCE: Eagle   COUNTY.   **Choctaw Nation**   **Choctaw Roll**   CARD NO.

POST OFFICE: Eagletown, I.T.   *(Not Including Freedmen)*   FIELD NO.   1345

Dawes' Roll No.	NAME	Relationship to Person First Named	AGE	SEX	BLOOD	TRIBAL ENROLLMENT Year	County	No.
3673	1 Thompson, George 51	First Named	48	M	Full	1896	Eagle	12246
3674	2 DIED PRIOR TO SEPTEMBER 25, 1902 Lucy	Wife	39	F	"	1896	"	12247
3675	3 " James 10	Son	7	M	"	1896	"	12249
3676	4 DIED PRIOR TO SEPTEMBER 25, 1902 Sophia	Dau	1	F	"			
	5							
	6							
	7	ENROLLMENT						
	8	OF NOS. 1 2 3 and 4 HEREON APPROVED BY THE SECRETARY						
	9	OF INTERIOR DEC 12 1902						
	10							
	11							
	12							
	13							
	14							
	15							
	16							
	17							

TRIBAL ENROLLMENT OF PARENTS

	Name of Father	Year	County	Name of Mother	Year	County
1	John Thompson	Dead	Eagle	Martha Thompson	Dead	Eagle
2	Eba-foh-ka	"	"		"	"
3	No 1			No 2		
4	No 1			No 2		
5						
6						
7			No 3 on 1896 roll as Jim Thompson			
8			No 2 died June 20, 1900; proof of death filed Dec 15, 1902.			
9		No 4 " Oct. 10, 1900; " " " " " " "				
10		No.2 died June 20 1900: Enrollment cancelled by Department [illegible] No.4 died Oct. 10, 1900: Enrollment cancelled by Department Sept. 6, 1904.				
11						
12						
13						
14						
15				DATE OF APPLICATION FOR ENROLLMENT. May 2/99		
16						
17						

Choctaw By Blood Enrollment Cards 1898-1914

RESIDENCE: Towson COUNTY. **Choctaw Nation** Choctaw Roll CARD NO.
POST OFFICE: Doaksville, I.T. (Not Including Freedmen) FIELD NO. **1346**

Dawes' Roll No.	NAME		Relationship to Person	AGE	SEX	BLOOD	TRIBAL ENROLLMENT		
							Year	County	No.
3677	1 Aaron, William	44	First Named	41	M	Full	1896	Towson	222
3678	2 " , Lucy	33	Wife	30	F	"	1896	"	223
3679	3 " , Elsie	20	Dau	17	"	"	1896	"	225
3680	4 " , Denison	16	Son	13	M	"	1896	"	224
3681	5 " , Bekinsie	13	"	10	"	"	1896	"	226
3682	6 " , Louina	11	Dau	8	F	"	1896	"	227
3683	7 " , Mary	7	"	4	"	"	1896	"	228
3684	8 " , Alex	6	Son	2	M	"			
3685	9 " , Leana	4	Dau	1/2	F	"			
3686	10 " , Selea	2	Dau	4mo	F	"			
	11								
	12	ENROLLMENT OF NOS. 123456789and10 HEREON APPROVED BY THE SECRETARY OF INTERIOR Dec. 12, 1902							
	13								
	14								
	15								
	16								
	17								

TRIBAL ENROLLMENT OF PARENTS

	Name of Father	Year	County	Name of Mother	Year	County
1	Caleb Aaron	Dead	Towson		Dead	Towson
2	Noka-sthea	"	"	Siline Aaron	1896	"
3	No 1			Sillen Bane	1896	"
4	No 1			No 2		
5	No 1			No 2		
6	No 1			No 2		
7	No 1			No 2		
8	No 1			No 2		
9	No 1			No 2		
10	No 1			No 2		
11						
12	No 4 on 1896 roll as Dennis Aaron					
13	No 5 " 1896 " " Mackenzie "					
14	No 6 " 1896 " " Lewinie "					
	No 10 enrolled May 17, 1901.					
15				Date of Application for Enrollment.	#1 to 9 inc	
16					May 2/99	
17						

Choctaw By Blood Enrollment Cards 1898-1914

Dawes' Roll No.		NAME	Relationship to Person	AGE	SEX	BLOOD	TRIBAL ENROLLMENT		
							Year	County	No.
3687	1	Byington, Davis ³¹	First Named	28	F	Full	1893	Eagle	P.R. 73
	2								
	3	ENROLLMENT OF NOS. 1 HEREON APPROVED BY THE SECRETARY OF INTERIOR DEC 12 1902							
	4								
	5								
	6								
	7								
	8								
	9								
	10								
	11								
	12								
	13								
	14								
	15								
	16								
	17								

TRIBAL ENROLLMENT OF PARENTS

	Name of Father	Year	County	Name of Mother	Year	County
1	Albert Byington	1896	Eagle	Nicey Byington	Dead	Eagle
2						
3						
4						
5		On 1893 Pay roll as Louis Byington, Page 7 No 73 Eagle County				
6						
7		Also on 1896 roll as Lewis Byington, Page 32, No 1289, Eagle Co.				
8						
9						
10						
11						
12						
13						
14					Date of Application for Enrollment.	
15						
16					May 2/99	
17						

Choctaw By Blood Enrollment Cards 1898-1914

Dawes' Roll No.	NAME	Relationship to Person First Named	AGE	SEX	BLOOD	TRIBAL ENROLLMENT		
						Year	County	No.
3688	1 Houston, Louie 23		20	M	Full	1896	Nashoba	5549
3689	2 Elsie DIED PRIOR TO SEPTEMBER 25, 1902	Wife	36	F	"	1893	"	PR 273
3690	3 Momintubbi, Sampson 6	Son	3	M	"			
	4							
	5	ENROLLMENT OF NOS. 1 2 and 3 HEREON APPROVED BY THE SECRETARY OF INTERIOR Dec 12, 1902						
	6							
	7							
	8							
	9							
	10							
	11							
	12							
	13							
	14							
	15							
	16							
	17							

TRIBAL ENROLLMENT OF PARENTS

	Name of Father	Year	County	Name of Mother	Year	County
1	Sampson Houston	Ded	Kiamatia[sic]		Ded	Kiamatia[sic]
2	Lotin Battiest	"	Nashoba	Josephine Battiest	"	Cedar
3	Silas Momintubbi	1896	"	No 2		
4						
5			No 1 on 1896 roll as Louis S. Houston			
6			No 2 " 1893 Pay roll as Elcy Haais			
7						
8			No2 died Aug-1899: Proof of death filed Dec. 18, 1902			
9			No3 has been legally adopted by Amos Wallace Choctaw Card #557 articles			
10			of adoption issued by County Court Rowson[sic] Dec 15, 1902 filed Jan 2, 1903.			
11			No.2 died Aug-1899. Enrollment cancelled by Department July 8, 1904.			
12						
13						
14					Date of Application for Enrollment.	
15						
16					May 1" 99	
17						

148

RESIDENCE: Red River COUNTY. **Choctaw Nation** **Choctaw Roll** CARD No.
POST OFFICE: Goodwater, I.T. *(Not Including Freedmen)* FIELD No. **1349**

Dawes' Roll No.	NAME	Relationship to Person	AGE	SEX	BLOOD	TRIBAL ENROLLMENT		
						Year	County	No.
3691	1 Thompson, Joe 31	First Named	28	M	Full	1896	Red River	12334
3692	2 " , Phillis 33	Wife	30	F	"	1896	" "	12335
3693	3 " , Jefferson 9	S.Son	6	M	"	1896	" "	12336
2694	4 DIED PRIOR TO SEPTEMBER 25, 1902 , Nellie	S.Dau	1	F	"			
3695	5 DIED PRIOR TO SEPTEMBER 25, 1902 , Hagerman	Son	1mo	M	"			
3696	6 " , Rosa 1	Dau	7mo	F	"			
	7							
	8							
	9							
	10							
	11	ENROLLMENT OF NOS. 1 2 3 4 5 and 6 HEREON						
	12	APPROVED BY THE SECRETARY OF INTERIOR Dec 12, 1902.						
	13							
	14							
	15							
	16							
	17							

TRIBAL ENROLLMENT OF PARENTS

	Name of Father	Year	County	Name of Mother	Year	County
1	Thompson Wilson	1896	Red River	Kanahotima	Ded	Red River
2	Eastman Willis	1896	Bok Tuklo	Yona	"	Bok Tuklo
3	Johnson William	1896	Red River	No 2		
4	No 1			No 2		
5	No 1			No 2		
6	No 1			No 2		
7						
8				No2 on 1896 roll as Sibbie Thompson		
9			No6 Born Nov. 1st 1901: Enrolled June 19th 1902.			
10						
11			No4 died in 1901: Proof of death filed Dec 2, 1902			
12		No5	" Oct. 1901: " " " " " " "			
13		No4 died – – 1901: No5 died Oct.-1901: Enrollment cancelled by Department Sept. 16, 1904.				
14						
15				No 5 enrolled Nov. 24/99		
16				Date of Application for Enrollment May 2" 99		
17				May 2nd 1899		

149

Choctaw By Blood Enrollment Cards 1898-1914

RESIDENCE: Towson   COUNTY.
POST OFFICE: Doaksville, I.T.

Choctaw Nation

Choctaw Roll
(Not Including Freedmen)

CARD NO.
FIELD NO. 1350

Dawes' Roll No.		NAME		Relationship to Person First Named	AGE	SEX	BLOOD	TRIBAL ENROLLMENT		
								Year	County	No.
3697	1	Loman Elias		DIED PRIOR TO SEPTEMBER 25, 1902	35	M	Full	1896	Towson	7928
3698	2	" Narcissy	48	Wife	45	F	"	1896	"	7929
3699	3	" Peter	10	Son	7	M	"	1896	"	7930
	4									
	5	ENROLLMENT								
	6	OF NOS. 1 2 and 3 HEREON APPROVED BY THE SECRETARY								
	7	OF INTERIOR DEC 12 1902								
	8									
	9									
	10									
	11									
	12									
	13									
	14									
	15									
	16									
	17									

TRIBAL ENROLLMENT OF PARENTS

	Name of Father	Year	County	Name of Mother	Year	County
1	James Loman	Ded	Towson	Hannah Loman	Ded	Towson
2	Kaniniata-bi	"	San Bois		"	"
3	No 1			No 2		
4						
5						
6						
7						
8	No1 died Nov 18, 1901: proof of death filed Dec 2, 1902					
9	No.1 died Nov. 18, 1901: Enrollment cancelled by Department July 8, 1904.					
10						
11						
12						
13						
14						
15					Date of Application for Enrollment.	
16					May 2" 99	
17						

Choctaw By Blood Enrollment Cards 1898-1914

RESIDENCE: Towson	COUNTY.	**Choctaw Nation**	**Choctaw Roll**	CARD NO.
POST OFFICE: Doaksville I.T.			*(Not Including Freedmen)*	FIELD NO. 1351

Dawes' Roll No.	NAME	Relationship to Person	AGE	SEX	BLOOD	TRIBAL ENROLLMENT		
						Year	County	No.
3700	1 Willis Emerson D ²²	First Named	19	M	Full	1896	Towson	13199
	2							
	3							
	4	ENROLLMENT						
	5	OF NOS. 1 HEREON APPROVED BY THE SECRETARY						
	6	OF INTERIOR DEC 12 1902						
	7							
	8							
	9							
	10							
	11							
	12							
	13							
	14							
	15							
	16							
	17							

TRIBAL ENROLLMENT OF PARENTS

	Name of Father	Year	County	Name of Mother	Year	County
1	Dixon Willis	De'd	Towson	Elizabeth Willis	Ded	Towson
2						
3						
4						
5						
6			Enrolled as Emerson D Wellis			
7			For child of No.1 see NB (March 3 1905) #1086			
8						
9						
10						
11						
12						
13						
14					Date of Application for Enrollment.	
15						
16					May 2" 99	
17						

151

Choctaw By Blood Enrollment Cards 1898-1914

RESIDENCE: Towson

POST OFFICE: Doaksville I.T.

Choctaw Nation (Not Including Freedmen)

Dawes' Roll No.	NAME	Relationship to Person First Named	AGE	SEX	BLOOD	TRIBAL ENROLLMENT Year	County
3701	1 William James 23	First Named	20	M	Full	1896	Kiamatia[sic]
	2						
	3 ENROLLMENT						
	4 OF NOS. 1 HEREON APPROVED BY THE SECRETARY						
	5 OF INTERIOR DEC 12 1902						
	6						
	7						
	8						
	9						
	10						
	11						
	12						
	13						
	14						
	15						
	16						
	17						

TRIBAL ENROLLMENT OF PARENTS

Name of Father	Year	County	Name of Mother	Year	County
1 Eaton William	Ded	Towson		Ded	
2					
3					
4					
5					
6					
7					
8					
9		Enrolled on 1896 Roll as James Williams			
10					
11					
12					
13					
14					
15					
16			Date of Application for Enrollment.		May 2-99
17					

Choctaw By Blood Enrollment Cards 1898-1914

RESIDENCE: Towson   COUNTY.   **Choctaw Nation**   Choctaw Roll   CARD NO.
POST OFFICE: Doaksville, I.T.   (Not Including Freedmen)   FIELD NO. 1353

Dawes' Roll No.		NAME	Relationship to Person First Named	AGE	SEX	BLOOD	TRIBAL ENROLLMENT		
							Year	County	No.
3702	1	Taylor, Sealy Ann ~~ED PRIOR TO SEPTEMBER 25, 1902~~	First Named	38	F	Full	1893	Towson	P R 360
3703	2	" Bicey 23	Dau	20	"	"	1893	"	361
3704	3	" Ellen 21	"	18	"	"	1893	"	362
3705	4	" Josiah Simpson 19	Son	16	M	"	1893	"	363
3706	5	" Becky 17	Dau	14	F	"	1893	"	364
3707	6	" Mary Jane 15	"	12	"	"	1893	"	366
3708	7	" Millie Jane 13	"	10	"	"	1893	"	365
3709	8	" Simmie 5	Son	2	M	"			
	9	ENROLLMENT							
	10	OF NOS. 1234567and8 HEREON APPROVED BY THE SECRETARY							
	11	OF INTERIOR DEC 12 1902							
	12	No 1 died January 9, 1901; proof of							
	13	death filed Dec 8, 1902.							
	14	No.1 died Jan. 9, 1902. Enrollment							
	15	cancelled by Department July 8, 1904							
	16								
	17								

TRIBAL ENROLLMENT OF PARENTS

	Name of Father	Year	County	Name of Mother	Year	County
1	Wilson Aaron	Dead	Towson	Elsie Aaron	Dead	Towson
2	John Taylor	"	"	No 1		
3	" "	"	"	No 1		
4	" "	"	"	No 1		
5	" "	"	"	No 1		
6	" "	"	"	No 1		
7	" "	"	"	No 1		
8	" "	"	"	No 1		
9		No1 on	1893 Pay roll Page 40 No 360 Towson County			
10		No2 "	1893 " " " 40 No 361 "	" as Nicey Taylor		
11		No3 "	1893 " " " 40 No 362 "	" "		
12		No4 "	1893 " " " 40 No 363 "	" as Joan Taylor		
13		No5 "	1893 " " " 40 No 364 "	" as Becca "		
14		No6 "	1893 " " " 40 No 366 "	" as Mede Jane "		
		No7 "	1893 " " " 40 No 365 "	" as Mary Jane "		
15	No 2 is now wife of Alexander H Reed on Choctaw card #819:					
16	evidence of marriage filed Dec. 6, 1902.			Date of Application for Enrollment	May 2/99	
17	No 7 Hugo I.T. 6/30/06					

For child of No 3 see NB (Apr 26 '06) Card #88

153

Choctaw By Blood Enrollment Cards 1898-1914

RESIDENCE: Eagle			COUNTY.	**Choctaw Nation**				**Choctaw Roll**	CARD NO.	
POST OFFICE: Eagle Town I.T.							*(Not Including Freedmen)*		FIELD NO.	1354

Dawes' Roll No.		NAME	Relationship to Person	AGE	SEX	BLOOD	TRIBAL ENROLLMENT			P NR.
							Year	County		
3710	1	Gardner Wilkin 37	First Named	34	M	Full	1893	Eagle		288
3711	2	" Nancy 51	Wife	48	F	"	1893	"		289
~~3712~~	3	~~DIED PRIOR TO SEPTEMBER 25, 1902 Wylis~~	~~Sis.~~	~~20~~	"	"	~~1893~~	"		~~291~~
3713	4	" Wilson 21	Bro.	18	M	"	1893	"		290
	5									
	6	ENROLLMENT								
	7	OF NOS. 1 2 3 and 4 HEREON APPROVED BY THE SECRETARY								
	8	OF INTERIOR DEC 12 1902								
	9									
	10									
	11									
	12									
	13									
	14									
	15									
	16									
	17									

TRIBAL ENROLLMENT OF PARENTS

	Name of Father	Year	County	Name of Mother	Year	County
1	Dennis E. Gardner	Ded	Eagle	Talowahoki	Ded	Eagle
2	Davis Colbert	"	"	Kanitima	"	"
3	~~Dennis E. Gardner~~	"	"	~~Talowahoki~~	"	"
4	" " "	"	"	"	"	"
5						
6						
7						
8						
9						
10						
11	No2 On 1893 Pay Roll Eagle Co. as Nancy Colbert					
12	No3 " 1893 " " " " " Willis Gardner					
13	Is not No4 duplicate enrollment of No 1 on 7-3732?					
	No.3 died Aug, 1902, proof of death filed Dec. 2, 1902					
14	~~No 3 died Aug — 1902: Enrollment cancelled by Department July 8, 1904~~					
15						
16				Date of Application for Enrollment	May 2" 99	
17						

154

Choctaw By Blood Enrollment Cards 1898-1914

RESIDENCE: Towson COUNTY.
POST OFFICE: Doaksville I.T.

Choctaw Nation

Choctaw Roll
(Not Including Freedmen)

CARD NO.
FIELD NO. 1355

Dawes' Roll No.	NAME	Relationship to Person	AGE	SEX	BLOOD	TRIBAL ENROLLMENT		
						Year	County	No.
3714	1 Aaron John 31	First Named	28	M	Full	1896	Towson	217
3715	2 " Sealy 53	Wife	50	F	"	1893	"	P.R. 257
3716	3 " Tama 16	Niece	13	"	"	1896	"	212
	4							
	5	ENROLLMENT						
	6	OF NOS. 1 2 and 3 HEREON APPROVED BY THE SECRETARY						
	7	OF INTERIOR DEC 12 1902						
	8							
	9							
	10							
	11							
	12							
	13							
	14							
	15							
	16							
	17							

TRIBAL ENROLLMENT OF PARENTS

	Name of Father	Year	County	Name of Mother	Year	County
1	James Aaron	Ded	Towson	Selina Aaron	Ded	Towson
2	Tik-ban-ta-bi	"	Kiamatia[sic]	"Shona"	"	Kiamatia[sic]
3	Pitman Aaron	Ded	Jack's Fork	"Innie"	"	Towson
4						
5						
6						
7						
8			No2 on 1893 Pay Roll Towson Co as Sallie Mellon.			
9						
10						
11						
12						
13						
14					Date of Application for Enrollment.	
15						
16			Date of application for enrollment May 2' 99			
17						

155

Choctaw By Blood Enrollment Cards 1898-1914

RESIDENCE: Towson COUNTY.
POST OFFICE: Fowlersville I.T.

Choctaw Nation

Choctaw Roll
(Not Including Freedmen)

CARD NO.

FIELD NO. 1356

Dawes' Roll No.	NAME		Relationship to Person First Named	AGE	SEX	BLOOD	TRIBAL ENROLLMENT		
							Year	County	No.
3717	1 Williams Charles	28	First Named	25	M	Full	1896	Towson	13169
3718	2 " James	3	Son	2½	M	1/2			
	3								
	4	ENROLLMENT							
	5	OF NOS. 1 and 2	HEREON						
	6	APPROVED BY THE SECRETARY OF INTERIOR DEC 12 1902							
	7								
	8								
	9								
	10								
	11								
	12								
	13								
	14								
	15								
	16								
	17								

TRIBAL ENROLLMENT

	Name of Father	Year	County	Name of Mother		
1	George Williams	Ded	Towson	Sattin Ann Williams		
2	N°1			Fitter Williams		non-c
3						
4						
5						
6						
7		N°1 is now the husband of Fitter Williams a non citizen. Evidence of				
8		marriage filed Aug. 15, 1902.				
9		N°2 Born March 1, 1900. Enrolled Aug. 18, 1902				
10						
11						
12						
13						
14						
15					#1	
16				Date of Application for Enrollment	May 2" 99	
17						

Choctaw By Blood Enrollment Cards 1898-1914

POST OFFICE: Fowlerville, I.T.

Dawes' Roll No.	NAME	Relationship to Person First Named	AGE	SEX	BLOOD	TRIBAL ENROLLMENT		
						Year	County	No.
3719	1 Christie Edward 20	First Named	17	M	Full	1896	Towson	2461
	2							
	3 ENROLLMENT OF NOS. 1 HEREON							
	4 APPROVED BY THE SECRETARY OF INTERIOR DEC 12 1902							
	5							
	6							
	7							
	8							
	9							
	10							
	11							
	12							
	13							
	14							
	15							
	16							
	17							

TRIBAL ENROLLMENT OF PARENTS

Name of Father	Year	County	Name of Mother			
1 Edward Christie	Dead	Towson	Mita Christie		ows	
2						
3						
4						
5						
6						
7						
8						
9						
10						
11						
12						
13						
14			Date of Application for Enrollment.			
15						
16			May 2/99			
17						

Choctaw By Blood Enrollment Cards 1898-1914

RESIDENCE: Red River COUNTY. **Choctaw Nation** Choctaw Roll CARD NO.
POST OFFICE: Goodwater, I.T. (Not Including Freedmen) FIELD NO. **1358**

Dawes' Roll No.	NAME		Relationship to Person First Named	AGE	SEX	BLOOD	TRIBAL ENROLLMENT		
							Year	County	No.
3720	1 Moore, Frances	31	First Named	28	F	Full	1896	Red River	2673
3721	2 Coxwell, Loston	8	Son	5	M	"	1896	" "	2674
14661	3 " , Louis	5	"	3	"	"			
3722	4 Moore , Allie	1	Dau	3mo	F	"			
15398	5 " , Ben	3	Son	2	M	"			
	6 ENROLLMENT								
	7 OF NOS. 1 2 and 4 HEREON APPROVED BY THE SECRETARY								
	8 OF INTERIOR Dec. 12, 1902								
	9 For child of No.1 see N.B. (Apr 26.06) Card No. 505								
	10 " " " " " " (Mar 3-05) " " 930								
	11								
	12 ENROLLMENT OF NOS. 3 HEREON								
	13 APPROVED BY THE SECRETARY OF INTERIOR May 20, 1903								
	14								
	15 ENROLLMENT OF NOS. ~~ 5 ~~ HEREON								
	16 APPROVED BY THE SECRETARY OF INTERIOR May 9 1904								
	17								

TRIBAL ENROLLMENT OF PARENTS

	Name of Father	Year	County	Name of Mother	Year	County
1	Daniel Coxwell	Dead	Red River	Siley Coxwell	Dead	Red River
2	Dixon Kemp	"	" "	No 1		
3	" "	"	" "	No 1		
4	John Moore	1896	" "	No 1		
5	" "	1896	" "	No 1		
6						
7			No 3 Affidavit of birth to be supplied Recd May 9/99			
8						
9			No1 on 1896 roll as Francis Coxwell			
10			No2 " 1896 " " Roston "			
11			No1 is now the wife of John Moore on Choctaw card #1324. Evidence of marriage filed March 15, 1902.			
12			No4 Born Janry 9, 1902. Enrolled April 3, 1902.			
13	No.5 Born Oct. 12, 1899 application first made Feby 1, 1901 No.5 enrolled April 7, 1904					
14						#1 to 3 inc
15					Date of Application for Enrollment.	
16					May 2/99	
17	P.O. America I.T. 4/11/05					

Choctaw By Blood Enrollment Cards 1898-1914

RESIDENCE: Towson COUNTY.
POST OFFICE: Fowlersville, I.T.

Choctaw Nation

Choctaw Roll
(Not Including Freedmen)

CARD NO.
FIELD NO. **1359**

Dawes' Roll No.	NAME	Relationship to Person	AGE	SEX	BLOOD	TRIBAL ENROLLMENT		
						Year	County	No.
3723	1 Harley, Mary Ann 48	First Named	45	F	Full	1893	Towson	221
	2							
	3	ENROLLMENT						
	4	OF NOS. 1 HEREON APPROVED BY THE SECRETARY						
	5	OF INTERIOR Dec. 12, 1902.						
	6							
	7							
	8							
	9							
	10							
	11							
	12							
	13							
	14							
	15							
	16							
	17							

TRIBAL ENROLLMENT OF PARENTS

	Name of Father	Year	County	Name of Mother	Year	County
1	Marshall Yale	Ded	Towson	Sarah Yale	Ded	Towson
2						
3						
4						
5						
6			On 1893 Pay Roll for Towson County as Mary An LeFlore			
7						
8		No 1 also on 1896 roll page 358. #13656 as Mary Willie				
9						
10						
11						
12						
13						
14						
15				Date of Application for Enrollment.		
16				May 2 – 99		
17						

159

RESIDENCE: **Nashoba** COUNTY.
POST OFFICE: **Smithville I.T.**

Choctaw Nation

Choctaw Roll
(Not Including Freedmen)

CARD NO.
FIELD NO. **1360**

Dawes' Roll No.	NAME		Relationship to Person First Named	AGE	SEX	BLOOD	TRIBAL ENROLLMENT		
							Year	County	No.
I.W. 512	₁ Mowdy, James M	(49)	First Named	47	M	I.W.	1896	Nashoba	14820
3724	₂ " Caroline	39	Wife	36	F	1/2	1896	"	8609
3725	₃ " Elsie E	13	Dau	10	"	1/4	1896	"	8610
3726	₄ " Margaret I	11	"	8	"	1/4	1896	"	8611
3727	₅ " Lola O	8	"	5	"	1/4	1896	"	8612
3728	₆ " Delta	6	Son	2	M	1/4			
3729	₇ " Delana	4	"	3mo	"	1/4			
3730	₈ " Nora Clemintine		Dau	2mo	F	1/4			
	9								
	10	ENROLLMENT OF NOS. 2 3 4 5 6 7 and 8 HEREON APPROVED BY THE SECRETARY OF INTERIOR Dec 12 1902							
	11								
	12								
	13 No 8 Born April 6th 1902: Enrolled June 26" 1902								
	14	ENROLLMENT OF NOS. ~ 1 ~ HEREON APPROVED BY THE SECRETARY OF INTERIOR Dec 24 1903							
	15								
	16								
	17								

TRIBAL ENROLLMENT OF PARENTS

	Name of Father	Year	County	Name of Mother	Year	County
1	James Mowdy	1896	Non Citz	Salane Mowdy	1896	Non Citz
2	Solomon Robison	Dead	Wade	Elizabeth Robison	1896	Nashoba
3	No 1			No 2		
4	No 1			No 2		
5	No 1			No 2		
6	No 1			No 2		
7	No 1			No 2		
8	No 1			No 2		
9						
10						
11	No 1 on 1896 roll as James M Mondy. He was also admitted by					
12	Dawes Commission as an Intermarried Citizen, Case No 356.					
13	No 2 on 1896 roll as Caroline Mondy					
	No 3 " 1896 " " Elsie A "					
14	No 4 " 1896 " " Margaret "					
15	No 5 " 1896 " " Lora O. "				Date of Application for Enrollment.	
16	Original marriage license on file in office of Dawes Commission, Muskogee I.T.				May. 2/99	
17	No.5 was also admitted by Dawes Commission in 1896: Choctaw case #356					

RESIDENCE: Eagle   COUNTY.   **Choctaw Nation**   **Choctaw Roll**   CARD NO.
POST OFFICE: Ultima Thule, Ark   (Not Including Freedmen)   FIELD NO. 1361

Dawes' Roll No.	NAME	Relationship to Person First Named	AGE	SEX	BLOOD	TRIBAL ENROLLMENT		
						Year	County	No.
3731	1 Dyer, David J. 23	First Named	20	M	Full	1896	Eagle	3415
3732	2 ~~Sadie~~ ED PRIOR TO SEPTEMBER 25, 1902	Wife	26	F	"	1896	"	4183
3733	3 ~~Cooper, Frances~~ DIED PRIOR TO SEPTEMBER 25, 1902	S.Dau	6	"	"	1896	"	2644
3734	4 " Johnny 7	S.Son	4	M	"	1896	"	2618
	5							
	6	ENROLLMENT OF NOS. 1 2 3 and 4 HEREON						
	7	APPROVED BY THE SECRETARY						
	8	OF INTERIOR DEC 12 1902						
	9							
	10							
	11							
	12							
	13							
	14							
	15							
	16							
	17							

TRIBAL ENROLLMENT OF PARENTS

	Name of Father	Year	County	Name of Mother	Year	County
1	Wilson Dyer	1896	Eagle	Emeline Dyer	De'd	Eagle
2	~~Thompson Haiakonabi~~	De'd	"	"Casey"	"	"
3	~~William Cooper~~	"	"	~~No 2~~		
4	" "	"	"	No 2		
5						
6			No2 on 1896 Roll as Sadie Fobb			
7			No4 " " "	" Johnny "		
8						
9			No2 died May 1901; proof of death filed Dec 6, 1902			
10			No3 " in 1901; " " " " " "			
11	No2 died May – 1901; No3 died - -, 1901: Enrollment cancelled by Department July 8, 1904					
12	For child of No1 see NB (Apr 26-06) Card #828					
13						
14						
15						
16				Date of Application for Enrollment. May 2" 99		
17						

Choctaw By Blood Enrollment Cards 1898-1914

POST OFFICE: Smithville, I.T.

Choctaw Nation

Choctaw Roll
(Not Including Freedmen)

CARD NO.
FIELD NO. 1362

Dawes' Roll No.	NAME	Relationship to Person	AGE	SEX	BLOOD	TRIBAL ENROLLMENT		
						Year	County	No.
3735	1 Robinson, Mary ⁵⁵	First Named	52	F	1/2	1896	Nashoba	10784
	2							
	3	ENROLLMENT						
	4	OF NOS. 1 HEREON APPROVED BY THE SECRETARY						
	5	OF INTERIOR DEC 12 1902						
	6							
	7							
	8							
	9							
	10							
	11							
	12							
	13							
	14							
	15							
	16							
	17							

TRIBAL ENROLLMENT OF PARENTS

	Name of Father	Year	County	Name of Mother	Year	County
1	Louis Robinson	Dead	Non Citz	Mary Robinson	Dead	Red River
2						
3						
4						
5						
6						
7						
8						
9						
10						
11						
12						
13						
14						
15						
16				Date of Application for Enrollment	May 2/99	
17						

Choctaw By Blood Enrollment Cards 1898-1914

RESIDENCE: Towson COUNTY.								
POST OFFICE: Fowlersville I.T.	**Choctaw Nation**		**Choctaw Roll** (Not Including Freedmen)			CARD NO. FIELD NO. **1363**		

Dawes' Roll No.	NAME	Relationship to Person	AGE	SEX	BLOOD	TRIBAL ENROLLMENT		
						Year	County	No.
3736	1 Austin, Legion 36	First Named	33	M	Full	1896	Towson	199
3737	2 " Molsey 25	Wife	22	F	"	1896	"	200
3738	3 " Lizzie 10	Dau	7	"	"	1896	"	201
3739	4 " James ~~DIED PRIOR TO SEPTEMBER 25, 1902~~	Son	1	M	"			
3740	5 " Adline 2	Dau	10mo	F	"			
	6							
	7	ENROLLMENT OF NOS. 1 2 3 4 and 5 HEREON APPROVED BY THE SECRETARY OF INTERIOR Dec 12 1902						
	8							
	9							
	10							
	11							
	12							
	13							
	14							
	15							
	16							
	17							

TRIBAL ENROLLMENT OF PARENTS

	Name of Father	Year	County	Name of Mother	Year	County
1	Ata-sa-ha-bi	Ded	Towson	Lotima	Ded	Towson
2	Brazil	"	Red River	"Siney"	"	Red Rive
3	No 1			No 2		
4	No 1			No 2		
5	No.1			No.2		
6						
7				No1 on 1896 roll as Legend Austin.		
8			No.5 Enrolled June 4th, 1901			
9						
10				No4 died April 1899: proof of death filed Dec 2, 1902.		
11			No.4 died April 1899: Enrollment cancelled by Department Sept. 16, 1904			
12						
13						
14						
15				# 1 to 4 inc		
16				Date of Application for Enrollment May 2 '99		
17						

Choctaw By Blood Enrollment Cards 1898-1914

RESIDENCE: Nashoba COUNTY. **Choctaw Nation** **Choctaw Roll** CARD NO.
POST OFFICE: Tushkahoma[sic], I.T. (Not Including Freedmen) FIELD NO. 1364

Dawes' Roll No.	NAME	Relationship to Person First Named	AGE	SEX	BLOOD	TRIBAL ENROLLMENT		
						Year	County	No.
3741	1 Frazier, Loren 21	First Named	18	M	Full	1896	Nashoba	4156
	2							
	3	ENROLLMENT						
	4	OF NOS. 1 HEREON APPROVED BY THE SECRETARY						
	5	OF INTERIOR DEC 12 1902						
	6							
	7							
	8							
	9							
	10							
	11							
	12							
	13							
	14							
	15							
	16							
	17							

TRIBAL ENROLLMENT OF PARENTS

	Name of Father	Year	County	Name of Mother	Year	County
1	Lolin Frazier	Dead	Wade	Jellicco Frazier	Dead	Wade
2						
3						
4						
5						
6						
7						
8						
9						
10						
11						
12						
13						
14						
15					Date of Application for Enrollment.	
16					May 2/99	
17						

164

Choctaw By Blood Enrollment Cards 1898-1914

RESIDENCE: Towson COUNTY. **Choctaw Nation** Choctaw Roll CARD NO.
POST OFFICE: Garvin, I.T. (Not Including Freedmen) FIELD NO. **1365**

Dawes' Roll No.	NAME	Relationship to Person	AGE	SEX	BLOOD	TRIBAL ENROLLMENT		
						Year	County	No.
3742	1 Willie, Leonidas ²⁴	First Named	21	M	Full	1896	Red River	13638
4743	2 ~~DIED PRIOR TO SEPTEMBER 25, 1932~~ ~~Viney~~	~~Wife~~	~~20~~	~~F~~	"	~~1893~~	~~Towson~~	P.R. 6
	3							
	4	ENROLLMENT						
	5	OF NOS. 1 and 2 HEREON APPROVED BY THE SECRETARY						
	6	OF INTERIOR DEC 12 1902						
	7							
	8							
	9							
	10							
	11							
	12							
	13							
	14							
	15							
	16							
	17							

TRIBAL ENROLLMENT OF PARENTS

	Name of Father	Year	County	Name of Mother	Year	County
1	Ranson	Dead	Bok Tuklo		1896	Red River
2	~~Legion Austin~~	~~1896~~	~~Towson~~	~~Netsey Austin~~	~~Dead~~	~~Towson~~
3						
4						
5		No 2 on 1893 Pay roll as Viney Austin, Page 1, No 6, Towson County.				
6						
7		No 2 died in January 1901; Proof of death filed Dec 2 1902				
8	No.2 died Jan. – , 1901: Enrollment cancelled by Department July 8, 1904					
9						
10						
11						
12						
13						
14						
15					Date of Application for Enrollment.	
16					May 2/99	
17						

165

Choctaw By Blood Enrollment Cards 1898-1914

RESIDENCE: **Red River** COUNTY. **Choctaw Nation** **Choctaw Roll** CARD No.

POST OFFICE: **Goodwater, I.T.** *(Not Including Freedmen)* FIELD No. **1366**

Dawes' Roll No.	NAME	Relationship to Person First Named	AGE	SEX	BLOOD	TRIBAL ENROLLMENT		
						Year	County	No.
I.W.**891**	1 Koozer, Charles 57	First Named	54	M	I.W	1896	Red River	14724
3744	2 " Charles H. 15	Son	12	M	1/8	1896	" "	7601
	3							
	4 ENROLLMENT							
	5 OF NOS. 2 HEREON APPROVED BY THE SECRETARY							
	6 OF INTERIOR DEC 12 1902							
	7							
	8 ENROLLMENT OF NOS 1 HEREON							
	9 APPROVED BY THE SECRETARY OF INTERIOR AUG 3 1904							
	10							
	11							
	12							
	13							
	14							
	15							
	16							
	17							

TRIBAL ENROLLMENT OF PARENTS

	Name of Father	Year	County	Name of Mother	Year	County
1	Fred Koozer	1896	Non Citz	Elizabeth Koozer	Dead	Non Citz
2	No 1			Lucretia Koozer	"	Red River
3						
4						
5						
6	No 2 on 1896 roll as Charles Kooza.					
7						
8						
9						
10						
11						
12						
13						
14						
15						
16				Date of Application for Enrollment:		May 2/99
17						

166

RESIDENCE: Eagle COUNTY.
POST OFFICE: Eagletown, I.T.

Choctaw Nation

Choctaw Roll
(Not Including Freedmen)

CARD NO.
FIELD NO. 1367

Dawes' Roll No.	NAME		Relationship to Person	AGE	SEX	BLOOD	TRIBAL ENROLLMENT		
							Year	County	No.
3745	1 Cooper, Martin	45	First Named	42	M	Full	1896	Eagle	2624
3746	2 " Susan	31	Wife	28	F	"	1896	"	2634
3747	3 " Edward	9	Son	6	M	"	1896	"	2601
3748	4 " Lucy	7	Dau	4	F	"	1896	"	2621
3749	5 " Lena	5	"	2	"	"			
3750	6 Fobb, Silas	19	Ward	16	M	"	1896	Eagle	2635
14662	7 Cooper, Phebe	2	Dau	19mo	F	"			
	8		ENROLLMENT						
	9		OF NOS. 1 2 3 4 5 and 6 HEREON						
	10		APPROVED BY THE SECRETARY OF INTERIOR DEC 12 1902						
	11								
	12		ENROLLMENT						
	13		OF NOS. 7 HEREON APPROVED BY THE SECRETARY						
	14		OF INTERIOR MAY 20 1903						
	15								
	16								
	17								

TRIBAL ENROLLMENT OF PARENTS

	Name of Father	Year	County	Name of Mother	Year	County
1	Ish-ti-chi	Dead	Nashoba	Chi-pi-oke	Dead	Eagle
2	John Talahala	"	Eagle	I-ya-na-hoke	"	Towson
3	No 1			No 2		
4	No 1			No 2		
5	No 1			No 2		
6	John Fobb	Dead	Eagle	Sallie Fobb	Dead	Eagle
7	Nº1			Nº2		
8						
9						
10						
11			No6 on 1896 roll as Silas Cooper			
12			Nº7 Born March 1, 1901 enrolled Oct. 20, 1902.			
13						#1 to 6
14						Date of Application for Enrollment.
15						
16						May 2/99
17						

167

Choctaw By Blood Enrollment Cards 1898-1914

RESIDENCE: Eagle   COUNTY.   **Choctaw Nation**   **Choctaw Roll**   CARD NO.

POST OFFICE: Eagle Town I.T.   *(Not Including Freedmen)*   FIELD NO. **1368**

Dawes' Roll No.	NAME	Relationship to Person	AGE	SEX	BLOOD	TRIBAL ENROLLMENT		
						Year	County	No.
3751	1 Gardner Anderson ²⁸	First Named	25	M	Full	1896	Eagle	4788
	2							
	3 ENROLLMENT							
	4 · OF NOS. 1 HEREON APPROVED BY THE SECRETARY							
	5 OF INTERIOR DEC 12 1902							
	6							
	7							
	8							
	9							
	10							
	11							
	12							
	13							
	14							
	15							
	16							
	17							

TRIBAL ENROLLMENT OF PARENTS

	Name of Father	Year	County	Name of Mother	Year	County
1	Tanisse	Ded	Eagle	Tonowahoke	Ded	Eagle
2						
3						
4						
5						
6						
7						
8						
9						
10						
11						
12						
13						
14						
15					Date of Application for Enrollment.	
16					May 2 – 99	
17						

168

Choctaw By Blood Enrollment Cards 1898-1914

RESIDENCE: Eagle   COUNTY.   **Choctaw Nation**   **Choctaw Roll**   CARD NO.
POST OFFICE: Eagletown, I.T.   *(Not Including Freedmen)*   FIELD NO. 1369

Dawes' Roll No.	NAME	Relationship to Person First Named	AGE	SEX	BLOOD	TRIBAL ENROLLMENT		
						Year	County	No.
3752	1 Cooper, Jinsy ³³	First Named	30	F	Full	1896	Eagle	2610
3753	2 Wesley, Agnes ~~DIED PRIOR TO SEPTEMBER 25, 1902~~	Dau	3	"	"	1896	"	2591
	3							
	4	ENROLLMENT						
	5	OF NOS. 1 and 2 HEREON						
	6	APPROVED BY THE SECRETARY						
	7	OF INTERIOR DEC 12 1902						
	8							
	9							
	10							
	11							
	12							
	13							
	14							
	15							
	16							
	17							

TRIBAL ENROLLMENT OF PARENTS

	Name of Father	Year	County	Name of Mother	Year	County
1	Abel Cooper	Dead	Eagle	Emiline Cooper	Dead	Eagle
2	~~Lije Wesley~~	1896	"	~~No 1~~		
3						
4						
5						
6						
7	~~No2 on 1896 roll as Agnes Cooper~~					
8	No 2 died Aug 6, 1902; proof of death filed Dec 12, 1902					
9	No.2 died Aug 6, 1901: Enrollment cancelled by Department July 8, 1904.					
10	For child of No.1 see NB (March 3 1905) #956					
11						
12						
13						
14						
15						
16					Date of Application for Enrollment	May 2/99
17						

169

Choctaw By Blood Enrollment Cards 1898-1914

RESIDENCE: Eagle COUNTY.
POST OFFICE: Eagletown, I.T.

Choctaw Nation

Choctaw Roll (Not Including Freedmen)

CARD NO.
FIELD NO. 1370

Dawes' Roll No.	NAME	Relationship to Person First Named	AGE	SEX	BLOOD	TRIBAL ENROLLMENT Year	County	No.
3754	1 Harrison, Thomas 29		26	M	Full	1893	Atoka	P.R. 501
3755	Susan PRIOR TO SEPTEMBER 25, 1902	Wife	30	F	"	1893	Eagle	152
3756	3 Haiakanubbi, Jonas 17	S.Son	14	M	"	1893	"	153
3757	4 " Sissy 15	S.Dau	12	F	"	1893	"	154
3758	5 " Colbert 12	S.Son	9	M	"	1893	"	155
	6 No1 is duplicate of Johnson Jacob No2 on Choctaw card 5607 Enroll							
	7 ment cancelled by Departmental instructions of September 27, 1905							
	8 I.T.D 12334 – 1905 D.C.#45441-1905							
	9							
	10 ENROLLMENT							
	11 OF NOS. 1 2 3 4 and 5 HEREON APPROVED BY THE SECRETARY							
	12 OF INTERIOR DEC 12 1902							
	13							
	14							
	15 No.2 died Sept 20, 1899: Enrollment							
	16 cancelled by Department July 8, 1904							
	17							

TRIBAL ENROLLMENT OF PARENTS

	Name of Father	Year	County	Name of Mother	Year	County
1	Caleb Harrison	Dead	Atoka	Sealy Harrison	Dead	Atoka
2	Abel Cooper	"	Eagle	Emiline Cooper	"	Eagle
3	Dixon Haiakanubbi	"	"	No2		
4	" "	"	"	No 2		
5	" "	"	"	No 2		
6						
7						
8						
9						
10	No1 on 1893 Pay roll as Thomas McGee, Page 57, No 601, Atoka County					
11	No2 " 1893 " " " Susan Hiakanabi, " 14, No 152, Eagle "					
12	No3 " 1893 " " " Jonas " 14 No 153 " "					
13	No4 " 1893 " " " Cissy " 14 No 154 " "					
14	No5 " 1893 " " " Colbert " 14 No 155 " "					
15	No2 on 1896 roll, Eagle Co, Page 137, No 5632 as Susan Hayakonubbi					
16	No3 " 1896 " " " 136, " 5593 " Jonas "					
	No4 " 1896 " " " 137, " 5636 " Sissie "					
	No5 " 1896 " " " 136, " 5596 as				Date of Application for Enrollment. May 2/99
17	Colbert Hayakonubbi					

170

Choctaw By Blood Enrollment Cards 1898-1914

RESIDENCE: Eagle   COUNTY.
POST OFFICE: Eagletown, I.T.

Choctaw Nation

Choctaw Roll
(Not Including Freedmen)

CARD NO.
FIELD NO.   1371

Dawes' Roll No.	NAME	Relationship to Person First Named	AGE	SEX	BLOOD	TRIBAL ENROLLMENT		
						Year	County	No.
3750	1 Cooper, Eason DIED PRIOR TO SEPTEMBER 25, 1902	First Named	24	M	Full	1896	Eagle	2600
	2							
	3	ENROLLMENT OF NOS. 1 HEREON						
	4	APPROVED BY THE SECRETARY OF INTERIOR DEC 12 1902						
	5							
	6							
	7							
	8							
	9							
	10							
	11							
	12							
	13							
	14							
	15							
	16							
	17							

TRIBAL ENROLLMENT OF PARENTS

Name of Father	Year	County	Name of Mother	Year	County
1 Abel Cooper	Dead	Eagle	Mary Cooper	Dead	Eagle
2					
3					
4					
5					
6	On 1896 roll as Elson Cooper				
7	No1 died April, 1900: proof of death filed Dec 12, 1902.				
8	No.1 died April – 1900: Enrollment cancelled by Department July 2, 1904.				
9					
10					
11					
12					
13					
14					
15					
16				Date of Application for Enrollment	May 2/99	
17					

Choctaw By Blood Enrollment Cards 1898-1914

RESIDENCE: Eagle COUNTY. **Choctaw Nation** **Choctaw Roll** CARD NO.
POST OFFICE: Eagletown, I.T. *(Not Including Freedmen)* FIELD NO. **1372**

Dawes' Roll No.	NAME	Relationship to Person First Named	AGE	SEX	BLOOD	TRIBAL ENROLLMENT		
						Year	County	No.
3760	1 Cooper, Sima ⁱ⁹		16	F	Full	1896	Eagle	2633
	2							
	3	ENROLLMENT OF NOS. 1 HEREON APPROVED BY THE SECRETARY OF INTERIOR Dec 12 1902						
	4							
	5							
	6							
	7							
	8							
	9							
	10							
	11							
	12							
	13							
	14							
	15							
	16							
	17							

TRIBAL ENROLLMENT OF PARENTS

Name of Father	Year	County	Name of Mother	Year	County
1 Kitson Wesley	Dead	Eagle	Sophie Hopiashuby	1896	Eagle
2					
3					
4					
5					
6		No 1 on 1896 Roll as Siney Cooper			
7					
8					
9					
10					
11					
12					
13					
14				Date of Application for Enrollment.	
15					
16				May 2/99	
17					

Choctaw By Blood Enrollment Cards 1898-1914

RESIDENCE: Nashoba COUNTY.
POST OFFICE: Alikchi I.T.

Choctaw Nation
Choctaw Roll
(Not Including Freedmen)

CARD NO.
FIELD NO. 1373

Dawes' Roll No.	NAME	Relationship to Person First Named	AGE	SEX	BLOOD	TRIBAL ENROLLMENT		
						Year	County	No.
I.W. 513	1 Woolery, John 57	First Named	53	M	I.W.	1896	Nashoba	15171
3761	2 " Nancy 33	Wife	30	F	Full	1896	"	13317
3762	3 " James 20	Son	17	M	1/2	1896	"	13318
3763	4 " Walker 18	"	15	"	1/2	1896	"	13319
3764	5 " Annie 16	Dau	13	F	1/2	1896	"	13320
3765	6 " Julia 11	"	8	"	1/2	1896	"	13321
3766	7 " John Jr. 9	Son	6	M	1/2	1896	"	13322
3767	8 " Carlston 8	"	5	"	1/2	1896	"	13323
3768	9 " Rhoda 5	Dau	2	F	1/2	ENROLLMENT OF NOS. ~1~ HEREON APPROVED BY THE SECRETARY OF INTERIOR Dec 24 1903		
3769	10 " Gilbert 2	Son	6mo	M	1/2			
14926	11 " Susan Anna 1	Gr.Dau	15mo	F	1/4			
	12	ENROLLMENT OF NOS. 23456789and10 HEREON APPROVED BY THE SECRETARY OF INTERIOR Dec 12 1902	For child of No3 see NB(Apr 26'06) Card #69	"	"	'No5 " " (Mar 3'05) " #1270		
	13							
	14							
	15	ENROLLMENT OF NOS. ~11~ HEREON APPROVED BY THE SECRETARY OF INTERIOR Oct 15 1903	No8 on 1896 roll as Colston Woolery No7 " 1896 " " John "					
	16							
	17							

	Name of Father	Year	County	Name of Mother	Year	County
1	John P. Woolery	De'd	Non Citz	Elsie Woolery	De'd	Non Citz
2	Moses Dyer	De'd	Eagle	Lottie Dyer	1896	Eagle
3	No 1			No 2		
4	No 1			No 2		
5	No 1			No 2		
6	No 1			No 2		
7	No 1			No 2		
8	No 1			No 2		
9	No 1			No 2		
10	No 1			No 2		
11	Nº 3			Donie Woolery		intermarried

12 It seems that evidence of marriage was left with Clerk of Circuit Court
13 of the County and that records have been destroyed. Evidence of himself and G.W. Thompson as to marriage taken – See same.
14 No.10 Enrolled July 9, 1901. No.11 Born April 30,1902. Enrolled July 27,1903
15 No3 is now husband of Dona Woolery on Choctaw
16 card 5772. Evidence of marriage of parent of No 11 filed July 27 1903
17 No3 Chula I.T. See affidavits of Joe Dyer and Jackson Hudson as to marriage of No1 to No2

Date of application for enrollment May-3-99
Date of Application for Enrollment

11/28/02
Valliant I.T.

according to Choctaw law filed July 3 1903.

173

Choctaw By Blood Enrollment Cards 1898-1914

RESIDENCE: Cedar COUNTY. **Choctaw Nation** Choctaw Roll CARD No.
POST OFFICE: Tuskahoma I.T. (Not Including Freedmen) FIELD No. **1374**

Dawes' Roll No.	NAME	Relationship to Person First Named	AGE	SEX	BLOOD	TRIBAL ENROLLMENT Year	County	No.
3770	1 Baker Hodgen 28	First Named	25	M	Full	1896	Nashoba	1148
3771	2 " Lecy Anna 31	Wife	28	F	"	1896	"	1147
3772	3 " Noel 16	S.Son	13	M	"	1896	"	1149
3773	4 " Annie 12	Dau	9	F	"	1896	"	1151
3774	5 " Lillie 11	"	8	"	"	1896	"	1152
3775	6 " Becky 6	"	3	"	"	1896	"	1154
3776	7 " Ida 5	"	1	"	"			
3777	8 Ward Eastman 8	Ward	5	M	"	1896	Jack's Fork	14113
	9							
	10	ENROLLMENT OF NOS. 1234567and8 HEREON APPROVED BY THE SECRETARY OF INTERIOR Dec 12 1902						
	11							
	12							
	13		For children of Nos 1&2 see NB (Mar 3-05) #854					
	14							
	15							
	16							
	17							

TRIBAL ENROLLMENT OF PARENTS

	Name of Father	Year	County	Name of Mother	Year	County
1	Simon Baker	De'd	Nashoba	Suky Edward	Ded	Nashoba
2	William Ward	"	"		"	"
3	Sam Hosa	"	"	No 2		
4	No 1			No 2		
5	No 1			No 2		
6	No 1			No 2		
7	No 1			No 2		
8	William Garland	1896	Nashoba	Nancy Ward	De'd	Cedar
9						
10						
11				No1 on 1896 roll as Hodges Baker		
12				No2 " " " " Louisiana Baker		
13				No5 " " " " Lillie "		
				No6 " " " " Beckie "		
14						Date of Application for Enrollment.
15						May 3-99
16						
17	P.O. Nashoba IT 4/11/05					

Choctaw By Blood Enrollment Cards 1898-1914

RESIDENCE: Nashoba COUNTY.

POST OFFICE: Alikchi, I.T.

Choctaw Nation

Choctaw Roll
(Not Including Freedmen)

CARD NO.

FIELD NO. 1375

Dawes' Roll No.	NAME	Relationship to Person First Named	AGE	SEX	BLOOD	TRIBAL ENROLLMENT		
						Year	County	No.
DEAD.	1 Watkins, Ben	First Named	70	M	I.W.	1896	Nashoba	15172
3778	2 Chapman, Kate K ²²	Dau	19	F	1/4	1896	"	13324
3779	3 Watkins Cora C ¹⁸	"	15	"	1/4	1896	"	13325
3780	4 " Waldo E ¹⁶	Son	13	M	1/4	1896	"	13326
3781	5 Chapman, James Emery	Son of No2	1mo	M	1/8			
I.W. 1095	6 " James M. ²⁶	Husband of No.2	26	M	I.W.			
	7							
	8 ENROLLMENT OF NOS. 2 3 4 and 5 HEREON APPROVED BY THE SECRETARY		For child of Nos 2 and 6 see NB(Apr. 26-06) No.555					
	9 OF INTERIOR DEC 12 1902							
	10					*Not* DISMISSED		
	11 No.2 is now the wife of James M Chapman							
	12 on Choctaw Card #D.637. 6/20/01.					APR 19 1906		
	13 No5 Born May 18ᵗʰ 1902: Enrolled June 28ᵗʰ 1901							
	14 ENROLLMENT							
	15 OF NOS. ~~~ 6 ~~~ HEREON APPROVED BY THE SECRETARY							
	16 OF INTERIOR NOV 16 1904							
	17							

TRIBAL ENROLLMENT OF PARENTS

	Name of Father	Year	County	Name of Mother	Year	County
1	Isham L. Watkins	Dead	Non Cit	Winnifred Watkins	Dead	Non Citz
2	No 1			Melvina Watkins	"	Bok Tuklo
3	No 1			" "	"	" "
4	No 1			" "	"	" "
5	James M. Chapman	on Choctaw Card #D637		No 2		
6	James Chapman		non citizen	Melvina Chapman	dead	non-citizen
7						
8	No2 on 1896 roll as Kate Watkins					
9	No4 " 1896 " " Waldo "					
10	No.6 transferred from Choctaw card #D-637, Oct. 31, 1904: See decision of Oct. 15, 1904					
11	No1 claims that the evidence of his marriage was					
12	left with the Clerk of Circuit Court, and that the					
13	records have been destroyed. Evidence of himself					
	and John Woolery as to marriage taken. See					
14	the same					
15	No.1 died May 5ᵗʰ 1900. See testimony of No2 taken June 20, 1901.					
16					Date of Application for Enrollment May 3/99	
17	No.6 P.O. Garvin I.T. 7/6/04					

175

Choctaw By Blood Enrollment Cards 1898-1914

Dawes' Roll No.	NAME	Relationship to Person First Named	AGE	SEX	BLOOD	TRIBAL ENROLLMENT		
						Year	County	No.
3782	1 Wilson, Cole 23	First Named	20	M	Full	1896	Eagle	13500
3783	2 " Viney 19	Wife	16	F	"	1893	"	P.R. 262
	3							
	4							
	5	ENROLLMENT						
	6	OF NOS. 1 and 2 HEREON APPROVED BY THE SECRETARY						
	7	OF INTERIOR DEC 12 1902						
	8							
	9							
	10							
	11							
	12							
	13							
	14							
	15							
	16							
	17							

TRIBAL ENROLLMENT OF PARENTS

	Name of Father	Year	County	Name of Mother	Year	County
1	David Wilson	1896	Eagle	Sealy Wilson	1896	Eagle
2	Wilson Dyer	Dead	"	Emiline Dyer	Dead	"
3						
4						
5	No1 on 1896 roll as Kolson Wilson					
6	No2 " 1893 Pay roll as Vincey Forb, Page 26, No 262, Eagle Co.					
7	For child of No2 see NB (Apr 26-06) Card #587 " " " " " " (Mar 3 1905) " #1019					
8						
9						
10						
11						
12						
13						
14						
15					Date of Application for Enrollment.	
16					May 3/99	
17						

Choctaw By Blood Enrollment Cards 1898-1914

RESIDENCE: Eagle   COUNTY.

POST OFFICE: Eagletown, I.T.

Choctaw Nation

Choctaw Roll
(Not Including Freedmen)

CARD NO.

FIELD NO. 1377

Dawes' Roll No.	NAME	Relationship to Person First Named	AGE	SEX	BLOOD	TRIBAL ENROLLMENT		
						Year	County	No.
3784	1 Jones, Winnie DIED PRIOR TO SEPTEMBER 25, 190?		60	F	Full	1896	Eagle	6930
	2							
	3							
	4	ENROLLMENT						
	5	OF NOS. 1 HEREON APPROVED BY THE SECRETARY						
	6	OF INTERIOR DEC 12 1902						
	7							
	8							
	9							
	10							
	11							
	12							
	13							
	14							
	15							
	16							
	17							

TRIBAL ENROLLMENT OF PARENTS

	Name of Father	Year	County	Name of Mother	Year	County
1	Ano-ko-be-la	Dead	Eagle	Na-wee	Dead	Eagle
2						
3						
4						
5						
6	No.1 died before Sept 25 1902. Enrollment cancelled by Department May 2 1906					
7						
8						
9						
10						
11						
12						
13						
14						
15						
16				Date of Application for Enrollment	May 3/99	
17						

177

Choctaw By Blood Enrollment Cards 1898-1914

Choctaw Nation

Choctaw Roll (Not Including Freedmen)

CARD NO.
FIELD NO. 1378

NAME	Relationship to Person First Named	AGE	SEX	BLOOD	TRIBAL ENROLLMENT		
					Year	County	No.
1 Wilson, Stewart 36 — DIED PRIOR TO SEPTEMBER 25, 1902		33	M	Full	1896	Eagle	13540
2 Sarah 39 — DIED PRIOR TO SEPTEMBER 25, 1902	Wife	36	F	"	1896	"	13523
3 Louie — DIED PRIOR TO SEPTEMBER 25, 1902	Son	5	M	"	1896	"	13520
4 " Frances 6	Dau	3	F	"	1896	"	13521
5 " Iden 5	Son	1/2	M	"			
6							
7							
8							
9							
10							
11							
12							
13							
14							
15							
16							
17							

3789

ENROLLMENT
OF NOS. 1 2 3 4 and 5 HEREON
APPROVED BY THE SECRETARY
OF INTERIOR DEC 12 1902

TRIBAL ENROLLMENT OF PARENTS

	Name of Father	Year	County	Name of Mother	Year	County
1	Alex Pisachubbee	1896	Nashoba	Emily Pisachubbee	Dead	Eagle
2	Summie Homer	Dead	Eagle	Melissa Homer	"	"
3	No 1			No 2		
4	No 1			No 2		
5	No 1			No 2		
6						
7	No 5 – Affidavit of birth to be supplied. Recd May 10/99					
8	N°3 Died May 15, 1901. Proof of death filed Dec 24, 1902					
9	N°2 Died Sept. 14, 1901. Proof of death filed Dec 24, 1902					
10	No2 died Sept 14 1901; No3 died May 15,1901; Enrollment cancelled by Department July 8 1904					
11	No1 died winter of 1900-1901; Enrollment cancelled by Department May 2-1906.					
12						
13						
14						
15						
16						
17						

Date of Application for Enrollment May 3/99

178

Choctaw By Blood Enrollment Cards 1898-1914

RESIDENCE: Nashoba COUNTY.
POST OFFICE: Smithville, I.T.

Choctaw Nation

Choctaw Roll
(Not Including Freedmen)

CARD NO.
FIELD NO. 1379

Dawes' Roll No.	NAME		Relationship to Person	AGE	SEX	BLOOD	TRIBAL ENROLLMENT		
							Year	County	No.
3790	1 Bohanan, Jonas	29	First Named	26	M	Full	1896	Nashoba	1120
3791	2 " Lucinda	20	Wife	17	F	1/2	1896	"	1113
3792	3 James, Sarah	6	S.Dau	3	"	3/4	1896	"	1114
3793	4 Bohanan, Impson	4	Son	10mo	M	3/4			
	5								
	6	ENROLLMENT OF NOS. 1 2 3 and 4 HEREON APPROVED BY THE SECRETARY OF INTERIOR DEC 12 1902							
	7								
	8								
	9								
	10								
	11								
	12								
	13								
	14								
	15								
	16								
	17								

TRIBAL ENROLLMENT OF PARENTS

	Name of Father	Year	County	Name of Mother	Year	County
1	Julius Bohanan	Dead	Nashoba	Sallie Bohanan	1896	Nashoba
2	Davis Benn	"	"	Martha Benn	Dead	Non Citz
3	Charley James	1896	Eagle	No 2		
4	Nº1			No 2		
5						
6						
7	No 2 on 1896 roll as Lucinda Benn					
8	No 3 " 1896 " " Sarah Ben					
9	No4 Affidavit of birth to be supplied. Recd May 12/99					
10	Evidence of Albert Carney taken as to marriage of father and mother of No2. See same.					
11	See testimony of Nº1 as to relationship of Nº4 to Nº1, taken July 10, 1903					
12	For child of Nos 1&2 see NB (March 3, 1905) #947					
13						
14						
15						
16					May	3/99
17						

179

Choctaw By Blood Enrollment Cards 1898-1914

Choctaw Nation

Choctaw Roll *(Not Including Freedmen)*   CARD NO.   FIELD NO. 1380

Dawes' Roll No.	NAME		Relationship to Person First Named	AGE	SEX	BLOOD	TRIBAL ENROLLMENT		
							Year	County	No.
3794	1 Johnson, Joseph	55	First Named	52	M	Full	1896	Nashoba	6817
3795	2 " Adeline	32	Wife	29	F	"	1896	"	6818
3796	3 " Noel	9	Son	6	M	"	1896	"	6819
~~3797~~	4 ~~DIED PRIOR TO SEPTEMBER 25, 1902 " William~~		~~"~~	~~4~~	~~"~~	~~"~~	~~1896~~	~~"~~	~~5820~~
3798	5 " Aggie	6	Dau	3	F	"	1896	"	6821
~~3799~~	6 ~~DIED PRIOR TO SEPTEMBER 25, 1902 " Lura~~		~~"~~	~~9mo~~	~~"~~	~~"~~			
3800	7 " Huston	1	Son	4mo	M	"			
	8								
	9	ENROLLMENT							
	10	OF NOS. 123456and7 HEREON APPROVED BY THE SECRETARY							
	11	OF INTERIOR DEC 12 1902							
	12								
	13								
	14								
	15								
	16								
	17								

TRIBAL ENROLLMENT OF PARENTS

	Name of Father	Year	County	Name of Mother	Year	County
1		Dead	in Mississippi		Dead	Wade
2	Geo. Watson	"	Nashoba	Netsie Watson	"	Nashoba
3	No 1			No 2		
4	No 1			No 2		
5	No 1			No 2		
6	No 1			No 2		
7	No 1			No 2		
8						
9	No2 on 1896 Roll as Adaline Johnson					
10	No5 on 1896 roll as Aiggy Johnson					
11	No7 Enrolled August 30, 1901.					
	No.4 died July, 1902: Proof of death filed Dec 23, 1902, as "Willie" Johnson					
12	Nº6 Died July 19, 1902: proof of death filed Jany. 29, 1903					
13	No4 died July 1902: No6 died July 19, 1902: Enrollment cancelled by Department July 8, 1904					
14	For child of No2 see NB (March 3 1905) #1033					
15						
16					Date of Application for Enrollment	For Nos 123 & 5
17						May 3/99

Choctaw By Blood Enrollment Cards 1898-1914

Dawes' Roll No.	NAME		Relationship to Person	AGE	SEX	BLOOD	TRIBAL ENROLLMENT		
							Year	County	No.
3801	1 Wilson, Charles	25	First Named	22	M	Full	1896	Nashoba	13228
3802	2 " Lucinda	26	Wife	23	F	"	1896	"	12162
3803	3 " Sherman	4	Son	5mo	M	"			
3804	4 " Milton	2	Son	5mo	M	"			
3805	5 " Brown	1	Son	6mo	M	"			
	6								
	7	ENROLLMENT OF NOS. 1 2 3 4 and 5 HEREON APPROVED BY THE SECRETARY OF INTERIOR Dec 12 1902							
	8								
	9								
	10								
	11								
	12								
	13								
	14								
	15								
	16								
	17								

TRIBAL ENROLLMENT OF PARENTS

	Name of Father	Year	County	Name of Mother	Year	County
1	Alex Wilson	1896	Nashoba	Eliza Wilson	1896	Nasahoba
2	James Taylor	Dead	"	Sophina Taylor	Dead	"
3	No 1			No 2		
4	No 1			No 2		
5	No 1			No 2		
6						
7						
8	No 2 on 1896 roll as Lucinda I Taylor					
9	No 4 Enrolled February 27, 1901.					
10	No 5 Born Dec. 15th 1901. Enrolled June 26th 1902. For child of Nos 1&2 see N.B. (March 3, 1905) #923					
11						
12						
13						
14					Date of Application for Enrollment.	
15						
16					May 3/99	
17	P.O. Hatfield Ark 4/7/05					

Choctaw By Blood Enrollment Cards 1898-1914

RESIDENCE: Nashoba COUNTY.   **Choctaw Nation**   Choctaw Roll   CARD NO.

POST OFFICE: Smithville I.T.   *(Not Including Freedmen)*   FIELD NO. 1382

Dawes' Roll No.	NAME		Relationship to Person First Named	AGE	SEX	BLOOD	TRIBAL ENROLLMENT		
							Year	County	No.
3806	₁ Carney, Albert	49	First Named	46	M	Full	1896	Nashoba	2487
3807	₂ " Amy	45	Wife	42	F	"	1896	"	2488
3808	₃ " Nora	11	Dau	8	"	"	1896	"	2490
3809	₄ DIED PRIOR TO SEPTEMBER 25, 1902 Ella		"	4	"	"	1896	"	2491
3810	₅ DIED PRIOR TO SEPTEMBER 25, 1902 Pearlie		"	1	"	"			
3811	₆ Robert Ben	16	S.Son	13	M	"	1896	Nashoba	10790
3812	₇ Carney Alzira	13	S Dau	10	F	"	1896	"	2489
	₈								
	₉ ENROLLMENT								
	₁₀ OF NOS. 123456and7 HEREON APPROVED BY THE SECRETARY								
	₁₁ OF INTERIOR DEC 12 1902								
	₁₂								
	₁₃								
	₁₄								
	₁₅								
	₁₆								
	₁₇								

TRIBAL ENROLLMENT OF PARENTS

	Name of Father	Year	County	Name of Mother	Year	County
₁	Kliotubbee	De'd	Nashoba	Walla	De'd	Nashoba
₂	Noli	"	"	Pisa hania	"	Eagle
₃	No 1			No 2		
₄	No 1			No 2		
₅	No 1			No 2		
₆	Immonbi Robert	De'd	Nashoba	No 2		
₇	Joe Johnson	1896	"	No 2		
₈						
₉						
₁₀			No 2 on roll of 1896 as Aimy Carney			
₁₁			No 3 " " " " " Narry "			
₁₂			No 7 " " " " " Zira " No.5 died Sept. 3, 1900: Enrollment cancelled by Department July 8 1904			
₁₃			For child of No7 see NB (Apr 26-06) card #603			
₁₄						
₁₅					Date of Application for Enrollment.	
₁₆					May 3"99	
₁₇	P.O. Beach I.T.					

Choctaw By Blood Enrollment Cards 1898-1914

RESIDENCE: Bok Tuklo   COUNTY.   **Choctaw Nation**   **Choctaw Roll** *(Not Including Freedmen)*   CARD NO.
POST OFFICE: Lukfata, I.T.   FIELD NO. **1383**

Dawes' Roll No.	NAME	Relationship to Person	AGE	SEX	BLOOD	TRIBAL ENROLLMENT		
						Year	County	No.
3813	1 Tekobbe, Bob 42	First Named	39	M	Full	1896	Bok Tuklo	122012
3814	2 Winnissie	Wife	23	F	"	1896	" "	12202
3815	3 " Susanna 6	Dau	3	"	"	1896	" "	12203
3816	4 Saul	Son	3mo	M	"			
3817	5 Nakishi, Watson 10	S.Son	7	"	"	1896	Bok Tuklo	9720
	6							
	7	ENROLLMENT OF NOS. 1 2 3 4 and 5 HEREON						
	8	APPROVED BY THE SECRETARY						
	9	OF INTERIOR DEC 12 1902						
	10							
	11							
	12							
	13							
	14							
	15							
	16							
	17							

DIED PRIOR TO SEPTEMBER 25, 1902 *(lines 2 and 4)*

TRIBAL ENROLLMENT OF PARENTS

	Name of Father	Year	County	Name of Mother	Year	County
1	Tekobbe	Dead	Bok Tuklo		Dead	Towson
2	Ka nich tubbee	"	" "	Salena	"	Bok Tuklo
3	No 1			No 2		
4	No 1			No 2		
5	Sim Nakishi	Dead	Bok Tuklo	No 2		
6						
7			No 2 on 1896 roll as Winnicy Tekobbe			
8			No 3 " 1896 " " Susie "			
9	No2 died in Summer of 1900: proof of death filed Dec 16, 1902.					
	No2 died 1900 No4 1900: Enrollment cancelled by Department July 8, 1904					
10	Nº1 is father of Sam Tekobbe on Choctaw card #4904					
11						
12						
13						
14					Date of Application for Enrollment.	
15						
16					May 3/99	
17						

183

Choctaw By Blood Enrollment Cards 1898-1914

RESIDENCE: **Nashoba** COUNTY. **Choctaw Nation** **Choctaw Roll** CARD NO.
POST OFFICE: **Smithville I.T.** *(Not Including Freedmen)* FIELD NO. **1384**

Dawes' Roll No.	NAME	Relationship to Person	AGE	SEX	BLOOD	TRIBAL ENROLLMENT		
						Year	County	No.
3818	1 McCoy Hilbon N. 43	First Named	40	M	Full	1896	Nashoba	9283
3819	2 " Mullim[sic] 51	Wife	48	F	"	1896	"	9284
	3							
	4	ENROLLMENT						
	5	OF NOS. 1 and 2 HEREON APPROVED BY THE SECRETARY						
	6	OF INTERIOR DEC 12 1902						
	7							
	8							
	9							
	10							
	11							
	12							
	13							
	14							
	15							
	16							
	17							

TRIBAL ENROLLMENT OF PARENTS

	Name of Father	Year	County	Name of Mother	Year	County
1	Nelson McCoy	De'd	Nashoba	Ho-lu-tie	Ded	Eagle
2	Sho-ma-ka	"	Eagle	Pis-a-la-ho-ka	"	Nashoba
3						
4						
5						
6						
7			No 1 on 1896 Roll as Hilben McCoy			
8			No 2 " " " " Mollen "			
9						
10						
11						
12						
13						
14						
15						
16				Date of Application for Enrollment	May 3" 99	
17						

184

Choctaw By Blood Enrollment Cards 1898-1914

RESIDENCE: Red River COUNTY.
POST OFFICE: Janis, I.T.

Choctaw Nation

Choctaw Roll
(Not Including Freedmen)

CARD NO.
FIELD NO. 1385

Dawes' Roll No.	NAME	Relationship to Person First Named	AGE	SEX	BLOOD	TRIBAL ENROLLMENT		
						Year	County	No.
3820	1 Jones, Jesse 8	First Named	5	M	Full	1896	Red River	7035
	2							
	3	ENROLLMENT						
	4	OF NOS. 1 HEREON APPROVED BY THE SECRETARY						
	5	OF INTERIOR DEC 12 1902						
	6							
	7							
	8							
	9							
	10							
	11							
	12							
	13							
	14							
	15							
	16							
	17							

TRIBAL ENROLLMENT OF PARENTS

	Name of Father	Year	County	Name of Mother	Year	County
1	Amon Jones	Dead	Red River	Sophie Jones	Dead	Red River
2						
3						
4						
5			On 1896 roll as Jessee Jones			
6						
7			Now living with Ben Williams, a white man, in			
8			Red River Co.			
9						
10			W.J. Whiteman of Goodwater is legal guardian of this child			
11			Original papers of appointment received and filed			
12			Nov 27, 1902.			
13						
14					Date of Application for Enrollment.	
15						
16					May 3/99	
17						

185

Choctaw By Blood Enrollment Cards 1898-1914

RESIDENCE: Nashoba COUNTY.				**Choctaw Nation**			**Choctaw Roll**	CARD NO.	
POST OFFICE: Smithville, I.T.							*(Not Including Freedmen)*	FIELD NO. 1386	

Dawes' Roll No.	NAME		Relationship to Person	AGE	SEX	BLOOD	TRIBAL ENROLLMENT		
							Year	County	No.
3821	1 Homer, Byington	26	First Named	23	M	Full	1896	Nashoba	5553
	2								
	3	ENROLLMENT							
	4	OF NOS. 1 HEREON APPROVED BY THE SECRETARY							
	5	OF INTERIOR DEC 12 1902							
	6								
	7								
	8								
	9								
	10								
	11								
	12								
	13								
	14								
	15								
	16								
	17								

TRIBAL ENROLLMENT OF PARENTS

	Name of Father	Year	County	Name of Mother	Year	County
1	Willis Homer	Dead	Eagle	Sallie Wilson	1896	Nashoba
2						
3						
4						
5	This is error No 1 now the Husband of Narcissa Homer No3 on Choctaw card #4252					
6	Evidence of marriage filed July 14th 1902					
7	No1 is know[sic] the husband of Nicey Harris on Choctaw card #2023, July 14, 1902					
8	this correction made Dec 6, 1902 For child of No1 see NB (March 3,1905) #798					
9						
10						
11						
12						
13						
14						
15					Date of Application for Enrollment.	
16					May 3/99	
17						

Choctaw By Blood Enrollment Cards 1898-1914

RESIDENCE: Bok Tuklo   COUNTY.   **Choctaw Nation**   **Choctaw Roll**   CARD NO.
POST OFFICE: Lukfata, I.T.   (Not Including Freedmen)   FIELD NO. **1387**

Dawes' Roll No.	NAME	Relationship to Person First Named	AGE	SEX	BLOOD	TRIBAL ENROLLMENT		
						Year	County	No.
3822	₁ Swarm, Inez ²⁴	First Named	21	F	Full	1893	Towson	P.R. 24
3823	₂ ~~Helen~~ DIED PRIOR TO SEPTEMBER 25, 1902	~~Dau~~	~~2mo~~	"	~~1/2~~			
3824	₃ " Nova Belle ¹	Dau	6wks	F	1/2			
	₄							
	₅	ENROLLMENT						
	₆	OF NOS. 1 2 and 3 HEREON APPROVED BY THE SECRETARY						
	₇	OF INTERIOR Dec 12 1902						
	₈							
	₉							
	₁₀							
	₁₁							
	₁₂							
	₁₃							
	₁₄							
	₁₅							
	₁₆							
	₁₇							

TRIBAL ENROLLMENT OF PARENTS

	Name of Father	Year	County	Name of Mother	Year	County
₁		Dead	Red River		1896	Red River
₂	F.M. Swarm	1896	Non Citz	No. 1		
₃	" "		" "	No 1		
₄						
₅						
₆						
₇		No 1 is niece of Eastman Jones, Goodwater and Granddaughter				
₈		of George Morris Arkindo				
₉		For children of No 1 see N.B. (March 3 1905) #1016				
₁₀		No 1 on 1893 Pay roll, Page 54, No 24, Towson Co, as Inez Jackson				
₁₁		No1 says that she was separated from her parents				
₁₂		when an infant and that she could never learn				
₁₃		their names.				
		No.3 Enrolled May 17, 1901				
₁₄	No2 died Nov. 2, 1900: proof of death filed Dec. 2, 1902.					
₁₅	No.2 died Nov. 2, 1900	Enrollment cancelled by Department July 8, 1904.			Date of Application for Enrollment.	
₁₆					May 3/99	
₁₇	P.O. Garvin I.T. 4/11/05					

187

Choctaw By Blood Enrollment Cards 1898-1914

RESIDENCE: Red River   COUNTY.   **Choctaw Nation**   **Choctaw Roll**   CARD NO.
POST OFFICE: Shawneetown, I.T.   (Not Including Freedmen)   FIELD NO.   1388

Dawes' Roll No.	NAME	Relationship to Person	AGE	SEX	BLOOD	TRIBAL ENROLLMENT Year	County	No.
5	1 Kaniatobe, Davis 44	First Named	41	M	Full	1896	Red River	7563
3	2 " Ellen 48	Wife	45	F	"	1896	" "	7564
7	3 Harley, Folsom 20	Ward	17	M	"	1896	" "	5665
	4							
	5 ENROLLMENT							
	6 OF NOS. 1 2 and 3 HEREON APPROVED BY THE SECRETARY							
	7 OF INTERIOR DEC 12 1902							
	8							
	9							
	10							
	11							
	12							
	13							
	14							
	15							
	16							
	17							

TRIBAL ENROLLMENT OF PARENTS

	Name of Father	Year	County	Name of Mother	Year	County
1	Kaniatobe	Dead	Red River	I-ma-to-na	Dead	Red River
2	Moses Frazier	"	" "	Pi-sak-ma-tema	"	" "
3	Calvin Harley	"	" "	Amy Harley	"	" "
4						
5						
6						
7			No 2 on 1896 roll as Helen Kamatobe			
8						
9						
10						
11						
12						
13						
14						
15				Date of Application for Enrollment.		
16				May 3/99		
17						

Choctaw By Blood Enrollment Cards 1898-1914

RESIDENCE: Red River   COUNTY.   **Choctaw Nation**   **Choctaw Roll** *(Not Including Freedmen)*   CARD NO. FIELD NO. **1389**

POST OFFICE: Kullituklo, I.T.

Dawes' Roll No.	NAME		Relationship to Person First Named	AGE	SEX	BLOOD	TRIBAL ENROLLMENT		
							Year	County	No.
3828	1 Walker, Semie	31	First Named	28	F	Full	1896	Red River	13591
3839	2 " Denison	15	Son	12	M	"	1896	" "	13592
3830	3 " Johnson	12	"	9	"	"	1896	" "	13593
3831	4 " Joe	9	"	6	"	"	1896	" "	13594
3832	5 " Nelie		Dau	4	F	"	1896	" "	13595
3833	6 " Loston	5	Son	1½	M	"			
14663	7 " Solen	2	Son	2	M	1/2			
	8								
	9								
	10								
	11								
	12								
	13								
	14								
	15								
	16								
	17								

(Row 5) DIED PRIOR TO SEPTEMBER 25, 1902

ENROLLMENT
OF NOS. 1 2 3 4 5 and 6 HEREON
APPROVED BY THE SECRETARY
OF INTERIOR Dec. 12 1902

ENROLLMENT
OF NOS. 7 HEREON
APPROVED BY THE SECRETARY
OF INTERIOR May 20, 1903

TRIBAL ENROLLMENT OF PARENTS

	Name of Father	Year	County	Name of Mother	Year	County
1	Lye Walker	Dead	Red River	Ellen Kaniatobe	1896	Red River
2	Cephus Frazier	"	" " "	No 1		
3	" "	"	" " "	No 1		
4	" "	"	" " "	No 1		
5	" "	"	" " "	No 1		
6	" "	"	" " "	No 1		
7	not known			No 1		
8	No 1 on 1896 roll as Cemy Walker					
9	No 5 " 1896 " " Malis "					
10						
11						
12	No5 died in 1899: proof of death filed Dec. 2, 1902					
13	No7 born June 11, 1900: enrolled Dec. 9, 1902					
14	No5 died – –, 1899: Enrollment cancelled by Department July 8, 1904.			For child of No1 see N.B. (Apr 26-06) card #861	#1 to 6 inc	
15					Date of Application for Enrollment.	
16					May 3/99	
17	P.O. Idabel, I.T. 3/16/07.					

189

Choctaw By Blood Enrollment Cards 1898-1914

RESIDENCE: **Red River** COUNTY. **Choctaw Nation** **Choctaw Roll** CARD NO.
POST OFFICE: **Albion, Texas.** *(Not Including Freedmen)* FIELD NO. **1390**

Dawes' Roll No.	NAME	Relationship to Person	AGE	SEX	BLOOD	TRIBAL ENROLLMENT		
						Year	County	No.
3834	1 Carn, Lucky 28	First Named	25	M	Full	1896	Red River	2658
I.W. 563	2 " Caldonia 25	Wife	21	F	I.W.			
	3							
	4 ENROLLMENT							
	5 OF NOS. 1 HEREON APPROVED BY THE SECRETARY							
	6 OF INTERIOR Dec. 12, 1902							
	7							
	8 ENROLLMENT							
	9 OF NOS. ~~ 2 ~~ HEREON APPROVED BY THE SECRETARY							
	10 OF INTERIOR Feb. 8, 1904							
	11							
	12							
	13							
	14							
	15							
	16							
	17							

TRIBAL ENROLLMENT OF PARENTS

	Name of Father	Year	County	Name of Mother	Year	County
1	Carn	Dead	Bok Tuklo	Maley Carn	Dead	Bok Tuklo
2	William Matlock	"	Non Citz	Sallie Matlock	"	Non Citz
3						
4						
5			No 1 on 1896 roll as Lancy Carn and on Page 33 No 205, 1893 Pay			
6			roll Bok Tuklo Co, as Lucy Carn			
7						
8			No 2 was married to Lucky Carn, as Lucky McKinney, on			
9			July 7, 1895			
10						
11			Is not No2 same as Dona Carn page 384 #14408 c.c. Roll 1896? Yes			
12			No2 also on 1896 Choctaw Census roll page 384 #14408 as Dona Carn			
13						
14				Date of Application for Enrollment		
15				May 4/99		
16						
17						

Choctaw By Blood Enrollment Cards 1898-1914

RESIDENCE: Eagle   COUNTY.
POST OFFICE: Eagle Town I.T.

Choctaw Nation

Choctaw Roll
(Not Including Freedmen)

CARD No.
FIELD No. 1391

Dawes' Roll No.	NAME		Relationship to Person First Named	AGE	SEX	BLOOD	TRIBAL ENROLLMENT		
							Year	County	No.
3835	1 Going David	19		16	M	Full	1896	Eagle	4793
	2								
	3	ENROLLMENT							
	4	OF NOS. 1 HEREON APPROVED BY THE SECRETARY							
	5	OF INTERIOR DEC 12 1902							
	6								
	7								
	8								
	9	No. 1 is duplicate of Simeon Ebafokla, No. 1 on Choctaw card #945, approved							
	10	roll 2545. Enrollment cancelled under Departmental authority of							
	11	October 12-1905; IT D13276-1905 DC 47932-1905							
	12								
	13								
	14								
	15								
	16								
	17								

TRIBAL ENROLLMENT OF PARENTS

	Name of Father	Year	County	Name of Mother	Year	County
1	Thomas Wilson	De'd	Eagle		De'd	Eagle
2						
3						
4						
5						
6						
7						
8						
9						
10						
11						
12			On 1896 Roll as Seamon Going.			
13						
14						
15						
16				Date of Application for Enrollment.	May 4" 99	
17						

Choctaw By Blood Enrollment Cards 1898-1914

| ENCE: Kiamatia[sic] COUNTY. OFFICE: Good-land I.T. | Choctaw Nation | | | | Choctaw Roll (Not Including Freedmen) | CARD NO. FIELD NO. | | |

es' No.	NAME	Relationship to Person	AGE	SEX	BLOOD	TRIBAL ENROLLMENT		
						Year	County	No.
92	1 Terry Jefferson J [55]	First Named	50	M	I.W.		Non Citz	
36	2 " Josephine [24]	Wife	21	F	3/8	1896	Kiamatia[sic]	3778
37	3 Hickman Emma B. [5]	S.Dau	1	"	3/8			
38	4 Terry, James Auther [3]	Son	4mo	M	3/16			
39	5 " Louis Victor [1]	Son	6wks	M	3/16			
	6							
	7	ENROLLMENT						
	8	OF NOS. 2,3,4 and 5 HEREON APPROVED BY THE SECRETARY						
	9	OF INTERIOR DEC 12 1902						
	10	ENROLLMENT						
	11	OF NOS. 1 HEREON APPROVED BY THE SECRETARY						
	12	OF INTERIOR AUG 3 1904						
	13							
	14							
	15							
	16							
	17							

TRIBAL ENROLLMENT OF PARENTS

Name of Father	Year	County	Name of Mother	Year	
1 Henderson Terry	De'd	Non Citz	Mary Terry	De'd	
2 Jimmie Gardner	"	Towson	Agnes Bohannan	1896	
3 Jimmie Hickman	1896	Eagle	No 2		
4 No.1			No.2		
5 Nº1			Nº2		
6					
7			No2 on 1896 Roll as Josephine Ervin		
8		No2 Evidence of divorce from James Hickman filed Dec. 17, 1902			
9					
10		For child of Nos 1&2 see NB (Mar 3-05) Card #101.			
11					
12		No.4 Enrolled May 24, 1900			
13		Nº5 Born Aug. 8, 1901, enrolled Sept 22, 1902.			
14					
15					
16				Date of Application for Enrollment	
17 Hugo I.T. 9/22/02					

Choctaw By Blood Enrollment Cards 1898-1914

RESIDENCE: Kiamatia[sic] COUNTY. **Choctaw Nation** **Choctaw Roll** *(Not Including Freedmen)* CARD NO.

POST OFFICE: Goodland I.T. FIELD NO. 1393

Dawes' Roll No.	NAME	Relationship to Person Named	AGE	SEX	BLOOD	TRIBAL ENROLLMENT		
						Year	County	No.
3840	1 Bohanan Agnes 56	First Named	53	F	1/4	1896	Kiamatia[sic]	8716
3841	2 Bacon Susan 15	Dau	12	"	5/8	1896	"	4822
	3							
	4	ENROLLMENT						
	5	OF NOS. 1 and 2 HEREON APPROVED BY THE SECRETARY						
	6	OF INTERIOR DEC 12 1902						
	7							
	8							
	9							
	10							
	11							
	12							
	13							
	14							
	15							
	16							
	17							

TRIBAL ENROLLMENT OF PARENTS

	Name of Father	Year	County	Name of Mother	Year	County
1	Jesse Bohanan	De'd	Eagle	Celeste Frazier	De'd	Cedar
2	John Bacon	"	Cedar	Agnes Bohanan	"	"
3						
4						
5						
6	No1 on roll as Agnes Murphy					
7	No2 " " " Susan Garvin					
8	For child of No.2, see N.B. (Apr. 26,1906) Card No. 164					
9						
10						
11						
12						
13						
14					Date of Application for Enrollment.	
15						
16					May 4" 99	
17	Erwin, OK 1/23/08					

193

Choctaw By Blood Enrollment Cards 1898-1914

RESIDENCE: Kiamatia[sic] COUNTY. **Choctaw Nation** Choctaw Roll (Not Including Freedmen)

POST OFFICE: Good-land I.T.

CARD NO.

FIELD NO. 1394

Dawes' Roll No.	NAME		Relationship to Person	AGE	SEX	BLOOD	TRIBAL ENROLLMENT		
							Year	County	No.
14664	1 Norman Eliza	71	First Named	68	F	Full	1896	Kiamatia[sic]	9775
	2								
	3								
	4	ENROLLMENT							
	5	OF NOS. 1 HEREON APPROVED BY THE SECRETARY							
	6	OF INTERIOR MAY 20 1903							
	7								
	8								
	9								
	10								
	11								
	12								
	13								
	14								
	15								
	16								
	17								

TRIBAL ENROLLMENT OF PARENTS

	Name of Father	Year	County	Name of Mother	Year	County
1	Jesse Bohanan	De'd	Eagle	Celeste Frazier	Ded	Cedar
2						
3						
4						
5						
6			On 1896 roll as Elza Norman.			
7						
8						
9						
10						
11						
12						
13						
14						
15						
16				Date of Application for Enrollment: May 4-99		
17	Antlers I.T. 12/2/02					

194

Choctaw By Blood Enrollment Cards 1898-1914

RESIDENCE: Towson COUNTY.
POST OFFICE: Doaksville, I.T.

Choctaw Nation

Choctaw Roll
(Not Including Freedmen)

CARD NO.
FIELD NO. 1395

Dawes' Roll No.	NAME	Relationship to Person First Named	AGE	SEX	BLOOD	TRIBAL ENROLLMENT Year	County	No.
3842	1 Folsom, Simpson N ~~ED PRIOR TO SEPTEMBER 25, 1902~~	~~First Named~~	~~71~~	~~M~~	~~1/2~~	~~1896~~	~~Towson~~	~~4136~~
DEAD ~~dead~~	2 " ~~Ollie N~~	~~Wife~~	~~30~~	~~F~~	~~I.W~~	~~1896~~	~~"~~	~~14529~~
3843	3 " Groves C ¹⁰	Son	7	M	1/4	1896	Towson	4137
	4							
	5 ENROLLMENT							
	6 OF NOS. 1 and 3 HEREON APPROVED BY THE SECRETARY							
	7 OF INTERIOR DEC 12 1902							
	8							
	9 No. 2 HEREON DISMISSED UNDER							
	10 ORDER OF THE COMMISSION TO THE FIVE							
	11 CIVILIZED TRIBES OF MARCH 31, 1905.							
	12							
	13							
	14							
	15							
	16							
	17							

TRIBAL ENROLLMENT OF PARENTS

	Name of Father	Year	County	Name of Mother	Year	County
1	David Folsom	Dead	Non Citz	Rhoda Folsom	Dead	
2	Martin V. Nance	"	" "	Lydia A. Nancy		Non Citz
3	No 1			No 2		
4						
5						
6			No 1 on 1896 roll as Sampson N. Folsom			
7			No.1 died March 1, 1901. Enrollment cancelled by Department May 2, 1906			
8			No 2 on 1896 roll as Ollie Folsom			
9			No3 lives with George W. Oakes on 7-1511			
10			No2 Died Jany 28, 1902, proof of death filed Dec 2 1904			
11						
12						
13						
14						
15						
16				Date of Application for Enrollment.	May 4/99	
17			No2 Evidence requested 3/28/04			

Choctaw By Blood Enrollment Cards 1898-1914

RESIDENCE: Towson COUNTY.
POST OFFICE: Doaksville, I.T.

Choctaw Nation

Choctaw Roll *(Not Including Freedmen)*

CARD NO. FIELD NO. **1396**

Dawes' Roll No.	NAME	Relationship to Person First Named	AGE	SEX	BLOOD	TRIBAL ENROLLMENT Year	County	No.
~~3844~~ 1	~~DIED PRIOR TO SEPTEMBER 25, 1902~~ ~~Rosenthal, Mary L.~~	First Named	~~41~~	~~F~~	~~1/4~~	~~1896~~	~~Kiamitia~~	~~10821~~
3845 2	" Ernestine 20	Dau	17	"	1/8	1896	"	10822
3846 3	" Jacob 19	Son	16	M	1/8	1896	"	10823
3847 4	" Maggie 13	Dau	10	F	1/8	1896	"	10824
3848 5	" Parker 11	Son	8	M	1/8	1896	"	10825
3849 6	" Ally Pate 5	Dau	2	F	1/8			
I.W. 1531 7	" Birdie	Wife of No 3	21	F	I.W.			
8								
9			For child of No 2 see NB (March 3-05) Card #1133					
10			" " " No 3 " " " " " #1419					
11			No 2 on 1896 as Pocahontas Rosenthal					
12	For child of No 3 see N.B. (Apr. 26/06) Card #371							
13								
16								
17								

Stamp over rows 8-10: ENROLLMENT OF NOS. 1 2 3 4 5 and 6 HEREON APPROVED BY THE SECRETARY OF INTERIOR Dec 12, 1902

Stamp over rows 13-15: ENROLLMENT OF NOS. ~~~ 7 ~~~ HEREON APPROVED BY THE SECRETARY OF INTERIOR Nov. 26, 1906

TRIBAL ENROLLMENT OF PARENTS

	Name of Father	Year	County	Name of Mother	Year	County
1	~~R.B. Willis~~	~~Dead~~	~~Non Citz~~	~~Margaret Willis~~	~~Dead~~	~~Kiamitia~~
2	Geo. Rosenthal	1896	" "	No 1		
3	" "	1896	" "	No 1		
4	" "	1896	" "	No 1		
5	" "	1896	" "	No 1		
6	" "	1896	" "	No 1		
7	Tom Earthman		non citizen	Jane Earthman		non-citizen
8						
9	No1 died Oct. 1901, proof of death filed Dec. 8, 1902					
10	No.1 died Oct. – 1901. Enrollment cancelled by Department July 8, 1904					
11	No7 placed hereon under order of Commissioner to Five Civilized Tribes of October 10, 1906 holding that application was made for her enrollment within					
12	the time provided by the Act of Congress approved April 26, 1906					
13	(Public No – 129)					
14	No 2 P.O. Fulton Ark 4/19/05					#1 to 6 inc Date of Application for Enrollment.
15	No 3 P.O. Spencerville					
16	Ashdown Ark 12/13/02					May. 4/99
17	P.O. Address of No 2 is Ft Towson			Granted	Oct. 10, 1906	

I.T. 6/1/04   Record forwarded Dept

Choctaw By Blood Enrollment Cards 1898-1914

RESIDENCE: Kiamitia COUNTY.	**Choctaw Nation**	Choctaw Roll	CARD NO.
POST OFFICE: Goodland, I.T.		*(Not Including Freedmen)*	FIELD NO. **1397**

Dawes' Roll No.	NAME	Relationship to Person First Named	AGE	SEX	BLOOD	TRIBAL ENROLLMENT Year	County	No.
3850	₁ Sanguin, Thomas E ³¹	First Named	28	M	1/8	1896	Towson	11368
I.W. 991	₂ " Zula C ²⁶	Wife	23	F	I.W.			
3851	₃ " Clyde ⁴	Son	7mo	M	1/16			
~~3852~~	₄ DIED PRIOR TO SEPTEMBER 25, 1902 ~~Virginia~~	~~Dau~~	~~6wks~~	~~F~~	~~1/16~~			
3853	₅ " Charles A ¹	Son	1mo	M	1/16			
	₆							
	₇ ENROLLMENT OF NOS. 1 3 4 and 5 HEREON							
	₈ APPROVED BY THE SECRETARY							
	₉ OF INTERIOR Dec. 12, 1902							
	₁₀							
	₁₁ ENROLLMENT OF NOS. ~ 2 ~ HEREON							
	₁₂ APPROVED BY THE SECRETARY							
	₁₃ OF INTERIOR Oct 21, 1904							
	₁₄							
	₁₅							
	₁₆							
	₁₇							

TRIBAL ENROLLMENT OF PARENTS

	Name of Father	Year	County	Name of Mother	Year	County
₁	Chas. Sanguin	Dead	Non Citz	Susan Sanguin		Towson
₂	J.B. Vaughn		" "	Jennie C. Vaughn		Non Citz
₃	No 1			No 2		
₄	~~No 1~~			~~No 2~~		
₅	No 1			No 2		
₆						
₇			No 4 Enrolled December 22, 1900.			
₈			No 5 Born July 11, 1901: enrolled Aug. 5, 1902.			
₉			~~No 4 died about Feb. 18, 1901, proof of death filed Dec. 12, 1902.~~ ~~No 1 is guardian of children on Choctaw card #808.~~			
₁₀			No.4 died Feb. 18, 1901; Enrollment cancelled by Department July 8, 1904.			
₁₁			For child of Nos 1&2 see N.B. (Apr. 26, 1906) Card No. 82.			
₁₂			" " " " " (March 3,1905) " " 1135			
₁₃						#1 to 3
₁₄				Date of Application for Enrollment.		May 8/99
₁₅						
₁₆	Hugo I.T. 12/19/02					
₁₇						

197

Choctaw By Blood Enrollment Cards 1898-1914

RESIDENCE: Kiamitia   COUNTY.   **Choctaw Nation**   **Choctaw Roll**   CARD NO.
POST OFFICE: Goodland, I.T.   *(Not Including Freedmen)*   FIELD NO. **1398**

Dawes' Roll No.	NAME	Relationship to Person First Named	AGE	SEX	BLOOD	TRIBAL ENROLLMENT Year	County	No.
3854	1 Spring, William 69	First Named	66	M	1/4	1896	Kiamitia	11474
	2							
	3	ENROLLMENT OF NOS. 1 HEREON APPROVED BY THE SECRETARY						
	4	OF INTERIOR Dec 12 1902						
	5							
	6							
	7							
	8							
	9							
	10							
	11							
	12							
	13							
	14							
	15							
	16							
	17							

TRIBAL ENROLLMENT OF PARENTS

	Name of Father	Year	County	Name of Mother	Year	County
1	Christopher Spring	Dead	Non Citz	Susan Spring	Dead	Kiamitia
2						
3						
4						
5						
6						
7						
8						
9						
10						
11						
12						
13						
14						Date of Application for Enrollment.
15						
16						May 8-99
17	Hugo I.T. 12/ [sic]					

Choctaw By Blood Enrollment Cards 1898-1914

RESIDENCE: Kiamitia   COUNTY.   **Choctaw Nation**   Choctaw Roll *(Not Including Freedmen)*   CARD NO.

POST OFFICE: Goodland, I.T.   FIELD NO. **1399**

Dawes' Roll No.	NAME	Relationship to Person First Named	AGE	SEX	BLOOD	TRIBAL ENROLLMENT Year	County	No.
3855	1 Spring, John ⁴²	First Named	39	M	1/2	1896	Kiamitia	11498
3856	2 " Nancy ⁴⁵	Wife	42	F	3/4	1896	"	11499
3857	3 " Eli ²²	Son	19	M	5/8	1896	"	11501
3858	4 " Isaac ²⁰	"	17	"	5/8	1896	"	11502
3859	5 " Melinda ¹⁷	Dau	14	F	5/8	1896	"	11503
3860	6 " Christopher ¹⁵	Son	12	M	5/8	1896	"	11504
3861	7 " John Jr ¹³	"	10	"	5/8	1893	"	P.R. 679
3862	8 " Jackson ¹¹	"	8	"	5/8	1896	"	11505
3863	9 " Benney ⁶	Son	3	M	5/8	1896	"	11507
	10							
	11							
	12							
	13							
	14							
	15							
	16							
	17							

ENROLLMENT
OF NOS. 12345678and9 HEREON
APPROVED BY THE SECRETARY
OF INTERIOR Dec 12 1902

15 For child of No 5 see NB (Apr 26/06) Card #340

TRIBAL ENROLLMENT OF PARENTS

	Name of Father	Year	County	Name of Mother	Year	County
1	William Spring	1896	Kiamitia	Jane Spring	Dead	Kiamitia
2	Dave McCoy	Dead	"	Bickey McCoy	"	"
3	No 1			No 2		
4	No 1			No 2		
5	No 1			No 2		
6	No 1			No 2		
7	No 1			No 2		
8	No 1			No 2		
9	No 1			No 2		
10						
11						
12						

13   No9 Name is Benney. Son of Nos 1-2. Correction authorized by
Departmental letter of November 6,1903 (G.O No 31431-1903)

14   No 7 on 1893 Pay roll Page 83, No 679, Kiamitia County

15   No.3 is now the husband of Mollie Jacob on Choctaw card #1586   Dec. 12, 1901

No.3 on 1896 roll as Ely Spring.

16   For child of No.1 see N.B. (Apr. 26, 1906) Card No. 122.

17   "   "   " No 3   "   "   (March 3,1905)   "   " 1194

  "   "   " No 5   "   "   "   "   "   " 1299

Date of Application for Enrollment.   #1 to 8&9   5/8/99

199

Choctaw By Blood Enrollment Cards 1898-1914

RESIDENCE: Kiamitia COUNTY. **Choctaw Nation** Choctaw Roll CARD NO.
POST OFFICE: Goodland, I.T. (Not Including Freedmen) FIELD NO. **1400**

Dawes' Roll No.	NAME		Relationship to Person First Named	AGE	SEX	BLOOD	TRIBAL ENROLLMENT		
							Year	County	No.
3864	1 Spring, Levi	60	First Named	57	M	1/4	1896	Kiamitia	11468
3865	2 " Sophia	45	Wife	42	F	Full	1896	"	11469
3866	3 " David	15	Son	12	M	5/8	1896	"	11470
3867	4 " Sarah	13	Dau	10	F	5/8	1896	"	11471
3868	5 " Franklin	10	Son	7	M	5/8	1896	"	11472
3869	6 " Jesse	6	"	3	"	5/8	1896	"	11473
3870	7 " Simeon	3	"	4mo	"	5/8			
	8								
	9	ENROLLMENT							
	10	OF NOS. 123456and7 HEREON APPROVED BY THE SECRETARY							
	11	OF INTERIOR Dec 12 1902							
	12								
	13								
	14								
	15								
	16								
	17								

TRIBAL ENROLLMENT OF PARENTS

	Name of Father	Year	County	Name of Mother	Year	County
1	Christopher Spring	Dead	Non Citz	Susan Spring	Dead	Kiamitia
2	Wm Boatman	"	Towson	Sallie Boatman	"	"
3	No 1			No 2		
4	No 1			No 2		
5	No 1			No 2		
6	No 1			No 2		
7	No 1			No 2		
8						
9						
10						
11						
12						
13						
14						
15						#1 to 6.
16					Date of Application for Enrollment	5/8/99
17	Hugo I.T. 12/4/02				No. 7 enrolled Oct 6/99	

Choctaw By Blood Enrollment Cards 1898-1914

RESIDENCE: Towson   COUNTY.   **Choctaw Nation**   **Choctaw Roll** *(Not Including Freedmen)*   CARD NO.

POST OFFICE: Grant, I.T.   FIELD NO.   1401

Dawes' Roll No.	NAME	Relationship to Person First Named	AGE	SEX	BLOOD	TRIBAL ENROLLMENT Year	County	No.
3871	1 Durant, Alexander R 63	First Named	60	M	1/2	1896	Kiamitia	3451
3872	2 " Annie L 26	Wife	23	F	3/4	1896	"	3452
DEAD.	3 " George E. F	Son	3	M	5/8	1896	"	3453
3873	4 " Etna R. 3	Dau	4mo	F	5/8			
	5							
	6	ENROLLMENT OF NOS. 1 2 and 4 HEREON						
	7	APPROVED BY THE SECRETARY OF INTERIOR DEC 12 1902						
	8							
	9							
	10	No 3 HEREON DISMISSED UNDER						
	11	ORDER OF THE COMMISSION TO THE FIVE						
	12	CIVILIZED TRIBES OF MARCH 31, 1905.						
	13							
	14							
	15							
	16							
	17							

TRIBAL ENROLLMENT OF PARENTS

	Name of Father	Year	County	Name of Mother	Year	County
1	Geo. Durant	Dead	Towson	Vicey Durant	Dead	Bok Tuklo
2	Ellis Choate	1896	Kiamitia	Patsey Choate	1896	Kiamitia
3	No 1			No 2		
4	No 1			No 2		
5						
6						
7			No 1 on 1896 roll as Alick R. Durant			
8			No 3 " 1896 " " Geo. E. F. "			
9			No.3 Proof of death filed March 13, 1901.			
10						
11						
12						
13						
14						
15					#1 to 3	
16				DATE OF APPLICATION FOR ENROLLMENT.	5/8/99	
17				No 4 enrolled Oct 6/99		

Born 6/24/1899

Choctaw By Blood Enrollment Cards 1898-1914

RESIDENCE: **Kiamitia** COUNTY.   **Choctaw Nation**   **Choctaw Roll** *(Not Including Freedmen)*   CARD NO.

POST OFFICE: **Goodland, I.T.**   FIELD NO. **1402**

Dawes' Roll No.	NAME		Relationship to Person	AGE	SEX	BLOOD	TRIBAL ENROLLMENT		
							Year	County	No.
3874	1 Spring, Joel	39	First Named	36	M	1/8	1896	Kiamitia	11476
3875	2 " Winnie R	33	Wife	30	F	1/8	1896	"	11477
3876	3 " Joel Jr	15	Son	12	M	1/8	1896	"	11478
3877	4 " Lawrence E	13	"	10	"	1/8	1896	"	11479
3878	5 " Jesse H	11	"	8	"	1/8	1896	"	11480
3879	6 " Winnie	8	Dau	5	F	1/8	1896	"	11481
3880	7 " Dewey L	4	Son	1	M	1/8			
3881	8 " Robert Murry	2	Son	3m	M	1/8			
	9								
	10								
	11	ENROLLMENT OF NOS. 1 2 3 4 5 6 7 and 8 HEREON							
	12	APPROVED BY THE SECRETARY							
	13	OF INTERIOR DEC 12 1902							
	14								
	15								
	16								
	17								

TRIBAL ENROLLMENT OF PARENTS

	Name of Father	Year	County	Name of Mother	Year	County
1	Sam Spring	Dead		Liza Spring	1896	Kiamitia
2	Henry Gooding	1896	Non Citz	Roseana Gooding	Dead	"
3	No 1			No 2		
4	No 1			No 2		
5	No 1			No 2		
6	No 1			No 2		
7	No 1			No 2		
8	No 1			No 2		
9						
10						
11						
12	No 3 on 1896 roll as Jodie Spring					
13	No 4 " 1896 " " Lawrence "					
14	No 5 " 1896 " " Henry "					
15	No 8 Enrolled January 22, 1901.					
16	For child of Nos 1&2 see NB (March 3, 1905) #1071					
17						

#1 to 7
Date of Application for Enrollment

Date of application for enrollment 5/8/99

Choctaw By Blood Enrollment Cards 1898-1914

| RESIDENCE: Kiamitia | COUNTY. | **Choctaw Nation** | Choctaw Roll | CARD No. |
| POST OFFICE: Goodland, I.T. | | | (Not Including Freedmen) | FIELD No. **1403** |

Dawes' Roll No.	NAME	Relationship to Person First Named	AGE	SEX	BLOOD	TRIBAL ENROLLMENT Year	County	No.
3882	1 Plank, Roseanna A 21	First Named	18	F	1/8	1896	Kiamitia	4819
3883	2 Plank, Inez 1	Dau	11 days	F	1/16			
I.W. 633	3 Plank, Jasper E. 36	Hus	36	M	I.W.			
	4							
	5 ENROLLMENT							
	6 OF NOS. 1 and 2 HEREON APPROVED BY THE SECRETARY							
	7 OF INTERIOR Dec 12 1902							
	8 ENROLLMENT							
	9 OF NOS. 3 HEREON APPROVED BY THE SECRETARY							
	10 OF INTERIOR Mar 26 1904							
	11							
	12							
	13							
	14							
	15							
	16							
	17							

TRIBAL ENROLLMENT OF PARENTS

	Name of Father	Year	County	Name of Mother	Year	County
1	Henry Gooding	1896	Non Citz	Rosanna Gooding	Dead	Kiamitia
2	Jasper E. Plank		Choctaw Card #D629 No 1			
3	Jasper Plank		non citizen	Eliza Plank		non citizen
4						
5						
6			No 3 transferred from Choctaw card D629 January 25, 1904			
7			See decision of January 7, 1904.			
8						
9			On 1896 roll as Rosie A. Gooding			
10			No.1 is now the wife of Jasper E. Plank on Choctaw Card #D629			
11			Evidence of marriage under a U.S. license, and subsequently			
12			under a Choctaw license filed this day April 19, 1902 in the records of Choctaw Case #D629.			
13			No.2 Born June 13th 1902: Enrolled June 24th 1902:			
14						
15					#1	
16				Date of Application for Enrollment.		5/8/99
17						

203

Choctaw By Blood Enrollment Cards 1898-1914

RESIDENCE: Kiamitia
POST OFFICE: Grant, I.T.

COUNTY. **Choctaw Nation**

Choctaw Roll (Not Including Freedmen)

CARD NO.
FIELD NO. **1404**

Dawes' Roll No.	NAME		Relationship to Person	AGE	SEX	BLOOD	TRIBAL ENROLLMENT		
							Year	County	No.
3884	1 Fulton, Jeff	44	First Named	41	M	Full	1896	Kiamitia	4235
3885	2 " Susan	35	Wife	32	F	"	1896	"	4236
3886	3 " Edgar	12	Son	9	M	"	1896	"	4231
3887	4 " Nancy	11	Dau	8	F	"	1896	"	4237
3888	5 " Robert	5	Son	2	M	"			
3889	6 " Arthur Daniel	1	Son	2mo	M	"			
	7								
	8								
	9								
	10								
	11								
	12								
	13								
	14								
	15								
	16								
	17								

ENROLLMENT OF NOS. 1 2 3 4 5 and 6 HEREON APPROVED BY THE SECRETARY OF INTERIOR Dec 12 1902

TRIBAL ENROLLMENT OF PARENTS

	Name of Father	Year	County	Name of Mother	Year	County
1	A-fa-ma-tubbee	Dead	Kiamitia		Dead	Kiamitia
2	Sam Hayes	"	"	Mary Hayes	"	"
3	No 1			No 2		
4	No 1			No 2		
5	No 1			No 2		
6	No.1			No.2		
7						
8			No.6 Enrolled May 17, 1901			
9						
10						
11						
12						
13						
14						#1 to 5 inc
15					Date of Application for Enrollment.	
16						5/8/99
17						

RESIDENCE: Kiamitia   COUNTY.   **Choctaw Nation**   **Choctaw Roll**   CARD NO.
POST OFFICE: Goodland, I.T.   *(Not Including Freedmen)*   FIELD NO. **1405**

Dawes' Roll No.	NAME		Relationship to Person	AGE	SEX	BLOOD	TRIBAL ENROLLMENT		
							Year	County	No.
3890	1 Sanguin, Henry	27	First Named	24	M	1/8	1896	Kiamitia	11492
I.W. **70**	2 " Alice J	25	Wife	22	F	I.W.			
3891	3 " Lena V.	3	Dau	2mo	F	1/16			
	4								
	5	ENROLLMENT							
	6	OF NOS. 1 and 3 HEREON							
	7	APPROVED BY THE SECRETARY OF INTERIOR DEC 12 1902							
	8								
	9	ENROLLMENT							
	10	OF NOS. ~~ 2 ~~ HEREON							
	11	APPROVED BY THE SECRETARY OF INTERIOR JUN 13 1903							
	12								
	13								
	14								
	15								
	16								
	17								

TRIBAL ENROLLMENT OF PARENTS

	Name of Father	Year	County	Name of Mother	Year	County
1	Chas Sanguin	Dead	Non Citz	Susan Sanguin	1896	Towson
2	Jerry O'Connell	1896	" "	Catherine O'Connell	1896	Non Citz
3	No. 1			No. 2		
4						
5						
6			For child of Nos 1&2 see NB (Mar 3rd 1905) Card No 211.			
7						
8						
9						
10						
11						
12						
13						
14						
15					#1&2	
16				DATE OF APPLICATION FOR ENROLLMENT.	5/8/99	
17	Hugo I.T. 12/11/02			No 3 Enrolled May 24, 1900		

Choctaw By Blood Enrollment Cards 1898-1914

Dawes' Roll No.	NAME	Relationship to Person First Named	AGE	SEX	BLOOD	TRIBAL ENROLLMENT 1406		
						Year	County	No.
3892	₁ Ervin, John N 14	First Named	11	M	Full	1896	Kiamitia	3779
3893	₂ " Edgar 12	Bro	9	"	"	1896	"	3780
3894	₃ DIED PRIOR TO SEPTEMBER 25, 190_ Benjamin F. Jr	"	6	"	"	1896	"	3781
I.W. 1096	₄ Ervin Charles W. 43	Father	43	M	I.W.	1896	Kiamitia	14496
	₅ ENROLLMENT							
	₆ OF NOS. 1 2 and 3 HEREON APPROVED BY THE SECRETARY							
	₇ OF INTERIOR DEC 12 1902							
	₈							
	₉ ENROLLMENT OF NOS. 4 HEREON							
	₁₀ APPROVED BY THE SECRETARY OF INTERIOR NOV 16 1904							
	₁₁							
	₁₂							
	₁₃ Petition W 91							
	₁₄							
	₁₅							
	₁₆							
	₁₇							

TRIBAL ENROLLMENT OF PARENTS

	Name of Father	Year	County	Name of Mother	Year	County
₁	Chas W. Ervin	1896	Kiamitia	Annie Ervin	Dead	Kiamitia
₂	" " "	1896	"	" "	"	"
₃	" " "	1896	"	" "	"	"
₄	William Ervin	Dead	non-citizen	Elizabeth Ervin	1896	non citz.
₅						
₆						
₇		Father of above children on Card No D143				
₈						
₉		No1 on 1896 roll as Jno. W. Ervin				
₁₀		No3 " 1896 " " Benj. "				
₁₁		No 3 died Aug. 27, 1899; proof of death filed Dec 5, 1902				
₁₂		No.3 died Aug. 27 1899; Enrollment cancelled by Department July 8, 1904				
₁₃		No.4 transferred from Choctaw card #D-143, Oct. 31, 1904: See decision of Oct. 15, 1904. For children of No 4 see NB (Apr 26'06) #1107				
₁₄						#1 2 &3
₁₅					Date of Application for Enrollment.	
₁₆					5/8/99	
₁₇						

Choctaw By Blood Enrollment Cards 1898-1914

RESIDENCE: Towson COUNTY **Choctaw Nation** **Choctaw Roll** CARD NO.
POST OFFICE: Doaksville, I.T. *(Not Including Freedmen)* FIELD NO. 1407

Dawes' Roll No.	NAME	Relationship to Person	AGE	SEX	BLOOD	TRIBAL ENROLLMENT		
						Year	County	No.
3895	1 Davis, Delilah F ⁵²	First Named	49	F	1/2	1896	Towson	3373
3896	2 Stalard, Jimmy ¹⁵	Dau	12	"	1/4	1896	"	11367
	3							
	4 ENROLLMENT							
	5 OF NOS. 1 and 2 HEREON APPROVED BY THE SECRETARY							
	6 OF INTERIOR DEC 12 1902							
	7							
	8							
	9							
	10							
	11							
	12							
	13							
	14							
	15							
	16							
	17							

TRIBAL ENROLLMENT OF PARENTS

	Name of Father	Year	County	Name of Mother	Year	County
1	Calvin Irvin	Dead	Non Citz	Sallie Irvin	Dead	Towson
2	Jim Stalard	"	" "	No 1		
3						
4						
5		No2 on 1896 roll as Jinnie Stalard				
6		No1 " 1896 " " Delilia Davis				
7						
8		For child of No 2 see NB (Apr 26-06) Card #718				
9						
10						
11						
12						
13						
14					Date of Application for Enrollment.	
15						
16					5/8/99	
17						

207

Choctaw By Blood Enrollment Cards 1898-1914

RESIDENCE: Kiamitia COUNTY. **Choctaw Nation** Choctaw Roll CARD NO.

POST OFFICE: Goodland, I.T. (Not Including Freedmen) FIELD NO. 1408

Dawes' Roll No.	NAME		Relationship to Person	AGE	SEX	BLOOD	TRIBAL ENROLLMENT		
							Year	County	No.
3897	1 Cole, Isaac	42	First Named	39	M	Full	1896	Kiamitia	2707
3898	2 " Sarah	47	Wife	44	F	"	1896	"	2708
	3								
	4	ENROLLMENT							
	5	OF NOS. 1 and 2 HEREON APPROVED BY THE SECRETARY							
	6	OF INTERIOR DEC 12 1902							
	7								
	8								
	9								
	10								
	11								
	12								
	13								
	14								
	15								
	16								
	17								

TRIBAL ENROLLMENT OF PARENTS

	Name of Father	Year	County	Name of Mother	Year	County
1	Mic-co	Dead	Jackson		Dead	Bok Tuklo
2	Sam McCann	"	Kiamitia	Ho-te-mi-ah	"	Kiamitia
3						
4						
5						
6						
7						
8						
9						
10						
11						
12						
13						
14						
15						
16				Date of Application for Enrollment.		5/8/99
17						

208

Choctaw By Blood Enrollment Cards 1898-1914

RESIDENCE: Jackson COUNTY. **Choctaw Nation** **Choctaw Roll** CARD NO.
POST OFFICE: Mayhew, I.T. *(Not Including Freedmen)* FIELD NO. 1409

Dawes' Roll No.	NAME	Relationship to Person	AGE	SEX	BLOOD	TRIBAL ENROLLMENT		
						Year	County	No.
3899	1 Allen, Joe 29	First Named	26	M	Full	1896	Kiamitia	366
	2							
	3 ENROLLMENT							
	4 OF NOS. 1 HEREON APPROVED BY THE SECRETARY							
	5 OF INTERIOR DEC 12 1902							
	6							
	7							
	8							
	9							
	10							
	11							
	12							
	13							
	14							
	15							
	16							
	17							

TRIBAL ENROLLMENT OF PARENTS

	Name of Father	Year	County	Name of Mother	Year	County
1	Jno. Tishohinloby	Dead	Jackson	Wicey Tishohinloby	Dead	Jackson
2						
3						
4						
5						
6			In penitentiary at Columbus, Ohio			
7						
8						
9						
10						
11						
12						
13						
14						
15				Date of Application for Enrollment.		
16				5/8/99		
17						

Choctaw By Blood Enrollment Cards 1898-1914

RESIDENCE: **Kiamitia** COUNTY.
POST OFFICE: **Goodland, I.T.**

Choctaw Nation

Choctaw Roll
(Not Including Freedmen)

CARD NO.
FIELD NO. **1410**

Dawes' Roll No.	NAME	Relationship to Person First Named	AGE	SEX	BLOOD	TRIBAL ENROLLMENT Year	County	No.
I.W. 1097	1 Kelly, William R. 40	First Named	37	M	I.W.	1896	Kiamitia	14728
3900	2 Roebuck, Isabella 35	Wife	32	F	1/4	1896	"	9771
3901	3 Kelly, Judia 12	Dau	9	"	3/8	1896	"	7604
3902	4 " Isaac 9	Son	6	M	3/8	1896	"	7603
3903	5 Nichols, Ben B. 8	S.Son	5	"	1/8	1896	"	9772
3904	6 Roebuck, Cephas 2	Son of No.2	6mo	M	3/8			
	7 ENROLLMENT							
	8 OF NOS. 2,3,4,5 and 6 HEREON APPROVED BY THE SECRETARY							
	9 OF INTERIOR Dec. 12, 1902							
	10							
	11							
	12 ENROLLMENT							
	13 OF NOS. ~~1~~ HEREON APPROVED BY THE SECRETARY							
	14 OF INTERIOR Nov. 16, 1904							
	15							
	16							
	17							

TRIBAL ENROLLMENT OF PARENTS

	Name of Father	Year	County	Name of Mother	Year	County
1	G.V. Kelly	1896	Non Citz	Ann M. Kelly	1896	Non Citz
2	John Lacey	Dead	" "	Sallie Lacey	Dead	Kiamitia
3	No 1			Sissy Kelly	Dead	Kiamitia
4	No 1			" "	"	"
5	Roberson Nichols	Dead	Non Citz	No 2		
6	William Roebuck	1896	Kiamitia	No 2		
7						
8	For child of No2 see NB (Apr 26'06) Card #204					
9	" " " " " " (March 3, 1905) " #1226					
10	No2 on 1896 roll as Isabella Nicholas					
	No3 " 1896 " " Judith Kelly					
11	No5 " 1896 " " Ben Nicholas					
12	No4 " 1896 " " Isaac P. Kelly					
	No1 " 1896 " " Wm R. "					
13	~~Nos 1&2 have been divorced certified copy of divorce proceedings filed July 8, 1901~~					
14	No2 is now the wife of William Roebuck on Choctaw card #1681. Evidence of marriage filed July 8, 1901					
15	No.6 Enrolled July 8, 1901					#1 to 5
16						Date of Application for Enrollment.
17	Hugo I.T. 12/11/02					5/8/99

No 2 P.O. Wilson I.T. 4/24/05

Choctaw By Blood Enrollment Cards 1898-1914

RESIDENCE: Kiamitia	COUNTY.	**Choctaw Nation**				**Choctaw Roll** *(Not Including Freedmen)*		CARD NO.	
POST OFFICE: Grant, I.T.								FIELD NO. 1411	

Dawes' Roll No.	NAME	Relationship to Person	AGE	SEX	BLOOD	TRIBAL ENROLLMENT		
						Year	County	No.
3905	1 Tanitubbi, Johnson ⁶⁸	First Named	65	M	Full	1896	Kiamitia	12345
3906	2 " Lucy ⁵⁹	Wife	56	F	"	1896	"	12346
3907	3 " James ²⁴	Son	21	M	"	1896	"	7067
	4							
	5 ENROLLMENT							
	6 OF NOS. 1 2 and 3 HEREON APPROVED BY THE SECRETARY							
	7 OF INTERIOR DEC 12 1902							
	8							
	9							
	10							
	11							
	12							
	13							
	14							
	15							
	16							
	17							

TRIBAL ENROLLMENT OF PARENTS

Name of Father	Year	County	Name of Mother	Year	County
1 Tan-i-tubbi	Dead	Bok Tuklo	Ah-cha-ya-hoke	Dead	Kiamitia
2 No-te-ma	"	Kiamitia		"	"
3 No 1			No 2		
4					
5					
6					
7		No 1 on 1896 roll as Johnson Tornatubby			
8		No 3 ' 1896 " " Jimmie Johnson			
9		No 2 ' 1896 " " Lucy Tornatubby			
10					
11					
12					
13					
14					
15					
16				Date of Application for Enrollment	5/8/99
17					

211

RESIDENCE: Kiamitia   COUNTY.
POST OFFICE: Grant, I.T.

Choctaw Nation

Choctaw Roll *(Not Including Freedmen)*

CARD NO.
FIELD NO. **1412**

Dawes' Roll No.		NAME		Relationship to Person First Named	AGE	SEX	BLOOD	TRIBAL ENROLLMENT		
								Year	County	No.
I.W. 71	1	Kirkpatrick, James C	46	First Named	43	M	I.W.			
3908	2	" Rena	23	Wife	20	F	Full	1896	Kiamitia	2682
DEAD	3	~~" Joe Cephus~~	5	~~Son~~	~~1½~~	~~M~~	~~1/2~~			
3909	4	" Dewey M	4	"	3mo	"	1/2			
	5									
	6	ENROLLMENT								
	7	OF NOS. 2 and 4 HEREON								
	8	APPROVED BY THE SECRETARY OF INTERIOR Dec 12, 1902								
	9									
	10	ENROLLMENT								
	11	OF NOS. ~~ 1 ~~ HEREON APPROVED BY THE SECRETARY								
	12	OF INTERIOR Jun 13, 1903								
	13									
	14	~~No 3 Hereon dismissed under order of~~								
	15	~~the Commission to the Five Civilized~~								
	16	~~Tribes of March 31, 1905.~~								
	17									

TRIBAL ENROLLMENT OF PARENTS

	Name of Father	Year	County	Name of Mother	Year	County
1	Jocephus Kirkpatrick	1896	Non Citz	Mary J Kirkpatrick	Dead	Non Citz
2	Adam Clark	Dead	Atoka	Jane Clark	"	Blue
3	~~No 1~~			~~No 2~~		
4	No 1			No 2		
5						
6						
7						
8			No 2 on 1896 roll as Rena Clark			
9			No 3 Died June 25, 1899, proof of death filed Oct. 15, 1902.			
10			For child of Nos 1&2 see N.B. (Apr 26, 1906) Card No. 83.			
11			" " " " " " (Mar. 3-1905) Card " 43.			
12						
13						
14						
15						
16					Date of Application for Enrollment	
17	P.O. Hugo I.T.				5/8/99	

Choctaw By Blood Enrollment Cards 1898-1914

RESIDENCE: **Kiamitia** COUNTY.
POST OFFICE: **Goodland, I.T.**

Choctaw Nation

Choctaw Roll
(Not Including Freedmen)

CARD NO.
FIELD NO. **1413**

Dawes' Roll No.	NAME	Relationship to Person First Named	AGE	SEX	BLOOD	Year	County	No.
I.W. 229	1 Kendrick, William D 49	First Named	45	M	I.W.	1896	Kiamitia	14729
3910	2 " Martha 38	Wife	35	F	1/4	1896	"	7605
3911	3 " William W. 18	Son	15	M	1/8	1896	"	7606
3912	4 " Annie M 16	Dau	13	F	1/8	1896	"	7607
3913	5 " Henry L 14	Son	11	M	1/8	1896	"	7608
3914	6 " Lelia J 11	Dau	8	F	1/8	1896	"	7609
3915	7 " John G. 8	Son	5	M	1/8	1896	"	7610
3916	8 " Emma E. 6	Dau	3	F	1/8	1896	"	7611
3917	9 " Mamie H. 5	"	1½	"	1/8			
3918	10 " Mary Stokes 2	"	2mo	"	1/8			
	11 No.10 Enrolled Dec. 14, 1900							
	12 ENROLLMENT OF NOS. HEREON							
	13 APPROVED BY THE SECRETARY OF INTERIOR							
	14							
	15 ENROLLMENT OF NOS. HEREON							
	16 APPROVED BY THE SECRETARY OF INTERIOR							
	17							

TRIBAL ENROLLMENT OF PARENTS

	Name of Father	Year	County	Name of Mother	Year	County
1	Henry E. Kendrick	Dead	Non Citz	Ann W. Kendrick	Dead	Non Citz
2	Wm Spring	1896	Kiamitia	Jane Spring	"	Kiamitia
3	No 1			No 2		
4	No 1			No 2		
5	No 1			No 2		
6	No 1			No 2		
7	No 1			No 2		
8	No 1			No 2		
9	No 1			No 2		
10	No 1			No 2		
11						
12		No 1 was admitted as an intermarried citizen by Dawes				
13		Commission as W.B. Kendrick Case No 1200 No appeal				
14		No 3 on 1896 roll as W. W. Kendrick				
		No 4 " 1896 " " Annie " No 7 on 1896 roll as Jno. G. Kendrick				
15		No 6 " 1896 " " Lelia J " #1 to 9 inc				
16		No 8 " 1896 " " Emma " Date of Application for Enrollment. 5/8/99				
17	Hugo I.T. 12/1/02	No 1 " 1896 " " W.D. "				

For child of No 4 see NB (Apr. 26 '06) Card #121
" " " No 3 " 2 1'3 (Mar 3-05) " #1271

Choctaw By Blood Enrollment Cards 1898-1914

Dawes' Roll No.	NAME	Relationship to Person	AGE	SEX	BLOOD	TRIBAL ENROLLMENT		
						Year	County	No.
3919	1 McCoy Reuben ⁱ⁴	First Named	11	M	Full	1896	Kiamitia	9388
3920	2 " Sopha[sic] ¹¹	Sister	8	F	"	1896	"	9389
	3							
	4							
	5							
	6							
	7							
	8							
	9							
	10							
	11							
	12							
	13							
	14							
	15							
	16							
	17							

ENROLLMENT
OF NOS. 1 and 2 HEREON
APPROVED BY THE SECRETARY
OF INTERIOR Dec. 12, 1902

TRIBAL ENROLLMENT OF PARENTS

	Name of Father	Year	County	Name of Mother	Year	County
1	Willie McCoy	Dead	Kiamitia	Bicey McCoy	Dead	Kiamitia
2	" "	"	"	" "	"	"
3						
4	No 1&2 now living with George Brashears Choc #1491.					
5						
6						
7						
8						
9						
10						
11						
12						
13						
14					Date of Application for Enrollment.	
15						
16					5/8/99	
17						

Choctaw By Blood Enrollment Cards 1898-1914

RESIDENCE: Kiamitia   COUNTY.

POST OFFICE: Mayhew, I.T.

Choctaw Nation

Choctaw Roll *(Not Including Freedmen)*

CARD NO. FIELD NO. **1415**

Dawes' Roll No.	NAME	Relationship to Person First Named	AGE	SEX	BLOOD	TRIBAL ENROLLMENT Year	County	No.
3921	1 Wade, Sissy ~~DIED PRIOR TO SEPTEMBER 25, 1902~~		38	F	Full	1896	Jackson	13842
3922	2 " Gilbert 11	Son	8	M	"	1896	"	13843
	3							
	4 ENROLLMENT							
	5 OF NOS. 1 and 2 HEREON APPROVED BY THE SECRETARY							
	6 OF INTERIOR DEC 12 1902							
	7							
	8							
	9							
	10							
	11							
	12							
	13							
	14							
	15							
	16							
	17							

TRIBAL ENROLLMENT OF PARENTS

	Name of Father	Year	County	Name of Mother	Year	County
1	Joseph King	Dead	Blue	Sallie King	Dead	Kiamitia
2	Levi Wade	"	Jackson	No 1		
3						
4						
5	No.1 died March 12, 1901; Enrollment cancelled by Department July 8, 1904.					
6						
7						
8						
9						
10						
11						
12						
13						
14						
15						
16				Date of Application for Enrollment		5/8/99
17						

Choctaw By Blood Enrollment Cards 1898-1914

RESIDENCE: Kiamitia   COUNTY.   **Choctaw Nation**   **Choctaw Roll** (Not Including Freedmen)   CARD NO.
POST OFFICE: Goodland, I.T.   FIELD NO. 1416

Dawes' Roll No.	NAME	Relationship to Person First Named	AGE	SEX	BLOOD	TRIBAL ENROLLMENT Year	County	No.
3923	1 Alexander, Alex 28	First Named	25	M	Full	1893	Kiamitia	6
3924	2 " Lucy 28	Wife	25	F	"	1893	"	100
3925	3 Carlister, Annie 10	S.Dau	7	"	"	1893	"	101
14665	4 Alexander William 1	Son	10mo	M	"			
	5							
	6	ENROLLMENT OF NOS. 1 2 and 3 HEREON						
	7	APPROVED BY THE SECRETARY						
	8	OF INTERIOR DEC 12 1902						
	9							
	10	ENROLLMENT						
	11	OF NOS. 4 HEREON APPROVED BY THE SECRETARY						
	12	OF INTERIOR MAY 20 1903						
	13							
	14							
	15							
	16							
	17							

TRIBAL ENROLLMENT OF PARENTS

	Name of Father	Year	County	Name of Mother	Year	County
1	Solomon Santa	Dead	Kiamitia	Sally Santa	Dead	Kiamitia
2	Davis Oklaby	1896	"	Hannah Oklaby	"	Jackson
3	Jacob Carlister	Dead	"	No 2		
4	No 1			No 2		
5						
6	No 1 on 1893 Pay roll Kiamitia County Page 1, No 6					
7	No 2 " 1893 " " " " " 13 No 100 as Lucy Carlister					
8	No 3 " 1893 " " " " " 13 No 101					
9	No.1 on 1896 Choctaw roll as Alexander Sounder, page 298, #1542					
	No.2 " " " " " Lucy " " " " #1543					
10	No.3 " " " " " Emmie Calister " 65 , #2738					
11	No 4 born Feb. 24, 1902: enrolled Dec 8 1902					
12						
13						
14						#1 to 3
15						Date of Application for Enrollment
16						5/8/99
17						

216

Choctaw By Blood Enrollment Cards 1898-1914

RESIDENCE: Blue   COUNTY.   **Choctaw Nation**

POST OFFICE: Durant, I.T.

Choctaw Roll (Not Including Freedmen)

CARD NO. FIELD NO. 1417

Dawes' Roll No.	NAME		Relationship to Person	AGE	SEX	BLOOD	TRIBAL ENROLLMENT		
							Year	County	No.
I.W.230	₁ Kelly, James J	54	First Named	51	M	I.W.	1896	Blue	14731
3926	₂ " Selina J	43	Wife	40	F	3/4	1896	"	7626
3927	₃ Spring Ida E	21	Dau	18	"	3/8	1896	"	7627
3928	₄ Kelly Louis A	15	Son	12	M	3/8	1896	"	7629
3929	₅ Spring, Edith Gayzelle	1	Grand Dau	3wks	F	7/16			
	6								
	7	ENROLLMENT							
	8	OF NOS. 2 3 4 and 5 HEREON APPROVED BY THE SECRETARY							
	9	OF INTERIOR DEC 12 1902							
	10	ENROLLMENT OF NOS. 1 HEREON							
	11	APPROVED BY THE SECRETARY OF INTERIOR SEP 12 1903							
	12								
	13								
	14								
	15								
	16								
	17								

TRIBAL ENROLLMENT OF PARENTS

	Name of Father	Year	County	Name of Mother	Year	County
1	Robert Kelly	Dead	Non Citz	Sarah Kelly	Dead	Non Citz
2	Thompson Tinnahaya	"	Atoka	Delilah Anderson	"	Red River
3	No 1			No 2		
4	No 1			No 2		
5	Joseph B. Spring	1893	Kiamitia	No 3		
6						
7						
8	For child of No.3 see N.B. (Apr. 26-06) No. 569					
9	No1 married a Choctaw Citz. Selina Richards,					
10	July 12, 1875. Record of marriage destroyed with Records of Towson Co, in 1897. See testimony of					
11	himself, Henry Williams, A.R. Durant and					
12	Columbus Irvin					
13	No.3 is now the wife of Joseph B. Spring on Choc. card #4241. Evidence of marriage filed Dec 4, 1901.					
	No 2 on 1896 roll as Selina Kelly					
14	No 4 " 1896 " " Louis B. "					
15	No 1 " 1896 " " Jas. J. "				DATE OF APPLICATION FOR ENROLLMENT.	
16	No.5 born Nov. 12, 1901: Enrolled Dec. 4, 1901.				5/8/99	
17						

Choctaw By Blood Enrollment Cards 1898-1914

RESIDENCE: Kiamitia COUNTY.   **Choctaw Nation**   **Choctaw Roll** CARD No.
POST OFFICE: Frogville, I.T.   *(Not Including Freedmen)*   FIELD No. **1418**

Dawes' Roll No.	NAME	Relationship to Person First Named	AGE	SEX	BLOOD	TRIBAL ENROLLMENT Year	County	No.
I.W. 231	1 Hibben, Thomas D 42	First Named	38	M	I.W.	1896	Kiamitia	14639
3930	2 " , Mary 38	Wife	35	F	1/8	1896	"	5751
3931	3 " , Ethel 16	Dau	13	"	1/8	1896	"	5752
3932	4 " , Sophia 13	"	11	"	1/8	1896	"	5753
3933	5 " , Samuel L 12	Son	9	M	1/8	1896	"	5754
3934	6 " , Eliza 10	Dau	7	F	1/8	1896	"	5755
3935	7 " , William T 8	Son	5	M	1/8	1896	"	5756
3936	8 " , Frances H 6	Dau	2	F	1/16			
3937	9 " , George Wellington 3	Son	6mo	M	1/16			
	10							
	11	ENROLLMENT OF NOS. 2345678and9 HEREON APPROVED BY THE SECRETARY						
	12	OF INTERIOR Dec. 12, 1902						
	13							
	14	ENROLLMENT						
	15	OF NOS. 1 HEREON APPROVED BY THE SECRETARY						
	16	OF INTERIOR Sep. 12, 1903.						
	17							

TRIBAL ENROLLMENT OF PARENTS

Name of Father	Year	County	Name of Mother	Year	County
1 W.B. Hibben	Dead	Non Citz	Eliza Hibben	Dead	Non Citz
2 Thos. W. Oakes	"	" "	Harriet N. Oakes	1896	Kiamitia
3 No 1			No 2		
4 No 1			No 2		
5 No 1			No 2		
6 No 1			No 2		
7 No 1			No 2		
8 No 1			No 2		
9 No 1			No 2		
10					
11 Surname appears on 1896 roll as "Hibbens"					
12 For child of No4 see N.B. (Apr. 26, 1906) Card No 115.					
13 No5 on 1896 roll as Samuel Hibbens. No.7 on 1896 " " Wm T. "					
14 For child of Nos. 1&2 see NB (March 3, 1905) #1088.			#1 to 8 inc		
15 No.8 Affidavit of birth to be supplied. Recd May 10/99.			Date of Application for Enrollment.		
16 No.9 Enrolled May 24, 1900.			5/8/99		
17					

Choctaw By Blood Enrollment Cards 1898-1914

RESIDENCE: Jacks Fork   COUNTY.   **Choctaw Nation**   **Choctaw Roll**
POST OFFICE: Antlers, I.T.   (Not Including Freedmen)   FIELD No. 1419

Dawes' Roll No.	NAME	Relationship to Person First Named	AGE	SEX	BLOOD	TRIBAL ENROLLMENT		
						Year	County	No.
3938	1 Cobb, Keener B. 28	First Named	25	M	Full	1896	Jacks Fork	3002
	2							
	3 ENROLLMENT							
	4 OF NOS. 1 HEREON APPROVED BY THE SECRETARY							
	5 OF INTERIOR DEC 12 1902							
	6							
	7							
	8							
	9							
	10							
	11							
	12							
	13							
	14							
	15							
	16							
	17							

TRIBAL ENROLLMENT OF PARENTS

	Name of Father	Year	County	Name of Mother	Year	County
1	Be-lin-che	Dead	Kiamitia	Casey	1896	Blue
2						
3						
4	On 1896 roll as K. B. Cobb					
5						
6						
7						
8						
9						
10						
11						
12						
13						
14						
15						
16				Date of Application for Enrollment.		5/8/99
17						

Choctaw By Blood Enrollment Cards 1898-1914

RESIDENCE: Kiamitia   COUNTY.   **Choctaw Nation**   Choctaw Roll   CARD No.
POST OFFICE: Grant, I.T.   *(Not Including Freedmen)*   FIELD No. **1420**

Dawes' Roll No.	NAME		Relationship to Person First Named	AGE	SEX	BLOOD	TRIBAL ENROLLMENT		
							Year	County	No.
I.W. 703	1 Combs, Edward	47	First Named	44	M	I.W.	1896	Kiamitia	14410
3939	2 " , Sarah	39	Wife	36	F	1/8	1896	"	2741
3940	3 " , Claude W.	20	Son	17	M	1/16	1896	"	2742
3941	4 Salter, Hattie	15	Dau	12	F	1/16	1896	"	2743
3942	5 Combs, Buster	11	Son	8	M	1/16	1896	"	2744
3943	6 " , Jesse J.	9	"	6	"	1/16	1896	"	2745
3944	7 " , Cora E.	6	Dau	3	F	1/16	1896	"	2746
3945	8 " , John	3	Son	3wks	M	1/16			
I.W. 1098	9 Salter, Henry J.	39	Husband of No. 4	37	M	I.W.			
	10								
	11	ENROLLMENT OF NOS. 2 3 4 5 6 7 and 8 HEREON APPROVED BY THE SECRETARY OF INTERIOR Dec. 12, 1902							
	12								
	13								
	14	For child of Nos 1&2 see NB (Mar 3'05) #1082							
	15	Nos.1-2: affidavit as to Marriage filed Dec. 29, 1902.							
	16								
	17								

TRIBAL ENROLLMENT OF PARENTS

	Name of Father	Year	County	Name of Mother	Year	County
1	William Combs	Dead	Non Citz	Dicey Combs	Dead	Non Citizen
2	Bill Harlin	"	" "	Lucinda Harlin	"	Kiamitia
3	No 1			No 2		
4	No 1			No 2		
5	No 1	ENROLLMENT OF NOS. ~~ 9 ~~ HEREON APPROVED BY THE SECRETARY OF INTERIOR Nov 16, 1904		No 2		
6	No 1			No 2		
7	No 1			No 2		
8	No 1			No 2		
9	Jesse Salter	Dead	Non-Citizen	Lula Salter	Dead	Non-Citizen
10	No1 see decision of March 2, 1904					
11	Surnames appear on 1896 Roll as "Comes" No4 on 1896 Roll as Hattie S. Comes					
12	No9 transferred from Choctaw card #D-660 Oct 31, 1904: See decision of Oct. 15, 1904					
13	Nos 1-2 were married in 1878, the wife being					
14	a Choctaw by Blood. License has			ENROLLMENT OF NOS. ~~ 1 ~~ HEREON APPROVED BY THE SECRETARY OF INTERIOR May-7-1904		
15	been lost or destroyed and no record found. See testimony of No.1 and Kate O'Brian					
16	No4 is now the wife of Henry J Salter on Choctaw			Date of Application for Enrollment.	#1 to 8	
17	Hugo, I.T.	card #D660. Evidence of marriage filed with papers in that case Aug 29, 1901.		May 8/99		

220

Choctaw By Blood Enrollment Cards 1898-1914

RESIDENCE: Kiamitia   COUNTY.
POST OFFICE: Goodland, I.T.

Choctaw Nation

Choctaw Roll
(Not Including Freedmen)

CARD NO.
FIELD NO. **1421**

Dawes' Roll No.	NAME		Relationship to Person First Named	AGE	SEX	BLOOD	TRIBAL ENROLLMENT		
							Year	County	No.
3946	1 Alfred, Morris	44	First Named	41	M	Full	1896	Kiamitia	334
I.W. 893	2 " , Elizabeth	40	Wife	37	F	I.W.			
3947	3 " , Maggie	10	Dau	7	"	1/2	1896	Kiamitia	335
	4								
	5	ENROLLMENT							
	6	OF NOS. 1 and 3 HEREON							
	7	APPROVED BY THE SECRETARY OF INTERIOR Dec. 12, 1902							
	8								
	9	ENROLLMENT							
	10	OF NOS. 2 HEREON APPROVED BY THE SECRETARY							
	11	OF INTERIOR Aug 3 1904							
	12								
	13								
	14								
	15								
	16								
	17								

TRIBAL ENROLLMENT OF PARENTS

	Name of Father	Year	County	Name of Mother	Year	County
1	Sampson Alfred	Dead	Kiamitia	Viney Coklin	Dead	Kiamitia
2	Wiley Jones	"	Non Citz	Katherine Jones	"	Non Citz
3	No 1			No 2		
4						
5						
6	No written evidence of marriage. See testimony of					
7	No.1 and Mrs. Sina Miller.					
8						
9						
10						
11						
12						
13						
14						
15						
16				Date of Application for Enrollment		5/8/99
17	Hugo I.T. 12/3/02					

Choctaw By Blood Enrollment Cards 1898-1914

RESIDENCE: Kiamitia   COUNTY.   **Choctaw Nation**   Choctaw Roll   CARD NO.
POST OFFICE: Goodland, I.T.   *(Not Including Freedmen)*   FIELD NO. **1422**

Dawes' Roll No.	NAME		Relationship to Person First Named	AGE	SEX	BLOOD	TRIBAL ENROLLMENT		
							Year	County	No.
3948	1 Lee, John M.	13	First Named	10	M	1/4	1893	Kiamitia	410
3949	2 " , Ella M.	11	Sister	8	F	1/4	1893	Kiamitia	411
	3								
	4	ENROLLMENT							
	5	OF NOS. 1 and 2 HEREON APPROVED BY THE SECRETARY							
	6	OF INTERIOR Dec 12, 1902							
	7								
	8								
	9								
	10								
	11								
	12								
	13								
	14								
	15								
	16								
	17								

TRIBAL ENROLLMENT OF PARENTS

	Name of Father	Year	County	Name of Mother	Year	County
1	Wax Lee	1896	Non Citz	Ella Taylor	Dead	Jackson
2	" "	1896	" "	" "	"	"
3						
4	Error – The names of these children are not found either on the					
5	1893 Pay Roll, or the Roll of 1896. Their mother, half					
6	blood Choctaw, Wife of Wax Lee died when No2 was in her infancy. The father of these children, Wax Lee,					
7	is in the Penitentiary and they are now in the					
8	custody of stepmother, present wife of Was Lee.					
9	See testimony of Nancy E. Lee and William Crowder hereto attached.					
10						
11						
12						
13						
14					Date of Application for Enrollment.	
15						
16					5/8/99	
17						

Choctaw By Blood Enrollment Cards 1898-1914

RESIDENCE: Kiamitia COUNTY. **Choctaw Nation** Choctaw Roll CARD NO.
POST OFFICE: Goodland, I.T. *(Not Including Freedmen)* FIELD NO. 1423

Dawes' Roll No.	NAME		Relationship to Person	AGE	SEX	BLOOD	TRIBAL ENROLLMENT		
							Year	County	No.
3950	₁ Ward, George	24	First Named	21	M	Full	1896	Kiamitia	13742
3951	₂ " Lucinda	21	Wife	18	F	"	1893	"	242
14666	₃ " Gilbert	1	Son of Nº 2	2mo	M	"			
	4								
	5	ENROLLMENT							
	6	OF NOS. 1 and 2 HEREON APPROVED BY THE SECRETARY							
	7	OF INTERIOR DEC 12 1902							
	8								
	9	ENROLLMENT							
	10	OF NOS. 3 HEREON APPROVED BY THE SECRETARY							
	11	OF INTERIOR MAY 2 1903							
	12								
	13								
	14								
	15								
	16								
	17								

TRIBAL ENROLLMENT OF PARENTS

	Name of Father	Year	County	Name of Mother	Year	County
1	Eden Ward	Dead	Kiamitia	Betty Ward	Dead	Kiamitia
2	Edmund Gardner	1896	"	Selina Gardner	"	"
3	Joseph Oklabe	1896	"	Nº2		
4						
5						
6			No2 on 1893 Pay roll as Lucinda Gardner, Page 30, No 242			
7			Kiamitia County.			
8			Nº3 Born sept. 3, 1902, enrolled Nov. 1, 1902			
9			Nº3 illegitimate			
10			No 1 in Jail at Atoka 12/2/02			
11						
12						
13						
14					#1&2	
15					Date of Application for Enrollment.	
16					5/8/99	
17	P.O. of No 2 is Nelson I.T. 12/2/02					

223

Choctaw By Blood Enrollment Cards 1898-1914

RESIDENCE: Kiamitia COUNTY.
POST OFFICE: Grant, I.T.

Choctaw Nation

Choctaw Roll
(Not Including Freedmen)

CARD NO.
FIELD NO. 1424

Dawes' Roll No.	NAME	Relationship to Person First Named	AGE	SEX	BLOOD	TRIBAL ENROLLMENT		
						Year	County	No.
I.W. 72	1 Nelson, Bethel A ³⁹	First Named	36	M	I.W.	1896	Kiamitia	14901
3952	2 " Fannie L ³⁷	Wife	34	F	1/4	1896	"	9750
3953	3 " Albert J ¹⁰	Son	7	M	1/8	1896	"	9751
3954	4 " Louise B ⁷	Dau	4	F	1/8	1896	"	9752
3955	5 " Florence ⁵	"	16mo	"	1/8			
3956	6 " William D ¹	Son	1mo	M	1/8			
	7							
	8 ENROLLMENT							
	9 OF NOS. 2 3 4 5 and 6 HEREON APPROVED BY THE SECRETARY							
	10 OF INTERIOR DEC 12 1902							
	11							
	12 ENROLLMENT							
	13 OF NOS. ~ 1 ~ HEREON APPROVED BY THE SECRETARY							
	14 OF INTERIOR JUN 12 1903							
	15							
	16							
	17							

TRIBAL ENROLLMENT OF PARENTS

	Name of Father	Year	County	Name of Mother	Year	County
1	W.D. Nelson	1896	Non Citz	Louise V. Nelson	Dead	Non Citz
2	Chas. D. Oakes	1896	Kiamitia	Judie Oakes	"	Kiamitia
3	No 1			No 2		
4	No 1			No 2		
5	No 1			No 2		
6	No.1			No.2		
7						
8						
9	For child of Nos 1&2 see NB (Mar 3-1905) Card #44					
10	No1 on 1896 roll as B.A. Nelson. He was admitted as an					
11	Intermarried Citz. by Dawes Commission, Case No 1135, as B. A. Nelson. Evidence of his marriage on file in the					
12	office of Dawes Commission, Muskogee, I.T.					
13	No2 on 1896 roll as Fannie W. Nelson					
14	No4 " 1896 " " Louisa "				Date of Application for Enrollment.	
15						
16	No5 Affidavit of birth to be supplied. Recd May 9/99 No6 Enrolled May 13, 1901				5/8/99	
17	No3 and 4 admitted by Dawes Com in 1896 as respectively Albert and Louisa Nelson					

224

Choctaw By Blood Enrollment Cards 1898-1914

RESIDENCE: **Kiamitia** COUNTY.
POST OFFICE: **Goodland, I.T.**

Choctaw Nation

Choctaw Roll
(Not Including Freedmen)

CARD NO.
FIELD NO. 1425

Dawes' Roll No.	NAME	Relationship to Person First Named	AGE	SEX	BLOOD	TRIBAL ENROLLMENT Year	County	No.
I.W. 634	1 Turnbull, Harriet E 57	First Named	56	F	I.W.	1896	Kiamitia	15106
3957	2 Pharis, Walter 21	Ward	18	M	1/4	1896	"	10436
3958	3 " Turner 17	"	14	"	1/4	1896	"	10437
	4							
	5 ENROLLMENT OF NOS. 2 and 3 HEREON							
	6 APPROVED BY THE SECRETARY							
	OF INTERIOR							
	7							
	8 ENROLLMENT OF NOS. 1 HEREON							
	9 APPROVED BY THE SECRETARY OF INTERIOR MAR 26 1904							
	10							
	11							
	12							
	13							
	14							
	15							
	16							
	17							

TRIBAL ENROLLMENT OF PARENTS

	Name of Father	Year	County	Name of Mother	Year	County
1	Samuel Willard	Dead	Non Citz	Martha Willard	Dead	Non Citz
2	Polk Pharis	"	" "	Eliza Pharis	"	Kiamitia
3	" "	"	" "	" "	"	"
4						
5						
6	No 1 on 1896 as Harriet Turnbull					
7						
8						
9						
10						
11						
12						
13						
14						
15						
16					Date of Application for Enrollment	5/8/99
17	Doaksville I.T. 12/3/02					

4-7-03

225

Choctaw By Blood Enrollment Cards 1898-1914

RESIDENCE: Towson COUNTY.
POST OFFICE: Doaksville, I.T.

Choctaw Nation

Choctaw Roll
(Not Including Freedmen)

CARD NO.
FIELD NO. **1426**

Dawes' Roll No.	NAME	Relationship to Person First Named	AGE	SEX	BLOOD	TRIBAL ENROLLMENT		
						Year	County	No.
3959	1 Wilson, Florance B. 31	First Named	28	F	1/4	1893	Towson	392
3960	2 " , John L 9	Son	6	M	1/8	1896	"	13181
3961	3 " , William E. 7	"	4	"	1/8	1896	"	13182
3962	4 " , Hattie I. 6	Dau	2	F	1/8	1896	"	13222
3963	5 " , Bessie B 5	"	14mo	"	1/8			
3964	6 " , Curtis B. 3	Son	2wks	M	1/8			
3965	7 DIED PRIOR TO SEPTEMBER 25, 1902 " , Leslie J.	Dau	1mo	F	1/8			
	8							
	9							
	10							
	11							
	12							
	13							
	14							
	15							
	16 see Card #5540							
	17							

ENROLLMENT OF NOS. 1 2 3 4 5 6 and 7 HEREON APPROVED BY THE SECRETARY OF INTERIOR Dec 12, 1902

TRIBAL ENROLLMENT OF PARENTS

	Name of Father	Year	County	Name of Mother	Year	County
1	William Frye	Dead	Jackson	Elizabeth Frye	1896	Jackson
2	John D Wilson	1896	Chick. Roll	No. 1		
3	" " "	1896	" "	No. 1		
4	" " "	1896	" "	No. 1		
5	" " "	1896	" "	No. 1		
6	" " "	1896	" "	No. 1		
7	" " "	1896	" "	No. 1		
8						
9	No 1 on 1893 Pay Roll as F.B. Wilson Page 44 No. 392, Towson Co.					
10	No 2 " 1896 roll as Jno. L. Wilson					
11	No 3 " 1896 roll as Aeyne "					
12	No 4 " 1896 roll as Harriet "					
	No 1 " 1896 roll as Emma " Page 346, No. 13180					
13	Towson Co.					
14	No7 died Aug 30, 1900: Enrollment cancelled by Department July 8, 1904.					#1 to 6
15	No7 Enrolled June 8 1900					Date of Application for Enrollment.
16	No7 died Aug 30, 1900: Proof of death filed Dec 5, 1902					5/8/99
17	see card 5469					

226

RESIDENCE: Kiamitia COUNTY: *#5 Box 405 Ark City, Ka 11-18-36* **Choctaw Nation** **Choctaw Roll** *(Not Including Freedmen)* CARD NO. FIELD NO. **1427**

POST OFFICE: Goodland, I.T.

Dawes' Roll No.	NAME	Relationship to Person First Named	AGE	SEX	BLOOD	TRIBAL ENROLLMENT		
						Year	County	No.
3966	₁ Colbert, Sam 40	First Named	37	M	Full	1896	Kiamitia	2686
3967	₂ " , Eliza 24	Wife	21	F	"	1896	"	4241
3968	₃ " , Frank 4	Son	5mo	M	"			
3969	₄ Holman, James ~~DIED PRIOR TO SEPTEMBER 25, 1902~~	Ward	13	"	"	1896	Kiamitia	5762
3970	₅ Colbert, Jimmy 1	Son	1mo	M	"			
	6							
	7 ENROLLMENT							
	8 OF NOS. 1 2 3 4 and 5 HEREON APPROVED BY THE SECRETARY							
	9 OF INTERIOR Dec. 12, 1902							
	10							
	11							
	12							
	13							
	14							
	15							
	16							
	17							

TRIBAL ENROLLMENT OF PARENTS

	Name of Father	Year	County	Name of Mother	Year	County
₁	James Colbert	Dead	Towson	Licey Colbert	Dead	Towson
₂	Stephen Frazier	"	Cedar	Louisa Frazier	"	Kiamitia
₃	No 1			No 2		
₄	Simon Holman	Dead	Towson	Susan Holman	Dead	Kiamitia
₅	No 1			No 2		
₆						
₇						
₈						
₉	No 2 on 1896 roll as Eliza Frazier					
₁₀	No 4 " 1896 " " James Holdman					
₁₁	No5 born Oct. 8th 1901: Enrolled Nov. 30, 1901.					
	No4 died Feb. 9, 1902: Proof of death filed Dec. 8, 1902					
₁₂	No.4 died Feb 9, 1902: Enrollment cancelled by Department July 8, 1904.					
₁₃						
₁₄				Date of Application for Enrollment.	#1 to 4	
₁₅					5/8/99	
₁₆						
₁₇						

Choctaw By Blood Enrollment Cards 1898-1914

RESIDENCE: Kiamitia   COUNTY.
POST OFFICE: Goodland, I.T.

Choctaw Nation

Choctaw Roll *(Not Including Freedmen)*

CARD NO.
FIELD NO. **1428**

Dawes' Roll No.	NAME		Relationship to Person	AGE	SEX	BLOOD	TRIBAL ENROLLMENT		
							Year	County	No.
3971	₁ Joe , Sim	44	First Named	41	M	Full	1896	Kiamitia	7068
3972	₂ " , Visey	29	Wife	26	F	"	1896	"	7069
3973	₃ " , Agnes	12	Dau	9	"	"	1896	"	7070
	₄								
	₅	ENROLLMENT							
	₆	OF NOS.1 2 and 3 HEREON APPROVED BY THE SECRETARY							
	₇	OF INTERIOR Dec 12, 1902.							
	₈								
	₉								
	10								
	11								
	12								
	13								
	14								
	15								
	16								
	17								

TRIBAL ENROLLMENT OF PARENTS

	Name of Father	Year	County	Name of Mother	Year	County
₁	Joe Te-hok-lo-tuby	Dead	Towson		Dead	Towson
₂	Solomon Sunta	"	Kiamitia	Sallie Sunta	"	Kiamitia
₃	No 1			No 2		
₄						
₅						
₆			No 1 on 1896 roll as I. Sim Joe.			
₇			No 2 " 1896 " " Wisey " .			
₈						
₉						
10						
11						
12						
13						
14					Date of Application for Enrollment.	
15						
16					5/8/99	
17						

RESIDENCE: Kiamitia   COUNTY.   **Choctaw Nation**   Choctaw Roll

POST OFFICE: Grant, I.T.   *(Not Including Freedmen)*

Dawes' Roll No.	NAME		Relationship to Person First Named	AGE	SEX	BLOOD	TRIBAL ENROLLMENT		
							Year	County	No.
3974	1 Ervin, Columbus C	53	First Named	50	M	1/2	1896	Kiamitia	3784
3975	2 " Lizzie H	37	Wife	34	F	1/2	1896	"	3785
3976	3 " Joel E	16	Son	13	M	1/2	1896	"	3786
3977	4 " Myrtle M	14	Dau	11	F	1/2	1896	"	3787
3978	5 " Walter P	12	Son	9	M	1/2	1896	"	3788
3979	6 " Abraham A	10	"	7	"	1/2	1896	"	3789
3980	7 " Turner L	9	"	6	"	1/2	1896	"	3790
3981	8 " Emmet	8	"	5	"	1/2	1896	"	3791
3982	9 " Harriet N	6	Dau	3	F	1/2	1896	"	3792
3983	10 " Mark H.	5	Son	20mo	M	1/2			
DEAD.	11 " ~~Thelma G~~		~~Dau~~	~~2mo~~	~~F~~	~~1/2~~	ENROLLMENT OF NOS. 1 2 3 4 5 6 7 8 9 10 11 12 and 13 HEREON		
3984	12 " Laura	2	Dau	2mo	F	1/2	APPROVED BY THE SECRETARY		
3985	13 " Archer Roy	1	Son	6wks	M	1/2	OF INTERIOR DEC 12 1902		
	14								
	15 Nº 11 Died Dec. 4, 1899, proof of same								
	16 filed Oct. 13, 1902.								
	17								

TRIBAL ENROLLMENT OF PARENTS

	Name of Father	Year	County	Name of Mother	Year	County
1	Calvin Ervin	Dead	Non Citz	Sallie Ervin	Dead	Towson
2	Joel Everidge	1896	Kiamitia	Sophronia Everidge	"	Kiamitia
3	No 1			No 2		
4	No 1			No 2		
5	No 1			No 2		
6	No 1			No 2		
7	No 1			No 2		
8	No 1	No. 11 HEREON DISMISSED UNDER		No 2		
9	No 1	ORDER OF THE COMMISSION TO THE FIVE		No 2		
10	No 1	CIVILIZED TRIBES OF MARCH 31, 1905.		No 2		
11	~~No 1~~			~~No 2~~		
12	No 1			No 2		
13	Nº 1			Nº 2		
14				For child of Nos 1&2 see NB (Mar 3'05) #668		
15	No2 on 1896 roll as Harriet E Ervin				Date of Application for Enrollment.	
16	No4 " 1896 " " Margaret P "				5/8/99	
16	Nºˢ 10-11 Affidavits of birth to be supplied. Recd May 9/99				*Enrolled*	1 to 11 inc
17	No12 Enrolled February 21, 1901					

Nº 13 Born July 5, 1902; enrolled Aug. 15, 1902

Choctaw By Blood Enrollment Cards 1898-1914

RESIDENCE: **Kiamitia**   COUNTY.   **Choctaw Nation**   **Choctaw Roll**
POST OFFICE: **Grant, I.T.**   *(Not Including Freedmen)*   FIELD NO. **1430**

Dawes' Roll No.	NAME			Relationship to Person	AGE	SEX	BLOOD	TRIBAL ENROLLMENT		
								Year	County	No.
I.W. 232	1	Jones, Frances A	53	First Named	50	F	I.W.	1896	Kiamitia	14695
3986	2	" John G.	19	Son	16	M	1/2	1896	"	7062
3987	3	" Margaret A	15	Dau	12	F	1/2	1896	"	7063
3988	4	" Katie B	13	"	10	"	1/2	1896	"	7064
	5									
	6	ENROLLMENT								
	7	OF NOS. 2 3 and 4 HEREON APPROVED BY THE SECRETARY								
	8	OF INTERIOR DEC 12 1902								
	9	ENROLLMENT								
	10	OF NOS. 1 HEREON APPROVED BY THE SECRETARY								
	11	OF INTERIOR SEP 12 1903								
	12									
	13									
	14									
	15									
	16									
	17									

TRIBAL ENROLLMENT OF PARENTS

	Name of Father	Year	County	Name of Mother	Year	County
1	S.M. Willard	Dead	Non Citz	Martha G. Willard	Dead	Non Citz
2	Wilson S. Jones	"	Kiamitia	No 1		
3	" " "	"	"	No 1		
4	" " "	"	"	No 1		
5						
6	No 2 on 1896 roll as Jno. G. Jones					
7	No 4 " 1896 " " Kittie B. "					
8	For child of No.2 see N.B. (Apr. 26, 1906) Card No. 89.					
9	" " " No.3 " " " " " " 90.					
10						
11						
12						
13						
14						
15						
16						5/8/99
17						

RESIDENCE: **Kiamitia** COUNTY. **Choctaw Nation** **Choctaw Roll** CARD NO.
POST OFFICE: **Goodland, I.T.** (Not Including Freedmen) FIELD NO. **1431**

Dawes' Roll No.	NAME	Relationship to Person First Named	AGE	SEX	BLOOD	TRIBAL ENROLLMENT Year	County	No.
3989	1 Gardner, Edmund ⁴⁸	First Named	45	M	Full	1896	Kiamitia	4830
3990	2 " , Nicey ⁴³	Wife	40	F	"	1896	Atoka	12482
3991	3 Williams, Isabel ¹⁶	S.Dau	13	"	"	1896	"	14072
3992	4 " , Enos ¹²	S.Son	9	M	"	1896	"	14073
~~3993~~	~~5 Thomas, Edmond~~ DIED PRIOR TO SEPTEMBER 25, 1902	~~" "~~	~~3~~	~~"~~	~~"~~	~~1896~~	~~"~~	~~12483~~
	6							
	7	ENROLLMENT						
	8	OF NOS. 1 2 3 4 and 5 HEREON APPROVED BY THE SECRETARY						
	9	OF INTERIOR Dec 12, 1902						
	10							
	11							
	12							
	13							
	14							
	15							
	16							
	17							

TRIBAL ENROLLMENT OF PARENTS

	Name of Father	Year	County	Name of Mother	Year	County
1	Geo. Gardner	Dead	Blue	Lucinda Gardner	Dead	Blue
2	Ho-stok-by	"	Kiamitia	Sally Hostokby	"	Atoka
3	Joe Homma	1896	Atoka	No 2		
4	Eastman Williams	Dead	"	No 2		
5	~~Edmond Thomas~~	~~Dead~~	~~Atoka~~	~~No 2~~		
6						
7	No2 on 1896 roll as Nicey Thomas					
8	No1 and 2 have seperated[sic] and No2 is now wife of					
9	Lafayette Homer on Choctaw No. 4254					
	No1 is now husband of Liney Holenlobi Choc 1515					
10	No5 died July 11-1901: Proof of death filed Nov. 25, 1902					
11	No.5 died July 11, 1901: Enrollment cancelled by Department July 8, 1904.					
12	For child of No3 see NB (Apr 26-06) Card #866.					
13						
14						
15						
16				Date of Application for Enrollment	5/8/99	
17	Nelson I.T. 12/2/02					

Choctaw By Blood Enrollment Cards 1898-1914

RESIDENCE: Jackson COUNTY.
POST OFFICE: Crowder, I.T.

Choctaw Nation

Choctaw Roll
(Not Including Freedmen)

CARD NO.
FIELD NO. 1432

Dawes' Roll No.	NAME	Relationship to Person First Named	AGE	SEX	BLOOD	TRIBAL ENROLLMENT		
						Year	County	No.
3994	1 Crowder, Mary A ⁴⁸	First Named	45	F	3/4	1896	Jackson	2820
3995	2 Spring, James F ¹⁹	Son	16	M	1/2	1896	"	11563
3996	3 " Zeno ¹⁶	"	13	"	1/2	1896	"	11564
3997	4 Crowder, Mary M ¹¹	Dau	8	F	5/8	1896	"	2822
3998	5 " John J ⁹	Son	6	M	5/8	1896	"	2823
	6							
	7							
	8	ENROLLMENT OF NOS. 1 2 3 4 and 5 HEREON						
	9	APPROVED BY THE SECRETARY OF INTERIOR DEC 2 1902						
	10							
	11							
	12							
	13							
	14							
	15							
	16							
	17							

TRIBAL ENROLLMENT OF PARENTS

	Name of Father	Year	County	Name of Mother	Year	County
1	Wᵐ Roebuck	Dead	Kiamitia	Mary A Roebuck	1896	Jackson
2	James O. Spring	"	"	No 1		
3	" " "	"	"	No 1		
4	Josh Crowder	"	"	No 1		
5	" "	"	"	No 1		
6						
7						
8			No1 on 1896 roll as W. A. Crowder			
9			No2 " 1896 " " James Spring			
10			No3 " 1896 " " Zena Spring			
			No5 " 1896 " " J.J. Crowder			
11			For child of No2 see NB (Apr 26-06) Card #450			
12						
13						
14					Date of Application for Enrollment.	
15						
16					5/8/99	
17	Hugo I.T. 12/5/02					

Choctaw By Blood Enrollment Cards 1898-1914

RESIDENCE: **Jackson** COUNTY. **Choctaw Nation** **Choctaw Roll** CARD NO.
POST OFFICE: **Crowder, I.T.** *(Not Including Freedmen)* FIELD NO. **1433**

Dawes' Roll No.	NAME		Relationship to Person	AGE	SEX	BLOOD	TRIBAL ENROLLMENT		
							Year	County	No.
~~3999~~	Roebuck, Annie	81	First Named	78	F	Full	1896	Kiamitia	10862
3999	2								
	3	ENROLLMENT							
	4	OF NOS. 1 HEREON APPROVED BY THE SECRETARY							
	5	OF INTERIOR DEC 12 1902							
	6								
	7								
	8								
	9								
	10								
	11								
	12								
	13								
	14								
	15								
	16								
	17								

TRIBAL ENROLLMENT OF PARENTS

	Name of Father	Year	County	Name of Mother	Year	County
1	John Homer	Dead	Blue	Lush-homma	Dead	Kiamitia
2						
3						
4						
5	No.1 Died Jan. 11-1901; Proof of Death filed Nov. 15-1902					
6	No.1 died Jan. 11, 1901; Enrollment cancelled by Department [Illegible]					
7						
8						
9						
10						
11						
12						
13						
14						
15						
16				Date of Application for Enrollment.	5/8/99	
17						

233

Choctaw By Blood Enrollment Cards 1898-1914

RESIDENCE: **Kiamitia** COUNTY.
POST OFFICE: **Goodland**, I.T.

Choctaw Nation

Choctaw Roll
(Not Including Freedmen)

CARD NO.
FIELD NO. 1434

Dawes' Roll No.		NAME	Relationship to Person	AGE	SEX	BLOOD	TRIBAL ENROLLMENT		
							Year	County	No.
4000	1	McIntire, Belshazzar ^{22}	First Named	19	M	1/2	1896	Kiamitia	9390
	2								
	3	ENROLLMENT							
	4	OF NOS. 1 HEREON APPROVED BY THE SECRETARY							
	5	OF INTERIOR DEC 12 1902							
	6								
	7								
	8								
	9								
	10								
	11								
	12								
	13								
	14								
	15								
	16								
	17								

TRIBAL ENROLLMENT OF PARENTS

	Name of Father	Year	County	Name of Mother	Year	County
1	James McIntire	Dead	Non Citz	Lucretia Roebuck	Dead	Kiamitia
2						
3						
4						
5			On 1896 roll as Balshizar McIntire			
6			Wife and children of No 1 on 7-2567			
7						
8						
9						
10						
11						
12						
13						
14						
15						
16				Date of Application for Enrollment.	5/8/99	
17						

Choctaw By Blood Enrollment Cards 1898-1914

RESIDENCE: **Kiamitia** COUNTY. POST OFFICE: **Goodland, I.T.**   **Choctaw Nation**   Choctaw Roll *(Not Including Freedmen)*   CARD NO. FIELD NO. **1435**

Dawes' Roll No.	NAME	Relationship to Person	AGE	SEX	BLOOD	TRIBAL ENROLLMENT		
						Year	County	No.
4001	1 Coone, Viney 30	First Named	27	F	Full	1896	Jackson	2835
4002	2 " , Charlie 9	Son	6	M	1/2	1896	"	2836
4003	3 " , Willie May 7	Dau	4	F	1/2	1896	"	2837
4004	4 " , David 2	Son	1 yr	M	1/2			
15782	5 " , Emma 1	Dau	1	F	1/2			
	6							
	7							
	8							
	9							
	10	ENROLLMENT OF NOS. 1 2 3 and 4 HEREON APPROVED BY THE SECRETARY OF INTERIOR Dec. 12, 1902							
	11								
	12								
	13	ENROLLMENT OF NOS. 5 HEREON APPROVED BY THE SECRETARY OF INTERIOR Mar. 15, 1905							
	14								
	15								
	16								
	17								

TRIBAL ENROLLMENT OF PARENTS

	Name of Father	Year	County	Name of Mother	Year	County
1	Dixon Peters	Dead	Red River	Mariah Hayes	Dead	Red River
2	Alvey Coone	1896	Non Citz	No 1		
3	" "	1896	" "	No 1		
4	" "	1896	" "	No 1		
5	Unknown			No 1		
6						
7	No4 Enrolled May 13, 1901					
8	No1 is now divorced from Alvey Coon[sic]. See application for					
9	enrollment of No.4 and letter of W.O. Surbaugh filed May 13, 1901 Father of Nos 2 and 3 is Alvy[sic] Coon on Choctaw Card #D728.					
10	No5: the illegitimate child of No1 was born Aug 26, 1902:					
11	application for her enrollment was made at Antlers, I.T.					
12	on Dec. 16, 1902 by John Parsons. (See evidence attached to affidavits of birth).					
13	No.5 placed on this card Nov. 22d, 1904.					
14	For child of No1 see NB (March 3, 1905) #574.			#1 to 3		
15				Date of Application for Enrollment.		
16				5/8/99		
17	P.O. Soper I.T. 3/31/05					

235

Choctaw By Blood Enrollment Cards 1898-1914

Dawes' Roll No.	NAME		Relationship to Person First Named	AGE	SEX	BLOOD	TRIBAL ENROLLMENT		
							Year	County	No.
4005	1 Gardner, Israel	26	First Named	23	M	Full	1896	Kiamitia	4823
4006	2 ~~Nancy~~ DIED PRIOR TO SEPTEMBER 25, 1902		Wife	23	F	"	1896	"	4824
4007	3 " Rosa	6	Dau	2	"	"			
4008	4 " ~~Adeline~~ DIED PRIOR TO SEPTEMBER 25, 1902		"	4mo	"	"			
	5								
	6								
	7								
	8								
	9								
	10								
	11								
	12								
	13								
	14								
	15								
	16								
	17								

ENROLLMENT
OF NOS. 1,2 3 and 4 HEREON
APPROVED BY THE SECRETARY
OF INTERIOR Dec 12, 1902

TRIBAL ENROLLMENT OF PARENTS

	Name of Father	Year	County	Name of Mother	Year	County
1	E mund[sic] Gardner	1896	Kiamitia	Lucy Gardner	Dead	Jackson
2	Levi Johnson	Dead	Blue	Liney Johnson	1896	Kiamitia
3	No 1			No 2		
4	No 1			No 2		
5						
6						
7						
8						
9	No2 died May 15, 1902; proof of death filed Dec 2, 1902.					
10	No4 " July 18, 1899; " " " " " 5, 1902					
11						
12	No1 is now husband of Winey Williams Choc 1474					
13	No2 died May 15,1902: No4 died July 18,1899: Enrollment cancelled by Department					
14					July 8, 1904.	
15					Date of Application for Enrollment.	
16					5/8/99	
17						

Choctaw By Blood Enrollment Cards 1898-1914

RESIDENCE: Towson COUNTY.
POST OFFICE: Doaksville, I.T.

Choctaw Nation

Choctaw Roll
(Not Including Freedmen)

CARD NO.
FIELD NO. 1437

Dawes' Roll No.	NAME	Relationship to Person First Named	AGE	SEX	BLOOD	TRIBAL ENROLLMENT Year	County	No.
4009	1 Tims, Edward W 61	First Named	58	M	1/2	1896	Towson	12121
I.W. 635	2 " Willie J 32	Wife	29	F	I.W.	1896	"	15102
4010	3 " Lucy 13	Dau	10	"	1/4	1896	"	12123
4011	4 " Minnie J 11	"	8	"	1/4	1896	"	12124
4012	5 " Edmond 9	Son	6	M	1/4	1896	"	12125
4013	6 " Benjamin W 6	"	2	"	1/4			
4014	7 Nanomantabbe, Adam 7	Ward	4	W	1/4	1896	Cedar	9654
4015	8 Tims, Myrtle 3	Dau	2mo	F	1/4			
4016	9 " Abel E 1	Son	2mo	M	1/4			
	10							
	11							
	12							
	13							
	14							
	15							
	16							
	17							

ENROLLMENT
OF NOS. 2 HEREON
APPROVED BY THE SECRETARY
OF INTERIOR MAR 26 1904

ENROLLMENT
OF NOS. 1345678and9 HEREON
APPROVED BY THE SECRETARY
OF INTERIOR DEC 12 1902

TRIBAL ENROLLMENT OF PARENTS

	Name of Father	Year	County	Name of Mother	Year	County
1	Vincent V. Tims	Dead	Non Citz	Betsy Tims	Dead	Towson
2	Maxwell	"	" "		"	Non Citz
3	No 1			No 2		
4	No 1			No 2		
5	No 1			No 2		
6	No 1			No 2		
7	Tobias Nanomantabbe	Dead	Cedar	Susan Nanomantabbe	Dead	Towson
8	No 1			No 2		
9	No 1			No 2		
10						
11		No1 on 1896 roll as Edward Tims				
12		No4 " 1896 " " Mamie "				
13	No9 born Dec. 14, 1901: Enrolled Feby. 14, 1902					
14	No8 enrolled Dec 19/99. Affidvit					
15	irregular and returned for correction.			Date of Application for Enrollment.	For Nos. 1 to 7 incl.	
16	Recd & filed Jany 17, 1902.				5/8/99	
17	No5 on 1896 roll as Edmund Tims.					
	Grant I.T. 12/8/02					

237

Choctaw By Blood Enrollment Cards 1898-1914

RESIDENCE: Towson COUNTY.
POST OFFICE: Doaksville, I.T.

Choctaw Nation

Choctaw Roll
(Not Including Freedmen)

CARD NO.
FIELD NO. 1438

Dawes' Roll No.	NAME	Relationship to Person	AGE	SEX	BLOOD	TRIBAL ENROLLMENT		
						Year	County	No.
4017	1 Fulsom, Lewis G. 49	First Named	46	M	1/4	1896	Towson	4135
	2							
	3							
	4							.
	5							
	6							
	7							
	8							
	9							
	10							
	11							
	12							
	13							
	14							
	15							
	16							
	17							

ENROLLMENT
OF NOS. 1 HEREON
APPROVED BY THE SECRETARY
OF INTERIOR DEC 12 1902

TRIBAL ENROLLMENT OF PARENTS

	Name of Father	Year	County	Name of Mother	Year	County
1	S. N. Fulsom	1896	Towson	Susan Fulsom	Dead	Towson
2						
3						
4						
5			On 1896 roll as Louis G. Folsom.			
6						
7						
8						
9						
10						
11						
12						
13						
14						
15						
16				Date of Application for Enrollment 5/8/99		
17						

Choctaw By Blood Enrollment Cards 1898-1914

RESIDENCE: Towson COUNTY. **Choctaw Nation**
POST OFFICE: Doaksville, I.T. **Choctaw Roll** (Not Including Freedmen) CARD NO. FIELD NO. 1439

Dawes' Roll No.	NAME	Relationship to Person	AGE	SEX	BLOOD	TRIBAL ENROLLMENT		
						Year	County	No.
4018	1 Garland, Osborne 23	First Named	20	M	3/4	1893	Blue	12
	2							
	3							
	4							
	5							
	6							
	7							
	8							
	9							
	10							
	11	ENROLLMENT						
	12	OF NOS. 1 HEREON APPROVED BY THE SECRETARY						
	13	OF INTERIOR DEC 12 1902						
	14							
	15							
	16							
	17							

TRIBAL ENROLLMENT OF PARENTS

	Name of Father	Year	County	Name of Mother	Year	County
1	Silas Garland	Dead	Towson	Lucinda Hall	Dead	Towson
2						
3						
4						
5						
6	On 1893 Pay roll, Blue County, Page 117, No 12 as Osborn Garland					
7						
8	Child of No1 on NB (Apr 26-06) Card #304					
9						
10						
11						
12						
13						
14						
15						
16				Date of Application for Enrollment.	5/8/99	
17	P.O. Ft Towson IT 10/24/05					

Choctaw By Blood Enrollment Cards 1898-1914

RESIDENCE: **Kiamitia** COUNTY. **Choctaw Nation** Choctaw Roll CARD NO.
POST OFFICE: **Goodland, I.T.** (Not Including Freedmen) FIELD NO. **1440**

Dawes' Roll No.	NAME	Relationship to Person First Named	AGE	SEX	BLOOD	TRIBAL ENROLLMENT Year	County	No.
Dead	1 Woods, Ellen DEAD.	First Named	26	F	3/4	1896	Jackson	10884
4019	2 Bacon, Ellen 9	Dau	6	"	5/8	1896	"	1513
	3							
	4							
	5 No 1 **DISMISSED**							
	6							
	7 FEB 11 1907							
	8							
	9							
	10							
	11 ENROLLMENT							
	12 OF NOS. 2 HEREON APPROVED BY THE SECRETARY							
	13 OF INTERIOR DEC 12 1902							
	14							
	15							
	16							
	17							

TRIBAL ENROLLMENT OF PARENTS

Name of Father	Year	County	Name of Mother	Year	County
1 Henry Goings	Dead	Jackson	Emma Goings	Dead	Jackson
2 Dave Bacon	1896	"	No 1		
3					
4					
5 No 1 is also on Pay roll for 1893, Page 32, No 281, Jackson					
6 County, as Ellen Goins					
7 No1 on 1896 roll as Ellen Russel.					
8 Proof of death of No1 requested 3 times [remainder illegible]					
9					
10					
11					
12					
13					
14					
15			Date of Application for Enrollment		
16 2/21/06 P.O. Hugo IT (?)				5/8/99	
17					

RESIDENCE: Kiamitia	COUNTY.	**Choctaw Nation**				Choctaw Roll *(Not Including Freedmen)*		CARD NO.
POST OFFICE: Grant I.T.							FIELD NO.	1441

Dawes' Roll No.	NAME	Relationship to Person	AGE	SEX	BLOOD	TRIBAL ENROLLMENT		
						Year	County	No.
I.W.233	1 Bearden Chas E. 31	First Named	29	M	I.W.			
4020	2 " Bessie 22	Wife	19	F.	1/16	P.R 1893	Kiamitia	528
4021	3 " Flora O 4	Dau	1	F.	1/32			
4022	4 " Oscar Payton 2	Son	New born	M.	1/32			
4023	5 " Florence Esther 1	Dau	1½mo	F	1/32			
	6							
	7							
	8							
	9 ENROLLMENT							
	10 OF NOS. 2 3 4 and 5 HEREON APPROVED BY THE SECRETARY							
	11 OF INTERIOR DEC 12 1902							
	12 ENROLLMENT							
	13 OF NOS. 1 HEREON APPROVED BY THE SECRETARY							
	14 OF INTERIOR SEP 12 1903							
	15							
	16							
	17							

TRIBAL ENROLLMENT OF PARENTS

Name of Father	Year	County	Name of Mother	Year	County
1 John Bearden	1896	Non Citizen	Rhoda Bearden	Dead	Non Citizen
2 Lem Oakes	1896	Kiamitia	Lucy Oakes	1896	Non Citizen
3 No. 1			No. 2		
4 No. 1			No. 2		
5 Nº1			Nº2		
6					
7 No.2 enrolled as Bessie Oakes on Page 66					
8 No 558 1893 Pay rolls[sic], Kiamitia Co					
9					
10 Certificate of marriage of LW Oakes and Lucy					
11 Smith, father and mother of Bessie Bearden, above					
12 dated December 29, 1879, exhibited					
13					
14 No.4 Enrolled June 23d, 1900				#1 to 3	
15 Nº5 Born Jany. 29,1902: enrolled March 18, 1902.					
16 Evidence of marriage of Nos 1 and 2 filed Dec 9, 1902				Date of Application for Enrollment. 5/8/99
For child of Nos 1&2 see NB (March 3,1905) #1077				
17 P.O. Hugo IT 4/12/05					

Choctaw By Blood Enrollment Cards 1898-1914

RESIDENCE: Kiamitia COUNTY.
POST OFFICE: Goodland, I.T.

Choctaw Nation

Choctaw Roll *(Not Including Freedmen)*

CARD NO.
FIELD NO. **1442**

Dawes' Roll No.	NAME		Relationship to Person First Named	AGE	SEX	BLOOD	TRIBAL ENROLLMENT		
							Year	County	No.
I.W. 234	1	Latimer, Osborne S. 34	First Named	30	M	I.W.	1896	Kiamitia	14770
4024	2	" Josephine B 29	Wife	26	F	1/4	1896	Kiamitia	8083
4025	3	" Mattie A 6	Dau	3	F	1/8	1896	"	8084
4026	4	" Ruby N 4	Dau	1mo	F	1/8			
4027	5	" Osborn W. 1	Son	1mo	M	1/8			
	6								
	7								
	8	ENROLLMENT							
	9	OF NOS. 2 3 4 and 5 HEREON APPROVED BY THE SECRETARY							
	10	OF INTERIOR Dec 12 1902							
	11								
	12	ENROLLMENT OF NOS. 1 HEREON							
	13	APPROVED BY THE SECRETARY							
	14	OF INTERIOR Sep 12 1903							
	15								
	16								
	17								

TRIBAL ENROLLMENT OF PARENTS

	Name of Father	Year	County	Name of Mother	Year	County
1	A.N. Latimer	1896	Non Citizen	Mattie Latimer	Dead	Non Citizen
2	Jas Usray	1896	Kiamitia	Malinda Usray	Dead	Kiamitia
3	No. 1			No 2		
4	No 1			No 2		
5	No 1			No 2		
6						
7						
8						
9	No1 on Roll as Osborne Latimer					
10	No3 " " " Mattie N. Latimer					
11	No1 admitted as an intermarried citizen in 1896					
12	by Dawes Commission, Choctaw Case #1219: No appeal No.5 Enrolled Sept. 10, 1901					
13						
14	For child of Nos 1&2 see NB (Mar 3-1905) Card #102					
15					#1 to 4	
16					Date of Application for Enrollment	5/8/99
17	Walker I.T. 10/25/02					

Choctaw By Blood Enrollment Cards 1898-1914

RESIDENCE: **Kiamitia**　　COUNTY.　**Choctaw Nation**　(Not Including Freedmen)　FIELD NO.　**1443**

POST OFFICE: **Grant, I.T.**

Dawes' Roll No.	NAME	Relationship to Person First Named	AGE	SEX	BLOOD	TRIBAL ENROLLMENT		
						Year	County	No.
4028 ₁	Everidge, Thomas W. ²⁹	First Named	26	M	1/4	P.R. 1893	Kiamitia	202
I.W. **235** ₂	"　Mollie ²⁹	Wife	25	F	I.W.		U.S.	
3								
4								
5								
6	ENROLLMENT							
7	OF NOS. 1 HEREON APPROVED BY THE SECRETARY							
8	OF INTERIOR DEC 12 1902							
9	ENROLLMENT							
10	OF NOS. 2 HEREON APPROVED BY THE SECRETARY							
11	OF INTERIOR SEP 12 1903							
12								
13								
14								
15								
16								
17								

TRIBAL ENROLLMENT OF PARENTS

	Name of Father	Year	County	Name of Mother	Year	County
1	Joe Everidge	1896	Kiamitia	Susan Everidge	Dead	Kiamitia
2	Robt Wilson	1896	Lamar (Tex)	Frances Wilson	1896	Lamar (Tex)
3						
4						
5						
6						
7			No 1 on P. 24 No 202 1893 Pay Rolls of Kiamitia Co.			
8			as Willie Everidge			
9			No1 Evidence of divorce from former wife, filed December 16, 1902			
			Nos 1 2 Evidence of marriage filed December 16, 1902			
10			For children of Nos 1&2 see NB (March 3, 1905) #1057			
11						
12						
13						
14						
15						
16					Date of Application for Enrollment 5/8/99	
17						

243

Choctaw By Blood Enrollment Cards 1898-1914

RESIDENCE: Kiamitia COUNTY. **Choctaw Nation** Choctaw Roll CARD NO.
POST OFFICE: Goodland I.T. *(Not Including Freedmen)* FIELD NO. 1444

Dawes' Roll No.	NAME		Relationship to Person	AGE	SEX	BLOOD	TRIBAL ENROLLMENT		
							Year	County	No.
4029	1 Spring Louis	24	First Named	21	M	1/2	1896	Kiamitia	11500
4030	2 " Lillie	20	Wife	17	F	1/16	1896	"	9944
4031	3 " Clarence E	4	Son	6mo	M	9/32			
4032	4 " Etta May	3	Dau.	5mo	F	9/32			
4033	5 " Essie M	1	Dau	1mo	F	9/32			
	6								
	7								
	8								
	9								
	10								
	11	ENROLLMENT							
	12	OF NOS. 1 2 3 4 and 5 HEREON APPROVED BY THE SECRETARY							
	13	OF INTERIOR DEC 12 1902							
	14								
	15								
	16								
	17								

TRIBAL ENROLLMENT OF PARENTS

	Name of Father	Year	County	Name of Mother	Year	County
1	John Spring	1896	Kiamitia	Nancy Spring	1896	Kiamitia
2	L.W. Oakes	1896	"	Lucy Oakes	1896	Non Citizen
3	No. 1			No 2		
4	No. 1			No. 2		
5	Nº1			Nº2		
6						
7			No 2 enrolled as Lillie Oakes			
8						
9						
10						
11						
12						
13			No 4 Enrolled May 24, 1900			
14			Nº5 Born June 18, 1902: enrolled July 30, 1902.			
15					#1 to 3	
16					Date of Application for Enrollment	5/8/99
17	Hugo I.T.					

244

Choctaw By Blood Enrollment Cards 1898-1914

Dawes' Roll No.	NAME	Relationship to Person	AGE	SEX	BLOOD	TRIBAL ENROLLMENT		
						Year	County	No.
	1 Crowder Richard [66]	First Named	63	M	1/4	1896	Jackson	2747
	2 " Fannie	Wife	58	F	1/2	1896	Kiamitia	2727
DEAD.	3 " Fannie DEAD.	Grand child	15	F	1/2	1896	"	2728
4035	4 Williams, Lena [1]	Dau of No 3	2mo	F	1/4	ENROLLMENT		
14667	5 Crowder John Richard [1]	Son	3mo	M	1/8	OF NOS. 6 HEREON APPROVED BY THE SECRETARY		
I.W. 810	6 " Mary Ellen [23]	Wife	23	F	I.W.	OF INTERIOR MAY 21 1904		
	7							

HEREON DISMISSED UNDER ORDER OF THE COMMISSION TO THE FIVE CIVILIZED TRIBES OF MARCH 31, 1905.

No. 2 and 3.

     ENROLLMENT
OF NOS. 1 and 4 HEREON
APPROVED BY THE SECRETARY
OF INTERIOR DEC 12 1902

For child of Nos 1&6 see NB (March 3, 1905) #848

No1 is now husband of Mary Ellen Crowder on Choctaw D 848

     ENROLLMENT
OF NOS. 5 HEREON
APPROVED BY THE SECRETARY
OF INTERIOR MAY 20 1903

No.3 Orphan N°3 died Jany 22, 1902. See affidavit of Richard C Crowder filed with application for enrollment of N°4 Feby 21, 1902.

N°5 was married Oct.10,1900, to J.A. Williams a non-citizen. License and certificate filed Feby 21,1902

N°4 Born Dec.8,1901; enrolled Feby 21, 1902

TRIBAL ENROLLMENT OF PARENTS

	Name of Father	Year	County	Name of Mother	Year	County
1	Eli Crowder	Dead	Jackson	Patsy Crowder	Dead	Jackson
2	Geo Durant	"	Towson	Viccy Durant	"	Bok Tuklo
3	Geo. Crowder	"	Kiamitia	Sarah Crowder	"	Red River
4	J.A. Williams		non-citizen	N°3		
5	N°1			Mary Ellen Crowder		intermarried
6	Wᵐ R Kelley		noncitizen	Lettitia Kelley	Dead	noncitizen
7						
8						
9	No1 It is said was never enrolled as a citizen until 1896. Investigate this matter.					
10	Also see if he was admitted or rejected by Commission in 1896. No record W.O.B.					
	N°2 Died March 26,1901, proof of death filed Oct. 15, 1902.					
11	No2 See Dawes Commission record 1896, Case 773					
12	No2 not the Fannie Crowder in 1896 Dawes Commission case Choctaw #773					
13	N°5 Born Sept. 3, 1902. Enrolled Dec. 24, 1902.					
14						
15						Date of Application for Enrollment.
16						5/8/99
17	Hugo I.T.					

No 6 transferred from Choctaw card D848 April 15,1904. See decision of March 15, 1904

Choctaw By Blood Enrollment Cards 1898-1914

RESIDENCE: **Kiamitia** COUNTY. **Choctaw Nation** **Choctaw Roll** CARD NO.

POST OFFICE: Goodland, I.T. *(Not Including Freedmen)* FIELD NO. 1446

Dawes' Roll No.	NAME	Relationship to Person	AGE	SEX	BLOOD	TRIBAL ENROLLMENT		
						Year	County	No.
4036	1 Homma, Annie 73	First Named	70	F	Full	1896	Kiamitia	5784
	2							
	3							
	4							
	5							
	6	ENROLLMENT						
	7	OF NOS. 1 HEREON APPROVED BY THE SECRETARY						
	8	OF INTERIOR DEC 12 1902						
	9							
	10							
	11							
	12							
	13							
	14							
	15							
	16							
	17							

TRIBAL ENROLLMENT OF PARENTS

	Name of Father	Year	County	Name of Mother	Year	County
1	Ya-cha-pie-e	Dead	Kiamitia	Min-te-ho-ke	Dead	Kiamitia
2						
3						
4						
5						
6						
7						
8						
9						
10						
11						
12						
13						
14						
15						
16				Date of Application for Enrollment	5/8/99	
17						

246

Choctaw By Blood Enrollment Cards 1898-1914

RESIDENCE: **Kiamitia**   COUNTY.   **Choctaw Nation**   CARD NO.
POST OFFICE: **Grant, I.T.**   *(Not Including Freedmen)*   FIELD NO. **1447**

Dawes' Roll No.	NAME		Relationship to Person	AGE	SEX	BLOOD	TRIBAL ENROLLMENT		
							Year	County	No.
4037	1 Hotema, Solomon	51	First Named	48	M	Full	1896	Kiamitia	5738
4038	2 " Nancy	41	Wife	38	F	"	1896	"	5739
4039	3 " Cornelia	15	Dau	12	"	"	1896	"	5740
4040	4 " Frank	9	Son	6	M	"	1896	"	5741
	5								
	6								
	7								
	8	ENROLLMENT							
	9	OF NOS. 1 2 3 and 4 HEREON APPROVED BY THE SECRETARY							
	10	OF INTERIOR DEC 12 1902							
	11								
	12								
	13								
	14								
	15								
	16								
	17								

TRIBAL ENROLLMENT OF PARENTS

	Name of Father	Year	County	Name of Mother	Year	County
1	John Hotema	Dead	Kiamitia		Dead	Kiamitia
2	John Coleman	"	Towson	Lucy Coleman	"	"
3	No1			No2		
4	No1			No2		
5						
6			For child of No.3 see NB (March 3, 1905) #1212			
7						
8			No.1 Died 4-23-02			
9						
10						
11						
12						
13						
14					Date of Application for Enrollment.	
15						
16					5/8/99	
17						

Choctaw By Blood Enrollment Cards 1898-1914

RESIDENCE: Towson   COUNTY.   **Choctaw Nation**   Choctaw Roll   CARD
POST OFFICE: Doaksville, I.T.   (Not Including Freedmen)   FIELD NO. 14

Dawes' Roll No.	NAME	Relationship to Person First Named	AGE	SEX	BLOOD	TRIBAL ENROLLMENT		
						Year	County	No.
I.W. 236	1 Howard, William H ⁴²	First Named	40	M	I.W.	1896	Towson	14625
4041	2 " Rhoda ³⁸	Wife	35	F	Full	1896	"	5501
4042	3 " Selma ¹²	Ward	9	"	"	1896	"	5502
	4							
	5							
	6							
	7	ENROLLMENT						
	8	OF NOS. 2 and 3 HEREON APPROVED BY THE SECRETARY						
	9	OF INTERIOR DEC 12 1902						
	10	ENROLLMENT						
	11	OF NOS. 1 HEREON APPROVED BY THE SECRETARY						
	12	OF INTERIOR SEP 12 1903						
	13							
	14							
	15							
	16							
	17							

TRIBAL ENROLLMENT OF PARENTS

	Name of Father	Year	County	Name of Mother	Year	County
1	J.W. Howard	1896	Non Citz	Sarah Howard	1896	Non Citz
2	Jesse Bryant	Dead			Dead	
3				Ellen Dennis	1896	Kiamitia
4						
5						
6		No 3 on 1896 Silinie Howard" As an illegitimate				
7		child, name of father unknown.				
8						
9		No1 on 1896 roll as Wᵐ H. Howard.				
10						
11						
12						
13						
14					Date of Application for Enrollment.	
15						
16	No1 P.O. Franks IT 1/1503		Date of application for enrollment 5/8/99			
17	No 3 in Wheelock Academy					

[Illegible]   11/28/02

248

Choctaw By Blood Enrollment Cards 1898-1914

RESIDENCE: Jackson COUNTY.
POST OFFICE: Crowder I.T.

Choctaw Nation
Choctaw Roll (Not Including Freedmen)

CARD NO.
FIELD NO. 1449

Dawes' Roll No.	NAME	Relationship to Person First Named	AGE	SEX	BLOOD	TRIBAL ENROLLMENT		
						Year	County	No.
15899	1 Crowder William J 53	First Named	50	M	1/4	1896	Jackson	2751
15900	2 " Abigail 16	Dau	13	F	1/8	1896	"	2754
15901	3 " Maggie 14	"	11	"	1/8	1896	"	2755
15902	4 " Rosa 13	"	10	"	1/8	1896	"	2756
15903	5 " William H 11	Son	8	M	1/8	1896	"	2757
15904	6 " John F 7	"	4	"	1/8	1896	"	2758
4043	7 " Mary 26	Dau	23	F	3/8	1896	"	2752
I.W. 1523	8 " Josephine 36	Wife	33	"	I.W.	1896	"	14413
15905	9 " Winnie Gertrude	Dau	2mo	F	1/8			

10 ~~Enrollment of Nos 1,2,3,4,5,6,7 and 9 cancelled by order of Department March 4, 1907~~

For child of No2 see NB #1037 (Act Apr 25'06)

11 Dec 6/99: No1-See Dawes Commission

12 record 1896,Case No760. See also Case No763 as No2   No2 Born Jan 13=05

13 ~~No.1 1885 Kiamitia No513 No8 1885 Kiamitia No514~~

14 ~~No7 also on 1896 roll, Page 67, No2819, Jackson Co.~~

15 Nos 1 to 6 inclusive were denied by Dawes Commission

16 in 1896:Choctaw case #760: no appeal

17 ~~No8 denied by Dawes Commission in 1896: Choctaw case #763: no appeal.~~

ENROLLMENT OF NOS 1 to 6 inc &9 HEREON APPROVED BY THE SECRETARY OF INTERIOR Aug 23 1905

ENROLLMENT OF NOS 8 HEREON APPROVED BY THE SECRETARY OF INTERIOR Mar 14 1906

TRIBAL ENROLLMENT OF PARENTS

	Name of Father	Year	County	Name of Mother	Year	County
1	Eli Crowder		Non Citz	Patsy Crowder	Ded	Jackson
2	No 1			No 8	No 8	
3	No 1			No 8	Granted	
4	No 1			No 8	Nov 6 – 1905	
5	No 1			No 8		
6	No 1			No 8		
7	No 1			Betsey Crowder	Dead	Jackson
8	Asa Taylor	Dead	Non Citz	Abigail Taylor	"	Non Citz
9	No 1			No 8		

10 For child of Nos 1&8 see NB (Apr 26,1906) Card No.10

11

No 1 on 1896 Roll as W.J. Crowder

12 No 4 " " " " Rosa A "

13 No 5 " " " " W.J. "

14 ~~No 6 " " " " J.F. "~~

15 ~~No 8 " " " " Dolly "~~

No.9 Enrolled Aug 12 1901

16

17 Nos 7-8 enrolled Aug 21/99

ENROLLMENT OF NOS. 7 HEREON APPROVED BY THE SECRETARY OF INTERIOR Dec 12, 1902

Date of Application for Enrollment.

May 8 '99

Nos 1,2,3,4,5,6,8 and 9 restored to roll by Departmental authority of January 19,1909 (File 5-51)

Choctaw By Blood Enrollment Cards 1898-1914

RESIDENCE: Kiamitia   COUNTY. **Choctaw Nation**   Choctaw Roll   CARD NO.

POST OFFICE: Goodland, I.T.   (Not Including Freedmen)   FIELD NO. 1450

Dawes' Roll No.	NAME		Relationship to Person	AGE	SEX	BLOOD	TRIBAL ENROLLMENT		
							Year	County	No.
4044	1 Crowder, Martin B	27	First Named	24	M	1/2	1896	Jackson	2824
4045	2 " Bessie L	24	Wife	21	F	1/2	1896	"	2825
4046	3 " Ophelia L	7	Dau	4	"	1/2	1896	"	2826
4047	4 " Benny F	5	Son	2	M	1/2			
	5								
	6								
	7								
	8	ENROLLMENT							
	9	OF NOS. 1 2 3 and 4 HEREON APPROVED BY THE SECRETARY							
	10	OF INTERIOR DEC 12 1902							
	11								
	12								
	13								
	14								
	15								
	16								
	17								

TRIBAL ENROLLMENT OF PARENTS

	Name of Father	Year	County	Name of Mother	Year	County
1	Josh. Crowder	Dead	Jackson	Sibbie Crowder	Dead	Kiamitia
2	James Spring	"	Kiamitia	Mary A. Spring	1896	Jackson
3	No 1			No 2		
4	No 1			No 2		
5						
6						
7			No 1 on 1896 roll as M.B. Crowder			
8			No 2 " 1896 " " Bessie "			
9			No 3 " 1896 " " Orprilla "			
10			For child of No. 1&2 see N.B. (Apr. 26, 1906) Card No. 86.			
11						
12						
13						
14					Date of Application for Enrollment	
15					5/8/99	
16						
17	Hugo I.T. 12/5/02					

250

Choctaw By Blood Enrollment Cards 1898-1914

RESIDENCE: Kiamitia   COUNTY.   **Choctaw Nation**   Choctaw Roll *(Not Including Freedmen)*   CARD NO.   FIELD NO. **1451**

POST OFFICE: Goodland I.T.

Dawes' Roll No.	NAME	Relationship to Person First Named	AGE	SEX	BLOOD	TRIBAL ENROLLMENT Year	County	No.
4048	1 Anderson Joe ⁴¹	First Named	38	M	Full	1896	Kiamitia	350
4049	2 " Nancy ²⁵	Wife	22	F	"	P R 1893	"	5
	3							
	4							
	5							
	6							
	7	ENROLLMENT						
	8	OF NOS. 1 and 2 HEREON APPROVED BY THE SECRETARY						
	9	OF INTERIOR DEC 12 1902						
	10							
	11							
	12							
	13							
	14							
	15							
	16							
	17							

TRIBAL ENROLLMENT OF PARENTS

	Name of Father	Year	County	Name of Mother	Year	County
1	Anderson	Dead	Kiamitia	Louisa Anderson	Dead	Kiamitia
2	Loman Lachatubbe	1896	"	Laury Lachatubbe	1896	"
3						
4						
5		No 1 enrolled on P. 1 No 4 1893 Pay Rolls		Kiamitia Co		
6		No 2 " " " 1 No 5 " " "		" "		
7						
8						
9						
10						
11						
12						
13						
14						
15						
16					5/8/99	
17	Hugo I.T. 12/5/					

251

Choctaw By Blood Enrollment Cards 1898-1914

RESIDENCE: Chickasaw Natn[sic] ~~COUNTY~~.
POST OFFICE: White, I.T.

Choctaw Nation

Choctaw Roll
(Not Including Freedmen)

CARD NO.
FIELD NO. 1452

Dawes' Roll No.	NAME	Relationship to Person First Named	AGE	SEX	BLOOD	TRIBAL ENROLLMENT		
						Year	County	No.
4050	1 Edwards, William 29	First Named	26	M	Full	1893	Blue	355
I.W. 894	2 " Donie 28	Wife	24	F	I.W			
4051	3 " Vinson 4	Son	5mo	M	1/2			
4052	4 Roebuck, William 18	Ward	15	"	Full	1896	Jackson	10887
	5							
	6							
	7	ENROLLMENT OF NOS. 1 3 and 4 HEREON APPROVED BY THE SECRETARY OF INTERIOR DEC 12 1902						
	8							
	9							
	10							
	11	ENROLLMENT OF NOS. 2 HEREON APPROVED BY THE SECRETARY OF INTERIOR AUG 3 1904						
	12							
	13							
	14							
	15							
	16							
	17							

TRIBAL ENROLLMENT OF PARENTS

	Name of Father	Year	County	Name of Mother	Year	County
1	Sam Edwards	Dead	Kiamitia	Tennessee Edwards	Dead	Kiamitia
2	Al Maxwell	1896	Non Citz	Manerva Maxwell	1896	Non Citz
3	No 1			No 2		
4	Ben Roebuck	Dead	Kiamitia	Annie Roebuck	Dead	Kiamitia
5						
6						
7	No 1 on 1893 Pay roll as William Edward, Page 34, No 355, Blue Co					
8						
9						
10	For child of Nos 1&2 see NB (Apr 26 '06) Card No 1309					
11						
12						
13						
14					Date of Application for Enrollment.	
15						
16					5/8/99	
17	Dolberg I.T. 1/1/03	No2 Evidence requested 3/28/02				

Choctaw By Blood Enrollment Cards 1898-1914

RESIDENCE: Kiamitia COUNTY. **Choctaw Nation** Choctaw Roll (*Not Including Freedmen*) CARD No.

POST OFFICE: Goodland I.T. FIELD No. 1453

NAME	Relationship to Person	AGE	SEX	BLOOD	TRIBAL ENROLLMENT		
					Year	County	No.
1 James Johnny ³³	First Named	30	M	Full	1896	Kiamitia	7078
2 Ellen	Wife	23	F	"	1896	"	4244
3							
4							
5							
6							
7	ENROLLMENT						
8	OF NOS. 1 and 2 HEREON APPROVED BY THE SECRETARY						
9	OF INTERIOR DEC 12 1902						
10							
11							
12							
13							
14							
15							
16							
17							

TRIBAL ENROLLMENT OF PARENTS

Name of Father	Year	County	Name of Mother	Year	County
1 Geo. James	Dead	Kiamitia	Mandy James	Dead	Kiamitia
2 Lone Coleman	"	"	Susie Coleman	"	"
3					
4					
5					
6	No 2 enrolled as Ellen Fulton				
7	For child of No.1 see N.B. (Apr. 26, 1906[sic]) Card No. 36				
8	No2 died January 8, 1902; proof of death filed Dec. 5, 1902				
9	No.1 is now husband of Lucy Cooper Choc 1516 12/2/02				

Date of Application for Enrollment.

May 8, 99

253

Choctaw By Blood Enrollment Cards 1898-1914

RESIDENCE: Jackson COUNTY. **Choctaw Nation** Choctaw Roll CARD NO.
POST OFFICE: Crowder, I.T. (Not Including Freedmen) FIELD NO. 1454

Dawes' Roll No.	NAME		Relationship to Person First Named	AGE	SEX	BLOOD	TRIBAL ENROLLMENT		
							Year	County	No.
4055	1 Bacon, Solomon	39	First Named	36	M	3/4	1896	Jackson	1501
4056	2 " Sinie	21	Wife	18	F	3/4	1896	"	7096
4057	3 " Devenworth	16	Son	13	M	3/4	1896	"	1503
4058	4 " Isabelle	13	Dau	10	F	3/4	1896	"	1504
4059	5 " Eliza	11	"	8	"	3/4	1896	"	1505
4060	6 " Silas	1	Son	4mo	M	3/4			
	7								
	8								
	9	ENROLLMENT							
	10	OF NOS. 12345and6 HEREON APPROVED BY THE SECRETARY							
	11	OF INTERIOR Dec 12 1902							
	12								
	13								
	14								
	15								
	16								
	17								

TRIBAL ENROLLMENT OF PARENTS

	Name of Father	Year	County	Name of Mother	Year	County
1	Thomas Bacon	Dead	Blue	Elizabeth Durant	1896	Jackson
2	William Jones	1896	Jackson	Isabelle Jones	Dead	"
3	No 1			Susan Bacon	"	"
4	No 1			" "	"	"
5	No 1			" "	"	"
6	Nº1			Nº2		
7						
8						
9						
10						
11	No2 on 1896 roll as Sinie Jones					
12	No3 " 1896 " " Deadenth Bacon					
13	No2 " 1896 " " Sinie " Page 38 No 1525, Jackson Co.					
14	No5 on 1896 roll as Eliza Bacon, Page 38 No 1531, Jackson Co					#1 to 5 inc
15						Date of Application for Enrollment.
16	Nº6 Born Feby 6, 1902: enrolled June 14, 1902					5/8/99
17						

Choctaw By Blood Enrollment Cards 1898-1914

RESIDENCE: Jackson COUNTY.
POST OFFICE: Mayhew, I.T.

Choctaw Nation

Choctaw Roll (Not Including Freedmen)

CARD NO.
FIELD NO. 1455

Dawes' Roll No.	NAME	Relationship to Person First Named	AGE	SEX	BLOOD	TRIBAL ENROLLMENT		
						Year	County	No.
4061	1 Cole, Minnie 68	First Named	65	F	Full	1896	Jackson	2722
15783	2 Tarney, Stephen 32	Grandson	32	M	"	1896	Kiamitia	12356
	3							
	4							
	5							
	6							
	7							
	8	ENROLLMENT						
	9	OF NOS. 1 HEREON APPROVED BY THE SECRETARY						
	10	OF INTERIOR DEC 12 1902						
	11							
	12	ENROLLMENT						
	13	OF NOS. 2 HEREON APPROVED BY THE SECRETARY						
	14	OF INTERIOR MAR 15 1905						
	15							
	16							
	17							

TRIBAL ENROLLMENT OF PARENTS

	Name of Father	Year	County	Name of Mother	Year	County
1	Ale-to-ko-tubbee	Dead	Bok Tuklo	Sarah	Died	in Mississippi
2	Gibson Tarney	"	" "	Minnie Tarney	"	Boktuklo[sic]
3						
4						
5						
6	No 1 on 1896 as Minnie Cole					
7	No.2 on 1896 roll as Stephen Tonitubbi					
8	No.2 on 1893 Pay Roll, Jackson Co., page 33, No. 294, as Stephen Tannitabbie No 2 also known as Stephen Cole. He is "idiotic and natural cripple" and					
9	has always lived with No.1					
10	No.2 originally listed for enrollment on Choctaw card #D145, 5/9/99. Transferred to this card Jan. 27, 1905.					
11						
12						
13						
14						
15						#1
16					Date of Application for Enrollment	5/9/99
17						

Choctaw By Blood Enrollment Cards 1898-1914

RESIDENCE: Jackson COUNTY.
POST OFFICE: Crowder, I.T.

Choctaw Nation

Choctaw Roll
(Not Including Freedmen)

CARD NO.
FIELD NO. 1456

Dawes' Roll No.	NAME		Relationship to Person	AGE	SEX	BLOOD	TRIBAL ENROLLMENT		
							Year	County	No.
4062	1 Crowder, Thomas C	57	First Named	54	M	1/4	1896	Jackson	2749
DEAD.	2 " Silva		Wife	35	F	Full	1896	"	2818
4063	3 " Green	23	Son	20	M	5/8	1896	"	2815
4064	4 " Emma	19	Dau	16	F	5/8	1896	"	2816
4065	5 DIED PRIOR TO SEPTEMBER 25, 1902 " Clay		Son	14	M	5/8	1896	"	2817
	6								
	7 No. 2 HEREON DISMISSED UNDER ORDER OF THE COMMISSION TO THE FIVE								
	8 CIVILIZED TRIBES OF MARCH 31, 1905.								
	9								
	10 ENROLLMENT								
	11 OF NOS. 1 3 4 and 5 HEREON APPROVED BY THE SECRETARY								
	12 OF INTERIOR DEC 12 1902								
	13								
	14								
	15								
	16								
	17								

TRIBAL ENROLLMENT OF PARENTS

	Name of Father	Year	County	Name of Mother	Year	County
1	Eli Crowder	Dead	Non Citz	Patsey Crowder	Dead	Jackson
2	Mason Pickens	"	Jackson	Amy Pickens	"	"
3	No1			No2		
4	No1			No2		
5	No1			No2		
6						
7			No2 on 1896 roll as Silsa Crowder			
8						
9			No 2 died April 27, 1902; proof of death filed Dec. 6, 1902.			
10			No 5 " Nov. 17, 1900; " " " " " " "			
11			No.5 died Dec. – 1901[sic]: Enrollment cancelled by Department Sept [illegible] For child of No 4 see NB (March 3, 1905) #1468			
12						
13						
14						
15						
16				DATE OF APPLICATION FOR ENROLLMENT.	5/9/99	
17						

256

Choctaw By Blood Enrollment Cards 1898-1914

Dawes' Roll No.	NAME		Relationship to Person	AGE	SEX	BLOOD	TRIBAL ENROLLMENT		
							Year	County	No.
I.W. 237	1 Ratliff, Lee U	40	First Named	36	M	I.W	1896	Kiamitia	14973
4066	2 " Sophia	28	Wife	25	F	1/2	1896	"	10813
	3								[or 16813]
	4								
	5								
	6								
	7								
	8	ENROLLMENT							
	9	OF NOS. 2 HEREON APPROVED BY THE SECRETARY							
	10	OF INTERIOR DEC 12 1902							
	11	ENROLLMENT							
	12	OF NOS. 1 HEREON APPROVED BY THE SECRETARY							
	13	OF INTERIOR SEP 12 1903							
	14								
	15								
	16								
	17								

TRIBAL ENROLLMENT OF PARENTS

	Name of Father	Year	County	Name of Mother	Year	County
1	John Ratliff	1896	Non Citz	Mary Ratliff	Dead	Non Citz
2	William Spring	1896	Kiamitia	Jane Spring	"	Kiamitia
3						
4						
5						
6						
7		No 1 on 1896 roll as Lee U. Ratlief				
8						
9						
10						
11						
12						
13						
14						
15						
16				DATE OF APPLICATION FOR ENROLLMENT	5/9/99	
17	Hugo IT 12/1/02					

257

Choctaw By Blood Enrollment Cards 1898-1914

RESIDENCE: Jackson   COUNTY. **Choctaw Nation**   Choctaw Roll   CARD NO.
POST OFFICE: Crowder, I.T.   *(Not Including Freedmen)*   FIELD NO. **1458**

Dawes' Roll No.	NAME	Relationship to Person First Named	AGE	SEX	BLOOD	TRIBAL ENROLLMENT		
						Year	County	No.
15906	1 Crowder, George W. [49]	First Named	46	M	1/4	1896	Jackson	2760
IW 1524	2 " Parlee C. [34]	Wife	30	F	I.W.	1896	"	14414
4067	3 Dowland Mattie [17]	Dau	14	"	3/8	1896	"	2765
4068	4 Crowder, Jesse [15]	Son	12	M	3/8	1896	"	2766
15907	5 " Louisa [12]	Dau	9	F	1/8	1896	"	2761
15908	6 " Joe [10]	Son	7	M	1/8	1896	"	2762
15909	7 " Belzori [6]	Dau	3	F	1/8	1896	"	2763
15910	8 " Willie [4]	Son	7mo	M	1/8			

9

ENROLLMENT
OF NOS. 3 and 4 HEREON
APPROVED BY THE SECRETARY
OF INTERIOR Dec. 12 1902

For child of Nos 1&2 see NB(Apr.26'06) Card #9
" " " " 3 " " " " " #346
" " " " 4 " " " " " #404

No8 Affidavit of birth to be
supplied:-Recd May 23/99   No1 – see Dawes Commission record
No 1 1885 Kiamitia No 509   1896, Case No 712, Dec 6/99
Dec 6/99. See Dawes Com.
record 1896, Case 699 – as to No2   ENROLLMENT
Crowder I.T. 12/8/02   OF NOS. ~~~ 2 ~~~ HEREON
APPROVED BY THE SECRETARY
OF INTERIOR Mar 14 1906

Nos1,2,5,6,6&8 restored to roll by Departmental authority of January 5,1909 (File 5-51)

TRIBAL ENROLLMENT OF PARENTS

	Name of Father	Year	County	Name of Mother	Year	County
1	Eli E Crowder	Dead	Non Citz	Patsey Crowder	Dead	Jackson
2	William Wallace	"	" "	Liasa Wallace	"	Non Citz
3	No 1			Roseann Crowder	"	Jackson
4	No 1			" "	"	"
5	No 1			No 2		
6	No 1			No 2		
7	No 1			No 2		
8	No 1			No 2		
9						
10						

ENROLLMENT
OF NOS. 1,5,6,7 & 8 HEREON
APPROVED BY THE SECRETARY
OF INTERIOR Aug 23 1905

11 No1 on 1896 Roll as G.W. Crowder
12 No2 " 1896 " " Pairlee "
13 No4 " 1896 " " Jessie "
    No5 " 1896 " " Liza "
14 No7 " 1896 " " Melzori "
15 Nº3 is now the wife of Frank Dowland on Choctaw
16 card #5706
17 P.O. Boswell I.T. /05

Date of Application for Enrollment.
May 9/99
No 2 enrolled June 15/99
no ticket issued

Over [No more information given]

Enrollment of Nos.1,2,5,6,7 and 8 cancelled by order of Department March 4, 1907

Choctaw By Blood Enrollment Cards 1898-1914

RESIDENCE: Jackson COUNTY. **Choctaw Nation** **Choctaw Roll** CARD NO.

POST OFFICE: Jackson, I.T. *(Not Including Freedmen)* FIELD NO. **1459**

Dawes' Roll No.		NAME		Relationship to Person First Named	AGE	SEX	BLOOD	TRIBAL ENROLLMENT		
								Year	County	No.
15911	1	Crowder, Van	59	First Named	56	M	1/4	1896	Jackson	2748
4069	2	" Louisa	55	Wife	52	F	1/2	1896	"	2813
4070	3	" Alice	14	Dau	11	"	3/8	1896	"	2814
	4									
	5									
	6									
	7									
	8									
	9	ENROLLMENT								
	10	OF NOS. 2 and 3 HEREON APPROVED BY THE SECRETARY								
	11	OF INTERIOR Dec 12 1902								
	12									
	13	ENROLLMENT								
	14	OF NOS. One HEREON APPROVED BY THE SECRETARY								
	15	OF INTERIOR Aug 23 1905								
	16									
	17									

TRIBAL ENROLLMENT OF PARENTS

	Name of Father	Year	County	Name of Mother	Year	County
1	Eli W. Crowder	Dead	Non Citz	Patsey Crowder	Dead	Jackson
2	Wᵐ Pitchlynn	"	Tobucksy	Rhoda Pitchlynn	"	Skullyville
3	No 1			No 2		
4						
5	No1 restored to roll by Departmental authority of January 19, 1909 (File 5-51)					
6	Enrollment of No.1 cancelled by order of Department March 4, 1907					
7	No.1 on 1885 Choctaw Census Roll Kiamitia County, No. 632.					
8	No3 on 1896 roll as Ellen Crowder					
9						
10	Denied Dec. 6/99. See Dawes Commission					
11	record 1896. Case 749, as to No1 – no appeal Papers sent to court thro' error					
12	No.1 originally listed hereon as Robert Crowder					
13	No.1 denied in 1896 as Robert Crowder Choctaw citizenship case No. 749					
14	For child of No 3 see N B (Mar 3 '05) #448					
15					Date of Application for Enrollment	
16	P.O. Boswell I.T. 9/6 – 04.					
17	Crowder I.T. 12/18/02					

259

Choctaw By Blood Enrollment Cards 1898-1914

RESIDENCE: Kiamitia COUNTY.   **Choctaw Nation**   Choctaw Roll *(Not Including Freedmen)*   CARD NO.
POST OFFICE: Goodland, I.T.   FIELD NO. **1460**

Dawes' Roll No.	NAME		Relationship to Person First Named	AGE	SEX	BLOOD	TRIBAL ENROLLMENT		
							Year	County	No.
4071	1 Oakes, Lemuel W	45	First Named	42	M	1/8	1896	Kiamitia	9942
I.W. 238	2 " Lucy E.	40	Wife	36	F	I.W.	1896	"	14911
4072	3 " Clarence A	19	Son	16	M	1/16	1896	"	9945
4073	4 " Frank	17	"	14	"	1/16	1896	"	9946
4074	5 " Mattie	15	Dau	12	F	1/16	1896	"	9947
4075	6 " Nola	13	"	10	"	1/16	1896	"	9948
4076	7 " Nona M.	11	"	8	"	1/16	1896	"	P.R. 534
	8								
	9								
	10	ENROLLMENT OF NOS. 1 3 4 5 6 and 7 HEREON APPROVED BY THE SECRETARY OF INTERIOR Dec 12 1902							
	11								
	12								
	13								
	14	ENROLLMENT OF NOS. 2 HEREON APPROVED BY THE SECRETARY OF INTERIOR Sep 12 1903							
	15								
	16								
	17								

TRIBAL ENROLLMENT OF PARENTS

	Name of Father	Year	County	Name of Mother	Year	County
1	Thos. W. Oakes	Dead	Non Citz	Harriet N. Oakes	1896	Kiamitia
2	Henry Smith	"	" "	Sarah Smith	Dead	Non Citz
3	No 1			No 2		
4	No 1			No 2		
5	No 1			No 2		
6	No 1			No 2		
7	No 1			No 2		
8						
9	No7 on 1893 Pay roll as Nona Oakes Page 66 No 534. Kiamitia County					
10						
11	For child of No.5 see NB (March 3, 1905) #1157					
12	Evidence of marriage of Nos 1 and 2 filed Dec 6, 1902					
13	No5 is now married to Joseph Collins Choc. #5634					
14	Evidence of marriage filed this day 12/3/02					
15					Date of Application for Enrollment.	
16					5/9/99	
17	Hugo I.T. 12/1/02					

260

Choctaw By Blood Enrollment Cards 1898-1914

RESIDENCE: Kiamitia COUNTY.
POST OFFICE: Grant, I.T.

Choctaw Nation

Choctaw Roll
(Not Including Freedmen)

CARD NO.
FIELD NO. **1461**

Dawes' Roll No.	NAME	Relationship to Person	AGE	SEX	BLOOD	TRIBAL ENROLLMENT		
						Year	County	No.
4077	1 Frederick, Mary E. ²⁹	First Named	26	F	3/4	1896	Kiamitia	4254
4078	2 " Nola ⁶	Dau	3	"	3/8	1896	"	4260
4079	3 ~~Richard J.~~ DIED PRIOR TO SEPTEMBER 25, 1902	Son	2mo	M	3/8			
4080	4 McCoy, Alex ¹⁰	"	7	"	3/8	1896	Kiamitia	9387
4081	5 Frederick Elbert ¹	Son	3mo	M	3/8			
	6							
	7							
	8	ENROLLMENT OF NOS. 1 2 3 4 and 5 HEREON APPROVED BY THE SECRETARY OF INTERIOR Dec 12 1902						
	9							
	10							
	11							
	12							
	13							
	14							
	15							
	16							
	17							

TRIBAL ENROLLMENT OF PARENTS

	Name of Father	Year	County	Name of Mother	Year	County
1	Tom Spring	1896	Kiamitia	Annie Spring	Dead	Kiamitia
2	T.G. Frederick	1896	Non Citz	No 1		
3	" "	1896	" "	No 1		
4	Chris McCoy	Dead	Kiamitia	No 1		
5	Tom Frederick		non citizen	No 1		
6						
7			No 1 on 1896 roll as Ella Frederick			
8			No 2 " 1896 " " Nola "			
9						
10			No 3 Affidavit of birth to be supplied. Recd May 12/99			
11			No 5 Born June 20 1902, enrolled Sept. 18, 1902.			
12		No.3 died Sept. 27, 1900: Enrollment cancelled by Department July 8, 1904				
13						
14					Date of Application for Enrollment.	
15						
16					For Nos 1 to 4 Incl. 5/9/99	
17						

261

Choctaw By Blood Enrollment Cards 1898-1914

RESIDENCE: **Jackson** COUNTY.   **Choctaw Nation**   **Choctaw Roll**   CARD NO.

POST OFFICE: **Mayhew, I.T.**   *(Not Including Freedmen)*   FIELD NO. **1462**

Dawes' Roll No.	NAME	Relationship to Person First Named	AGE	SEX	BLOOD	TRIBAL ENROLLMENT Year	County	No.
4082	1 Gardner, Zachariah 31	First Named	28	M	Full	1893	Jackson	296
D.P.	2 " Edna Harriet	Dau	2½	F	1/2			
	3							
	4							
	5							
	6	ENROLLMENT						
	7	OF NOS. 1 HEREON APPROVED BY THE SECRETARY						
	8	OF INTERIOR Dec 12 1902						
	9							
	10							
	11							
	12							
	13							
	14							
	15							
	16							
	17							

TRIBAL ENROLLMENT OF PARENTS

	Name of Father	Year	County	Name of Mother	Year	County
1	Edmund Gardner	1896	Kiamitia	Lucy Gardner	Dead	Jackson
2	No 1			Florence R Gardner		White woman
3						
4	On 1893 Pay roll as Sick Gardner, Page 34, No 296 Jackson Co.					
5						
6	N°2 Born June 16, 1900. Enrolled Dec 24, 1902.					
7	Evidence of marriage of parents of No2 to be supplied. Requested Nov. 22, 1903					
8	#2 Refused Feb 21 1907 Action approved by Mar 4 – 1907			" March 25 1904		
9	Secretary of Interior			" Aug 10 1904 Also		
10	Notice of Departmental action forwarded Attorneys for Choctaw					
11	and Chickasaw Nations Apr 5 – 1907			Apr 5-1907		
12	Notice of Departmental action forwarded Attorney for Applicant					
13	Notice of Departmental action mailed applicant Apr 5 – 1907					
14					Date of Application for Enrollment.	
15	Franks I.T. 8/19/04					
16	P.O. McAlester IT				5/9/99	
17						

262

Choctaw By Blood Enrollment Cards 1898-1914

No.3 P.O. Graham I.T. 3/27/05

RESIDENCE: Jackson　　　COUNTY.　**Choctaw Nation**　**Choctaw Roll**　CARD NO.
POST OFFICE: Crowder, I.T.　　*(Not Including Freedmen)*　FIELD NO.　**1463**

Dawes' Roll No.	NAME	Relationship to Person First Named	AGE	SEX	BLOOD	TRIBAL ENROLLMENT		
						Year	County	No.
4083	₁ Going, James	First Named	43	M	3/4	1896	Jackson	4844
15399	₂ " Zarabelle	Wife	33	F	1/4	1896	"	4845
4084	₃ " Frances	Dau	14	"	1/2	1896	"	4848
4085	₄ " Rosie	"	12	"	1/2	1896	"	4847
4086	₅ " Jim	Son	10	M	1/2	1896	"	4849
4087	₆ " David	"	8	"	1/2	1896	"	4850
4088	₇ " Thomas	"	5	"	1/2	1896	"	4851
4089	₈ ~~Gibson~~ (DIED PRIOR TO SEPTEMBER 25, 1902)	"	1	"	1/2			
4090	₉ " Frank	Son	1	"	1/2			
	₁₀ No 8 Affidavit of birth to be							
	₁₁ supplied. Rec'd May 17/99							
	₁₂							
No 2	Admitted in 1896 by Dawes Commission							
	as Ziarriabelle Gowens Choctaw Case #994							
	No appeal.							
	₁₅							
	₁₆ No.8 died Dec-1899: proof of							
	₁₇ death filed Dec. 8, 1902							

ENROLLMENT
OF NOS. 1345678and9 HEREON
APPROVED BY THE SECRETARY
OF INTERIOR Dec 12 1902

TRIBAL ENROLLMENT OF PARENTS

	Name of Father	Year	County	Name of Mother	Year	County
₁	Gibson Going	Dead	Jackson	Sokey Going	Decd	Jackson
₂	Tour Crowder	1896	"	Flora Crowder	"	"
₃	No 1			No.2		
₄	No 1			No 2		
₅	No 1		ENROLLMENT	No 2		
₆	No 1		OF NOS. ~~~2~~~ HEREON	No 2		
₇	No 1		APPROVED BY THE SECRETARY OF INTERIOR May 9 1904	No 2		
₈	~~No 1~~			~~No 2~~		
₉	No 1			No 2		

No.2 on 1896 roll as Isabelle Goings }
No.7 " 1896 " " Tommie " }
Surnames appear on 1896 roll as Goings }

No.2 has never applied as Cherokee
nor is her name on any Cherokee roll
See letter of Cherokee Land Office
of December 12, 1903

Mother of No.2, Cherokee Citz. recognized as such. She, No.2,
always resided in Choctaw Nation after her marriage. Said
not to be registered in Cherokee Nation. See if correct No.[sic]
No.8 Enrolled Sept. 4, 1901

For child of No 3 see NB(Mar-3'-05) #505
" " " Nos1&2 " " " " " #1046

#1 to 8
Date of Application for Enrollment.
5/9/99

(5/22/08 P.O. Boswell I.T.)

No.8 died Feb.8,1900: Enrollment cancelled by Department July 8, 1904

263

Choctaw By Blood Enrollment Cards 1898-1914

RESIDENCE: Towson COUNTY.
POST OFFICE: Doaksville, I.T.

Choctaw Nation

Choctaw Roll
(Not Including Freedmen)

CARD NO.
FIELD NO. 1464

Dawes' Roll No.	NAME	Relationship to Person	AGE	SEX	BLOOD	TRIBAL ENROLLMENT		
						Year	County	No.
I.W.239	1 Self, William D. 27	First Named	25	M	I.W.			
4091	2 Ellie [DIED PRIOR TO SEPTEMBER 25, 1902]	Wife	24	F	3/4	1896	Kiamitia	4225
	3							
	4							
	5							
	6							
	7							
	8	ENROLLMENT						
	9	OF NOS. 2 HEREON APPROVED BY THE SECRETARY						
	10	OF INTERIOR DEC 12 1902						
	11	ENROLLMENT						
	12	OF NOS. 1 HEREON APPROVED BY THE SECRETARY						
	13	OF INTERIOR SEP 12 1903						
	14							
	15							
	16							
	17							

TRIBAL ENROLLMENT OF PARENTS

	Name of Father	Year	County	Name of Mother	Year	County
1	William Self	1896	Non Citz	Caroline Self	1896	Non Citz
2	M.H. Fisher	1896	Kiamitia	Sillen Fisher	1896	Kiamitia
3						
4						
5						
6		No2 on 1896 roll as Ellie Fisher				
7						
8		No 2 died April 6, 1901; proof of death filed Dec 5, 1902				
9		No.2 died April 6, 1901: Enrollment cancelled by Department [illegible]				
10						
11						
12						
13						
14						
15						
16					Date of Application for Enrollment.	5/9/99
17	Spencerville I.T.					

264

Choctaw By Blood Enrollment Cards 1898-1914

RESIDENCE: Kiamitia COUNTY. **Choctaw Nation** Choctaw Roll CARD NO.
POST OFFICE: Goodland, I.T. *(Not Including Freedmen)* FIELD NO. **1465**

Dawes' Roll No.	NAME	Relationship to Person First Named	AGE	SEX	BLOOD	TRIBAL ENROLLMENT Year	County	No.
4092	₁ Roebuck, Malina 57	First Named	54	F	7/8	1896	Kiamitia	10815
4093	₂ " Willie 19	Son	16	M	7/8	1896	"	10817
4094	₃ " Zack 20	G.Son	17	"	3/4	1896	Wade	9253
DEAD	Yale, Jackson DEAD	Ward	18	"	3/4	1893	Blue	39
I.W. 811	₅ Roebuck Minnie (21)	Wife of No 2	21	F	I.W.			
	6							
	7 ENROLLMENT							
	8 OF NOS. 1 2 and 3 HEREON APPROVED BY THE SECRETARY							
	9 OF INTERIOR Dec 12 1902							
	10							
	11 ENROLLMENT							
	12 OF NOS. 5 HEREON APPROVED BY THE SECRETARY							
	13 OF INTERIOR May 21 1904							
	14 No. 4 hereon dismissed under order of							
	15 the Commission to the Five Civilized							
	16 Tribes of March 31, 1905.							
	17							

TRIBAL ENROLLMENT OF PARENTS

Name of Father	Year	County	Name of Mother	Year	County
₁ Louis Austin	Dead	Gaines	Mollie Austin	Dead	Gaines
₂ David Roebuck	"	Kiamitia	No 1		
₃ Chas Koneubbee	"	"	Mary Koneubbee	Dead	Kiamitia
₄ Umphus Yale	"	"	Adeline Yale	"	"
₅ Zack Isabell		noncitizen	Alice Isabell		noncitizen
6					
7 No5 transferred from Choctaw card D783, April 15, 1904					
8 See decision of March 15, 1904.					
9					
10 No3 on 1896 roll as Zack Moody					
11 No4 " 1893 Payroll, Page 119, No 39, Blue County					
12 No1 " 1896 roll as Malina A. Roebuck					
No4 Died July 4 1900: proof of death filed Sept. 18, 1902.					
13 N°2 is now the husband of Minnie Roebuck on Choctaw card #D783 Sept 3, 1902					
14 Child of No3 on NB (Apr 26 06) Card #303					
15 " " No2 " " " " " " #418			Date of Application for Enrollment.		
16			Nos 1 to 4 5/9/99		
17					

P.O. of No 2 Hugo I.T. Dec 1ˢᵗ '03.

Choctaw By Blood Enrollment Cards 1898-1914

RESIDENCE: Kiamitia COUNTY.
POST OFFICE: Nelson, I.T.

Choctaw Nation

Choctaw Roll
(Not Including Freedmen)

CARD NO.
FIELD NO. **1466**

Dawes' Roll No.	NAME	Relationship to Person First Named	AGE	SEX	BLOOD	TRIBAL ENROLLMENT Year	County	No.
4095	1 Homer, Silan	36 First Named	33	M	Full	1896	Kiamitia	5774
4096	2 , Annie (DIED PRIOR TO SEPTEMBER 25, 1902)	Wife	40	F	"	1896	"	5775
	3							
	4							
	5							
	6							
	7							
	8							
	9							
	10							
	11	ENROLLMENT OF NOS. 1 and 2 HEREON APPROVED BY THE SECRETARY OF INTERIOR Dec. 12, 1902						
	12							
	13							
	14							
	15							
	16							
	17							

TRIBAL ENROLLMENT OF PARENTS

	Name of Father	Year	County	Name of Mother	Year	County
1	Chubby Homer	Dead	Jacks Fork	Eau-la-tema	Dead	Jacks Fork
2	Capt Okchiya	"			"	
3						
4						
5						
6						
7						
8	No.2 died Dec - 1900: Enrollment cancelled by Department July 8, 1904					
9	No2 died Dec. - 1900: Proof of death filed Dec 5, 1902					
10	No1 is now husband of Sissie Lohen, a Cherokee: evidence of					
11	marriage filed December 15, 1902. Enrolled As Sissy Homer, No.3 on Choctaw Card #1621 approved roll Number #[sic] 16204.					
12	For child of No1 see NB (March 3,1905) #1072.					
13						
14						
15						
16					Date of Application for Enrollment 5/9/99	
17						

266

Choctaw By Blood Enrollment Cards 1898-1914

RESIDENCE: Kiamitia   COUNTY.   **Choctaw Nation**   Choctaw Roll   CARD No.
POST OFFICE: Goodland, I.T.   *(Not Including Freedmen)*   FIELD No. **1467**

Dawes' Roll No.	NAME	Relationship to Person	AGE	SEX	BLOOD	TRIBAL ENROLLMENT Year	County	No.
4097	1 Oakes, Thomas E. 55	First Named	52	M	1/8	1896	Kiamitia	9949
4098	2 " , Margaret J. 49	Wife	46	F	1/2	1896	"	9950
4099	3 " , Daniel W. 28	Son	25	M	5/16	1896	"	9951
4100	4 " , Thomas J. 22	"	19	"	5/16	1896	"	9952
4101	5 " , Susan 20	Dau	17	F	5/16	1896	"	9953
4102	6 " , Rosa 13	"	10	"	5/16	1896	"	9954
4103	7 " , Edgar O. 11	Son	8	M	5/16	1896	"	9955
	8							
	9							
	10	ENROLLMENT OF NOS. 123456and7 HEREON APPROVED BY THE SECRETARY OF INTERIOR Dec 12, 1902						
	11							
	12							
	13							
	14							
	15							
	16							
	17							

TRIBAL ENROLLMENT OF PARENTS

	Name of Father	Year	County	Name of Mother	Year	County
1	Thos. W. Oakes	Dead	Non Citz	Harriet N. Oakes	1896	Kiamitia
2	Calvin Ervin	"	" "	Sally Ervin	Dead	Towson
3	No 1			No 2		
4	No 1			No 2		
5	No 1			No 2		
6	No 1			No 2		
7	No 1			No 2		
8						
9	No 3 on 1896 roll as Dan W. Oakes.					
10	No 4 " 1896 " " Thos. J. "					
11	No.3 is now the husband of Mary A. Freeney on Choctaw card #3897, Aug 24, 1901					
12	For child of No3 see NB (March 3, 1905) Card #572.					
13						
14					Date of Application for Enrollment.	
15						
16	Hugo, I.T. 12/3/02				5/9/99	
17						

267

Choctaw By Blood Enrollment Cards 1898-1914

RESIDENCE: Kiamitia   COUNTY.   **Choctaw Nation**   Choctaw Roll   CARD NO.

POST OFFICE: Goodland, I.T.   *(Not Including Freedmen)*   FIELD NO. 1468

Dawes' Roll No.	NAME	Relationship to Person First Named	AGE	SEX	BLOOD	TRIBAL ENROLLMENT		
						Year	County	No.
4104	1 Oakes, Susan M 25	First Named	22	F	5/16	1896	Kiamitia	9977
	2							
	3							
	4							
	5							
	6							
	7							
	8							
	9							
	10							
	11							
	12							
	13							
	14							
	15							
	16							
	17							

ENROLLMENT
OF NOS. 1 HEREON
APPROVED BY THE SECRETARY
OF INTERIOR DEC 12 1902

TRIBAL ENROLLMENT OF PARENTS

	Name of Father	Year	County	Name of Mother	Year	County
1	C.D. Oakes	1896	Kiamitia	Judie Oakes	Dead	Kiamitia
2						
3						
4						
5		No 1 is now wife of Dr Ben L Denison (White) Garvin I.T.				
6		For child of No.1 see NB (March 3,1905) #972				
7						
8						
9						
10						
11						
12						
13					Date of Application for Enrollment.	
14						
15						
16					Date of Application for Enrollment	5/9/99
17						

Choctaw By Blood Enrollment Cards 1898-1914

RESIDENCE: Kiamitia COUNTY. **Choctaw Nation** Choctaw Roll CARD NO.
POST OFFICE: Frogville, I.T. (Not Including Freedmen) FIELD NO. 1469

Dawes' Roll No.	NAME	Relationship to Person	AGE	SEX	BLOOD	TRIBAL ENROLLMENT		
						Year	County	No.
4105	1 Oakes, Harriet N 78	First Named	75	F	1/4	1896	Kiamitia	9975
	2							
	3							
	4							
	5							
	6							
	7							
	8							
	9							
	10							
	11	ENROLLMENT OF NOS. 1 HEREON						
	12	APPROVED BY THE SECRETARY						
	13	OF INTERIOR DEC 12 1902						
	14							
	15							
	16							
	17							

TRIBAL ENROLLMENT OF PARENTS

	Name of Father	Year	County	Name of Mother	Year	County
1	Thos. Everidge	Dead	Non Citz	Eve Everidge	Dead	Kiamitia
2						
3						
4						
5						
6						
7						
8						
9						
10						
11						
12						
13						
14						
15				Date of Application for Enrollment.		
16				5/9/99		
17						

Choctaw By Blood Enrollment Cards 1898-1914

RESIDENCE: Kiamitia	COUNTY.	Choctaw Nation	Choctaw Roll	CARD NO.
POST OFFICE: Goodland, I.T.			(Not Including Freedmen)	FIELD NO. 1470

Dawes' Roll No.		NAME		Relationship to Person	AGE	SEX	BLOOD	TRIBAL ENROLLMENT		
								Year	County	No.
4106	1	Martin, Rogers	15	First Named	12	M	Full	1896	Kiamitia	8699
	2									
	3									
	4									
	5									
	6									
	7									
	8									
	9									
	10									
	11									
	12									
	13									
	14									
	15									
	16									
	17									

ENROLLMENT
OF NOS. 1 HEREON
APPROVED BY THE SECRETARY
OF INTERIOR DEC 12 1902

TRIBAL ENROLLMENT OF PARENTS

	Name of Father	Year	County	Name of Mother	Year	County
1	John Martin	Dead	Kiamitia	Lucy Martin	Dead	Kiamitia
2						
3						
4						
5						
6						
7						
8						
9						
10						
11						
12						
13						
14				Date of Application for Enrollment.		
15						
16					5/9/99	
17						

270

Choctaw By Blood Enrollment Cards 1898-1914

RESIDENCE: Kiamitia   COUNTY.   **Choctaw Nation**   **Choctaw Roll**   CARD NO.

POST OFFICE: Grant, I.T.   *(Not Including Freedmen)*   FIELD NO. 1471

Dawes' Roll No.	NAME		Relationship to Person	AGE	SEX	BLOOD	TRIBAL ENROLLMENT		
							Year	County	No.
4107	1 Hayes, Lucy	55	First Named	52	F	Full	1896	Kiamitia	5785
	2								
	3								
	4								
	5								
	6								
	7								
	8								
	9								
	10								
	11	ENROLLMENT							
	12	OF NOS. 1 HEREON APPROVED BY THE SECRETARY							
	13	OF INTERIOR DEC 12 1902							
	14								
	15								
	16								
	17								

TRIBAL ENROLLMENT OF PARENTS

	Name of Father	Year	County	Name of Mother	Year	County
1	Wallace Byington	Dead	Kiamitia	Hannah Byington	Dead	Kiamitia
2						
3						
4						
5						
6						
7						
8						
9						
10						
11						
12						
13						
14						
15				Date of Application for Enrollment.		
16				5/9/99		
17						

Choctaw By Blood Enrollment Cards 1898-1914

RESIDENCE: Kiamitia COUNTY.
POST OFFICE: Goodland, I.T.

Choctaw Nation

Choctaw Roll *(Not Including Freedmen)*

CARD NO.
FIELD NO. 1472

Dawes' Roll No.	NAME	Relationship to Person First Named	AGE	SEX	BLOOD	TRIBAL ENROLLMENT		
						Year	County	No.
4108	1 Roberts, Mollie 20	First Named	17	F	1/4	1896	Kiamitia	336
4109	2 Roberts, Beulah May 1	Dau	2mo	F	1/8			
	3							
	4							
	5							
	6							
	7	ENROLLMENT OF NOS. 1 and 2 HEREON						
	8	APPROVED BY THE SECRETARY						
	9	OF INTERIOR DEC 12 1902						
	10							
	11							
	12							
	13 For child of No1 see NB (Apr 26-06) Card #479							
	14							
	15							
	16							
	17							

TRIBAL ENROLLMENT OF PARENTS

	Name of Father	Year	County	Name of Mother	Year	County
1	Wesley Anderson	Dead	Non Citz	Patsey Taylor	1896	Kiamitia
2	A.L. Roberts		" "	No. 1		
3						
4						
5						
6	On 1896 roll as Mollie Anderson					
7						
8	No1 now the wife of AL. Roberts, non-citizen. Evidence of marriage requested 7/14/02. Filed July 31, 1902.					
9	No.2 Born May 12" 1902: Enrolled July 14" 1902.					
10						
11						
12						
13						
14						
15						
16				Date of Application for Enrollment	5/9/99	
17	Hart I.T.					

272

Choctaw By Blood Enrollment Cards 1898-1914

RESIDENCE: Kiamitia COUNTY.
POST OFFICE: Grant, I.T.

Choctaw Nation

Choctaw Roll
(Not Including Freedmen)

CARD NO.
FIELD NO. 1473

Dawes' Roll No.	NAME	Relationship to Person First Named	AGE	SEX	BLOOD	TRIBAL ENROLLMENT		
						Year	County	No.
4110	1 Houston, Beckie DIED PRIOR TO SEPTEMBER 25, 1902		85	F	Full	1896	Kiamitia	5760
	2							
	3							
	4							
	5							
	6	ENROLLMENT						
	7	OF NOS. 1 HEREON APPROVED BY THE SECRETARY						
	8	OF INTERIOR DEC 12 1902						
	9							
	10							
	11							
	12							
	13							
	14							
	15							
	16							
	17							

TRIBAL ENROLLMENT OF PARENTS

Name of Father	Year	County	Name of Mother	Year	County
1 Che-le-tubbee		Died in Mississippi		Dead	
2					
3					
4					
5					
6		On 1896 roll as Mrs. Houston			
7		No. 1 died October 8, 1899; Enrollment cancelled by [illegible]			
8					
9					
10					
11					
12					
13					
14					
15					
16				Date of Application for Enrollment	5/9/99
17					

Choctaw By Blood Enrollment Cards 1898-1914

RESIDENCE: **Kiamitia** COUNTY. **Choctaw Nation** Choctaw Roll CARD NO.
POST OFFICE: Grant, I.T. *(Not Including Freedmen)* FIELD NO. 1474

Dawes' Roll No.	NAME		Relationship to Person First Named	AGE	SEX	BLOOD	TRIBAL ENROLLMENT		
							Year	County	No.
4111	1 Williams, Tobias	DIED PRIOR TO SEPTEMBER 25, 1902	Named	31	M	Full	1893	Kiamitia	834
4112	2 " Winey	46	Wife	43	F	"	1893	"	867
4113	3 " Jincy	10	Dau	7	F	"	1896	"	13725
4114	4 " Eli	8	Ward	5	M	"	1896	"	13728
	5								
	6								
	7	ENROLLMENT OF NOS. 1 2 3 and 4 HEREON							
	8	APPROVED BY THE SECRETARY							
	9	OF INTERIOR DEC 12 1902							
	10								
	11								
	12								
	13								
	14								
	15								
	16								
	17								

TRIBAL ENROLLMENT OF PARENTS

	Name of Father	Year	County	Name of Mother	Year	County
1	Billy William	Dead	Kiamitia	Lidia Foster	Dead	Kiamitia
2	John Candy	"	"	Beckie Houston	1896	"
3	No 1			No 2		
4	Eastman Williams	Dead	Kiamitia	Eliz. Williams	Dead	Kiamitia
5						
6	No 1 on 1893 Pay roll, Page 102, No 834, Kiamitia Co. as Tobias William					
7	No 2 " 1893 " " " 105, No 867 " " " Viney Williams					
8	No.2 also on 1896 Choctaw census roll, Kiamitia County; No.13724 as Willie Williams					
9	No.1 died Feb 12, 1900; proof of death filed Dec 5, 1902					
10	No 2 now wife of Israel Gardner Choc #1436					
11	No.1 died Feb. 12, 1900; Enrollment cancelled by Department [illegible]					
12						
13						
14					Date of Application for Enrollment.	
15						
16					5/9/99	
17						

Choctaw By Blood Enrollment Cards 1898-1914

RESIDENCE: Kiamitia   COUNTY.   **Choctaw Nation**   **Choctaw Roll**   CARD NO.
POST OFFICE: Grant, I.T.   (Not Including Freedmen)   FIELD NO. **1475**

Dawes' Roll No.	NAME	Relationship to Person	AGE	SEX	BLOOD	TRIBAL ENROLLMENT		
						Year	County	No.
4115	1 Ervin, Nellie ²⁸	First Named	25	F	5/8	1896	Kiamitia	3793
4116	2 " , James ⁶	Son	3	M	5/16	1896	"	3795
4117	3 " , Mary ⁴	Dau	1	F	5/16			
	4							
	5							
	6							
	7							
	8							
	9	ENROLLMENT OF NOS. 1 2 and 3 HEREON APPROVED BY THE SECRETARY OF INTERIOR Dec. 2, 1902						
	10							
	11							
	12							
	13							
	14							
	15							
	16							
	17							

TRIBAL ENROLLMENT OF PARENTS

	Name of Father	Year	County	Name of Mother	Year	County
1	James Spring	Dead	Kiamitia	Mary Spring now Crowder	1896	Jackson
2	William Ervin	1896	Non Citz	No 1		
3	" "	1896	" "	No 1		
4						
5						
6						
7	No2 on 1896 roll as Jimmie Ervin					
8	For child of No.1 see NB (March 3,1905) #1190					
9						
10						
11						
12						
13						
14					Date of Application for Enrollment.	
15						
16					5/9/99	
17	Hugo I.T. 12/2/02					

Choctaw By Blood Enrollment Cards 1898-1914

RESIDENCE: Blue COUNTY.
POST OFFICE: Bennington, I.T.

Choctaw Nation

Choctaw Roll
(Not Including Freedmen)

CARD NO.
FIELD NO. 1476

Dawes' Roll No.	NAME		Relationship to Person	AGE	SEX	BLOOD	TRIBAL ENROLLMENT		
							Year	County	No.
4118	1 Fry, Samuel	33	First Named	30	M	Full	1896	Blue	4379
4119	2 " , Sophia	23	Wife	20	F	"	1896	"	4380
4120	3 " , Joseph	7	Son	4	M	"	1896	"	4381
4121	4 " , Cornelia	4	Dau	10mo	F	"			
14668	5 Homer, Solomon	2	son of No2	21mo	M	"			
	6								
	7								
	8								
	9	ENROLLMENT							
	10	OF NOS. 1 2 3 and 4 HEREON APPROVED BY THE SECRETARY							
	11	OF INTERIOR Dec 12, 1902							
	12								
	13	ENROLLMENT							
	14	OF NOS. 5 HEREON APPROVED BY THE SECRETARY							
	15	OF INTERIOR May 20, 1903							
	16								
	17								

TRIBAL ENROLLMENT OF PARENTS

	Name of Father	Year	County	Name of Mother	Year	County
1	Billy Fry	1896	Blue	Wisey Fry	1896	Blue
2	Solomon Yale	Dead	Jackson	Winey Williams	1896	Kiamitia
3	No 1			No 2		
4	No 1			No 2		
5	Dana Homer	1896	Blue	No 2		
6						
7						
8	No2 on 1896 roll as Sophie Fry					
9	No5 Born March 8, 1901. Enrolled Dec. 22, 1902.					
10	No5 is illegitimate					
11						
12						
13						
14					#1 to 4 inc	
15					Date of Application for Enrollment.	
16					5/9/99	
17						

Choctaw By Blood Enrollment Cards 1898-1914

RESIDENCE: Kiamitia   COUNTY.

POST OFFICE: Goodland, I.T.

Choctaw Nation

Choctaw Roll
(Not Including Freedmen)

CARD NO.

FIELD NO.   1477

Dawes' Roll No.	NAME		Relationship to Person First Named	AGE	SEX	BLOOD	TRIBAL ENROLLMENT		
							Year	County	No.
4122	1 Willis, Elmira	33	First Named	30	F	Full	1896	Kiamitia	13717
4123	2 Coston, Lina	12	Dau	9	"	1/2	1896	"	2683
4124	3 Willis, Irena	9	"	6	"	3/4	1896	"	13718
4125	4 " Jimmy	7	Son	4	M	3/4	1896	"	13719
14669	5 " Thomas	3	Son	2 10/mo	M	3/4			
	6								
	7								
	8	ENROLLMENT							
	9	OF NOS. 1 2 3 and 4 HEREON APPROVED BY THE SECRETARY							
	10	OF INTERIOR DEC 12 1902							
	11								
	12	ENROLLMENT							
	13	OF NOS. 5 HEREON APPROVED BY THE SECRETARY							
	14	OF INTERIOR MAY 20 1903							
	15								
	16								
	17								

TRIBAL ENROLLMENT OF PARENTS

	Name of Father	Year	County	Name of Mother	Year	County
1	Jim Willis	Dead	Kiamitia	Minney Willis	Dead	Kiamitia
2	Tom Coston	1896	Non Citz	No 1		
3	Epriam Roebuck	Dead	Kiamitia	No 1		
4	" "	"	"	No 1		
5	Unknown			Nº 1		
6						
7						
8						
9						
10						
11	Nº 5 Born Dec 12, 1899, enrolled Oct. 20, 1902					
12	For child of No.1 see NB (March 3, 1905) #1099					
13	" " " No 2 " " " " " #1339					
13	No.3 died Jan 15, 1908, (reported by U.S. Indian Supt. 7/31/11)					
14						
15					#1 to 4	
16				Date of Application for Enrollment		5/9/99
17						

Choctaw By Blood Enrollment Cards 1898-1914

RESIDENCE: Kiamitia COUNTY. **Choctaw Nation** Choctaw Roll CARD NO.

POST OFFICE: Goodland, I.T. (Not Including Freedmen) FIELD NO. 1478

Dawes' Roll No.	NAME	Relationship to Person First Named	AGE	SEX	BLOOD	TRIBAL ENROLLMENT Year	County	No.
4126	1 Gooding, Osborne A 24	First Named	21	M	1/16	1896	Kiamitia	4825
4127	2 " Fannie B. 19	Sister	16	F	1/16	1896	"	4820
	3							
	4							
	5							
	6	ENROLLMENT						
	7	OF NOS. 1 and 2 HEREON APPROVED BY THE SECRETARY						
	8	OF INTERIOR DEC 12 1902						
	9							
	10							
	11							
	12							
	13							
	14							
	15							
	16							
	17							

TRIBAL ENROLLMENT OF PARENTS

	Name of Father	Year	County	Name of Mother	Year	County
1	Henry L Gooding	1896	Intermarried	Rosana Gooding	Dead	Kiamitia
2	" " "	1896	"	" "	"	"
3						
4						
5						
6						
7	No2 enrolled as Annie B. Gooding					
8						
9	Father on Card No D148					
10	For child of No2 see NB (March 3, 1905) #1131					
11						
12						
13						
14						
15						
16				Date of Application for Enrollment	5/9/99	
17						

278

RESIDENCE: **Kiamitia** COUNTY.								
POST OFFICE: **Goodland, I.T.**		**Choctaw Nation**				**Choctaw Roll** *(Not Including Freedmen)*	CARD NO. FIELD NO.	**1479**

Dawes' Roll No.	NAME	Relationship to Person First Named	AGE	SEX	BLOOD	TRIBAL ENROLLMENT		
						Year	County	No.
4128 ₁	Gooding, Charles H ³⁷	First Named	34	M	1/16	1896	Towson	4736
4129 ₂	" Louie ¹⁵	Son	12	"	3/8	1896	"	4738
4130 ₃	" Josie ¹³	Dau	10	F	3/8	1896	"	4739
4131 ₄	" Henry ¹¹	Son	8	M	3/8	1896	"	4740
4132 ₅	" Lettie Lee ¹	Dau	3mo	F	1/32			
I.W.**704** ₆	" Minnie Lee ²¹	Wife	21	F	I.W.			
₇								
₈	ENROLLMENT							
₉	OF NOS. 1 2 3 4 and 5 HEREON APPROVED BY THE SECRETARY							
₁₀	OF INTERIOR DEC 12 1902							
₁₁								
₁₂	ENROLLMENT							
₁₃	OF NOS. ~~ 6 ~~ HEREON APPROVED BY THE SECRETARY							
₁₄	OF INTERIOR MAY -7 1904							
₁₅								
₁₆								
₁₇								

TRIBAL ENROLLMENT OF PARENTS

Name of Father	Year	County	Name of Mother	Year	County
₁ Henry L. Gooding	1896	Intermarried	Rosana Gooding	Dead	Kiamitia
₂ No 1			Annie Gooding	"	"
₃ No 1			" "	"	"
₄ No 1			" "	"	"
₅ No 1			Minnie Gooding		non citizen
₆ Pleasant David Hall		non citizen	Sarah Hall	" "	
₇					

₈ Nº6 transferred from Choctaw card #D782. See decision of Feby 27, 1904

₉ No1 on 1896 roll as Chas. H Gooding Kiamitia County #4815

₁₀ No1 is now the husband of Minnie Gooding a non-citizen: Feby 15, 1902
No.5 born Nov.24, 1901: Enrolled Feby 15, 1901: Evidence of marriage ^ Feby. 15, 1902. filed

₁₁ Nº2 on 1896 Roll as Louis Gooding, Kiamitia Co. #4815

₁₂ Nº3 " 1896 " " Josephine Gooding Kiamitia Co #4817

₁₃ Nº4 " 1896 " " Henry Gooding jr[sic] Kiamitia Co #4818

₁₄ Nº1-2-3 and 4 also on Choctaw card #1678 Which was cancelled this day Sept 2, 1902

₁₅ Nº1 is the husband of Minnie Lee Gooding on Choctaw card #D782 Sept, 1902

#1 to 4 inc

₁₅ No1 is father of Nos 4 and 5 on Choc card #3338

₁₆ For child of Nos 1&6 see NB (Mar 3-1905) Card #103

Date of Application for Enrollment.

₁₇ P.O. Grant IT 3/17/05

5/9/99

279

Choctaw By Blood Enrollment Cards 1898-1914

RESIDENCE: Kiamitia   COUNTY.

POST OFFICE: Grant, I.T.

Choctaw Nation

Choctaw Roll
(Not Including Freedmen)

CARD NO.

FIELD NO. 1480

Dawes' Roll No.	NAME		Relationship to Person	AGE	SEX	BLOOD	TRIBAL ENROLLMENT		
							Year	County	No.
4133	1 Phillips, Rosey	23	First Named	20	F	1/2	1896	Kiamitia	11484
14888	2 " Vivian	1	Dau	16mo	F	1/4			
	3								
	4								
	5								
	6								
	7	ENROLLMENT							
	8	OF NOS. 1 HEREON APPROVED BY THE SECRETARY							
	9	OF INTERIOR DEC 12 1902							
	10								
	11	ENROLLMENT							
	12	OF NOS. 2 HEREON APPROVED BY THE SECRETARY							
	13	OF INTERIOR MAY 21 1903							
	14								
	15								
	16								
	17								

TRIBAL ENROLLMENT OF PARENTS

	Name of Father	Year	County	Name of Mother	Year	County
1	Tom Spring	1896	Kiamitia	Melissie Spring	Dead	Kiamitia
2	Press Phillips		non-citizen	Nº1		
3						
4						
5						
6	On 1896 roll as Rosey Spring					
7	No.2 proof of birth to be supplied					
8	Nº2 Born Aug. 1, 1901, application made Dec 13, 1902. Proof of birth received 3/7/03.					
9						
10						
11						
12						
13						
14					Date of Application for Enrollment.	
15						
16					5/9/99	
17	Hugo I.T. 12/3/02					

Choctaw By Blood Enrollment Cards 1898-1914

RESIDENCE: Kiamitia COUNTY.
POST OFFICE: Goodland, I.T.

Choctaw Nation

Choctaw Roll
(Not Including Freedmen)

CARD No.
FIELD No. 1481

Dawes' Roll No.	NAME	Relationship to Person First Named	AGE	SEX	BLOOD	TRIBAL ENROLLMENT		
						Year	County	No.
I.W.73	1 Oliver, Samuel R ³⁴	First Named	31	M	I.W.	1896	Kiamitia	14910
4134	2 " Josephine ²⁵	Wife	22	F	1/4	1896	"	9936
	3							
	4							
	5							
	6							
	7	ENROLLMENT						
	8	OF NOS. 2 HEREON APPROVED BY THE SECRETARY						
	9	OF INTERIOR DEC 12 1902						
	10							
	11	ENROLLMENT OF NOS. ~~~ 1 ~~~ HEREON						
	12	APPROVED BY THE SECRETARY OF INTERIOR JUN 13 1903						
	13							
	14							
	15							
	16							
	17							

TRIBAL ENROLLMENT OF PARENTS

	Name of Father	Year	County	Name of Mother	Year	County
1	Frank Oliver	Dead	Non Citz	Mattie [Illegible]	1896	Non Citz
2	Tom Spring	1896	Kiamitia	Melissie Spring	Dead	Kiamitia
3						
4						
5						
6						
7			No 1 on 1896 roll as Sam Oliver.			
8						
9						
10						
11						
12						
13						
14						
15						
16				Date of Application for Enrollment	5/9/99	
17	Hugo I.T. 12/4/02					

281

Choctaw By Blood Enrollment Cards 1898-1914

Choctaw Nation

Choctaw Roll
(Not Including Freedmen)

CARD NO.
FIELD NO. **1482**

Dawes' Roll No.		NAME	Relationship to Person First Named	AGE	SEX	BLOOD	TRIBAL ENROLLMENT		
							Year	County	No.
4135	1	Williams, Isham ⁴¹	First Named	38	M	Full	1896	Kiamitia	13729
DEAD	2	" , Carrie A.	Wife	34	F	I.W.	1896	"	15182
4136	3	" , Fannie ¹⁷	Dau	14	"	1/2	1896	"	13730
4137	4	" , William A ¹²	Son	9	M	1/2	1896	"	13731
4138	5	" , Mary C. ¹⁰	Dau	7	F	1/2	1896	"	13732
4139	6	" , Alma ⁸	"	5	"	1/2	1896	"	13733
4140	7	" , George C. ⁷	Son	4	M	1/2	1896	"	13734
4141	8	" , Oscar R. ⁵	"	2	"	1/2			
	9	ENROLLMENT							
	10	OF NOS. 1 3 4 5 6 7 and 8 HEREON							
	11	APPROVED BY THE SECRETARY OF INTERIOR Dec 12, 1902							
	12								
	13	No. 2 hereon dismissed under order of							
	14	the Commission to the Five Civilized Tribes of March 31, 1905.							
	15								
	16								
	17								

TRIBAL ENROLLMENT OF PARENTS

	Name of Father	Year	County	Name of Mother	Year	County
1	Simon Williams	Dead	Towson	Mary Williams	Dead	Towson
2	Owen Tucker	1896	Non Citz	Sarah Tucker	1896	Non Citz
3	No 1			Frances Williams	Dead	Intermarried
4	No 1			No 2		
5	No 1			No 2		
6	No 1			No 2		
7	No 1			No 2		
8	No 1			No 2		
9						
10	No2 on 1896 roll as Carrie E. Williams					
11	No4 " 1896 " " Wᵐ A. William					
12	No6 " 1896 " " Elma Williams					
13	No7 " 1896 " " Geo. C. "					
13	No 2 died May 29, 1902· Proof of death filed Dec 13, 1902					
14						
15						
16					Date of Application for Enrollment.	5/9/99
17	Hugo I.T.					

RESIDENCE: Jackson	COUNTY.	**Choctaw Nation**			Choctaw Roll *(Not Including Freedmen)*		CARD NO.	
POST OFFICE: Crowder, I.T.							FIELD NO.	**1483**

Dawes' Roll No.	NAME		Relationship to Person First Named	AGE	SEX	BLOOD	TRIBAL ENROLLMENT		
							Year	County	No.
4142	1 Bacon, David	36	First Named	33	M	1/2	1896	Jackson	1496
4143	2 " , Mame	23	Wife	20	F	1/2	1896	"	1497
4144	3 " , Elmer	11	Son	8	M	1/2	1896	"	1498
4145	4 " , Bob	9	"	6	"	1/2	1896	"	1499
4146	5 " , Pearlie	8	Dau	5	F	1/2	1896	"	1500
4147	6 " , Phoebe	6	"	3	"	1/2	1896	"	1532
4148	7 " , Solomon	4	Son	5wks	M	1/2			
4149	8 " , Mittie Belle	1	Dau	3mo	F	1/2			
	9								
	10								
	11	ENROLLMENT OF NOS. 1234567and8 HEREON							
	12	APPROVED BY THE SECRETARY							
	13	OF INTERIOR Dec. 12, 1902							
	14								
	15	For child of Nos 1&2 see NB (Apr 26-06) Card #338.							
	16	" " " " " " " (Mar 3-05) " #604.							
	17								

TRIBAL ENROLLMENT OF PARENTS

	Name of Father	Year	County	Name of Mother	Year	County
1	Thos Bacon	Dead	Blue	Elizabeth Bacon	1896	Jackson
2	Morrison		Non Citz	Permelia Drake	Dead	Sans Bois
3	No.1			No.2		
4	No.1			No.2		
5	No.1			No.2		
6	No.1			No.2		
7	No.1			No.2		
8	No.1			No.2		
9						
10			No.2 on 1896 roll as Minnie Bacon.			
11			No.4 " 1896 " " Bobbie " .			
12						
13			No.7 affidavit of birth to be supplied. Recd May 17/99			
14			No8 born August 21, 1901: Enrolled Nov. 27, 1901.			
15						
16					Date of Application for Enrollment	5/9/99
17	P.O. Boswell I.T. 3/30/05					1 to 7 inc

Choctaw By Blood Enrollment Cards 1898-1914

RESIDENCE: Kiamitia   COUNTY.
POST OFFICE: Goodland, I.T.

Choctaw Nation

Choctaw Roll *(Not Including Freedmen)*

CARD NO.
FIELD NO. 1484

Dawes' Roll No.		NAME		Relationship to Person	AGE	SEX	BLOOD	TRIBAL ENROLLMENT		
								Year	County	No.
4150	1	Homma, Mary	59	First Named	56	F	1/4	1896	Kiamitia	5743
	2									
	3									
	4									
	5									
	6									
	7									
	8	ENROLLMENT								
	9	OF NOS. 1 HEREON APPROVED BY THE SECRETARY								
	10	OF INTERIOR DEC 12 1902								
	11									
	12									
	13									
	14									
	15									
	16									
	17									

TRIBAL ENROLLMENT OF PARENTS

	Name of Father	Year	County	Name of Mother	Year	County
1	William Walker	Dead	Creek Roll	Elsie Walker	Dead	Kiamitia
2						
3						
4						
5						
6						
7						
8						
9						
10						
11						
12						
13						
14						
15				Date of Application for Enrollment.		
16				5/9/99		
17						

Choctaw By Blood Enrollment Cards 1898-1914

RESIDENCE: Kiamitia COUNTY.
POST OFFICE: Goodland, I.T.

Choctaw Nation

Choctaw Roll
(Not Including Freedmen)

CARD NO.
FIELD NO. 1485

Dawes' Roll No.	NAME	Relationship to Person First Named	AGE	SEX	BLOOD	TRIBAL ENROLLMENT		
						Year	County	No.
51	₁ Hart, Lemon Sr.		64	M	1/4	1896	Kiamitia	5737
52 4152	₂ Monkus, Samuel ¹⁷	G.Son	14	"	1/4	1896	"	8702
	3							
	4							
	5							
	6							
	7							
	8							
	9							
	10							
	11							
	12							
	13							
	14							
	15							
	16							
	17							

DIED PRIOR TO SEPTEMBER 25, 1902

ENROLLMENT
OF NOS. 1 and 2 HEREON
APPROVED BY THE SECRETARY
OF INTERIOR DEC 12 1902

TRIBAL ENROLLMENT OF PARENTS

	Name of Father	Year	County	Name of Mother	Year	County
1	Cornelius Hart	Dead	Non Citz	Elsie Walker	Dead	Kiamitia
2	Sam Monkus	"	" "	Elmira Monkus	"	"
3						
4						
5						
6						
7						
8	No 1 died Dec 18, 1901; proof of death filed Dec 5, 1902.					
9	No.1 died Dec. 18, 1901; Enrollment cancelled by Department [illegible]					
10						
11						
12						
13						
14						
15					Date of Application for Enrollment.	
16					5/9/99	
17						

Choctaw By Blood Enrollment Cards 1898-1914

RESIDENCE: Towson COUNTY. **Choctaw Nation** Choctaw Roll CARD NO.
POST OFFICE: Doaksville, I.T. (Not Including Freedmen) FIELD NO. 1486

Dawes' Roll No.	NAME		Relationship to Person	AGE	SEX	BLOOD	TRIBAL ENROLLMENT		
							Year	County	No.
I.W. 705	1 Hankins, Levi	26	First Named	23	M	I.W.	1896	Towson	14623
4153	2 " Sarah	26	Wife	23	F	1/2	1896	"	5489
4154	3 " Henry	7	Son	4	M	1/4	1896	"	5490
4155	4 DIED PRIOR TO SEPTEMBER 25, 1902 James		"	14mo	"	1/4			
4156	5 " Granderson	3	Son	5mo	M	1/4			
14670	6 " Charley	1	Son	1mo	M	1/4			
	7		ENROLLMENT						
	8		OF NOS. ~~~ 1 ~~~ HEREON						
	9		APPROVED BY THE SECRETARY OF INTERIOR MAY -7 1904						
	10								
	11	ENROLLMENT							
	12	OF NOS. 2 3 4 and 5 HEREON APPROVED BY THE SECRETARY							
	13	OF INTERIOR DEC 12 1902							
	14		ENROLLMENT						
	15		OF NOS. 6 HEREON						
	16		APPROVED BY THE SECRETARY OF INTERIOR MAY 20 1903						
	17								

TRIBAL ENROLLMENT OF PARENTS

	Name of Father	Year	County	Name of Mother	Year	County
1	David Hankins	1896	Non Citz	Mary Hankins	1896	Non Citz
2	Silas Garland	Dead	Towson	Lucinda Garland	Dead	Towson
3	No 1			No 2		
4	No 1			No 2		
5	No.1			No.2		
6	Nº1			Nº2		
7						
8			No1 See Decision of March 2 '04			
9			No4 Affidavit of birth to be supplied. Recd May 17/99			
10			No.5 Enrolled July 16, 1900. Nº6 Born Sept. 10, 1902. Enrolled Oct 15, 1902			
11						
12			No4 died in Aug. 1899: proof of death filed Dec. 2, 1902.			
13	No.4 died Aug. - 1899 Enrollment cancelled by Department [illegible]					
14						
15						
16				Date of Application for Enrollment	5/9/99	
17	P.O. Miah I.T. 5/25/03				1 to 4	

Choctaw By Blood Enrollment Cards 1898-1914

RESIDENCE: Kiamitia   COUNTY.   **Choctaw Nation**   **Choctaw Roll**   CARD No.
POST OFFICE: Goodland, I.T.   *(Not Including Freedmen)*   FIELD No.   1487

Dawes' Roll No.		NAME	Relationship to Person First Named	AGE	SEX	BLOOD	TRIBAL ENROLLMENT		
							Year	County	No.
4157	1	Spring, Thomas ~~DIED PRIOR TO SEPTEMBER 25, 1902~~	First Named	51	M	1/4	1896	Kiamitia	11482
4158	2	" Walter ²¹	Son	18	"	5/8	1896	"	11485
	3								
	4								
	5								
	6	ENROLLMENT							
	7	OF NOS. 1 and 2 HEREON APPROVED BY THE SECRETARY							
	8	OF INTERIOR DEC 12 1902							
	9								
	10								
	11								
	12								
	13								
	14								
	15								
	16								
	17								

TRIBAL ENROLLMENT OF PARENTS

	Name of Father	Year	County	Name of Mother	Year	County
1	Christopher Spring	Dead	Non Citz	Susan Spring	Dead	Kiamitia
2	No 1			Melissie Spring	"	"
3						
4						
5						
6	No1 died January 1, 1902: proof of death filed Dec 6, 1902					
7	No.1 died Jan. 1, 1902: Enrollment cancelled by Department [illegible]					
8						
9						
10						
11						
12						
13						
14						
15						
16					Date of Application for Enrollment	5/9/99
17	Hugo I.T. 12/3/02					

287

Choctaw By Blood Enrollment Cards 1898-1914

RESIDENCE: **Kiamitia**   COUNTY.   **Choctaw Nation**   **Choctaw Roll**   CARD NO.

POST OFFICE: **Grant, I.T.**   *(Not Including Freedmen)*   FIELD NO.   **1488**

Dawes' Roll No.		NAME		Relationship to Person	AGE	SEX	BLOOD	TRIBAL ENROLLMENT		
								Year	County	No.
4159	1	Fisher, Morris H.	50	First Named	47	M	Full	1896	Kiamitia	4223
4160	2	" Sillain	43	Wife	40	F	"	1896	"	4224
4161	3	" Robert	22	Son	19	M	"	1896	"	4226
4162	4	" Willie	18	"	15	"	"	1896	"	4227
4163	5	" Thomas	14	"	11	"	"	1896	"	4228
4164	6	" Frank	10	"	7	"	"	1896	"	4229
4165	7	" Georgie	7	Dau	4	F	"	1896	"	4230
	8									
	9									
	10									
	11									
	12									
	13									
	14									
	15									
	16									
	17									

ENROLLMENT
OF NOS. 123456and7 HEREON
APPROVED BY THE SECRETARY
OF INTERIOR DEC 12 1902

TRIBAL ENROLLMENT OF PARENTS

	Name of Father	Year	County	Name of Mother	Year	County
1	John Fisher	Dead	Kiamitia	Liley Fisher	Dead	Kiamitia
2	Wm Simpson	"	"	Vicey Simpson	"	Cedar
3	No 1			No 2		
4	No 1			No 2		
5	No 1			No 2		
6	No 1			No 2		
7	No 1			No 2		
8						
9						
10						
11						
12						
13						
14					Date of Application for Enrollment.	
15						
16					5/9/99	
17						

RESIDENCE: Atoka COUNTY. **Choctaw Nation** **Choctaw Roll** CARD NO.
POST OFFICE: Coalgate, I.T. (Not Including Freedmen) FIELD NO. 1489

Dawes' Roll No.	NAME		Relationship to Person	AGE	SEX	BLOOD	TRIBAL ENROLLMENT		
							Year	County	No.
4166	1 Randall, Mattie	21	First Named	18	F	3/8	1896	Jackson	10881
4167	2 " Ruth	6	Dau	3	"	3/16	1896	"	10882
4168	3 " Lazerus	4	Son	1	M	3/16			
4169	4 " Willie	1	"	1 wk	M	3/16			
	5								
	6								
	7								
	8								
	9								
	10								
	11	ENROLLMENT							
	12	OF NOS. 1 2 3 and 4 HEREON APPROVED BY THE SECRETARY							
	13	OF INTERIOR DEC 12 1902							
	14								
	15								
	16								
	17								

TRIBAL ENROLLMENT OF PARENTS

	Name of Father	Year	County	Name of Mother	Year	County
1	John Rushing	Dead	Non Citz	Nannie J Rushing	Dead	Jackson
2	Gus Randell	1896	" "	No 1		
3	" "	1896	" "	No 1		
4	" "			No.1		
5						
6						
7						
8			No.4 Enrolled Sept. 4, 1901.			
9			For child of No.1 see NB (March 3, 1905) #1273			
10						
11						
12						
13					#1 to 3	
14				Date of Application for Enrollment		
15						
16				5/9/99		
17	Swink I.T. 12/4/02					

289

RESIDENCE: Kiamitia   COUNTY.   **Choctaw Nation**   Choctaw Roll   CARD NO.

POST OFFICE: Goodland, I.T.   (Not Including Freedmen)   FIELD NO. **1490**

Dawes' Roll No.	NAME	Relationship to Person	AGE	SEX	BLOOD	TRIBAL ENROLLMENT		
						Year	County	No.
I.W. 1400	1 Rice, Ambrose L. ³⁰	First Named	27	M	I.W.	1896	Kiamitia	14974
	2							
	3							
	4							
	5	ENROLLMENT						
	6	OF NOS. ~~~ 1 ~~~ HEREON APPROVED BY THE SECRETARY						
	7	OF INTERIOR Jun 12, 1905						
	8							
	9	No 1 restored to roll by Departmental authority of January 19, 1909 (File 5-51)						
	10	~~Enrollment of No.1 cancelled by order of Department of March 4, 1907~~						
	11							
	12							
	13							
	14							
	15							
	16							
	17							

TRIBAL ENROLLMENT OF PARENTS

	Name of Father	Year	County	Name of Mother	Year	County
1	G.W. Rice	1896	Non Citz	Ithema Rice	1896	Non Citz
2						
3			No1 formerly husband of Annie L. Rice			
4			1893 Kiamiatia[sic] No 710 and who died in 1896			
5			On 1896 roll as Embro L Rice			
6			~~No1 denied by Davis Commission in 1896~~			
7			~~Choctaw case #662; no appeal.~~			
8			See testimony of No.1 taken October 17, 1902.			
9						
10			No1 is now the husband of Isabelle Huland on Choctaw Card #1510			
11			Evidence of marriage filed Dec. 12-1902			
12						
13						
14						
15						
16					Date of Application for Enrollment	5/9/99
17	Dibble I.T. 1/8/04					

Choctaw By Blood Enrollment Cards 1898-1914

RESIDENCE: Kiamitia   COUNTY.   **Choctaw Nation**   Choctaw Roll   CARD NO.
POST OFFICE: Goodland, I.T.   *(Not Including Freedmen)*   FIELD NO.   **1491**

Dawes' Roll No.	NAME	Relationship to Person First Named	AGE	SEX	BLOOD	TRIBAL ENROLLMENT Year	County	No.
4170	1 Brashears, George ⁴⁴	First Named	41	M	1/2	1896	Kiamitia	1460
4171	2 DIED PRIOR TO SEPTEMBER 25, 1902 , Mary	Wife	24	F	Full	1896	"	1461
4172	3 " , Edward ⁶	Son	2	M	3/4			
4173	4 DIED PRIOR TO SEPTEMBER 25, 1902 , Betsy	Dau	4mo	F	3/4			
	5							
	6							
	7							
	8							
	9							
	10							
	11	ENROLLMENT						
	12	OF NOS. 1 2 3 and 4 HEREON APPROVED BY THE SECRETARY						
	13	OF INTERIOR Dec 12, 1902						
	14							
	15							
	16							
	17							

TRIBAL ENROLLMENT OF PARENTS

	Name of Father	Year	County	Name of Mother	Year	County
1	Wᵐ Brashears	Dead	Kiamitia	Caroline Brashears	Dead	Kiamitia
2	Ompsion Homa	"	"	Sophia Homa	"	"
3	No 1			No 2		
4	No 1			No 2		
5		No1 is husband of Susan M. Coy, a Choc-Freedman Card #615.				
6		No1 on 1896 roll as George Bershears				
7		No2 " 1896 " " Mary "				
8						
9		Nos 3-4 Affidavits of birth to be supplied. Recd May 10/99.				
10						
11	No2 died Oct. 11, 1900. Proof of death filed Dec 6, 1902.					
12	No4 " Aug 15, 1899. " " " " " " "					
13	No2 died Oct.11,1900: No4 died Aug.15,1899: Enrollment cancelled by Department July 8,1904.					
14						
15						
16	Hugo I.T.			Date of Application for Enrollment 5/9/99		
17						

RESIDENCE: **Kiamitia**   COUNTY.   **Choctaw Nation**   Choctaw Roll   CARD NO.

POST OFFICE: **Nelson, I.T.**   *(Not Including Freedmen)*   FIELD NO. **1492**

Dawes' Roll No.	NAME	Relationship to Person First Named	AGE	SEX	BLOOD	TRIBAL ENROLLMENT Year	County	No.
IW240	1 Jeter, Joshua B. 50	First Named	47	M	I.W.	1896	Kiamitia	14696
4174	2 " , Sarah E. 41	Wife	38	F	1/8	1896	"	7080
4175	3 " , Gertrude 24	Dau	21	"	1/16	1896	"	7081
4176	4 " , Hattie 22	"	19	"	1/16	1896	"	7082
4177	5 " , James T. 18	Son	15	M	1/16	1896	"	7083
4178	6 " , William W. 14	"	11	"	1/16	1896	"	7084
4179	7 " , Olive M. 7	Dau	4	F	1/16	1896	"	7085
	8							
	9 ENROLLMENT							
	10 OF NOS. 23456and7 HEREON APPROVED BY THE SECRETARY OF INTERIOR Dec 12, 1902							
	11							
	12 ENROLLMENT							
	13 OF NOS. 1 HEREON APPROVED BY THE SECRETARY							
	14 OF INTERIOR Sep. 12, 1903.							
	15							
	16							
	17							

TRIBAL ENROLLMENT OF PARENTS

	Name of Father	Year	County	Name of Mother	Year	County
1	James Jeter	Dead	Non Citz	Selena Jeter	Dead	Non Citz
2	Thos. W. Oakes	"	" "	Harriet Oakes	1896	Kiamitia
3	No 1			No 2		
4	No 1			No 2		
5	No 1			No 2		
6	No 1			No 2		
7	No 1			No 2		
8						
9	No1 on 1896 roll as Joshua B. Jetter					
10	No5 " 1896 " " Thomas Jeter					
11	No6 " 1896 " " William "					
	No7 " 1896 " " Oliver M. "					
12	No.7 " Choc. Census Roll as a Male 2/27/03.					
13	See statement of No.1 regarding his marriage					
14	hereto attached					
	No1 was admitted as an intermarried citizen in					
15	1896 by Dawes Commission Choctaw Case #1047. No appeal					
16	For child of No4 see NB (Apr. 26'06) Card No.153.				Date of Application for Enrollment	
17	P.O. Altus I.T. 3/16/03				5/9/00	

RESIDENCE: Towson COUNTY.
POST OFFICE: Doaksville, I.T.

Choctaw Nation

Choctaw Roll
(Not Including Freedmen)

CARD No.
FIELD No. **1493**

Dawes' Roll No.	NAME	Relationship to Person First Named	AGE	SEX	BLOOD	TRIBAL ENROLLMENT		
						Year	County	No.
IW992	1 Roberts, John W. 46		43	M	I.W.			
4180	2 " Susan 47	Wife	44	F	1/2	1896	Towson	7932
4181	3 Sanguin, William M 25	S.Son	22	M	1/4	1896	"	11377
4182	4 Le Flore, Carrie 21	S.Dau	18	F	1/2	1896	"	7933
4183	5 " Basil L. 17	S.Son	14	M	1/2	1896	"	7935
4184	6 " Rosanna 15	S.Dau	12	F	1/2	1896	"	7936
4185	7 " Osborne 12	S.Son	9	M	1/2	1896	"	7937
4186	8 " Landry G. 10	S.Dau	7	F	1/2	1896	"	7938
4187	9 " Susie 9	"	6	"	1/2	1896	"	7939
	10							
	11	ENROLLMENT						
	12	OF NOS. 2 3 4 5 6 7 8 and 9 HEREON APPROVED BY THE SECRETARY						
	13	OF INTERIOR Dec 12, 1902						
	14							
	15							
	16							
	17							

TRIBAL ENROLLMENT OF PARENTS

	Name of Father	Year	County	Name of Mother	Year	County
1	Robert Roberts	Dead	Non Citz	Elizabeth Roberts	Dead	Non Citz
2	William Spring	1896	Kiamitia	Jane Spring	"	Kiamitia
3	Chas Sanguin	Dead	Non Citz	No 2		
4	Zeddick Le Flore	"	Towson	No 2		
5	" "	"	"	No 2		
6	" "	"	"	No 2		
7	" "	"	"	No 2		
8	" "	"	"	No 2		
9	" "	"	"	No 2		
10						
11	8/29/13 For child of No5 see N.B. (Apr.26-06) card No.233					
12	For child of No 4 see N.B. (Mar.3-1905) Card No 45.					
13	No 3 on 1896 roll as Billy Sanguin					
14	No 5 " 1896 " " Brasill Le Flore					
15	No 6 " 1896 " " Rosa "			ENROLLMENT		Date of Application for Enrollment.
16	No 7 " 1896 " " Osie "			OF NOS. ~ 1 ~ HEREON APPROVED BY THE SECRETARY OF INTERIOR Oct 21, 1904		
17	No 8 " 1896 " " Landry "					5/9/99
	No 2 " 1896 " " Susan "					
	Nos 1 and 2 have seperated[sic] see testimony of No 1 – 12/9/02					

Choctaw By Blood Enrollment Cards 1898-1914

RESIDENCE: Towson COUNTY.
POST OFFICE: Doaksville, I.T.

Choctaw Nation

Choctaw Roll
(Not Including Freedmen)

CARD NO.
FIELD NO. **1494**

Dawes' Roll No.	NAME	Relationship to Person First Named	AGE	SEX	BLOOD	TRIBAL ENROLLMENT		
						Year	County	No.
4188	1 Blankenship, Winnie ¹⁹	First Named	16	F	1/2	1896	Towson	7934
	2							
	3							
	4							
	5							
	6							
	7							
	8							
	9							
	10							
	11							
	12							
	13							
	14							
	15							
	16							
	17							

ENROLLMENT
OF NOS. 1 HEREON
APPROVED BY THE SECRETARY
OF INTERIOR Dec. 12, 1902

TRIBAL ENROLLMENT OF PARENTS

	Name of Father	Year	County	Name of Mother	Year	County
1	Zeddick Le Flore	Dead	Towson	Susan Le Flore	1896	Towson
2						
3						
4						
5						
6		On 1896 roll as Winnie Le Flore				
7						
8		For child of No. 1 see N.B. (Apr. 26-06) card #513				
9						
10						
11						
12						
13						
14					Date of Application for Enrollment.	
15						
16					5/9/99	
17						

Choctaw By Blood Enrollment Cards 1898-1914

RESIDENCE: Kiamitia COUNTY.   **Choctaw Nation**   **Choctaw Roll**   CARD NO.
POST OFFICE: Goodland, I.T.   *(Not Including Freedmen)*   FIELD NO. **1495**

Dawes' Roll No.	NAME	Relationship to Person First Named	AGE	SEX	BLOOD	TRIBAL ENROLLMENT		
						Year	County	No.
4189	1 Miller, Melvina ~~DIED PRIOR TO SEPTEMBER 25, 1902~~		52	F	Full	1896	Kiamitia	8723
4190	2 " Henry ²⁶	Son	23	M	"	1896	"	8704
4191	3 Guess, Amelia ²²	Dau	19	F	"	1896	"	8705
4192	4 Miller Sophia ²⁰	"	17	"	"	1896	"	8706
4193	5 " Frances ¹⁸	"	15	"	"	1896	"	8707
4194	6 " Ida ¹⁵	"	12	"	"	1896	"	8708
4195	7 Guess, Henry ⁵	G.Son	1½	M	1/2			
4196	8 " Michael ~~DIED PRIOR TO SEPTEMBER 25, 1902~~	"	9mo	M	1/2			
14672	9 " Rosa ¹	Dau of No4	3mo	F	1/4			
	10							
	11	ENROLLMENT OF NOS. 1234567and8 HEREON APPROVED BY THE SECRETARY OF INTERIOR Dec. 12, 1902						
	12							
	13	No9 born Sept.24,1902:enrolled Dec.8,1902						
	14	No1 died Aug 12,1901: proof of ~~death filed Dec. 9, 1902.~~						
	15	No8 died April, 1901, proof of						
	16	death filed Dec. 9, 1902.						

No.1 died Aug 12,1901: No.8 died April -, 1901: Enrollment cancelled by Department July 8, 1904.

TRIBAL ENROLLMENT OF PARENTS

	Name of Father	Year	County	Name of Mother	Year	County
1	~~Joe Taylor~~	~~Dead~~	~~Kiamitia~~	~~Mary Taylor~~	~~Dead~~	~~Kiamitia~~
2	Alfred Miller	"	"	No 1		
3	" "	"	"	No 1		
4	" "	"	"	No 1		
5	" "	"	"	No 1		
6	" "	"	"	No 1		
7	Martin Guess	1896	Non Citz	No 3		
8	" "	"	~~Choc freedman~~	~~No 3~~		
9	Billy Guess	"	"	No 4		

No.5 P.O. Kent, OK 2/15/08

For child of No3 see NB (Apr 26/06) Card #129
No3 on 1896 roll as Permelia Miller
For child of No5 see NB (Apr 26'06) Card #309
~~No3 is the wife of Martin Guess, a Choctaw freedman on~~
~~Choctaw freedman card #613~~
Father of Nos 7and8 is a Choctaw freedman
Evidence of marriage of No.3 and Martin Guess to be
supplied. For child of No.4 see NB (March 3,1905) #1343.
No 8 Born April 24 1900 enrolled Jany 17, 1901
Hamden I.T. 12/9/02.

ENROLLMENT
OF NOS. 9 HEREON
APPROVED BY THE SECRETARY
May 20 1903

Date of Application for Enrollment. #1 to 7

5/9/99

295

Choctaw By Blood Enrollment Cards 1898-1914

RESIDENCE: Towson   COUNTY.
POST OFFICE: Clear Creek, I.T.

Choctaw Nation

Choctaw Roll
(Not Including Freedmen)

CARD NO.
FIELD NO. **1496**

Dawes' Roll No.	NAME	Relationship to Person First Named	AGE	SEX	BLOOD	TRIBAL ENROLLMENT		
						Year	County	No.
DEAD	₁ Brown, Julius DEAD		26	M	IW			
4197	₂ Herndon Lottee ²⁴	Wife	21	F	1/2	1893	Towson	52
ᴵᵂ812	₃ Herndon Ezekiel K ³²	Hus	32	M	IW			
	₄							
	₅ No. 1. Hereon Dismissed under order							
	₆ of the Commission to the Five Civilized Tribes of March 31, 1905.							
	₇							
	₈ ENROLLMENT							
	₉ OF NOS. 2 HEREON APPROVED BY THE SECRETARY							
	₁₀ OF INTERIOR Dec. 12, 1902							
	₁₁ Affidavit of death of No1 filed							
	₁₂ April 17ᵗʰ 1900.							
	₁₃							
	₁₄ ENROLLMENT OF NOS. 3 HEREON							
	₁₅ APPROVED BY THE SECRETARY OF INTERIOR May 21, 1904							
	₁₆							
	₁₇							

TRIBAL ENROLLMENT OF PARENTS

Name of Father	Year	County	Name of Mother	Year	County
₁ Mike Brown	1896	Non Citz	Matilda Brown	1896	Non Citz
₂ John McEvers	Dead	" "	Silvie McEvers	Dead	Atoka
₃ Harrison H. Herndon		noncitizen	Alice R. Herndon		noncitizen
₄					
₅ No 3 transferred from Choctaw card D849, April 15, 1904					
₆ See decision of March 15, 1904					
₇					
₈ No 2 on 1893 Pay roll ∧ as Sarah Lottie McEvers of Atoka County,					
₉ Page 56 No 52. Also on 1896 roll Lottie McCannis, Page 238, No 9456, Atoka Co.					
₁₀					
₁₁ Dixon Sexton is said to have known mother of Lottie					
₁₂ Brown and can appear for examination at					
₁₃ Atoka, I.T. May Harris, wife of Bert Harris, is a sister of No 2.					
₁₄ No 2 is now the wife of E.K Herndon on Choctaw card D849					
₁₅ a United States citizen			April 4ᵗʰ, 1900		
₁₆				Date of Application for Enrollment 5/9/99	
₁₇ Valiant I.T. 12/18/02					

RESIDENCE: Towson   COUNTY.   **Choctaw Nation**   **Choctaw Roll** CARD NO.
POST OFFICE: Doaksville, I.T.   *(Not Including Freedmen)* FIELD NO. **1497**

Dawes' Roll No.	NAME		Relationship to Person	AGE	SEX	BLOOD	TRIBAL ENROLLMENT		
							Year	County	No.
4198	1 Harkins, James	39	First Named	36	M	3/4	1896	Towson	5497
I.W.74	2 " Viney	28	Wife	25	F	I.W.	1896	"	14624
4199	3 " Silas	11	Son	8	M	3/8	1896	"	5498
4200	4 " Lena	9	Dau	6	F	3/8	1896	"	5499
4201	5 " Novey	7	"	4	"	3/8	1896	"	5500
4202	6 " Susie	5	"	1½	"	3/8			
4203	7 " Carry	2	Dau	3mo	F	3/8			
	8								
	9	ENROLLMENT OF NOS. 1 3 4 5 6 and 7 HEREON APPROVED BY THE SECRETARY OF INTERIOR Dec. 12, 1902							
	10								
	11								
	12 13	ENROLLMENT OF NOS. ~~~ 2 ~~~ HEREON APPROVED BY THE SECRETARY OF INTERIOR Jun 13, 1903							
	14								
	15								
	16								
	17								

TRIBAL ENROLLMENT OF PARENTS

	Name of Father	Year	County	Name of Mother	Year	County
1	Richard Harkins	Dead	Red River	Silbie Harkins	Dead	Towson
2	Silas Garland	"	Towson	Martha Wilson	1896	Non Citz
3	No 1			No 2		
4	No 1			No 2		
5	No 1			No 2		
6	No 1			No 2		
7	No 1			No 2		
8						
9			No 7 Enrolled Aug. 18 1900			
10			For child of Nos 1&2 see N.B. (March 3, 1905) #1340			
11						
12						
13						
14						
15					#1 to 6	
16					Date of Application for Enrollment	
17	P.O. Swink I.T. 4/22/05					5/9/99

Choctaw By Blood Enrollment Cards 1898-1914

RESIDENCE: Kiamitia   COUNTY.   **Choctaw Nation**   **Choctaw Roll** *(Not Including Freedmen)*   CARD NO.

POST OFFICE: Goodland, I.T.   FIELD NO. **1498**

Dawes' Roll No.	NAME		Relationship to Person First Named	AGE	SEX	BLOOD	TRIBAL ENROLLMENT		
							Year	County	No.
I.W.75	1 Self, Thomas	32	First Named	29	M	I.W.	1896	Kiamitia	15051
4204	2 " Annie	28	Wife	25	F	1/4	1896	"	11512
4205	3 " William P	11	Son	8	M	1/8	1896	"	11513
4206	4 " Harvey E	8	"	5	"	1/8	1896	"	11514
4207	5 " James E.	5	"	2	"	1/8			
4208	6 " William O	3	"	10mo	M	1/8			
	7								
	8								
	9	ENROLLMENT OF NOS. 2 3 4 5 and 6 HEREON APPROVED BY THE SECRETARY OF INTERIOR Dec 12, 1902							
	10								
	11								
	12	ENROLLMENT OF NOS. 1 HEREON APPROVED BY THE SECRETARY OF INTERIOR Jun 13, 1903							
	13								
	14								
	15								
	16								
	17								

TRIBAL ENROLLMENT OF PARENTS

	Name of Father	Year	County	Name of Mother	Year	County
1	William Self	1896	Non Citz	Carrie Self	1896	Non Citz
2	James Usrey	1896	" "	Melinda Usrey	Dead	Kiamitia
3	No 1			No 2		
4	No 1			No 2		
5	No 1			No 2		
6	No 1			No 2		
7						
8			No 3 on 1896 roll as Billy Self			
9			No 4 " 1896 " " Harvey "			
10			No.6 Enrolled Oct. 8th, 1900			
			Nos 1-2: Evidence of marriage filed December 22, 1902			
11						
12						
13						
14						
15					Date of Application for Enrollment.	#1 to 5 inc
16						
17	Hugo I.T.					5/9/99

298

Choctaw By Blood Enrollment Cards 1898-1914

RESIDENCE:	Jackson	COUNTY.								
POST OFFICE:	Crowder, I.T.		**Choctaw Nation**		Choctaw Roll *(Not Including Freedmen)*			CARD NO. FIELD NO. **1499**		

Dawes' Roll No.	NAME		Relationship to Person First Named	AGE	SEX	BLOOD	TRIBAL ENROLLMENT		
							Year	County	No.
15912	₁ Wright, Betsy	25	First Named	22	F	1/4	1896	Jackson	13812
15913	₂ " Thomas E.	6	Son	3	M	1/8	1896	"	13813
15914	₃ " Mary M.	4	Dau	3mo	F	1/8			
15915	₄ " Lenard Dalco	1	Son	6wks	M	1/8			
	₅ ENROLLMENT								
	₆ OF NOS. 1, 2, 3 & 4 HEREON APPROVED BY THE SECRETARY								
	₇ OF INTERIOR Aug 23, 1905								
	₈ Nos 1,2,3&4 retored to roll by Departmental authority of								
	₉ Jan 19 1909 (File 5-51) Nos 1 and 2 denied by Dawes								
	₁₀ Commission in 1896, Choctaw case #507: no appeal. None of above applicants has made application for								
	₁₁ enrollment as Cherokee: see letter of Cherokee land								
	₁₂ office of December 12, 1903, nor is any of them on								
	₁₃ Cherokee Rolls.								
	₁₄								
	₁₅								
	₁₆								
	₁₇								

TRIBAL ENROLLMENT OF PARENTS

	Name of Father	Year	County	Name of Mother	Year	County
₁	Thos C. Crowder	1896	Jackson	Flora Crowder	Dead	Cherokee Roll
₂	J.W. Wright	1895	Non Citz	No 1		
₃	" "	1896	" "	No 1		
₄	" "		" "	No 1		

₅ No.1 on 1885 Choctaw Census Roll, Kiamitia Co., No 585 as Betsy Crowder
₆ No 1 on 1893 Choctaw Pay Roll, Jackson Co. page 12, No 100 as Elizabeth "
₇ No 1 on 1896 roll as Battie Wright
No 2 " 1896 " " Ella T. "
₈ For child of No1 see N.B. (Apr. 26, 1906) Card No. 20.
₉ Mother of No 1 was a Cherokee, No1 is not known to be
₁₀ enrolled as a Cherokee, has drawn no money as a Cherokee
in the last six years. See testimony of husband of W. Wright, also
₁₁ if enrolled as a Cherokee.
₁₂
₁₃ No 3 Affidavit of birth to be supplied. Recd May 17/99
₁₄ No 4 Enrolled July 2, 1901 ~~order of~~
₁₅ Enrollment of Nos 1,2,3,and 4 cancelled by ~~order of~~ Department March 4, 1907

	#1 to 3 inc
₁₆	Date of Application for Enrollment 5/9/99
₁₇ P.O. Boswell I.T. 11/30/04	

Choctaw By Blood Enrollment Cards 1898-1914

RESIDENCE: Kiamitia COUNTY. **Choctaw Nation** Choctaw Roll CARD NO.
POST OFFICE: Nelson, I.T. *(Not Including Freedmen)* FIELD NO. **1500**

Dawes' Roll No.	NAME		Relationship to Person	AGE	SEX	BLOOD	TRIBAL ENROLLMENT		
							Year	County	No.
4209	1 Bond, Ida	14	First Named	11	F	Full	1896	Kiamitia	1452
	2								
	3								
	4								
	5	ENROLLMENT OF NOS. 1 HEREON							
	6	APPROVED BY THE SECRETARY OF INTERIOR Dec. 12, 1902							
	7								
	8								
	9								
	10								
	11								
	12								
	13								
	14								
	15								
	16								
	17								

TRIBAL ENROLLMENT OF PARENTS

	Name of Father	Year	County	Name of Mother	Year	County
1	Bond	Dead	Sans Bois	Phoebe Chitto	Dead	Sans Bois
2						
3						
4						
5			Living with T. L. Greggs			
6						
7			For child of No 1 see N.B. (Mar 3-1905) Card #41			
8						
9						
10						
11						
12						
13						
14					Date of Application for Enrollment.	
15						
16					5/9/99	
17						

AARON
    Alex 146
    Annie 72
    Austin 100
    Bekinsie 146
    Caleb 146
    Denison 146
    Dennis 146
    Elsie 100,146,153
    Felin 88
    Frances 72
    Itey 72
    James 155
    Janie 59
    Jim 59
    John 155
    Johnson 72
    Leana 146
    Lewinie 146
    Liley 59
    Louina 146
    Lucy 146
    Mackenzie 146
    Martha 88
    Mary 146
    Moses 72
    Nebus 94
    Phelan 100
    Pitman 10,155
    Sallie 100
    Sarah 72
    Sealy 155
    Sekea 146
    Selina 88,155
    Sibbie 100
    Siline 146
    Stephen 59,72,94
    Susan 94
    Tama 155
    Thomas 10
    William 146
    Wilson 153
A-BA-LA-TEBY 80
ABA-WHEE-LY 70
A-CHE-NO-TA 124
ACHUKMAHONA 135
ACHUK-MA-HO-YO 107

A-FA-MA-TUBBEE 204
AHAYOTUBBE 101
    Betay 101
    Leson 100
    Solomon 100
    Taylor 101
AH-CHA-YA-HOKE 211
AHEKATABI 92
AH-LE-MUH-TUBBEE 69
AH-NE-TUBBY 49
AH-NIT-TUBBEE 51,52
AH-NO-HUN-TABY 21
AH-TEGL 127
AH-TOOK-CHE-NUBY 54
A-LAH-TA-HO-NA 37
ALEMATUBE
    Agnes 57
    Steson 57
ALE-MOH-TABI 61
ALEMOHTUBBI 42
    David 57
    Eleus 42
    Elus 42
    Emma 57
    Ilas 42
    Ina 57
    Inez 57
    Israel 42
    Kesin 57
    Leannie 42
    Leon 42
    Litey 57
    Litty 42
    Sidney 42
    Silis 42
    Sillis 42
    Steson 57
ALE-TO-KO-TUBBEE 255
ALEXANDER
    Alex 216
    Lucy 216
    William 216
ALFRED
    Elizabeth 221
    Maggie 221
    Morris 221
    Sampson 221

ALLEN
Joe 209
Liney...17
Solomon 17
AMA-HE-TA-BI 106
AMOS
Amancy 17
Amanda 17
Esanis 17
Esias 17
Kana 17
Meley...117
Sam...117
Susie 17
William 17
AMY..132
ANDERSON 251
Camel 28
Daniel 80
Delilah 217
Isaac...80
Joe 251
Louisa..251
Mollie 272
Nancy 251
Selina 28
Silas...18
Sillie 18
Wesley..272
Winey 80
ANO-KO-BE-LA 177
ANOLIMANA 39
ANSON, Silas 132
A-PO-AN-TUBBE 79
APOTANTUBBE, Selina 28
ARKINDO, George Morris 187
ASHLEY...75
ATA-SA-HA-BI 163
A-TOOK-CHI-NUBBEE 55
AUSTIN
Adline...163
Becky.. 8
Benjamin 7
James 163
Legend...163
Legion..163,165
Lena... 8

Lizzie 163
Louie... 8
Louis...265
Mollie 265
Molsey 163
Netsey 165
Pauline 8
Tobias 7,8
Viney 165
BACON
Bob 283
Bobbie 283
Dave 240
David 283
Deadenth.......................................254
Devenworth 254
Eliza..254
Elizabeth.......................................283
Ellen 240
Elmer 283
Isabelle 254
John 193
Mame...283
Minnie 283
Mittie Belle...................................283
Pearlie...283
Phoebe 283
Silas 254
Sinie..254
Solomon 254,283
Susan 193,254
Thomas 254
Thos...283
BAH-NA-BY....................................122
BAKER
Annie 174
Beckie 174
Becky..174
Hodgen 174
Hodges...174
Ida...174
Lecy Anna 174
Lillie 174
Louisiana 174
Noel...174
Simon 174
BANABBE..71

BANE, Sillen.....................................146
BANON
   Isabell O 86
   Jack O..86
BAR-NA-BY..53
BARNEY
   Ellis 126
   Isabelle 126
   Viney..126
BARTEE
   Deide 115
   Virgil 115
BAR-TI-TUBBEE................................32
BA-TA-LE-HUNA..............................70
BATHEST
   Allington....................................106
   Lizzie...106
   Pitchlynn.....................................93
   Samblin......................................106
BATTIEST 93
   Aaron...67
   Allington....................................106
   Amy...67
   Frances 67
   Josephine 148
   Lotin 148
   Sibbie...67
   Simpson.....................................106
   William.......................................67
BEARDEN
   Bessie 241
   Chas E 241
   Flora O.......................................241
   Florence Esther..........................241
   John 241
   Oscar Payton..............................241
   Rhoda 241
BE-LIN-CHE.....................................219
BEN, Sarah.......................................179
BENN
   Davis..179
   Lucinda......................................179
   Martha 179
BERSHEARS
   George 291
   Mary 291
BETSY 64

BETTAST, Phycia...............................96
BILLY 137
   Austin 131
   Delilah 93
   Eleus..137
   Eliza...131
   Ellen 43,137
   Frances 20
   George 137
   James 137
   Jency...20
   Jim 127
   Johnnis...43
   Lena 137
   Naaman..43
   Nora...43
   Pikey..137
   Simon 137
   Susan 137
   Tom 20
   Wesley 131
BIRLEN
   Albert...36
   Betsy...36
   Catherine 36
   Filena..36
   Joe 36
   Rebecca.......................................36
   Stephen.......................................36
BIRLOW
   Albert...36
   Stephen.......................................36
BISSIE...42
BLANKENSHIP, Winnie................294
BOATMAN
   Sallie..200
   Wm..200
BOB
   Johnson..90
   Sarah...77
BOBB
   Aalin 118
   Betty 102
   Ellen 118
   Ellis 118
   Emily 90
   Frelin 90

Johnson..................................90
Joseph..................................102
Mitchell 118
Nancy 102
BOHANAN
   Agnes..................................193
   Impson................................179
   Jesse..............................193,194
   Jonas..................................179
   Juliua 179
   Lucinda................................179
   Sallie..................................179
BOHANNAN, Agnes 192
BOLING
   Asay....................................132
   Billy......................................61
BOND......................................300
   Ida......................................300
BRASHEARS
   Betsy..................................291
   Caroline 291
   Edward 291
   George 214,291
   Mary 291
   Wm......................................291
BRAZIL 163
BROWN
   Annie..................................122
   Arnes 122
   Bicey..............................122,123
   Eastman 122
   Eight 122
   Elias..................................122
   Emma 122
   Frank..................................122
   John 23
   Josephine 123
   Julius..................................296
   Ketsie..................................122
   Kitsie 122
   Lottie 296
   Louisa..................................122
   Matilda 296
   Mike 296
   Minnie 122
   Nicholas................................122
   Seldon..................................23

Susan 23
BRYANT, Jesse 248
BUTTER, Abel.............................134
BYINGTON
   Albert................................66,147
   Alfred 66,119
   Annie..................................21
   Basie....................................66
   Davis..................................147
   Francis..................................21
   Hannah 271
   Israel..................................117
   Lewis..................................147
   Louis..................................147
   Maxwell................................117
   Moody 21
   Nicey 147
   Philis..................................66
   Phillis..................................66
   Sallie..................................21
   Sibbie..................................21
   Thos....................................21
   Wallace................................271
   Zona..................................... 6
CALISTER, Emmie.......................216
CAMPBELL, Louis.........................99
CANDY, John 274
CARBY
   Betsy..................................85
   Eli......................................85
   Josiah..................................85
   Louis..................................85
   Nicholas................................85
CARLISTER
   Annie..................................216
   Jacob..................................216
   Lucy..................................216
CARN......................................190
   Caldonia 190
   Dona..................................190
   Lancy..................................190
   Lucky..................................190
   Lucy..................................190
   Maley..................................190
CARNEY
   Aimy..................................182
   Albert........................117,179,182

Alzira......................................182
Amy..182
Ella 182
Ephraim 117
Jinsey.....................................117
Julius......................................117
Narry......................................182
Nora.......................................182
Pearlie....................................182
Zira..182
CASEY..........................161,219
CHA-FA-HO-NA 66
CHAPMAN
James.....................................175
James Emery...........................175
James M..................................175
Kate K 175
Melvina...................................175
CHE-LE-TUBBEE 273
CHELONIE................................43
CHIFFIE...................................21
CHIMULIHOKE.......................137
CHI-PI-OKE............................167
CHITTO, Phoebe......................300
CHOATE
Ellis 201
Patsey 201
CHRISTIE
Edward 157
Mita 157
Sarah......................................22
CLARK
Adam 212
Jane..212
Rena.......................................212
CLAY
Arthur 35
Betsy.................................34,35
Bycey......................................35
Bycy 35
Calvin 35
Isabella 35
Simon 35
Wolsey....................................37
COBB
K B 219
Keener B.................................219

COKLIN, Ciney 221
COLBERT
Davis......................................154
Eliza.......................................227
Frank......................................227
Jimmy 227
Jonas..31
Nancy 154
Sallie..31
Sam...227
Sinie...31
William J 31
Wm J 31
COLE
Isaac.......................................208
Mimie.....................................255
Minnie 255
Sarah......................................208
Stephen...................................255
COLEMAN
John 247
Lone.......................................253
Lucy.......................................247
Susie 253
COLLINS, Joseph 260
COLUMBUS, Melwessie...............106
COMBS
Buster 220
Claude W................................220
Cora E.....................................220
Dicey......................................220
Edward 220
Jesse J 220
John 220
Sarah......................................220
William....................................220
COMES 220
Hattie S...................................220
COON
Alvey 235
Alvy..235
COONE
Alvey 235
Charlie 235
David 235
Emma 235
Viney 235

Willie May 235
COOPER
   Abel 169,170,171
   Agnes 169
   Eason 171
   Edward 167
   Elson 171
   Emiline 169,170
   Frances 161
   Jinsy 169
   Johnny 161
   Lena 167
   Lucy 167,253
   Martin 5,167
   Mary 171
   Mean 5
   Phebe 167
   Silas 167
   Sima 172
   Siney 172
   Susan 167
   William 161
   Wincy 5
CORNELIUS, Mary 114
COSTON
   Lina 277
   Tom 277
COTTON, Rebecca 89
COXWELL
   Daniel 116,158
   Frances 124
   Francis 158
   Johnson 116
   Loston 158
   Louis 158
   Roston 158
   Sallie 116
   Siley 158
COY, Susan M 291
CRAVEN 34
CROSBY, Susan 121
CROSSBILL
   Josiah 41
   Silyn 41
CROWDER
   Abigail 249
   Alice 259

Belzori 258
Benny F 250
Bessie 250
Bessie L 250
Betsey 249
Betsy 299
Clay 256
Dolly 249
Eli 245,249,256
Eli E 258
Eli W 259
Elizabeth 299
Ellen 259
Emma 256
Fannie 245
Flora 263,299
G W 258
Geo 245
George W 258
Green 256
J F 249
J J 232
Jesse 258
Jessie 258
Joe 258
John F 249
John J 232
John Richard 245
Josephine 249
Josh 232,250
Liza 258
Louisa 258,259
M B 250
Maggie 249
Martin B 250
Mary 249,275
Mary A 232
Mary Ellen 245
Mary M 232
Melzori 258
Ophelia L 250
Orprilla 250
Pairlee 258
Parlee C 258
Patsey 256,258,259
Patsy 245,249
Richard 245

Richard C...................................245
Robert.......................................259
Rosa...249
Rosa A......................................249
Roseann....................................258
Sarah..245
Sibbie.......................................250
Silsa...256
Silva...256
Thomas C.................................256
Thos C......................................299
Tom..263
Van..259
W A..232
W J...249
William......................................222
William H..................................249
William J...................................249
Willie..258
Winnie Gertrude........................249
DAVID
   Loin..98
   Wister..98
DAVIS
   Delilah F...................................207
   Delilia.......................................207
   Fannie..84
   Rose Ella....................................84
   Z T..84
DENISON, Dr Ben L....................268
DENNIS, Ellen............................248
DICKSON, Minerva......................89
DOWLAND
   Frank..258
   Mattie.......................................258
DRAKE, Permelia........................283
DURANT
   Alexander R...............................201
   Alick R.....................................201
   Annie L.....................................201
   Elizabeth...................................254
   Etna R......................................201
   Geo.....................................201,245
   Geo E F....................................201
   George E F................................201
   A R...217
   Selina.......................................114

Vicey...................................201,245
DYER
   David J......................................161
   Emeline.....................................161
   Emiline......................................176
   Granson......................................17
   Joe..173
   Lottie..173
   Louis...17
   Moses..173
   Sadie..161
   Sallie..141
   Wilson.................................161,176
EARTHMAN
   Jane..196
   Tom..196
EAU-LA-TEMA............................266
EBA-FOH-KA..............................145
EDWARD
   Suky..174
   William......................................252
EDWARDS
   Donie..252
   John..46
   Sam...252
   Tennessee..................................252
   Vinson......................................252
   William......................................252
ELA-YO-TO-NA............................43
ELEAH.......................................109
ELEHOMAHI.................................40
ELIKANCLAITABI..........................66
ELIMA...1
ELLIS...24
E-LO-MA......................................46
ELOMA, Marsie.............................46
E-MI-L-TO-NA...............................19
EMI-LYA.....................................127
E-MOLLIE.....................................11
E-MO-NAH-ABY...........................125
ERVIN
   Abraham A................................229
   Annie..206
   Archer Roy................................229
   Benj..206
   Benjamin F, Jr............................206
   Calvin..................................229,267

Charles W 206
Chas W 206
Columbus C 229
Dan W 267
Edgar 206
Elizabeth.....................................206
Emmet 229
Harriet E 229
Harriet N....................................229
James 275
Jimmie..275
Jno W...206
Joel E 229
John N 206
Josephine 192
Laura...229
Lizzie H 229
Margaret P 229
Mark H 229
Mary 275
Myrtle M 229
Nellie..275
Sallie...229
Sally..267
Thelma G.....................................229
Thos J 267
Turner L.......................................229
Walter P.......................................229
William..206,275
EVERIDGE
Eve...269
Joe 87,243
Joel 229
Mollie 243
Sophronia.....................................229
Susan 243
Susie..87
Thomas W 243
Thos...269
Willie...243
E-YA-HOKE-TUBBY 50
EYATONA.....................................28
FA-LE-SEN...................................119
FEH-NA-HOHKE 47
FI-LAM-I-TABI............................60
FINNEY 137
FISHER

Amy...122
Daniel 126
Elizabeth......................................33
Ellie 264
Frank..288
Georgie 288
Harris...33
Hicks..33
John 288
Liley 288
M H 264
Malis..126
Morris H 288
Robert..33,288
Rogers..9
Sillen..264
Sillian 288
Sose 33
Susan 126
Thomas...288
Viney..126
Willie...288
Wilson..126
FOBB 117
Adeline 140
Alice 44
Battes...104
Chaslin...119
Eastman 141
Ellen 140
Frances...103
Francis 103
Ida..116
Impson 140
Jenkin 119
Jinkin 119
Joe 119
John 103,167
Johnny 161
Lee 119
Lewis 74
Lizzie 44,140
Louis...44,140,141
Lucy..44
Philis..119
Phillis...119
Rhoda 103

Robert 119
Sadie 161
Sallie 103,167
Silas 167
Sophia 141
Sophie 74
Watkin 44
FOLSOM
David 195
Groves C 195
Ollie 195
Ollie N 195
Rhoda 195
Sampson N 195
Simpson N 195
FORB, Vincey 176
FOSTER, Lidia 274
FOWLER, H L 118
FRANCES 76
FRAZIER
Aaron 99
Bakie 99
Betsie 99
Celeste 193,194
Cephus 189
Eliza 227
Jellicco 164
Jennie 99
Lolin 164
Loren 164
Louisa 227
Martha 99
Moses 188
Rebecca 99
Stephen 227
FREDERICK
Elbert 261
Ella 261
Mary E 261
Nola 261
Richard J 261
T G 261
Tom 261
FREENEY, Mary A 267
FRY
Billy 276
Cornelia 276

Joseph 276
Samuel 276
Sophia 276
Sophie 276
Wisey 276
FRYE
Elizabeth 226
William 226
FULSOM
Lewis G 238
Lou 4
Louis G 238
S N 238
Susan 238
FULTON
Arthur Daniel 204
Edgar 204
Ellen 253
Jeff 204
Nancy 204
Robert 204
Susan 204
FURGESON
Frances 46
Tom 46
GABEL
Ansie 131
Willman 131
GARDNER
Adeline 236
Alfred 115
Anderson 168
Dennis E 154
E mund 236
Edmond 105
Edmund 223,231,262
Edna Harriet 262
Emma L 115
Florence R 262
Geo 231
Israel 236,274
Jeff 49
Jennie 115
Jerry 105,115
Jimmie 192
Jinnie 105
Laura B 105

Lela 105
Lucinda 223,231
Lucy 236,262
Lydia 105
Mattie 115
Nancy 154,236
Nicey 231
Rena M 115
Rosa 236
Selina 223
Sick 262
Wilkin 154
William J 105
Willis 154
Wilson 154
Wylis 154
Zachariah 262

GARLAND
Lucinda 286
Nicholas 8
Osborn 239
Osborne 239
Pauline 8
Silas 239,286,297
William 174

GARVIN
Henry 56
Susan 193

GHOING, Sillis 5
GIBSON 88
Jane 88
Peter 88
Selina 88

GOING
David 191,263
Frances 263
Frank 263
Gibson 263
Isom 97
James 263
Jim 263
John 11
Rosie 263
Seamon 191
Semaye 97
Semiya 97
Sokey 263

Thomas 263
Zarabelle 263
GOINGS 263
Emma 240
Henry 240
Isabelle 263
Littie 64
Tommie 263
GOINS, Ellen 240
GOODING
Annie 279
Annie B 278
Charles H 279
Chas H 279
Fannie B 278
Henry 202,203,279
Henry L 278,279
Henry, Jr 279
Josephine 279
Josie 279
Lettie Lee 279
Louie 279
Louis 279
Minnie 279
Minnie Lee 279
Osborne A 278
Rosana 278,279
Rosanna 203
Roseana 202
Rosie A 203
GOODWATER, Eastman Jones 187
GOWENS, Ziarriabelle 263
GRAVY
James 14
Jane 14
GUESS
Amelia 295
Billy 295
Henry 295
Martin 295
Michael 295
Rosa 295
HAAIS
Cotton 30
Elcy 148
HAIAKANUBBI 24
Amblin 24

Colbert................................170
Dixon.................................170
Hamplin.............................24
Jonas..................................170
Louisiana...........................24
Lucy Ann...........................24
Sissy 170
Wellington.........................24
HAIAKONABI, Thompson.............161
HALL
    Lucinda.............................239
    Pleasant David...................279
    Sarah.................................279
HAMPTON
    Ben 110
    Bennie...............................110
    Benson...............................110
    Carrie................................136
    Mary 110
HANKINS
    Charley.............................286
    David................................286
    Granderson 286
    Henry................................286
    James................................286
    Levi...................................286
    Mary 286
    Sarah.................................286
HARKINS
    Carry.................................297
    Dave..................................89
    James.................................297
    Lena..................................297
    Minerva.............................89
    Novey 297
    Richard..............................297
    Silas..................................297
    Silbie.................................297
    Susie.................................297
    Viney................................297
HARLAN, Ishtona.............................99
HARLAND
    Agnes................................99
    Bil.....................................99
    Jennie................................99
    Raybin 99
HARLEY

Amy.....................................16,188
Calvin 16,17,188
Folsom................................188
Jane....................................16
Maggie...............................17
Mary Ann 159
Mikey 17
Thomas 16
Yousen................................16
HARLIN
    Bill....................................220
    Lucinda.............................220
    Raybin 99
HARNER
    Wilbum..............................9
    Wilmon..............................9
HARRIET..............................76
HARRIS
    Bert...................................296
    May...................................296
    Nicey 186
HARRISON
    Caleb.................................170
    Emiline 50
    Sealy.................................170
    Stephen..............................137
    Susan.................................170
    Thomas 170
HART
    Cornelius...........................285
    Lemon, Sr 285
HAYAKONUBBI
    Colbert...............................170
    Jonas.................................170
    Sissie.................................170
    Susan 170
HAYES
    Abel 108
    Eliza..................................108
    Fannie................................108
    Lucy...................................271
    Mariah 235
    Mary 204
    Sam...................................204
    Viney 108
HE-NA-KE...........................40
HE-O-HO-NO 117

HERNDON
Alice 47
Alice R...296
E K 296
Ezekiel K 296
Harrison..47
Harrison H 296
Isabelle 47
John C...47
Lottee...296
HESHAYA, Jim 10
HIAKANABI
Cissy..170
Colbert..170
Jonas..170
Susan 170
HIBBEN
Eliza..218
Ethel 218
Frances H......................................218
George Wellington 218
Mary 218
Samuel L 218
Sophia...218
Thomas D 218
W B 218
William T 218
HIBBENS..218
Samuel...218
Wm T...218
HICKMAN
Eliza..131
Emma B...192
James 192
Jimmie 192
John 131
HICKS
Anna 130
Mishaid..130
William...130
HINEY 10
HLEOHTAMB 40
HLEOHTAMBI...........................41,54
Betsey...54
Betsy...41
Charley 54
Eleciana 54

Eliona 54
Esias 41
Margaret 54
Olacie 41
Oleasy..41
Selile...54
Silili..54
HLEOTAMBI 40
Betsy...40
Nisey...40
HOH-NA 69
HO-K-ABE
Joseph...10
Missie..10
Sallie...10
HOKABE
Joseph.. 7
Susan 7
HOKI...60
HOLDER
Jackson 36
Mandy...36
HOLDMAN, James.........................227
HOLENLOBI, Liney 231
HOLMAN
Ben Denison 65
Charles R 65
James 65,227
Licey...227
Rosa..65
Sarah...65
Simon 227
Susan 227
HOLO..133
HO-LU-TIE 184
HOMA
Elijah 112
Ompsion...291
Solomon 112
Sophia...291
HOMER
Annie..266
Byington 186
Chubby 266
Dana 276
John 233
Lafayette...231

Melissa 178
Narcissa 186
Silan..266
Sissy 266
Solomon 276
Summie......................................178
Willis 186
HOMMA
    Annie 246
    Flora 117
    Jincy 117
    Joe 231
    Mary 284
    Simeon.....................................117
    Simpson......................................16
HOPAKONOBI, Elizabeth................20
HO-PA-KON-UBBY......................128
HOPAKONUBBY, Liswe................128
HOPIASHUBY, Sophie 172
HOPYISHUBBEE, John 45
HOSA, Sam................................174
HO-STOK-BY................................231
HOSTOKBY, Sally 231
HOTEMA
    Cornelia....................................247
    Frank..247
    John 247
    Nancy 247
    Solomon 247
HO-TE-MI-AH..............................208
HO-TIN-LOBI................................48
HOTINLOBI
    Joe 48
    Lasin..48
    Louisiana.....................................48
HOUSTON
    Beckie..............................273,274
    Davison.....................................125
    Elsey...30
    Elsie...148
    Lewieson...................................125
    Louie...148
    Louis S......................................148
    Mrs 273
    Sampson 148
    Sopha..125
    Sophia.......................................125

HOWARD
    J W 248
    Rhoda 248
    Sarah..248
    Selma.......................................248
    Silinie 248
    William H..................................248
    Wm H.......................................248
HUDSON, Jackson........................173
HULAND, Isabelle........................290
ICHUKENATABI............................133
I-LIP-HON-NA 91
I-MA-TO-NA 188
INEY 10
INNIE 155
IRVIN
    Calvin 207
    Columbus...................................217
    Sallie..207
ISABELL
    Alice 265
    Zack...265
ISH-NOAH.............................122,123
ISH-TA-BA-WE-LA 128
ISHTAHNUBE................................17
ISHTAHONA................................109
ISH-TA-LA-MA............................... 2
ISH-TAN-TUBBEE 143
ISHTEMONA 92
ISHTIAHONOBBE
    Hettie 45
    Leniy..45
    Tom 45
ISH-TIATA-BI................................60
ISH-TI-CHI 167
ISHTONAKE, Sis 109
ISHTONTOBE, Thomas 143
I-YA-NA-HOKE.............................167
I-YO-KA-LA.................................118
JACKSON 118
    Inez...187
    Lizzie...26
JACOB 90
    Johnaon.....................................170
    Mollie 199
    Netsy..43
JACOBS

Colman 7
Houston B... 7
Rhoda 7
JAMES
  Aaron...118
  Alfred 36,114
  Bob...47
  Calvin 47
  Charles..102
  Charley 105,179
  Ellen..253
  Garvin..47
  Geo 253
  George 103
  Isham...90
  Janey...47
  Joe 114
  John 86
  Johnny 253
  Jones..104
  Joseph...104
  Mandy...253
  Marcy 102
  Margaret 102,104
  Marswis 114
  Mary L...105
  Masaris 114
  Nancy 114
  Nannie 102
  Netsie...114
  Patterson 118
  Rebecca 36
  Sally..86
  Sarah...179
  Sheb...47
  Shub...47
  Simeon..114
  Siney..97
  Wilson 102,104
JEFFERSON
  Adam...2,142
  Alin...140
  Anna 2
  Caesar...137
  Catharine 2
  Catherine 2
  Cornelius 120

Daniel 138
Jamison..120
Jennie...138
Jincy 138
Josephus 138
Julius..2,53
Lewis 137
Maggie..2
Mahaley 113,120
Mary 44,140
Mykie 2
Philip 137
Pikey...137
Rhoda 142
Simeon...44,140
Simpson 2
Solomon 2
Stephen 138
Susan 138
Thomas 138
Winnie 2
Winsy 142
JETER
  Gertrude..292
  Hattie 292
  James 292
  James T..292
  Joshua B 292
  Olive M 292
  Oliver M 292
  Selena 292
  Susan E..292
  Thomas 292
  William..292
  William W 292
JETTER, Joshua B............................292
JOE
  Agnes..228
  J Sim..228
  Sim 228
  Visey..228
  Wisey...228
JOHN
  Amos 109
  Hagan 45
  Lena..45
  Lily 45

Mary 45
Simon 45
JOHNSON
  Adaline 180
  Adeline 180
  Aggie 180
  Aiggy 180
  Anthony 9
  Elsie 9
  Huston 180
  Isabel 63
  Isabelle 63
  Jimmie 211
  Joe 182
  Joseph 180
  Levi 236
  Liney 236
  Lura 180
  Noel 180
  Sibbie 63
  Tennessee 60
  Tennissa 60
  Tom 63
  Watson 60
  William 180
  Willie 180
JONES
  Amon 185
  Amos 11
  Crason 5
  Eastman 11
  Frances A 230
  Grayson 5
  Hattie 119
  Isabelle 254
  Isham 11
  Isom 5,50
  Jefferson 76
  Jesse 185
  Jessee 185
  Jimmie 76
  Jno G 230
  John G 230
  Katherine 221
  Katie B 230
  Kittie B 230
  Latis 77

Louis 11
Margaret A 230
Sarah 77
Silis 11
Sillis 11,50
Sinie 254
Sophie 185
Sylvester 11
Thomas 11
Wiley 221
William 254
Wilson S 230
Winey 5
Winnie 177
JUZAN
  Isaac 139
  Philliston 139
  Sattie 139
JUZAR, Celia 17
KALAHA 100
KAMATOBE, Helen 188
KANA-A-TUBE, Mary 17
KANA-HAMA 69
KANAHAMBIE 1
KANAHIMA 70
KA-NA-HO-TEMA 142
KANAHOTIMA 138,149
KANASHAMBE 79
  Chostin 79
  Israel 79
  Malissa 79
  Milissa 79
  Sinie 79
  Stephen 1
KANASHAMBIE, Stephen 1
KANIATOBE 19,188
  Davis 188
  Ellen 188,189
  Sallie 19
  Sam 19
KA-NICH-TUBBEE 183
KANINIATA-BI 150
KANITIMA 154
KANIYOTABI, Sam 14
KATY 39
KELLEY
  Letitia 245

Wm R 245
KELLY
Ann M 210
G V..210
Isaac..210
Isaac P 210
James J......................................217
Jas J 217
Judia 210
Judith...210
Louis A......................................217
Louis B 217
Robert..217
Sarah...217
Selina...217
Selina J 217
Sissy 210
William R 210
Wm R 210
KEMP
Cornelius 123
Dixon...158
KENDRICK
Ann W 213
Annie...213
Annie M.....................................213
Emma 213
Emma E 213
Henry E 213
Henry L 213
Jno G 213
John G 213
Lelia J 213
Lelin J 213
Mamie H.....................................213
Martha 213
Mary Stokes...............................213
W B 213
W D 213
W W 213
William D....................................213
William W 213
KING
Anna 128
Arlington 6
Beslin..128
Bessie 128

Charlisson Isaac...........................128
Elsie...128
Emily 128
Hinson 67
Joseph..215
Melissie 6
Sallie..215
Silas... 6
Solomon 128
Wicklis 128
Wilkin...128
KIRBY
Alice 136
Asa...136
Murtie..136
KIRKPATRICK
Dewey M 212
James C 212
Jocephus 212
Joe Cephus...................................212
Mary J..212
Rena...212
KLIOTUBBEE 182
KONEUBBEE
Chas...265
Mary 265
KOOZA, Charles............................166
KOOZER
Charles...166
Charles H......................................166
Elizabeth......................................166
Fred...166
Lucretia..166
LACEY
John 210
Sallie..210
LACHANTUBBE
Laury..251
Loman..251
LATIMER
Josephine B..................................242
Mattie 242
Mattie A.......................................242
Mattie N.......................................242
A N...242
Osborn W 242
Osborne 242

Osborne S 242
Ruby N 242
LAWITAYA
   Hodges 73
   Isabell 73
   John 73
   Sophie 73
LE-A-MUS 49
LEAMUS, Emily 49
LEE
   Ella M 222
   John M 222
   Nancy E 222
   Wax 222
LEFLORE
   Basil L 293
   Brasill 293
   Carrie 293
   Henry 99
   Landry 293
   Landry G 293
   Mary An 159
   Osborne 293
   Osie 293
   Rosa 293
   Rosanna 293
   Susan 293,294
   Susie 293
   Winnie 294
   Zeddick 293,294
LEWIS 108
   Betsy 108
   Jacob 66
   King 68
   Mawey 68
   Nancy 68,90
LILA 73
LINNA 79
LOHEN, Sissie 266
LOMAN
   Anna 130
   Annie 46
   Elias 150
   Frank 130
   Hannah 150
   James 150
   Josiah 13

Joson 13
Mollie 130
Narcissy 150
Oscar 46
Peter 150
Suky 13
Susan 46
Thomas 46
Wilson 130
LOTIMA 163
LOUIS
   Johnson 121
   Silman 121
   Sukey 121
LOWITAYA 73
LUCY 79
LUSH-HOMMA 233
MA-HLI-TABI 108
MA-HO-NA 76
MALINDY 78
MARTIN
   John 270
   Lucy 270
   Rogers 270
MA-SEY 53
MATLOCK
   Sallie 190
   William 190
MAXWELL 237
   Al 252
   Manerva 252
MCAFEE, Selina 102
MCCANN
   Frances 132
   Sam 208
MCCANNIS, Lottie 296
MCCLURE
   Absalom 139
   Absolom 139
   Acy 132
   Alex 132
   Babis 74
   Bicky 139
   Ellen 74
   Elsie 132
   Elson 132
   Fannie 74

Freeman............................132,134
Gleason............................135,139
Isabel....................74,75,134,135
Isabelle......................................75
Isom...139
Jennie...74
Jinnie...74
Josephine................................134
Lena...132
Lottie.......................................135
Mason......................................134
Mollis...74
Newton.......................................74
Oscar..74
Reuben..74
Stephen............................132,134
Taylor......................................139
Viney..74
Wallace.......................................74
Wallis...............................134,135
Wesley.....................................132
MCCOY
    Alex......................................261
    Bicey....................................214
    Bickey..................................199
    Chris.....................................261
    Dave.....................................199
    Hilben..................................184
    Hilbon N..............................184
    Mollen.................................184
    Mullim.................................184
    Nelson.................................184
    Reuben.................................214
    Sopha...................................214
    Willie...................................214
MCEVERS
    John......................................296
    Sarah Lottie.........................296
    Silvie...................................296
MCFARLAND
    Abbie...................................136
    Abby.....................................136
    Anna L.................................136
    Daniel Zac............................136
    Ina Juanita...........................136
    J B..136
    James A................................136

Jno E..136
John E.......................................136
Mary Ann.................................136
MCGEE.......................................37
    Austin................................37,49
    Ed...37
    Jennie....................................49
    Lizzie.....................................37
    Louisa....................................37
    Thomas................................170
MCINTIRE
    Balshizar.............................234
    Belshazzar...........................234
    James...................................234
    Lucretia...............................234
MCINTOSH
    Ida.......................................116
    A J.......................................144
    Melissa................................144
MCKEE
    Austin....................................37
    Ed...37
    Lizzie.....................................37
    Louisa....................................37
MCKENNON, Commissioner..........84
MCKINNEY
    Anderson................................72
    Ishlea.....................................28
    John.......................................28
    Lucky...................................190
    Seama....................................28
    Silway....................................72
    Simmie...................................28
    Sisten.....................................28
MEASHETUBBI
    Sally......................................48
    Wm..48
ME-ASH-IN-TUBBY....................55
ME-HE-TUBBI..............................93
MELLON, Sallie.........................155
MESHAYA
    Hicks.....................................10
    James.....................................10
MIC-CO.....................................208
MIHYACHUBBE
    Elie..85
    Josiah.....................................85

MILLER
    Alfred 295
    Frances 295
    Henry..295
    Ida...295
    Melvina.....................................295
    Mrs Sina 221
    Permelia....................................295
    Sophia.......................................295
MIN-TE-HO-KE 246
MINTICHUBY
    Weiney..53
    Wright...53
MINTIHEMA...................................61
MINTO-HOYO 67
MISHAYA, James.............................10
MITCHELL
    Albert...80
    Elcie...80
MOMINTUBBI, Silas 148
MONDY
    Caroline....................................160
    Elsie A 160
    James M.....................................160
    Lora O 160
    Margaret 160
MONINTUBBI, Sampson 148
MONKUS
    Elmira.......................................285
    Sam...285
    Samuel 285
MON-LA-TUB-BI 33
MONTE-MA 11
MON-TO-NA 40
MOODY, Zack 265
MOORE
    Ainsworth 124
    Allie..158
    Ben 158
    Frances 158
    John 124,158
    Linnie 124
    Martha 124
    Philliston...................................124
    Rayson......................................124
    Sarlin 124
    Sealy 124

MORRIS...136
MORRISON 283
MOWDY
    Carolione 160
    Delana.......................................160
    Delta 160
    Elsie E 160
    James 160
    James M.....................................160
    Lola O 160
    Margaret I 160
    Nora Clemintine 160
    Salane..160
MUELLENR, M J 129
MULLEN, James.............................130
MURPHY
    Agnes...193
    Joe 32
    Molsey 32
    Serena...32
    Stephen.......................................32
NAKISHI
    Sim 183
    Watson.......................................183
NANAMANTUBE, Mary 95
NANCE
    Lydia A......................................195
    Martin V 195
NANOMANTABBE
    Adam 237
    Susan 237
    Tobias..237
NANOMANTUBBE, Mary.............98
NANO-MAN-TUBBEE 98
NANOMANTUBE, Mary 95
NA-TAK-CHO-PA, Davis 37
NA-WEE 177
NEHKA, Noel 43
NEISE..77
NELSON
    Albert..224
    Albert J 224
    B A 224
    Bethel A.....................................224
    Fannie L.....................................224
    Fannie W 224
    Florence.....................................224

Louisa 224
Louise B 224
Louise V 224
Millie 9
W D 224
William D 224
NETSIE 39
NICHOLAS
  Ben 210
  Isabella 210
NICHOLS
  Ben B 210
  Roberson 210
NICHOLSON, Omer R 47
NIHKA, Siney 131
NOKA-STHEA 146
NOLI 182
NORMAN
  Eliza 194
  Elza 194
NO-TE-MA 211
OAKES
  Bessie 241
  C D 268
  Chas D 224
  Clarence A 260
  Daniel W 267
  Edgar O 267
  Frank 260
  George W 195
  Harriet 292
  Harriet N 218,260,267,269
  Judie 224,268
  L W 241,244
  Lem 241
  Lemuel W 260
  Lillie 244
  Lucy 241,244
  Lucy E 260
  Margaret J 267
  Mattie 260
  Nola 260
  Nona 260
  Nona M 260
  Rosa 267
  Susan 267
  Susan M 268

Thomas E 267
Thomas J 267
Thos W 218,260,267,292
OBANNON
  Bill 86
  Elizabeth 86
  Isabel 86
  Jack 86
O'BRIAN, Kate 220
O'CONNELL
  Catherine 205
  Jerry 205
OKCHIYA, Capt 266
OKLABE, Joseph 223
OKLABY
  Davis 216
  Hannah 216
OKLAESHI 28
OKLAHAMBI
  Joseph 48
  Mary 48
  Miney 48
  Ramsey 48
OKLA-HAY-SHE 50
OLIVER
  Frank 281
  Josephine 281
  Sam 281
  Samuel R 281
ONA 42
ONTAIYABI 39
  Netsie 39
  Stephen 39
ONTOHYOBE, Stephen 39
O-SH-SHE-HUMA 47
PA-LA-TABY 71
PA-LE-BY 117
PARSONS, John 235
PEBSWORTH
  Sam 89
  Vivian 89
PEKY 75
PE-SA-HU-NA 19
PESA-HU-NA 20
PE-SA-KA-CHE-HOKE 24
PETER
  Davison 30

Gooden 30
PETERS, Dixon...............................235
PHARIS
    Eliza..225
    Polk 225
    Turner 225
    Walter 225
PHILLIPS
    Annie 4
    Bob 3,4
    Dora 4
    Jeffie J 4
    Julia Margarett............................... 4
    Press 280
    Rosey 280
    Sallie... 4
    Sally 3
    Tobe.. 4
    Vivian 280
PICKEN
    Ellis 19
    Elsie 19
    Isabel 19
PICKENS
    Amy...256
    Mason 256
PISA HANIA 182
PISA-BUN-ABY 19,20
PISACHUBBEE
    Alex 178
    Emily 178
PISACHUBBI 77
    Case..77
    Sarah...77
    Sebit..77
PISAHAMBE
    Betsy 88
    David 88
    Willie 88
PISAHEKABI, Sam 28
PISAHINLABI 80
    Winney 80
PI-SAK-MA-TEMA......................188
PIS-A-LA-HO-KA 184
PISALETUBBI, Gooden 30
PISA-LU-KA-BI 9
PISATIMMA.....................................77

PISA-TOK-CUBBEE 98
PISCHUBBI, Nancy 78
PISLIN 27,29
    Aleck 27
    Alexander 27
    Guelis 29
    Sincy 27
    Snillis...29
PISSACHABBE, King 77
PITCHLYNN
    Rhoda 259
    Wm...259
PLANK
    Eliza..203
    Inez...203
    Jasper..203
    Jasper E 203
    Rosenna A 203
PO-SHE-MAR.................................17
PUSH, Henry.....................................80
RANDALL
    Lazerus 289
    Mattie 289
    Ruth 289
    Willie 289
RANDELL, Gus...............................289
RANSON...165
RATLIEF, Lee U 257
RATLIFF
    John 257
    Lee U 257
    Mary 257
    Sophia..257
REED, Alexander H 153
RICA
    Annie L..290
    Embro L...290
RICE
    Ambrose L 290
    G W 290
    Ithema...290
RICHARDS, Selina..........................217
ROBERT
    Ben 182
    David 17
    Immonbi 182
    John 107

Mollie 107
Sarah..107
Silas..107
ROBERTS
Buelah May 272
Elizabeth....................................293
John W.......................................293
A L 272
Mollie 272
Robert..293
Susan 293
ROBINSON
Louis...162
Mary 162
ROBISON
Elizabeth....................................160
Solomon 160
ROEBUCK
Annie 233,252
Ben 252
Cephas 210
Dvid...265
Epriam 277
Isabella 210
Malina..265
Mary A 232
Minnie 265
William....................................210,252
Willie..265
Wm..232
Zack...265
ROSENTHAL
Ally Pate 196
Birdie..196
Ernestine....................................196
Geo 196
Jacob..196
Maggie.......................................196
Mary E.......................................196
Parker 196
Pocahontas................................196
RUSHING
John 289
Nannie J.....................................289
RUSSEL, Ellen.............................240
SALENA 183
SALLY 14

SALTER
Hattie 220
Henry J 220
Jesse...220
Lula..220
SAM
Bill 127
Winnie 127
SANGUIN
Alice J..205
Billy..293
Charles A 197
Chas.......................................197,205
Chs...293
Clyde 197
Henry..205
Lena V 205
Susan 197,205
Thomas E...................................197
Virginia......................................197
William M 293
Zula C..197
SANTA
Sally...216
Solomon 216
SARAH 255
SELF
Annie 298
Billy..298
Caroline 264
Carrie...298
Ellie 264
Harvey 298
Harvey E....................................298
James E......................................298
Thomas 298
William...................................264,298
William O 298
William P...................................298
SELINA...101
SHAW
Bessie 109
Bob 109
Collin..109
David 109
Keith...109
Samuel 109

SHO-MA-KA 184
SHONA 155
SHO-NABI 73
SIBBIE 93,106
SILINA..28
SIMPSON
   Viney 288
   Wm..288
SINE...10
SINEY 29,163
SISSY 9,48
SI-YOH-KE....................................85
SMITH
   Henry....................................260
   Lucy......................................241
   Sarah....................................260
SNEAD
   Dewey.....................................98
   Emiline 98
   Josephine 98
   Louis.......................................98
SOUNDER
   Alexander 216
   Lucy......................................216
SPAULDING, G A............................84
SPRING
   Annie.....................................261
   Benney...................................199
   Christopher 198,199,200,287
   Clarence E 244
   David 200
   Dewey L 202
   Edith Gayzelle 217
   Eli 199
   Ely 199
   Essie M 244
   Etta May 244
   Franklin 200
   Henry....................................202
   Ida E 217
   Isaac.....................................199
   Jackson 199
   James 232,250,275
   James F 232
   James O 232
   Jane......................199,213,257,293
   Jesse.....................................200

   Jesse H..................................202
   Jodie 202
   Joel 202
   Joel, Jr..................................202
   John 199,244
   John, Jr 199
   Joseph B 217
   Lawrence 202
   Lawrence E.............................202
   Levi......................................200
   Lillie 244
   Liza......................................202
   Louis.....................................244
   Mary 275
   Mary A 250
   Melinda..................................199
   Melissie 280,281,287
   Nancy 199,244
   Robert Murry 202
   Rosey....................................280
   Sam.......................................202
   Sarah.....................................200
   Simeon...................................200
   Sophia....................................200
   Susan 198,200,287
   Thomas 287
   Tom 261,280,281
   Walter....................................287
   William..................198,199,257,293
   Winnie 202
   Winnie R 202
   Wm.......................................213
   Zena......................................232
   Zeno......................................232
STALARD
   Jim.......................................207
   Jimmy 207
   Jinnie 207
STEKA..61
STEPHEN
   Cety..50
   Lemus......................................50
   Linas.......................................50
STEPHENS, Lucin 48
SUNTA
   Sallie....................................228
   Soloman..................................228

323

SURBAUGH, W O 235
SWARM
    F M 187
    Helen 187
    Inez...187
    Nova Belle...................................187
SWILLA.......................................134
TA-HO-KA-TUBBEE.....................69
TA-HO-NA 32
TAKABI, Bobb 77
TAKALITUBBI 133
TALAHALA, John........................167
TALOWAHOKI.............................154
TALVATONA 61
TA-MA-HUNA 49,51,52
TA-NAP-NO-WA 40
TANISSE.......................................168
TAN-I-TUBBI................................211
TANITUBBI
    James 211
    Johnson.......................................211
    Lucy..211
TANNITABBIE, Stephen................255
TAR-KA-HAR-JO 95
TARNEY
    Gibson 255
    Minnie 255
    Stephen.......................................255
TASHKA
    Kissie..56
    Levi...56
TAYLOR
    Abigail..249
    Asa..249
    Becca 153
    Becky..153
    Bicey..153
    Ella 222
    Ellen 153
    Jacob...88
    James 181
    Joan...153
    Joe 295
    John 153
    Johnson.......................................101
    Josiah Simpson 153
    Latis..77

Lodus..77
Lucinda J 181
Mary 295
Mary Jane 153
Mede Jane....................................153
Millie Jane...................................153
Nicey 153
Patsey 272
Sealy Ann 153
Simmie 153
Sophina..181
Sukey...88
Watson...77
TE-HOK-LO-TUBY, Joe 228
TE-HOL-BA-TA-BI........................78
TEKOBBE.....................................183
    Bob 183
    Sam 183
    Saul...183
    Susianna 183
    Susie 183
    Winnicy 183
    Winnissie.....................................183
TERRY
    Henderson....................................192
    James Auther 192
    Jefferson 192
    Josephine 192
    Louis Victor................................192
    Mary 192
THOMAS
    Chostin 79
    Edmond 231
    Hudson 9
    Jason...9
    John 9,18
    Josiah..18
    Nicey 231
    Philiston......................................18
    Philliston.....................................18
    Sallie...18
    Silway...18
    Wilson 114
THOMPSON 58,125
    [?]agerman..................................149
    Alexander 83
    Alexander B.................................83

Betsy................................83
Craymon 58
Ella 83
Ella N..............................83
Emma 142
G W 173
George 145
Hampton...........................88
Henry...............................82
Henry W 82,88
Illie 82,88
Jack.................................76
James 145
Jefferson 149
Jim 145
Joe 149
Joel 83
Joel J...............................83
John 83,145
Joseph..............................83
Joseph P...........................83
Josiah...............................85
Lena...............................142
Louisa..............................58
Lucy..........................82,145
Martha 145
Nellie 149
Peter B.............................83
Peter P 83
Phillis.............................149
Robert............................142
Rosa...............................149
Sibbie.............................149
Simon 82,83
Sophia............................145
Stephen..........................142
Thompson.......................142
Wilson 149
Wincey 142
TIHBAMBI, Geo..............39
TIK-BAN-TA-BI..............155
TIKBOMBE, Amy 18
TIMS
    Abel E.........................237
    Benjamin W.................237
    Benson..........................81
    Betsy..........................237

Columbus.........................38
E W...................................38
Edmond 237
Edmund 237
Edward 237
Edward W.......................237
Emiline 68,81,83
Lucy...............................237
Mamie.............................237
Minnie J..........................237
Myrtle 237
Mzy..................................68
Polly 38
Roberson...........................68
Rosanna 81
Vincent 68,83
Vincent V 237
Willie................................68
Willie J 237
TINNAHAYA, Thompson 217
TISHOHINLOBY
    Jno 209
    Wicey 209
TOANTABI.......................76
TOLUBBI, Kissi................76
TOM
    Jesse..............................92
    Jimmie 92
    Sally..............................92
    Sarah.............................92
TOMS, Harrison................92
TONIHKA
    Otson 49
    Richmond 49
    Salean 51
TONITUBBI, Stephen.......255
TONOWAHOKE 168
TORNATUBBY
    Johnson.........................211
    Lucy.............................211
TOSHOAHONA 104
TO-TUBBI
    Battiest...........................76
    Kissie.............................76
TUCKER
    Owen 282
    Sarah............................282

TURNBULL
  Harriet..............................225
  Harriet E 225
TUSHKA..............................56
  Alfred 126
  Felin................................ 2
  Kissie...............................56
  Levi.................................56
  Maggie............................. 2
  Netsey..............................56
  Silway.............................. 2
UA-KA-TEMA......................55
UNA-HA-TEMA....................124
UNT-A-MAH 57
UNTEMABE
  Lorin................................45
  Rosie................................45
USRAY
  Jas..................................242
  Malinda...........................242
USREY
  James 298
  Lelinda.............................298
VAUGHN
  J B..................................197
  Jennie C 197
WADE
  Anna................................21
  Barnet 50
  Ben 69
  Bickny 50
  Bitny 50
  Elsie................................50
  Formy 50
  Frances 50
  Gilbert.............................215
  Leasin 69
  Lemus 50
  Levi................................215
  Louina..............................69
  Melvina.............................69
  Nancy 12
  Nicholas E 50
  Sissy 69,215
  Williston...........................50
WAIB, Starling...................... 9
WA-KA-YA 17

WAKAYA, Siney.....................17
WALKER
  Cemy 189
  Denison............................189
  Elsie...........................284,285
  Joe 189
  Johnson............................189
  Loston..............................189
  Lye..................................189
  Malis................................189
  Nelie 189
  Semie...............................189
  Solen...............................189
  William.............................284
WALLA 182
WALLACE
  Amos 148
  Liasa 258
  William.............................258
WALLIN
  Lucy.................................33
  Simon 33
WARD
  Amy.................................70
  Betty 223
  Celliny 14
  Cillin................................14
  Eastman 174
  Eden................................223
  Emma 70
  George 223
  Gilbert..............................223
  Harris............................14,15
  Liswee 70
  Lorancy.............................15
  Lucinda.............................223
  Lucy.................................98
  Lyman...............................70
  Mary 15
  Moses 14
  Nancy 174
  Reed.................................14
  Robert..............................15
  Silena...............................14
  Sillan.............................14,15
  Simon 14
  Sissy 14

W S 14
William...174
William S 14
Willie 15
WARDEN, William S 128
WASHINGTON
    Anthony 131
    Eliza...131
    Eny 90
    Isham 90
    Isom 90
    Lucy...113
    Patterson 90
    Willis 113
WATKIN, Gibson 9
WATKINS
    Ben 175
    Cora C 175
    Gibson 9
    Isham L.......................................175
    Kate 175
    Melvina.......................................175
    Mollie 91
    Waldo 175
    Waldo E.......................................175
    Winnifred.....................................175
WATSON
    Geo 180
    Netsie..180
    Nicie 80
    Thomas 80
WEBSTER
    Byington 65
    Daniel 65
    Lavisa 65
    Michael 22
    Sarah..65
    Wilson 22
WELLIS, Emerson D 151
WESLEY
    Agnes...169
    Betty 49
    Bicey..96
    Edward 26
    Elias...49
    Elizabeth.......................................96
    Elsey 52

John 49
Jonis..26
Kitson 172
Lemus 51
Lenas 51
Lije 169
Lucy..49
Malissy 49
Mishontutta.....................................96
Winnie 26
WHITEMAN, W J..........................185
WILLARD
    Martha 225
    Martha G 230
    S M 230
    Samuel..225
WILLIAM
    Billy..274
    Cillen 16
    Dennis...25
    Eaton...152
    James 152
    Johnson...............................129,149
    Mary 15
    Michael 16
    Tobias 274
WILLIAMS
    Alma 282
    Ben 185
    Benj 25
    Billy...15,16
    Byington 63
    Carrie A 282
    Carrie E 282
    Charles..156
    Dennis...25
    Eastman 231,274
    Eli 274
    Eliz 274
    Elma 282
    Elton 156
    Enos...231
    Fannie 282
    Fitter 156
    Frances 282
    Geo C..282
    George 156,282

Henry............................217
Isabel 231
Isham 282
J A 245
James 152,156
Jincy 274
Lena.............................245
Mary 282
Mary B.........................15
Mary C.........................282
Michael.........................16
Oscar R........................282
Sallie Ann 156
Sillan............................16
Simon 282
Simpson........................16
Siney.....................15,16,25
Tobias 274
Viney 274
William A.....................282
Willie............................274
Winey 236,274,276
Wm A 282

WILLIE
Leonidas 165
Mary 159
Viney 165

WILLIS
Andrew 84
Bunneta.........................84
Davis.............................53
Dixon...........................151
Eastman 149
Elizabeth......................151
Elmira..........................277
Emerson D....................151
Frances M 84
Inis................................53
Irena.............................277
Ismon............................31
Jim...............................277
Jimmy 277
Joe 18
Jones.............................18
Margaret 196
May J 31
Minney 277

R B 196
Sarphim 53
Sinie.............................31
Soyou...........................114
Tennessee 18
Thomas 277
Wallace.........................53

WILLISTON
Mary 24
Payson 35
Sarah.............................35

WILSON 137
Aeyne 226
Alex 181
Alma.............................87
Ambrose 126
Anna 4
Bessie Ann....................143
Bessie B.......................226
Betsey...........................54
Betsy.........................1,55
Bissiam 143
Brown 181
Caesar..........................137
Charles..........................181
Cole 176
Commise........................62
Curtis B 226
David 176
Easter............................64
Edward 87
Edward H.......................87
Eliza.............................181
Emma 87,226
Ennis............................127
Eva................................89
F B 226
Florance B 226
Foston...........................127
Frances 127,178,243
Frank..........................64,89
Hantima 143
Harriet..........................226
Hattie I.........................226
Iden..............................178
Ilomtima 144
Isabelle 64

Isbam 81
J Dace 87
Jacob 64
James 57,81,87,127
Jno L 226
Joe 66
Joel 1
John 127,135
John D 226
John L 226
Kase 77
Kolson 176
Lenus 137
Leslie J 226
Lila 64
Lou 3
Louie 178
Lucinda 181
Maggie 144
Mamie 55
Mannie 55
Martha 297
Mary 64
Matihena 64
Melissie 81
Milton 181
Nellie 127
Nelson 144
Ollie M 3
Philip 137
Raphael 89
Rhoda 1
Roah 127
Robt 243
Rosanna 81
Sallie 186
Sally 57
Sarah 178
Sarphin 53
Sealy 176
Senie 127
Sherman 181
Sillena 144
Sillie 124
Sillin 77
Simon 81
Stewart 178

Thomas 143,144,191
Thompson 124,138
Tobias 62
Tom 62
Viney 176
Walter 64
Ward 53
Wiley 55
William E 226
William P 64
Willie 3,4
Willie H 87
Winny 62
Wm P 64
WINNIE 73
WISBY, Dicy 96
WOODS, Ellen 240
WOOLERY
    Annie 173
    Carlston 173
    Colston 173
    Dona 173
    Donie 173
    Elsie 173
    Gilbert 173
    James 173
    John 173,175
    John P 173
    John, Jr 173
    Julia 173
    Nancy 173
    Rhoda 173
    Susan Anna 173
    Walker 173
WRIGHT
    Battie 299
    Betsy 299
    Ella T 299
    J W 299
    Lenard Dalco 299
    Mary M 299
    Thomas E 299
    W 299
YA-CHA-PIE-E 246
YAH-A-NO-LA 128
YA-HO-KA-BI 10
YA-HO-KEBABI 28

YA-KAB-IM-NIA 33
YAKOHTINA 34
YALE
   Adeline 265
   Amos 46,111
   Elisha 111
   Jackson 265
   Marshall 159
   Sarah 159
   Solomon 276
   Umphus 265
YO-CHI-MON
   James 40
   Louisa 40
YONA 149
YOUNG
   Annie 99
   Johnson 99